CRITICAL ISSUES IN
AMERICAN PSYCHIATRY AND THE LAW

Publication Number 1047
AMERICAN LECTURE SERIES®

A Monograph in
The BANNERSTONE DIVISION *of*
BEHAVIORAL SCIENCE AND LAW

Edited by
RALPH SLOVENKO, B.E., LL.B., M.A., Ph.D.
Wayne State University
Law School
Detroit, Michigan

CRITICAL ISSUES IN AMERICAN PSYCHIATRY AND THE LAW

By

RICHARD ROSNER, M.D.

Diplomate in Forensic Psychiatry
Clinical Associate Professor
Department of Psychiatry
School of Medicine
New York University
and
Medical Director
Forensic Psychiatry Clinic
for the New York Criminal and Supreme Courts
(First Judicial District)
New York, New York

With a Foreword by

Herbert E. Thomas, M.D.

President
American Academy of Psychiatry and the Law
New York, New York

CHARLES C THOMAS • PUBLISHER
Springfield • Illinois • U.S.A.

Published and Distributed Throughout the World by
CHARLES C THOMAS • PUBLISHER
2600 South First Street
Springfield, Illinois 62717 U.S.A.

©*1982, by* CHARLES C THOMAS • PUBLISHER
ISBN 0-398-04578-X
Library of Congress Catalog Card Number 81-9059

*With THOMAS BOOKS careful attention is given to all details of
manufacturing and design. It is the Publisher's desire to present books
that are satisfactory as to their physical qualities and artistic possibilities
and appropriate for their particular use. THOMAS BOOKS will be
true to those laws of quality that assure a good name and good will.*

Critical issues in American psychiatry and the law.

(American lecture series; publication no. 1047)
"Collected papers, revised . . . given at the annual
series of postgraduate medical education programs in
New York City by the regional membership of the
American Academy of Psychiatry and the Law" —
Introd.
"A monograph in the Bannerstone Division of
behavioral science and law."
Bibiography: p.
Includes index.
1. Forensic psychiatry — United States — Addresses,
essays, lectures. I. Rosner, Richard. II. American
Academy of Psychiatry and the Law. III. Series.
[DNLM: 1. Forensic psychiatry. W 740 C934]
KF8922.C75   614'.1   81-9059
ISBN 0-398-04578-X   AACR2

Printed in the United States of America
S-RX-1

to the memory of
Arthur Donald Herrick, LL.B.,
who introduced the editor to the
interface of law and medicine

CRITICAL ISSUES IN
AMERICAN PSYCHIATRY AND THE LAW

was edited for

THE AMERICAN ACADEMY OF PSYCHIATRY AND THE LAW
(TRI-STATE CHAPTER)

CONTRIBUTORS

MORTON BIRNBAUM, M.D., LL.B., Executive Director, The Center for Law and Health Care Policy, Brooklyn, New York

PETER M. CRAIN, M.D., Clinical Assistant Professor, Department of Psychiatry, Albert Einstein College of Medicine, Yeshiva University, Bronx, New York

HENRY H. FOSTER, LL.B., LL.M., Professor of Law (retired), School of Law, New York University, New York, New York

ROBERT LLOYD GOLDSTEIN, M.D., Clinical Assistant Professor of Psychiatry, New York University School of Medicine, Chief, Psychiatric Outpatient Services, New York Veterans Administration Medical Center, New York, New York

SAMUEL GOROVITZ, Ph.D., Professor and Chairman, Department of Philosophy, University of Maryland, College Park, Maryland

PETER D. GUGGENHEIM, M.D., Medical Director, Family Court Mental Health Services of the City of New York, and Clinical Associate Professor, Department of Psychiatry, School of Medicine, New York University, New York, New York

ABRAHAM L. HALPERN, M.D., Chairman, Department of Psychiatry, United Hospital, Port Chester, New York, and Clinical Professor of Psychiatry, New York Medical College, New York, New York

MICHAEL G. KALOGERAKIS, M.D., Clinical Professor, Department of Psychiatry, School of Medicine, New York University, New York, New York

MICHAEL L. PERLIN, J.D., Director, Division of Mental Health Advocacy, Department of the Public Advocate, Trenton, New Jersey

IRWIN N. PERR, M.D., J.D., Professor of Psychiatry, Professor of Environmental and Community Medicine, Rutgers Medical School, College of Medicine and Dentistry of New Jersey, Piscataway, New Jersey

vii

Hon. JUSTINE WISE POLIER, Judge (retired), Family Court of the City of New York, New York, New York

STANLEY L. PORTNOW, M.D., Clinical Associate Professor of Psychiatry, New York University School of Medicine, New York, New York, and Diplomate, American Board of Forensic Psychiatry

STEPHEN RACHLIN, M.D., Acting Chairman, Department of Psychiatry and Psychology, Nassau County Medical Center, East Meadow, New York, and Associate Professor of Clinical Psychiatry, State University of New York at Stony Brook School of Medicine, Stony Brook, New York

JONAS R. RAPPEPORT, M.D., Clinical Professor of Psychiatry, School of Medicine, University of Maryland, Baltimore, Maryland

JONAS ROBITSCHER, J.D., M.D., formerly Henry R. Luce Professor of Law and Behavioral Sciences, Emory University, Atlanta, Georgia

RICHARD ROSNER, M.D., Diplomate in Forensic Psychiatry, Clinical Associate Professor, Department of Psychiatry, School of Medicine, New York University, and Medical Director, Forensic Psychiatry Clinic for the New York Criminal and Supreme Courts (First Judicial District), New York, New York

FAUST F. ROSSI, J.D., Professor of Law, School of Law, Cornell University, Ithaca, New York

ROBERT L. SADOFF, M.D., Clinical Professor of Psychiatry, Director, Center for Studies in Social-Legal Psychiatry, University of Pennsylvania, Lecturer in Law, Villanova University School of Law, Philadelphia, Pennsylvania

RICHARD SCHUSTER, Ph.D., Chief Psychologist, Family Court Mental Health Services of the City of New York, and Clinical Director, Mental Health Services, Bronx Family Court, New York, New York

RALPH SLOVENKO, LL.B., Ph.D., Professor of Law and Psychiatry, School of Law, Wayne State University, Detroit, Michigan

EMANUEL TANAY, M.D., Clinical Professor of Psychiatry, Wayne State University School of Medicine, Detroit, Michigan

HENRY C. WEINSTEIN, LL.B., LL.M., M.D., Clinical Associate Professor, Department of Psychiatry, School of Medicine, and Adjunct Professor of Law, School of Law, New York University, New York, New York

FOREWORD

As the current president of The American Academy of Psychiatry and the Law, I am indeed privileged to write a foreword to this book.

This represents the first major publishing activity of the academy outside of the bulletin and the newsletter. The credit for this must go entirely to Dr. Richard Rosner, whose contributions to the field of forensic psychiatry are both numerous and significant. To name but one, I would point to his organizing the first local branch of the academy. Its annual January meeting in New York City has already become something of a tradition.

This book will appeal to any serious student of the field. Articles on civil law and psychiatry represent wide-ranging studies of an area that forensic psychiatrists are often accused of overlooking in order to focus on the criminal law. I would hasten to add that the latter is also fully covered in these pages.

In his chapter entitled "A Conceptual Model for Forensic Psychiatry," Dr. Rosner focuses on the need to determine what psychiatric findings are germane to the legal issue. To many psychiatrists this will be understood to mean that forensic psychiatry is simply a by-product of clinical psychiatry. In my opinion, those areas which are dealt with in forensic psychiatry may in fact represent areas for clinical research largely unavailable to other psychiatrists. For an example of this, one only need recall that twenty years ago the diagnosis of traumatic neurosis was actively discouraged by many clinical psychiatrists. This entity was usually equated with malingering. However, today in DSM III one reads of post-traumatic stress disorders and one of the stressors mentioned is that of car accidents. I would suggest that this is in large measure due to the forensic psychiatrists' recognition that such an entity did, in fact, exist. Another example is the opportunity for psychiatrists working in maximum security prisons to understand stress-related regressive phenomena and to share such understanding with clinical psychiatrists who have not had the opportunity to study in such settings.

On behalf of the officers and members of The American Academy of Psychiatry and the Law, I congratulate Dr. Rosner and those of his colleagues who have contributed to this most worthwhile publication.

HERBERT E. THOMAS, M.D.

INTRODUCTION

The first book to have been conceived and produced for The American Academy of Psychiatry and the Law, under the auspices of its Tri-State Chapter, *Critical Issues in American Psychiatry and the Law* is a record of an adventure in ideas.

Here are the collected papers, revised for this presentation and brought up to date, that were given at the annual series of postgraduate medical education programs in New York City by the regional membership of The American Academy of Psychiatry and the Law. In several instances in order to make this volume even more comprehensive, entirely new chapters were added to the basic core. One result is an intentional diversity of style. Some of these papers retain the flavor of their original oral format, and their ideas are presented in an informal, almost intimate manner. Other chapters are so filled with data that, although they may have been read to an attentive audience, they gain substantially by being available for leisurely study in written form. In all cases, the essays represent sophisticated minds engaged in approaching some of the most complex problems at the interface of two professions, namely, mental health and the law.

The Tri-State Chapter, as an idea, was born in Boston at the October 1975 meeting of The American Academy of Psychiatry and the Law. At that time, it was determined that so many complex issues were evolving in the field of forensic psychiatry that a single, national convention did not provide sufficient opportunity for serious consideration and advanced postgraduate education. On November 13, 1975, the first meeting of the New York regional membership group of A.A.P.L. was held. The minutes of that meeting read, "It was suggested that a modest goal might be set: furthering the education of all psychiatrists who were interested in the interface of psychiatry and the law."

The most public aspect of that "modest goal" has been the annual training programs held at New York University Medical

Center and jointly sponsored by the Post-Graduate Medical School of New York University and the Tri-State Chapter of A.A.P.L., with the assistance of the Forensic Psychiatry Clinic for the Criminal and Supreme Courts of New York (First Judicial Department). In 1977 the program was devoted to the topic "Legal Activism: Its Impact on Psychiatric Practice and Social Structures." In 1978 the focus was on the subject "The Expert Witness in Forensic Psychiatry." In 1979 the theme was "Family Law, Domestic Relations and Forensic Psychiatry." In 1980 the topic was, "Psychiatric Treatment and the Law." These four areas are represented in the four major sections of this text.

In each instance, the executive board of the regional chapter sought to have diverse needs addressed. Some members of the audience would be novices in forensic psychiatry; others would be leading educators in the field. Each program had to offer introductory materials, which would bring the beginners up to baseline levels of information necessary for informed discussion. However, each program also had to offer advanced and subtle state-of-the-art data so that the most learned professor would come away with the legitimate feeling of being stimulated to further thought. The task was to find superb lecturers, with scholarly depth and clinical wisdom—not such a modest goal as we had initially anticipated.

One of the concerns was to avoid premature closure of discussion. We did not want the audience to leave with the feeling that problems had been solved; rather, we wanted them to come to a deeper understanding of the facets of the problems, to share in the intellectual process of reasoning about issues with some of the best minds in America. To that end, we encouraged each lecturer to present his or her ideas firmly, to stake out a position on an issue, and to argue it cogently. We attempted to balance these presentations against each other, in the best tradition of an adversary system so that no one view would be accepted as authoritative. It was hoped that this conflict and ferment of ideas would make for *active learning,* not passive participation in a didactic exercise.

It is our belief that we have largely succeeded. Each year the attendance at the annual meetings has increased, and the quality of the questions from the audience has become impressive. In truth, these are mutual educational experiences, wherein the principal speakers enter into a sophisticated dialogue with the audience.

This book is an invitation to a wider public to join in that dialogue, to experience personally the adventure in ideas that has made "the education of all psychiatrists who were interested in the interface of psychiatry and the law" such a rewarding enterprise.

CONTENTS

SECTION III
FAMILY LAW, DOMESTIC RELATIONS,
AND FORENSIC PSYCHIATRY

SECTION IV
PSYCHIATRIC TREATMENT AND THE LAW

CRITICAL ISSUES IN
AMERICAN PSYCHIATRY AND THE LAW

SECTION I

LEGAL ACTIVISM

Chapter 1

A CONCEPTUAL MODEL
FOR FORENSIC PSYCHIATRY:
A GUIDE FOR THE PERPLEXED

RICHARD ROSNER, M.D.

A major source of confusion in psychiatry and the law is the absence of a uniform conceptual framework for practitioners in the field. This stands in contradistinction to the uniform medical model of organizing information about a particular patient. Such organizing frameworks facilitate communication between professionals. More importantly, a good conceptual model permits clarity of thought by directing attention to relevant considerations. The thrust of this chapter is that such a framework can be designed for forensic psychiatry and that it will enhance the quality of psychiatric-legal thought and psychiatric-legal reports.

The model that is used in medical practice is well known. It is a format used in the presentation of cases by physicians at all levels of experience, from medical students to practitioners to professors. In this model, the relevant facts are marshalled in a systematic manner. An outline of the model is as follows:

1. Chief complaint of the patient
2. History of the present illness
3. History of past medical illnesses
4. Review of social, vocational, and familial considerations
5. Review of physical systems
6. Review of mental status
7. Physical examination
8. Laboratory data
9. Differential diagnoses

Understandably, many physicians who enter into the practice of forensic psychiatry attempt to organize their ideas using this well-

5

known medical model. They do not routinely consider whether or not that model is appropriate to work at the interface of mental health and the law. They do not consider whether another organizational framework would be better for the purposes of interprofessional communication. They do not consider whether the traditional medical framework may actually interfere with understanding the nature of psychiatric-legal problems. One result may be that reports by forensic psychiatrists are often irrelevant to the needs of the legal system. Also, the reports may be so cumbersome for legally trained persons to decipher that the value of the reports are undermined. More important, the traditional model of organizing data may not be designed to accommodate the relevant legal data base and may not be designed to permit rational consideration of psychiatric-legal issues.

To put this matter in bold relief, it may be useful to note that the system for the organization of facts into a meaningful conceptual framework that is used by lawyers is quite different from that used by doctors. The usual legal outline, such as might be employed when a law school student essays to "brief" a case, is entirely different from the medical model. An outline of the legal model is as follows:

1. Who are the parties to the case?
2. What is the nature of the specific legal proceeding?
3. What are the pertinent facts in the case?
4. What are the applicable rules of law in the case?
5. What is the issue in this specific case?
6. What is the decision (holding, finding, verdict)?
7. What rule (and potential precedent for the future) has been the outcome of the case?
8. What is the reasoning process used by the court, how did it apply the relevant rules of law to the specific facts of the case in order to reach its decision on the issue of the case?
9. What concurring or dissenting opinions were presented by the other judges who heard the case?
10. What terms were given specific legal meaning (as opposed to colloquial English usage) during this court decision?[1]

---

[1]For an interesting variation on the legal conceptual model, *see* Harold J. Grilliot, *Introduction to Law and the Legal System* (Boston, Houghton Mifflin Company, 1975), pp. 12 and 13.

There are several striking differences between these two styles of organizing facts. Perhaps it is most important to note that most lawyers are as unfamiliar with the traditional medical model of data organization as most doctors are unfamiliar with the traditional legal model of data organization. Yet each of these models has been designed over the course of time to permit intraprofessional communication, to facilitate reasoning about the data that is relevant to the respective functions of the two separate professions. These models are not merely arbitrary, albeit different doctors will make some minor alterations in the exact sequence of the sections of the medical conceptual framework and different lawyers will make their personal modifications of the basic outline of the legal conceptual model.

One outcome of these different models is that medical reports are usually quite intelligible to doctors but are not readily readable by attorneys. On the simplest level, they do not recognize the headings we use to organize our information. They do not understand what weight to give to one portion of the report as opposed to another portion of the report. Most irritatingly, they are confused by our system of putting "the answer," i.e. the differential diagnoses, at the *end* of the report, as conspicuously contrasted to their system of putting "the answer," i.e. the court's holding/finding/verdict, near the *start* of the report. This does not even begin to address the fact that the nature and quality of a medical answer is quite distinct from the nature and quality of a legal answer. Without belaboring the point, it follows that the reverse is also most often true—legal reports are usually quite understandable to lawyers but are not readily readable by physicians. One of the basic tasks in training beginning fellows in forensic psychiatry is to teach them how to read a formal report of a case. They can read all of the individual words, phrases, and sentences; they are not able to organize the information into a meaningful conceptual framework. Certainly, it may be easier to fit a square peg into a round hole than to fit legal data into the medical framework, or vice versa.

Any conceptual model that is used in psychiatric-legal thinking and report writing must borrow from both professional frameworks. Such a model must direct the attention of the physician and the lawyer to the considerations that are paramount at the interface of mental health and the law, while deleting those portions of the two frameworks that are not germane to the specific medical-legal enterprise. In fact, such a model for psychiatric-legal thinking and report writing should be logically derivative from the very nature of forensic psychiatry.

If one accepts, as this author does, the definition proposed by Dr. Seymour Pollack, Professor of Psychiatry at the University of Southern California and Director of its Institute of Psychiatry and the Law, that forensic psychiatry is the application of psychiatric expertise for legal ends, then the nature of the task becomes relatively straightforward. First, one must be clear on the specific legal end, i.e. the legal issue that is under specific consideration. Is the issue competence to stand trial? Is the issue competence to make a will? Is the issue Who should have custody of a child? There is no such entity as a general psychiatric-legal report; there is only a specific psychiatric-legal report addressed to a specific legal issue. Unless the forensic psychiatrist and the lawyer agree on the legal issue to be the focus of the psychiatric-legal evaluation, there will be much waste of time, talent, and money.

Second, every legal issue exists within a legal context. That context depends upon the court that has competent jurisdiction over the case. There is no single body of law in the United States. Each state has its own statutes and case law and administrative codes; the federal government has its own set of statutes, case law, and administrative codes. That means that every issue has the chance of being in, at the minimum, fifty-one different legal contexts. The legal context will be the determining factor in the legally prescribed criteria that govern the interpretation of the specific legal issue. For example, the criteria for determining whether or not a person is "not guilty by reason of insanity" depend on whether the legal context is one that uses the M'Naghten rule, the American Law Institute's Model Penal Code rule, or, in the past, the Durham rule. Unless the forensic psychiatrist and the lawyer can agree to the legally binding criteria that determine the issue in the particular jurisdiction, the result will be wasted effort, ineffectual reasoning, miscommunication, and an irrelevant report.

Third, the focus of the clinical psychiatric examination of the specific individual(s) at the center of the specific legal issue must be directed to the clarification of *relevant* data, i.e. clinical data that are relevant to the legally mandated (by statute, case law, and code) criteria for the specific issue. This is an area of some controversy. Many psychiatrists who are asked to interview a patient/client/ defendant for legal purposes engage in the same type of interview that they would use in their clinical practice, use the same type of reasoning processes as in clinical practice, and write the same type of comprehensive clinical report as in clinical practice. However, the ends of psychiatric-clinical practice are clinical, whereas the ends of psychiatric-legal practice are legal. The different ends require different data. Not all of the data that are relevant for psychiatric-clinical ends are relevant for psychiatric-legal ends. Much psychiatric-clinical data is extraneous and distracting in a psychiatric-legal setting. As a corollary, much of the data that is essential in a psychiatric-legal setting will not be ordinarily considered in a psychiatric-clinical setting. To cite a glaring example, I have seen reports submitted to the court on the issue of testamentary capacity, i.e. competence to make a will, which describe in exquisite clinical detail the adolescent masturbatory fantasies of a geriatric patient but which did not address whether or not the patient had been asked the nature and extent of her property, the natural heirs of her estate, and the purpose of a final will. The test of relevance is essential. To determine what is relevant, one must have a knowledge of the legal issue (step one) and a knowledge of the applicable criteria that determine the meaning of the legal issue (step two). The collection of germane psychiatric data (step three) follows naturally thereafter.

Fourth, as has been argued persuasively by Dr. Seymour Pollack,[2] the crucial step in a psychiatric-legal evaluation is the reasoning process by which the relevant psychiatric data are applied to the mandatory legal criteria so as to resolve the legal issue under consideration. The immediate applicability of even the most pertinent psychiatric materials is not self-evident. The forensic psychiatrist *must* explain the reasoning process by which he applies

---

[2]Seymour Pollack, "Psychiatric Consultation for the Court," in W. Mendel and P. Solomon, ed., *Psychiatric Consultation* (New York, Grune and Stratton, 1967) and Seymour Pollack, "Forensic Psychiatry—A Specialty," *Bulletin of the American Academy of Psychiatry and the Law, II(1),* 1974.

his psychiatric materials to the legal criteria to settle the issue. In all too many instances, the general psychiatrist who is asked to provide a psychiatric-legal evaluation is unable to make a logical connection between his clinical material and his opinion. Partly that is the result of the unaccustomed situation of having to explain one's thought processes. Partly it is the result of the thought processes being poorly organized and not directed to the legal ends at issue. This fourth step, however, is essentially simple. It is merely the verbalization of what has already taken place in the logical sequence of a good psychiatric-legal evaluation. It is the articulation in words of what the relevant data are, i.e. a report on the pertinent findings of the psychiatric examination, the ways they directly respond to the legally mandated criteria, and, given these data and those criteria, the way the issue is answered (in the opinion of the particular examiner). The main reason this fourth step so often seems impossible for the general psychiatrist is that it has not been preceded by the first three logical steps.

The outline for the psychiatric-legal conceptual model for organizing data and communicating data is thus seen to be logically derived from the inherent nature of the psychiatric-legal evaluation itself. The psychiatric-legal model is as follows:

1. A determination of the specific legal issue(s) to which the psychiatric-legal report is directed.
2. A determination of the specific mandatory legal criteria (statutes, case law, and codes) that interpret the operational meaning of the legal issue(s).
3. A determination of the relevant clinical psychiatric data, i.e. those psychiatric findings which are germane to the criteria.
4. An expression/articulation/formulation of the reasoning process by which step 3 is applied to step 2 to resolve step 1.

It is the experience of this author, and the express contention of this paper, that the psychiatric-legal conceptual framework that has been outlined is adequate to *all* problems in the field of forensic psychiatry, in so far as those problems are understood to be based on the application of psychiatric expertise to legal ends.

The last statement must be understood to be quite distinct from the claim that forensic psychiatry can always provide satisfactory answers to psychiatric-legal problems. It may be that the law has been poorly conceived, so the specific issue is vague or may not refer to a "real" entity. For example, no law directed to the selection of satanic witches can be dealt with in the absence of satanic witches. This is the issue that periodically surfaces when persons talk of the myth of mental illness. If there is no such thing as mental illness then laws about mental illness are meaningless (it is alleged).

In a similar manner, if the legal criteria that determine the meaning of the law are vague or have no definite operational content, then it will be difficult or impossible to provide germane psychiatric data. In the Durham rule for criminal responsibility, for example, the operational definition of product was imprecise, making psychiatric testimony of dubious value.

Alternately, it may be that there is no firm psychiatric data to offer. Some persons have suggested that the prediction of dangerous behavior is not within psychiatric expertise, no matter how vital the legal issue and no matter how clear the operational criteria.

Finally, the reasoning process itself may be faulty, no matter how clearly it is articulated. Different psychiatrists, looking at the same defendant, may reach different conclusions. One may have used a different reasoning process than the other. The court will have to decide which of the two reasoning processes is to be accepted.

The conceptual model is only a framework for organizing and communicating data. It is not a foolproof method that can produce answers to all the psychiatric-legal problems of society. However, it may serve a useful purpose in pointing out the locus of the difficulty, i.e. in vague law, in imprecise operational criteria, in basic lacunae in psychiatric knowledge, in faulty logic.

The absence of a uniform conceptual model in forensic psychiatry has contributed to many of the difficulties in the practice of the physician in this field. It is hoped that the proposed psychiatric-legal framework will enhance the quality of thought, testimony, and reports.

Chapter 2

THE RIGHT TO TREATMENT: SOME INNOVATIONS IN SEEKING TO ACCOMPLISH ITS GOALS

MORTON BIRNBAUM, M.D., LL.B.

PARTIAL HISTORY OF THE RIGHT TO TREATMENT

In May, 1960, I wrote an article in the American Bar Association Journal entitled *The Right to Treatment*.[1] It proposed what was then a novel concept in American law. It advocated the *realistic* recognition, definition, enforcement, and implementation of the legal right of a state mental hospital patient to adequate care and treatment. For convenience, I called this concept the right to treatment. It was pointed out that although our society undoubtedly recognized a moral right to treatment, our law had not recognized this concept—especially for the involuntarily civilly committed state mental hospital patient.

The article first pointed out the need for the right to treatment. It showed that several hundred thousand Americans were treated in our state mental hospitals every year. Most of these patients, whether voluntarily or involuntarily hospitalized, received inadequate care and treatment due to overcrowding, understaffing, and other factors—all due primarily, but not solely, to insufficient funding.

While every state had statutes regulating who should be hospitalized in state mental hospitals and how one should be hospitalized—

This chapter is based on a paper originally presented at a conference on legal activism at the annual meeting of the New York State Chapter of the American Academy of Psychiatry and the Law held in New York City on January 29, 1977.

[1]Birnbaum, *The Right to Treatment*, 46 AMER. BAR ASSN. J. 499(1960).

12

whether voluntarily or involuntarily, by contrast, no state had an effective statute compelling adequate care for these patients during hospitalization. It was proposed that this failure to provide minimally adequate care and treatment constituted a deprivation of liberty without the due process of law required by the fourteenth amendment to the United States Constitution. The contention was made that effective enforcement of a constitutional right to treatment—the releasing of inadequately treated patients through habeas corpus proceedings—would compel the state to provide minimally adequate care. Moreover, federal aid would probably be needed to supplement state funding.

In an accompanying editorial entitled "A New Right,"[2] the journal commented that if such a precedent could be established, it would be "the dawn of a new day" for thousands of the mentally ill. It compared the possibilities to the results of such legal milestones as *Marbury v. Madison*,[3] which established the Constitution as superior to the laws of Congress.

In this chapter, I shall first review certain unfortunately minimal improvements in state mental hospital care achieved in the last two decades because of the circumscribed recognition and enforcement of this right.

Then I shall discuss some recently proposed innovations in this constitutional concept. I believe that these innovations are needed by the problems posed by, and the solutions available for, inadequate state mental hospital care in the 1980s.

IN THE SIXTIES, A RIGHT WHOSE TIME HAD NOT COME

Throughout the 1960s, although the need for the right to treatment continued, no legislature enacted an effective right to treatment statute, and no court recognized this concept for the noncriminal state mental hospital patient.

On at least seven separate occasions, the United States Supreme Court persistently refused to hear cases involving this concept, although the facts of grossly inadequate and inhumane care and treatment were clear and were undisputed by the state mental hos-

---

[2]*Editorial, A New Right*, 46 AMER. BAR ASSN. J. 516 (1960).
[3]Marbury v. Madison, 5 U.S. 137 (1803).

pital personnel who were the nominal defendents in these actions.

For example, on four separate occasions, the Court repeatedly refused to hear a Florida case, *Donaldson v. O'Connor.*[4] In that case, there was only 1 doctor and 1 nurse for more than 1,000 patients; patients were often not seen by any doctor for more than two years; completely illiterate aides who were in full charge of wards often brutally physically assaulted patients; and many of the buildings were in a complete state of obsolescence, some having been built more than 150 years before.

The foregoing inhumane conditions were clearly set forth in a Florida legislative report prepared by Richardson Smith,[5] a distinguished Florida lawyer, who went on to become the president of the American Bar Association. This horrifying report had been repeatedly submitted to the Supreme Court in support of Donaldson's petitions for certiorari and, in effect, repeatedly rejected by the Supreme Court.

On three other separate occasions, the Court again persistently refused to hear a New York case, *Stephens v. LaBurt.*[6] In that case, there was only 1 doctor for more than 500 patients; the patient had not been seen by any doctor for more than one year; and the ward attendant who was in sole and full charge of the patient's ward at night, and who was subsequently found to be criminally insane, routinely sexually assaulted helpless, bedridden elderly patients, even murdering one patient during such an assault by choking him to death.

During the 1960s, therefore, the concept of a legal right to treatment had done nothing to raise care and treatment in state mental hospitals to minimally adequate levels for patients not accused, or convicted, of committing a crime. In the 1970s, how-

---

[4]Donaldson v. O'Connor, 400 U.S. 869 (1970);
Donaldson v. O'Connor, 390 U.S. 971 (1968);
Donaldson v. Florida, 371 U.S. 806 (1963);
in re Donaldson, 364 U.S. 808 (1960).

[5]Committee on State Institutions, Florida Legislative Council, Final Report of the General Findings Relating to the Conditions at Florida State Hospital and the Alleged Mistreatment of Patients, May 1, 1961 (mimeograph).

[6]New York *ex rel.* Anonymous v. LaBurt, 385 U.S. 936 (1966);
United States *ex rel.* Anonymous v. LaBurt, 373 U.S. 928 (1963);
New York *ex rel.* Anonymous v. LaBurt, 369 U.S. 428 (1962).

ever, this concept appeared to have become, on the surface at least, a right whose time had come — primarily because of the impetus of the case of *Wyatt v. Stickney*.

IN THE SEVENTIES, A RIGHT WHOSE TIME HAD COME?

Wyatt v. Stickney

In March, 1971, in the case of *Wyatt v. Stickney*,[7] United States District Court Judge Frank M. Johnson, Jr., held that involuntarily civilly committed patients in an Alabama state mental hospital were entitled to minimally adequate care and treatment or they were being deprived of their liberty without the due process of law required by the fourteenth amendment to the United States Constitution. Commentators invariably overlook that a significant breakthrough occurred when the defendants, led by Dr. Stonewall B. Stickney, then Alabama Mental Health Commissioner, conceded at the outset of the proceedings, and before Judge Johnson's decision was handed down, that these patients had such a right. *Wyatt*, therefore, not only marked the first time that an American court clearly recognized this concept. It also marked the first time that state mental hospital personnel agreed during litigation that their patients had this right.

In subsequent orders, the scope of the hearings was extended to all patients in Alabama state mental hospitals and state schools for the retarded; therefore, all patients, both voluntary and involuntary, in these facilities were included in the court's follow-up orders.

Judge Johnson said that the three major aspects of an adequate treatment program are the following: (1) a humane physical and psychological environment, (2) staffing adequate in numbers and training to provide treatment, and (3) an individual treatment plan for each patient.[8] Subsequently, he ordered the defendants to implement a specific set of objective standards of care and treatment.[9] Again, commentators usually overlook that although these standards improved care in Alabama facilities, they were still

---

[7] Wyatt v. Stickney, 325 F. Supp. 781 (1971).

[8] Wyatt v. Stickney, 334 F. Supp. 1341 (1971).

[9] 344 F. Supp. 373 (1972).

low standards for minimally adequate care in state hospitals and undoubtedly would be unacceptable for the usual voluntary or private mental inpatient facility — especially in the area of patient-professional staff ratios.

Subsequently, more than twenty "right to treatment" and similar cases have been started throughout the nation involving not only state mental hospitals but also state schools for the retarded and state prisons.

The Supreme Court, however, still refuses to hear and determine whether this concept is a valid constitutional requirement.

For example, it is often generally overlooked that in the case of *O'Connor v. Donaldson*,[10] decided by the Court in June, 1975, the Court specifically ordered that the decision of the United States Court of Appeals for the Fifth Circuit that had recognized the concept of "the right to treatment" not be considered to be of precedential effect.

I would like to digress now to make three comments that one should bear in mind while reading this chapter.

First, I was a counsel in all the *Donaldson, Stephens,* and *Wyatt* cases that were discussed and in the *Woe* case that will be discussed. Accordingly, as Judge Learned Hand once noted, an advocate comes to these discussions more with the sword of Luther than the reasoning found in the book of Erasmus.

Second, I wish to emphasize that no blanket adverse criticism of any state mental hospital personnel is intended by any comment in this chapter. The understaffing and lack of adequate physical facilities in our state mental hospitals are not their doing; rather they are the doing of our society. Our society should be grateful to, rather than censorious of, the personnel who continue to work in these institutions under the present trying conditions.

Third, in truth, I originally agreed to come to the convention because of the opportunity of meeting old friends. I developed other motives.

To continue, I shall first point out that the need for the *realistic* recognition, definition, enforcement, and implementation of this right exists as validly now as it did when I first proposed this concept in 1960. Then I shall advocate a novel constitutional

---

[10]O'Connor v. Donaldson, 422 U.S. 563 (1975).

reform—that the care and treatment of the state mental hospital patient be *realistically equalized* and *integrated* with the care and treatment of the general hospital psychiatric inpatient. This advocacy will take the form of a discussion of a current lawsuit, *Woe v. Carey*,[11] that I am now prosecuting in the United States District Court in Brooklyn.

THE PRESENT NEED FOR THE RIGHT TO TREATMENT

Over 500,000 severely mentally ill Americans are institutionalized annually in our state mental hospitals.[12] Disproportionately frequently, they are socially disadvantaged—being poor, black, and/or uneducated. Frequently, they require only short-term mental hospitalization—thirty days or less. Usually, they are involuntarily civilly committed. Almost invariably, they receive only inadequate custodial care and treatment primarily because there is no significant federal funding for these facilities.

At best, this custodial care is aimed only at the temporary control of the most flagrant abnormal behavior that brought the person to the state facility.

This too often inhumane treatment of these severely mentally ill Americans is the major nationwide unsolved problem in the delivery of adequate health care to the socially disadvantaged.

It is conventional for most reformers—including myself in the past—to attempt to upgrade the inadequate care in our state mental hospitals by asking the state legislatures and our courts only for marginal improvements. It is also conventional for other reformers to consider the entire state mental hospital system as being inadequate beyond redemption; therefore, they seek to totally phase out the state mental hospital system. Unfortunately, however, they invariably do not offer alternative nonstate mental hospital facilities that are adequate both in number and quality to treat

---

[11]Walter Woe et al. v. Hugh Carey et al., United States District Court, Eastern District of New York, Civ. No. 75 C 1029.

[12]U.S. Dept. Health and Human Services, Public Health Service, Alcohol, Drug Abuse, and Mental Health Administration, National Institute of Mental Health, Division of Biometry and Epidemiology, Survey and Reports Branch, Statistical Note No. 154, Trends in Patient Care Episodes in Mental Health Facilities, 1955–1977 (DHHS Pub. No. [ADM] 180–158, 1980).

the socially disadvantaged inmates of our state hospitals.[13]

Various groups supported by several foundation and federal government grants are now engaged in lawsuits throughout the nation attempting to achieve these inadequate conventional goals. Frequently, the Civil Rights Division of the United States Department of Justice is actively participating in these lawsuits, as they are aimed only at state and local governments. Tragically, these well-publicized but futile efforts have served to obscure the simple truth.

Neither the federal government, any state government, any national health care group, nor any public law group has a realistic plan to solve this major nationwide problem — the inadequate delivery of needed mental hospital care to the severely mentally ill, socially disadvantaged Americans now being institutionalized in our state mental hospitals. Furthermore, inmates of state mental hospitals do not routinely riot and seize and kill attendants as do inmates of Attica and other state penal institutions. Neither do they protest their treatment by openly speaking out and lobbying as have blacks, women, and homosexuals. Accordingly, it should not be expected that our legislators, our governors or our president will originate efforts to fully correct conditions in our state facilities.

It is to be expected, therefore, that since nothing seems to invite more rejection in our society than being both socially disadvantaged and severely mentally ill — a form of bigotry that I have labeled "sanism"[14] — the future reform efforts by our society in general and by our legal and medical communities in particular will turn elsewhere. I believe, however, that if groups such as A.A.P.L. were to help, our society's present unjust treatment of state mental hospital patients could be corrected.

First, the current treatment of the socially advantaged voluntary general hospital psychiatric inpatient establishes the goal we *should* achieve for the state mental hospital patient.

Second, lawsuits such as the one I shall now discuss, *Woe v. Carey*, show us how we *can* achieve this goal. The *Woe* case sets forth a

---

[13]Birnbaum, *The Right to Treatment*, 10 *Duquesne L. Rev.* 579, at 597–606 (1972).

[14]Birnbaum, *The Right to Treatment: Some Comments on its Development*, in MEDICAL, MORAL AND LEGAL ISSUES IN MENTAL HEALTH CARE 97 (F. J. Ayd ed. 1974).

unique, needed, and novel constitutional claim of first instance. It asks of our courts—and indirectly of our legislatures—that the care and treatment of the state mental hospital patient be *equal to, and integrated with,* the care of the general hospital psychiatric inpatient.

THE GOAL THAT WE SHOULD ACHIEVE

Another 500,000 equally severely mentally ill Americans are hospitalized annually in our general hospital psychiatric inpatient facilities—80 percent in nonpublic general hospital psychiatric inpatient facilities.[15]

Compared with the state mental hospital population, the patients in this nonpublic sector are, disproportionately frequently, socially advantaged, being middle or upper class, white and/or educated. Nearly always these patients are voluntarily hospitalized. Usually, they require only short-term hospitalization.

Almost invariably, these patients in the nonpublic facilities receive necessary adequate care and treatment frequently due to huge amounts of federal funds, e.g. Medicaid, amounting to more than $1 billion annually. By contrast, the state mental hospital patient between twenty-one and sixty-five years of age is arbitrarily excluded from any Medicaid benefit no matter how impoverished he is.

The humane treatment of these socially advantaged severely mentally ill Americans in our nonpublic general hospital psychiatric inpatient facilities shows that our nation has both the medical and financial capabilities to provide adequate care and treatment for the severely mentally ill when it chooses to do so.

A METHOD OF ACHIEVING THIS GOAL—*WOE V. CAREY*

Woe v. Carey is a certified class action brought on behalf of all the involuntarily civilly committed patients in all New York state mental hospitals. It is the primary goal of this lawsuit to obtain medically needed and adequate mental hospital care for these patients.

---

[15]U.S. Dept. Health and Human Services, *supra* note 12.

The complaint alleges that in the state of New York and throughout the nation, there are invidious discriminations between the socially advantaged and the socially disadvantaged as to the *place* of, as to the *method of obtaining,* and as to the *quality* of mental hospital care.

De facto, and not *de jure,* under state law when the socially disadvantaged, the poor, the black, and the uneducated, become so severely mentally ill as to require mental hospitalization, they are disproportionately frequently steered, usually by involuntary civil commitment, to the state mental hospital.

By contrast, when the middle and upper classes, the white, and the educated similarly become so severely mentally ill as to require mental hospitalization, they are usually steered, invariably by voluntary hospitalization, to the general hospital psychiatric facility.

Subsequent to the utilization of these invidious two-tier procedures for mental hospitalization, there follows equally, if not even more invidious, two-tier provisions for mental hospital care that are directly and causally related to unfair procedures for mental hospitalization. These unjust two-tier provisions for mental hospital care exist *de jure,* both under state and federal laws, and *de facto.*

The socially disadvantaged patients of the state mental institutions receive only unneeded, and actually potentially harmful, inadequate custodial care frequently at a total cost of less than $50.00 a day.

By contrast, the socially advantaged general hospital psychiatric facility patients receive needed, and potentially curative, adequate and active care at a total cost that is at least $250.00 a day.

Neither ability to pay nor financial sponsorship in building the general hospital psychiatric unit is a factor in usually steering the socially disadvantaged to the state mental institution and then providing them only with unneeded and potentially harmful short-term care.

As to ability to pay, the socially disadvantaged, because of their poverty and their severe mental illness, are eligible for federal Medicaid benefits. Medicaid is ready, willing, and able to pay the complete $250.00 a day or more cost for any beneficiary who had been steered to, and treated in, the general hospital. Furthermore, the majority of psychiatric patients in the upper-tier general hospital psychiatric facility receive Medicaid benefits. For although this majority is middle-class, they are usually considered to be medically indigent, and therefore eligible for Medicaid. This occurs because the usual Blue Shield and other third-party hospitalization insurance contract often excludes mental hospitalization.

As to financial sponsorship of the building of the general hospital psychiatric units, almost all these facilities were built since 1960 and almost 100 percent with federal funds.

Admittedly, more money and better care may not always improve the prognosis and result for the socially disadvantaged state mental hospital patient who now usually receives only inadequate and custodial care at a cost of $50.00 a day. This patient claims, however, that he is constitutionally entitled to at least the same opportunity for cure or failure that is invariably routinely accorded to the upper and middle class, white, and educated general hospital mental patient at a cost of $250.00 a day or more.

For relief, the plaintiffs claim that they have a constitutional right to adequate care and treatment, as they had been involuntarily civilly committed by means of loosely construed remedial substantive and procedural state mental hospitalization laws. Ostensibly, the *sole* reason for their involuntary incarceration was that the state of New York claimed that these inmates needed active and adequate mental hospital care.

The inmates claim, therefore, that as they had been involuntarily civilly committed, *quid pro quo,* they have a constitutional right to receive adequate care at the mental facility to which they had been committed by a justice of the New York Supreme Court.

The prayer for relief, however, does not limit itself to making the conventional, orthodox, and expected request that the budgets of state mental institutions be increased—through increased state appropriations, through Medicaid eligibility and other federal funding, etc.—so that the state institution would be able to approach the $250.00 a day level of expenditures of the general hospital psychiatric facility. Realistically, at most this could only result in still invidious two-tier procedures for mental hospitalization that would be subsequently followed by "separate but only theoretically equal" provisions for mental hospital care.

The inmates have, therefore, made an unconventional, unorthodox, and unique constitutional claim of first instance. They claim that it is constitutionally required to have a single "integrated and equal" mental hospitalization procedure for the socially disadvantaged and for the socially advantaged. Furthermore, they claim that this must constitutionally be directly related to, and subsequently followed by, a single "integrated and equal" active and adequate mental hospital care system.

Thereby, both the socially advantaged and the socially disadvantaged would usually be primarily voluntarily hospitalized, and both groups would be treated within the same adequate facilities.

CONCLUSION

In this chapter, I have set forth innovations in the concept of the right to treatment that I believe enable this concept to meet present needs and problems.

These innovations concern themselves with the need to ask our legislatures and our courts that the care and treatment of the state mental hospital patient be equal to, and integrated with, the care of the general hospital psychiatric inpatient, especially with the nonpublic general hospital psychiatric inpatient.

I hope that these innovations merit consideration, frank criticism, and support.

Chapter 3

LEGAL ACTIVISM AND ITS IMPACT ON PSYCHIATRIC PRACTICE: THE RIGHT TO REFUSE TREATMENT

HENRY C. WEINSTEIN, LL.B., LL.M., M.D.

Changes in the practice of a medical specialty are usually slow. Clinical experiences and research findings are announced, replicated, accepted by the professional community, then gradually incorporated into the teaching curriculum and into individual practices. Social changes and changes in the economic and political situation, as well as changes in the law, rarely immediately and directly alter clinical practice. Within the past decade, however, changes, as the result of the impact of the law on or the intrusion of the judicial process into psychiatric practice have taken place with dizzying speed. Lawyers, judges, and lawmakers (legislators) are eschewing their usually conservative posture—here in regard to mental health issues—and taking a more active stance to bring about specific changes in psychiatric practice. I refer to this phenomena as legal activism.

This chapter will use the development of the principle of the patient's right to refuse psychiatric treatment to demonstrate this activism and the resulting impact on psychiatric practice.

The innumerable subsidiary legal and psychiatric issues and the profound philosophical and ethical questions that are raised by any consideration of a right to refuse treatment cannot be included here. However, because much of the initial controversy surrounding the right to refuse treatment is the result of conflicting social trends and conflicting perspectives, some of these trends

---

This chapter is adapted from an earlier article, which was presented at a symposium of the New York State chapter of The American Academy of Psychiatry and the Law on January 25, 1977, and was published as The Right to Treatment in *The Bulletin of the American Academy of Psychiatry and the Law,* 5:425, 1977.

and perspectives will be presented first. This will be followed by a brief discussion of certain central issues—involuntary commitment and informed consent. Then, a number of legal decisions that have set forth some of the parameters of the right to refuse treatment will precede a discussion of some attempts at solutions to the problems raised. Finally, regarding the impact that the development of the right to refuse treatment has had on psychiatric practice, this chapter will conclude with some suggestions on how we might better cope with the resulting difficulties.

Of the various modern social trends that are epitomized by the right to refuse treatment, the demand for greater civil rights and civil liberties is perhaps the most dramatic. That the American Civil Liberties Union has been so active in the mental health area is not a coincidence. One by one different groups have demanded greater social, political, and economic equality. A whole segment of the legal industry is now devoted to such issues—the civil rights lawyers. Where the clients themselves cannot articulate their dissatisfactions, as is often the case with psychiatric patients, the lawyer's role is particularly evident. This takes the form of a new style of legal practice—advocacy.

A related trend, often surfacing under the banner of the right to privacy, stresses the right to be left alone. Justice Brandeis is often quoted when he said that the makers of the constitution "conferred as against the government, the right to be let alone—the most comprehensive of rights and the right most valued by civilized men."[1] Our most basic rights are set forth in the Bill of Rights, but this followed by eleven years the Declaration of Independence that listed "certain unalienable rights . . . life, liberty, and the pursuit of happiness." Thus, again and again the emphasis has been on rights, and in order to start our considerations in this chapter, it must at the outset be emphasized that the right to refuse treatment is a right against the government, and "the government" in these situations is represented by the physician—the practitioner. This fact must be kept in mind in the cases where psychiatric treatment is refused; the psychiatrist represents the government, and this is the way legal advocates and legal activists see him.

---

[1]Olmstead v. U.S., 277 U.S. 438, 478 (1928).

Another significant social trend that must be taken into account in understanding some of the issues related to the right to refuse treatment is the changing attitude of the public toward vested authority. On the campus, in the church, and in the professional's office, the effects of this trend are evident. The medical profession is not alone. Clients of all professionals (again, often aided by legal activists) are demanding more say in the service being delivered and more accountability from the professional. These changes are frequently expressed in legal terms, the change from a fiduciary relationship to a more contractual or quasi-contractual relationship. What this means, in essence, is that there is a demand for more equality between the parties, and, as a result in the psychiatric situation, an increased emphasis on the patient's right to know with greater specificity about the treatment proposed and, as a corollary, his right to refuse treatment.

Turning from such larger social trends to certain critical legal issues relating to the refusal of psychiatric treatment, we must, at the outset, distinguish between the refusal to be hospitalized and the refusal of a particular treatment while in a psychiatric hospital. The former encompasses the legal issues relating to involuntary incarceration, the latter, the legal issues relating to informed consent.

Cases and statutes usually refer to the status of the patient, i.e. whether the patient is a voluntary or an involuntary psychiatric patient. One would think that there would be little question that a voluntary patient clearly has the right to refuse treatment. However, the voluntary patient is usually, by statute, subject to a number of restrictions. He usually must give notice before he can leave the psychiatric hospital, and during this period of time, the hospital director has the opportunity to convert the patient to involuntary status. So, in truth, the voluntary psychiatric patient is not quite in the same position as the ordinary medical patient. But is the status of a hospitalized patient a truly valid distinction on which to base a difference of rights, e.g. here the right to refuse treatment? Some legal scholars have noted that the realities of why a particular patient is hospitalized under either status do *not* permit the conclusion to be drawn that there is an invariable relationship between the status of a patient (whether he is voluntary or involuntary) and the severity of his illness and therefore the denial of his right to refuse treatment.

However, should the involuntary commitment itself be taken to imply that the patient cannot refuse treatment? Certainly a strong argument can usually be made that this was the intention of the commitment statute, the intent of the legislature in involuntary hospitalization of a psychiatric patient. And, in my own experience, it was certainly the stated intent of the judges who had committed patients in our court at the Bellevue Psychiatric Hospital, i.e. that the patient is being involuntarily committed in order to be treated, whether the patient wanted to be treated or not.

Putting the question differently, Does the finding that a patient is not competent to remain at large (outside of a psychiatric hospital) imply an incompetency to participate in treatment decisions while within the hospital? This is not invariably the case in practice. Involuntary patients are often able to participate in treatment decisions. Furthermore, this capacity usually changes during the course of a period of hospitalization (the patient improves) without a change in status.

In regard to the treatment while a patient is hospitalized, restrictions on the use of particular treatments are usually imposed in the context of the consent to the treatment. The innumerable issues relating to informed consent cannot all be detailed here. While the general principles apply to all medical and surgical patients, there are special issues that arise in relation to certain populations such as prisoners, minors, and, of course, psychiatric patients. The basic principles of informed consent have been set forth by many authors. Stone, for example, presents the issues in the tripartite formula of "competent, informed, consent."[2] The threshold question is the competence of the patient to give consent—here, whether the involuntarily committed is competent to participate in treatment decisions. We note that the trend has been to expand rather than contract the rights of the involuntary patient and therefore to hold him competent to exercise such rights as the right to vote, make a contract, etc. However, the very purpose of involuntary hospitalization, as contrasted to imprisonment, is to

---

[2]Stone, *Mental Health and Law: A System in Transition*, N.I.M.H., 1975.

administer treatment.

The next part of the formula, the informed part of competent, informed consent, i.e. the knowledge to be imparted by the doctor to the patient, is complicated because it may be inappropriate in a particular case to list side effects and dangers to a particular psychiatric patient — even assuming we could predict these effects prior to treatment.

In the last part of the tripartite formula, the consent, the actual agreement on the part of the patient to undergo treatment is complicated, under the best of circumstances, by such questions as ambiguous communications, the doctor's influence over the patient — the transference if you will, both positive and negative — the coerciveness of the hospital setting itself, etc.

This brief look at some of the background issues that impinge upon the topic of the right to refuse treatment will assist us in reviewing a number of illustrative cases, which demonstrate the impact of legal activism on psychiatric practice.

In 1972 in the reknowned case of *Wyatt v. Stickney*,[3] Judge Johnson set forth a list of "minimum constitutional standards for the adequate treatment for the mentally ill," and under the heading "Humane Psychological and Physical Environment" stated that "patients have a right not to be subjected to treatment procedures such as lobotomy, electro-convulsive treatment, aversive reinforcement conditioning or other unusual or hazardous treatment procedures without their express and informed consent after consultation with counsel or an interested party of the patient's choice."[4] Thus, the participants in the informed consent procedure are no longer to be limited to the patient and his doctor. There is an increase in the cast of characters and, more importantly for our purposes, diminution of the physician's authority and power.

In 1975 in the same case, now known as *Wyatt v. Hardin*[5] (in the Alabama United States District Court), Judge Johnson re-

---

[3]Wyatt v. Stickney, 325 F. Supp. 781 (M.D. Ala. 1971); 334 F. Supp. 1341 (M.D. Ala. 1971); *enforced by* 344 F. Supp. 373; 344 F. Supp. 387, *appeal docketed sub nom.*, Wyatt v. Aderholt, No. 72-2634 (5th Cir. Aug. 2, 1973).

[4]*Id.*

[5]Wyatt v. Hardin, *unreported* (M.D. Ala. 1975), *reprinted in* F. MILLER, THE MENTAL HEALTH PROCESS, at 556 (2d ed. 1976).

vised this court ordered standard.

For our inquiry here of the impact on psychiatric practice, it is interesting to note that at the onset of his order Judge Johnson felt constrained to add a disclaimer that the court is not determining which forms of treatment are appropriate.

"It must be emphasized that . . . the court is not undertaking to determine which forms of treatment are appropriate in particular situations." We must wonder why it is necessary "to be emphasized . . ."? What doubts does this denial cover? He goes on: "But the determination of what procedural safeguards must accompany the use of extraordinary or potentially hazardous modes of treatment on patients in the state's mental institutions is a fundamentally legal question and one which the parties to this law suit have put in issue."[6]

This is the critical distinction—the determination of what is appropriate treatment from what he terms procedural safeguards. Certainly, on the face of it this seems an easy and neat distinction, but as practitioners now know, not only do procedural safeguards of sufficient burdensomeness and complexity in essence prohibit a course of action, and eliminate a particular choice of treatment, but also the mere existence of such procedural safeguards may have a chilling effect and inhibit the clinician in the exercise of his responsibilities to provide adequate care.

In any event, in this case Judge Johnson again orders standards to be applied in Bryce Hospital in regard to psychosurgery, aversive therapy, and shock treatment. First, he holds that psychosurgery is to be absolutely prohibited. Whatever one's attitude toward psychosurgery, it must be questioned whether this is merely a procedural safeguard.

Then, in regard to aversive therapy, he sets out strict conditions. Prior approval is required by a committee made up of a psychiatrist, a neurologist or internist, "and at least one member shall be an attorney."[7] The patient must be represented by counsel throughout all proceedings. All striking changes in usual medical practice. Near the end of his list of conditions he adds: "No patient

---

[6]*Id.*

[7]*Id.*, at 557.

shall be subjected to an aversive conditioning program that attempts to extinguish or alter socially appropriate behavior or to develop new behavior patterns for the sole or primary purpose of institutional convenience."[8] Again, what has this to do with procedural safeguards?

In regard to shock treatment, he listed fourteen conditions that must be met. The competency of the patient to give consent is to be determined *by the attorney* appointed to represent him and an "Extraordinary Treatment Committee." It is interesting to note that among those listed conditions is the prohibition of certain types of shock therapy. "Regressive, multiple or depatterning electro-convulsive techniques shall not be utilized."[9] Perhaps *this* is a "procedural safeguard." The point need not be reiterated. These court orders are seriously affecting psychiatric practice. Indeed, the power to administer certain types of psychiatric treatment is taken from the physician.

Judge Johnson's order related specifically to psychosurgery, ECT and aversive conditioning and cases that deal with the right to refuse treatment are generally grouped according to the type of psychiatric treatment involved. The case of *Kaimowitz v. Department of Mental Hygiene* arose in 1973 in a County Circuit Court in Michigan.[10] Kaimowitz was an outside lawyer (a legal "activist"), who brought this habeas corpus action on behalf of a patient, John Doe, who was a detainee under a sexual psychopath law. Doe was charged with the rape and murder of a student nurse while he had been a patient at a state hospital. He had been selected for experimental psychosurgery to "control his uncontrollable aggression." He had signed consent and his parents had also signed. Two committees had reviewed the study and the validity of the consent. At that point Kaimowitz found out and notified the press. Considerable newspaper publicity ensued, and this suit was filed. (Later, funding for the research project was stopped as were plans to pursue the research.)

---

[8]*Id*, at 558.

[9]*Id*, at 560.

[10]Kaimowitz v. Dep't. of Mental Health, *unreported* C.V. #73-1943 (Cir. Ct. Cty. Wayne, Mich. 1973), *reprinted in* F. MILLER. THE MENTAL HEALTH PROCESS. at 567 (2d ed. 1976).

The court, holding that informed consent for experimental psychosurgery *cannot* be given by a patient *involuntarily detained,* stated that "it is obvious that there must be close scrutiny of the adequacy of the consent when an experiment, as in this case, is dangerous, intrusive, irreversible, and of uncertain benefit to the patient and society."[11] This seems reasonable—"close scrutiny." The special psychological problems relating to consent in a medical context had been presented. The lawyers for the Department of Mental Hygiene and the doctors had noted that anyone who has ever been treated for any relatively serious illness recognizes that a doctor can usually get nearly any patient to consent to almost anything because, first, patients do not want to make decisions about complex medical matters and, second, there is the general tendency to avoid decision making in stress situations. The lawyers for the doctors further argued that "a patient is always under duress when hospitalized and that in a hospital or institutional setting there is no such thing as a volunteer."

The court retorted that it did not agree that a truly informed consent cannot be given for a regular surgical procedure by a patient, institutionalized or not. "The law has long recognized that such valid consent can be given. But we do hold that informed consent cannot be given by an involuntarily detained patient for experimental psychosurgery."[12] Thus, as a matter of law, no matter *what* efforts are made to attain fair and proper informed consent, a particular previously accepted medical treatment *cannot* be administered under these circumstances. This, on the basis of *constitutional* principles. After a long discussion of informed consent, reviewing the requirements of (1) capacity to consent, (2) the knowledge of the risks involved and the procedures to be undertaken, and finally (3) the voluntariness of the consent, the court turns to the "compelling constitutional considerations" that *preclude* the involuntary detained mental patient from giving effective consent to this type of surgery. The court cited the first amendment as protecting the freedom to express ideas and to generate ideas. Then the court turned to the right of privacy, relying on the first, fifth, and

---

[11]*Id,* at 593.

[12]*Id.*

fourteenth amendments, saying: "Intrusion into ones intellect, when one is involuntarily detained and subject to the control of institutional authorities, is an intrusion into ones constitutionally protected right of privacy. If one is not protected in his thoughts, behavior, personality and identity, then the right of privacy becomes meaningless."[13] Finally, the court also based its decision on the the eighth amendment, stating that the psychosurgery proposed would constitute cruel and unusual punishment.

I cite these details to indicate the extent to which constitutional arguments have been used here to hold, as a matter of law, that in this case not only is there a right to refuse treatment, but that the procedure of informed consent *cannot be utilized.*

The 1973 case of *Knecht v. Gillman*[14] (in the United States Circuit Court in Iowa) involved aversive conditioning, or behavior modification. Two prisoners in the custody of the state of Iowa alleged that the drug apomorphine—a vomit-inducing drug—was utilized as aversion therapy for various offenses such as not getting up, swearing, lying, and so forth. Noting that the use of apomorphine could only be justified as being used as *treatment,* the court made it clear that the mere characterization of an act as treatment does not insulate it from eighth amendment scrutiny (cruel and unusual punishment). In other words, the court will not take the physician's word for it. And, in this instance, "Whether it is called 'aversive stimuli' or punishment, the act of forcing someone to vomit for a fifteen minute period for committing some minor breach of the rules can only be regarded as cruel and unusual unless the treatment is being administered to a patient who knowingly and intelligently has consented to it."[15]

Recalling that the court's order in *Wyatt v. Hardin* cited previously related to psychosurgery, aversive conditioning therapy and ECT, and having examined the impact of legal activism on the first two, we now turn to ECT (shock treatment) and note that as contrasted to psychosurgery or aversive conditioning, this area is generally a more controversial one, and not only as relates to the right to

---

[13]*Id.*, at 577.

[14]Knecht V. Gillman, 488 F.2d 1136 (8th Cir. 1973).

[15]*Id.*, at 1139.

refuse treatment. This is probably because there are considerable differences of opinion within the profession about ECT. First, as to whether ECT as a form of treatment is severe or hazardous, and second, whether it is the appropriate treatment in particular psychiatric illnesses.

To demonstrate the rapidity of changes as well as the impact of legal activism on this aspect of psychiatric practice, I note a 1977 front page article in the *APA Psychiatric News*[16] on the regulation of ECT, which discussed at length California's newly enacted statute outlining very strict criteria for informed consent before any ECT (or psychosurgery) can be performed on any patient, voluntary or involuntary. The consent forms were prepared by the lawyers of the Patient's Rights Unit of the California Department of Health!

Yet in 1966 — only eleven years previously — in *Campbell v. Glenwood Hills Hospital, Inc.,*[17] which was a case for damages claiming *unauthorized treatment*, the supreme court of Minnesota held there would be no recovery in tort (assault and battery) for ECT and medication administered during a hospitalization because there was a valid court order in which the patient, plaintiff, was found to be "in need of care and treatment," and the statute provided for "institutional care and treatment." The court said, "The course of treatment was determined and effected by competent institutional doctors who would have been at fault if they had not attempted to help the plaintiff [patient]."[18] The court ended this part of its opinion by stating, "If defendants [the doctors and other personnel] are to be held liable to plaintiff in this case, then every psychiatric hospital, state or private, and its superintendent would be liable in tort to patients inspite of full compliance with valid court orders and applicable statutory provisions."[19] in other words, a valid involuntary hospitalization and proper determinations by the professional staff were all that was required to administer ECT. Things were soon to change, and six years later in 1972 a

---

[16]McDonald, *The Regulation of ECT.* XXI PSYCHIATRIC NEWS (Jan. 21, 1977).

[17]Campbell v. Glenwood Hills Hospital, Inc., 142 N.W.2d (1966).

[18]*Id.,* at 262.

[19]*Id.*

New York court, in *Stein v. N.Y.C. Health and Hospitals Corporation*, held that an involuntary patient could refuse ECT in spite of the valid involuntary hospitalization and despite the fact that a parent also consented to this treatment.[20] This case was brought on behalf of this patient by the Mental Health Information Service, a New York State agency under the aegis of the court system, which was originally instituted as an impartial advisory service to the courts and has since positioned itself as an advocacy group. Furthermore, in this case the Judge himself spoke to the patient and decided both that she was competent to decide whether she wanted ECT or not and that in this case she did not want ECT!

From cases dealing with the right to refuse psychosurgery, aversion therapy, and ECT, we turn to the right to refuse medication. In the 1966 *Campbell* case mentioned previously, the court said the doctors would have been at fault if they had not treated the patient despite his refusal. In a 1965 New York case, *Whitree v. State*,[21] damages had been awarded to a patient because he was confined without treatment. Why? Because the patient should have been given certain medication despite his refusals, because he was, in the words of the court, "entitled to it." The court noted, with disapproval, that the patient, Mr. Whitree, had *not* been "treated with any of the modern tranquilizing drugs . . . during his entire stay at the hospital." And it noted, with an air of disbelief, "that the reason for not using such drugs was that Whitree refused them." The court said, "We consider such a reason to be illogical, unprofessional, and not consonant with prevailing medical standards."[22] Thus, not only did this court not recognize or discuss a right to refuse treatment, but it cited a "duty to treat" and raised the spector of a malpractice suit if a patient's refusal is improperly honored. This was 1965, and within six years the pendulum had swung to the opposite side. It was in 1971 that the United States Court of Appeals in New York decided the case of *Winters v. Miller*.[23] A fifty-nine-year-old woman on welfare had been trans-

---

[20]New York City Health and Hospitals Corp. v. Stein, 70 Misc.2d 944, 335 N.Y.S. 2d 461 (Sup. Ct. 1972).

[21]Whitree v. State, 290 N.Y.S.2d 486 (Ct. Cl. 1968).

[22]*Id.*, at 501.

[23]Winters v. Miller, 446 F.2d 65 (2d Cir. 1971); *cert. denied* 404 U.S. 985 (1972).

ferred to a different welfare hotel after living for ten years in one hotel. There, she created a problem for the manager by refusing to change rooms as he had requested, and the police were called. She was taken to a psychiatric hospital where she was involuntarily committed. At the hospital she refused to take medication on the grounds that she was a practicing Christian Scientist. She was medicated over her protests. The issue in this case was whether she was entitled to relief under the federal civil rights statutes. The trial court said no, but the appellate court reversed and re-manded the case for trial, noting that the finding of mental illness in New York State did not raise a presumption of incompetence.

"Absent a specific finding of incompetence, the mental patient retains the right to sue or defend in his own name, to sell or dispose of his property, to marry, draft a will, and in general to manage his own affairs.... It is clear ... that if we were dealing here with an ordinary patient suffering from a physical ailment, the hospital authorities would have no right to impose compul-sory medical treatment against the patient's will and indeed that to do so would constitute a common-law assault and battery. The question then becomes at what point, if at all, does the patient suffering from a mental illness lose the rights he would otherwise enjoy in this regard?"[24] The answer: When there is a specific judicial finding of incapacity. The court clearly distinguished between the involuntary hospitalization issue and the competency to consent to treatment issue. "Appellant [the patient], however, is not suggesting in this case that the authorities could not legally retain her in the hospital, but rather only that her First Amend-ment rights were violated as a result of compulsory medication."[25] Again, involuntary hospitalization does not automatically permit involuntary treatment—here, the administration of medication.

Yet, the dissenting judge in this case had the opposite view. His opinion was that an involuntary admission "constitutes a quasi-judicial determination under State law authorizing medical care of an individual notwithstanding her lack of consent thereto,"[26]

---

[24]*Id*, at 68.

[25]*Id*, at 70.

[26]*Id*, at 74.

and that the doctors "should be entitled to rely on such quasi-judicial authorization."[27]

However, it is clear that whatever had been the practice before, it is now necessary for the clinician in an institutional setting to consider hospitalization and treatment separately—even with medication.

A subsequent case relating to the administration of medication without consent was *Scott v. Plante*,[28] a 1976 federal case in New Jersey. Though the district court concluded that the involuntary administration of psychotherapeutic substances was not the basis of a claim of constitutional deprivation, the court of appeals disagreed, holding that "case law points to at least three conceivable constitutional deprivations that may accompany the involuntary administration of such substances by state officers acting under color of state law to inmates confined in a state institution."[29]

These constitutional deprivations included the first, fifth, and eighth amendments and perhaps a possible fourth constitutional deprivation, the invasion of the patient's right to bodily privacy. Thus, again constitutional arguments are arrayed against the psychiatrist's clinical judgment in regard to treatment.

Here, too, the court noted that the patient, "though perhaps properly commitable, has never been adjudicated an incompetent who is incapable of giving an informed consent to medical treatment."[30]

Some other relevant cases in regard to the right to refuse medication include the famous *Lessard* case,[31] a leading case in regard to the due process safeguards required in the civil commitment process, where the court held that a patient should be able to appeal at an initial commitment hearing without being *incapacitated* "by medication." Stone, discussing the potential impact of this deter-

---

[27]*Id.*

[28]Scott v. Plante, 530 F.2d 939 (1976).

[29]*Id.*, at 946.

[30]*Id.*

[31]Lessard v. Schmidt, 349 F. Supp. 1078 (E.D. Wisc. 1972); *vacated and remanded* 414 U.S. 473 (1974).

mination, points to the difficulties in psychiatric practice faced by an administering institutional psychiatrist under these circumstances. "A violently disturbed patient can disrupt not only an entire ward, but an entire hospital, if staff have to be brought to subdue him and struggles ensue. Without medication, mental hospitals would be back to straightjackets, padded cells, and the 19th century. What such struggles do to the staff in terms of physical injury, morale and therapeutic attitude are critical costs which affect other patients as well." He then points out the difficulties that ensue when the court gets too involved in clinical decisions. "The uneasy compromises allowed by [one of the judges] was to permit drugs to be used at dosages or of a kind which would 'restrain' but not 'treat.' Is it possible to translate this legal distinction into pharmacology? One might administer sodium amytal . intramuscularly rather than phenothiazines. But query, which drug would permit a more effective hearing? Clearly, this is one of those human situations where human judgment rather than rigid rules are the sensible alternative." Then, perhaps in dismay or exasperation, he goes on to suggest that "if even [the Judge's] solution were to be found legally unacceptable, then mentally ill patients who are violent should be taken to jails rather than hospitals until their probable cause hearing. Bad as that would be, it surely would be more sensible than transforming hospitals into jails."[32]

In our review of the range of treatments, we have proceeded from hazardous and intrusive therapies, such as psychosurgery, to aversive therapy to shock treatment to medication. What about milieu therapy?

While there are no cases directly on point, some legal activists and advocates have cited articles that indicate that this form of therapy may be harmful to certain patients,[33] and I am certain that some lawyers are considering litigation to enforce a right to refuse treatment by milieu therapy.

I cannot help but comment at this point and note that in certain

---

[32]Stone, *supra* note 2, at 53.

[33]*See, e.g.,* Van Potten, *Milieu Therapy: Contraindications?,* 29 ARCHIVES OF GENERAL PSYCHIATRY 640 (1973). *See also,* Pardes et al., 46 PSYCHIATRIC QUARTERLY 29 (1972).

respects what we now call milieu therapy was long ago called moral therapy, which if eliminated might leave only immoral therapy.

For the practicing psychiatrist, the problem is How and by whom is the decision to be made? In other words, assuming that a question has been raised whether a patient is competent to participate in a treatment decision, How is this question to be decided?

First, let us look at a draft report of the APA task force on the right to treatment published in 1975, which contained a section titled "The Right To Refuse Treatment."[34]

> The American Psychiatric Association is aware of the possibility that the right to adequate care and treatment may be misunderstood and even be used in some cases in a coercive manner. We, therefore, wish to clearly indicate that our concern is that adequate care and treatment be available. If a patient declines to accept or participate in one or more forms of treatment, we support that patient's right to refuse. We recommend that the courts be the final arbiters of such disagreement, should the hospital staff feel that such treatment is essential. In cases where the patient refuses treatment which is deemed essential by the medical staff, and where this refusal is supported by the judiciary, the medical staff should review whether this patient should remain in an active treatment setting, or whether his right to care should be implemented in another facility. Appropriate facilities should be available for alternative placement of selected individuals, who because of their refusal of treatment, may not belong in a hospital devoted to active treatment.[35]

Dr. Rachlin and others in a series of trenchant articles and letters raised serious questions in regard to these principles and questioned the feasibility and the propriety of such "appropriate facilities."[36, 37]

In the final draft of this document, the title was changed to "Authorization for Treatment," and states the following: "The

---

[34]Proposed Position Paper: *The Right to Adequate Care and Treatment for the Mentally Ill and Mentally Retarded,* (prepared for The Task Force on The Right To Treatment, Jonas R. Rappeport, M.D., Chairman, Oct. 19, 1974, *unpublished* Fourth Draft).

[35]*Id,* at 6.

[36]*See, e.g.,* Rachlin, *One Right Too Many, presented at* the 7th Annual Meeting of the American Academy of Psychiatry and the Law, Boston, Oct. 23, 1975.

[37]Talbott, J. (unpublished letters) (Aug. 1, 1975); Rappeport, J. (unpublished letters) (Aug. 12, 1975).

American Psychiatric Association is aware of the possibility that the right to adequate care and treatment may be used in some cases in a coercive manner. We, therefore, wish to clearly indicate that our concern is that adequate care and treatment be available. As is the practice generally in medicine, the patient's informed consent for treatment is required except for emergent situations."[38] Thus, the APA acknowledges the centrality of informed consent. Then it continues, "No patient should be treated against his will unless some procedural safeguards are instituted." Here is the phrase procedural safeguards again. The APA adopts the very wording of the *legal* decisions. But, the matter, it now points out, is not so simple.

"Since a patient's refusal of necessary treatment may not be in his best interest, some means of allowing him to receive proper medical care with the least amount of time consuming procedures must be developed." Notice the careful use of words — not *forced,* involuntary treatment, but allowed proper medical care. And note the phrase "his best interest"! A discussion of this concept, in this context could fill a philosophical treatise. Nonetheless, decisions must be made on the following:

> Depending on the circumstances, any of the following may be appropriate:
>
> 1. Court-authorized treatment at the time of commitment.
>
> 2. Court evaluation for competency to consent to or refuse treatment.
>
> 3. In-hospital patient rights review committees (with outside representatives).
>
> 4. Administrative-judicial hearings.
>
> These alternatives may represent a new departure from usual past procedures and therefore will require further study and trial.[39]

One specific example of an attempt to solve the problem of decision making took the form of a New York State Department of Mental Hygiene regulation promulgated in September 1975 titled "Care and Treatment: Right to Object and Appeal."[40] It begins with the statement that "patients may object to any form of care

---

[38]Proposed Position Paper, *supra* note 34.

[39]*Id,* at 6.

[40]14 N.Y.C.R.R. § 278 (1975) *(Care and Treatment: Right to Object and Appeal).*

and treatment and may appeal decisions with which they disagree."

A general provision is first made for emergency treatment. Next it is stated that patients on voluntary or informal status may not be given treatment over their objection but must be discharged or converted to involuntary status. Involuntary patients may be given treatment over their objection only under certain circumstances. Four categories are set forth:

1. Emergencies.
2. Those who object on the basis of religious belief—in which case a court order must be obtained.
3. Those for whom the treatment recommended is surgery, ECT, a major medical treatment, experimental drugs, or aversive stimuli—in such case, a separate set of regulations requiring consent of a relative or court order.
4. Finally, the fourth category—for all others—establishes a special review procedure.

The review procedure is in two steps. First, the objection is reviewed by the head of service, and his decision is communicated to the patient or his representative. If any object, an appeal can then be taken to the director of the facility. The director's decision is apparently final for the purpose of this regulation, though it is clear that an appeal to the court is available. Although the regulation is clear on the procedure for decision making, it should be noted that there are no *criteria* set forth as to the basis of such a decision.

To study the impact that this regulation had on hospital practice, questionnaires were sent to the thirteen inpatient psychiatric facilities in Manhattan (New York County) a year after this regulation was put into effect. Replies were widely varied. Some facilities responded that they had no problems. Others related such problems as concerns that treatment had been delayed, claims that the lawyers assigned to particular facilities were encouraging patients to refuse medication, a story of a patient who committed suicide after discharge, and so forth.

To obtain additional data, a pilot study was carried out on the five adult units in Bellevue Psychiatric Hospital with a total capacity of 250 patients. The period covered was the year from

October 1, 1975, through September 30, 1976. Bellevue is a short-term hospital, and during that time there were approximately 4,000 admissions to these units (including readmissions). At any time about 30 percent of the patients were on involuntary status. During this period only *five* cases were appealed to the director—approximately .0025 percent of admissions! In *all* cases the director supported the doctor's wish to medicate the patient even after refusal.

A senior member of the facility commented that the regulation did not seem to have profoundly affected clinical practice in the hospital. An informal survey of psychiatrists and lawyers at the hospital agreed that the impact was minimal. It is worth pausing to reflect upon this. A somewhat complex procedural safeguard is put into place but has minimal impact. Certainly a more rigidly *administered* set of regulations might have a greater chance of having an impact on sophisticated practice—but at what cost?

Another attempt to resolve the issue of decision making was suggested by Stone, who concluded that the practical, legal solutions in the area of the right to refuse treatment would ultimately have to be linked to the development of PSROs and effective psychiatric utilization procedures.[41] But, for the moment, he suggested the appointment of a *third party* as decision maker.[42] However, he noted that unless the decision maker is a judge, questions would be raised whether the patient's civil liberties had been protected. He therefore went on to suggest a two-step procedure involving a preliminary judicial hearing on whether the patient requires commitment and then a second judicial hearing, of a more formal type, which would deal with a number of questions including patient's competency to object to some part of the treatment plan. He noted, however, the *tremendous cost* in terms of medical time and other factors, as well as the dangers of delaying treatment. Therefore, he suggested that the full procedural safeguards be made mandatory only for "the more severe therapies."[43]

Two recent cases that dealt with the decision-making process

---

[41]Wyatt v. Stickney, *supra* note 3.

[42]*Id*, at 104.

[43]*Id*, at 105.

regarding the right to refuse treatment were *Rennie v. Klein,*[44] decided in the federal court in New Jersey, and *Rogers v. Okin,*[45] from the federal court in Massachusetts. Briefly, in the first *Rennie* case under the rubric of "procedural due process," Judge Brotman found that such due process required a hearing, counsel for the patient, and an outside psychiatrist of the patient's choosing. In an enlarged class action suit that followed (known as *Rennie 2*),[46] Judge Brotman set forth requirements (replacing those noted previously), which included the following: A system of informed consent forms, which must be signed prior to administration of medication. A system of patient advocates is established who obtain in-hospital and independent review for the patient if the treating physician certifies that a patient is incapable of providing informed consent. Additionally, the advocates serve as counsel to patients wishing to refuse treatment. An independent psychiatrist reviews the medical director's order to medicate forcibly. The independent psychiatrist considers whether forced medication would violate the patient's right to privacy and the principles of the first and eighth amendments. The independent psychiatrist may hold an informal hearing without compulsory access to witnesses or cross examination. The psychiatrist sets a time limit, which may not exceed sixty days, in which the patient may continue to be medicated.

In other words, under Judge Brotman's system, an *independent psychiatrist* makes the ultimate treatment decision.

In the *Rogers* case,[47] also a class action, the court required an adjudication of incompetency and an appointment of a *guardian* who is not to act "as a third person," but is to stand and act in the place of the patient. Here, medical or psychiatric judgment is no longer determinative, but the treatment decision is rather made by a lay person, the so-called guardian.

Thus, while the *Rennie* case still deferred to psychiatric opinion (in the form of an independent psychiatrist), both these cases continue the trend that, in the context of the refusal of treatment, drastically limits the scope and authority of psychiatric judgments.

---

[44]Rennie v. Klein, 462 F. Supp. 1131 (D.N.J. 1978); 476 F.Supp. 1294 (D.N.J. 1979).

[45]Rogers v. Okin, 478 F.Supp. 1342 (D.Mass. 1979).

[46]Rennie v. Klein, 476 F.Supp. 1294 (D.N.J. 1979).

[47]Rogers v. Okin, 478 F.Supp. 1342 (D.Mass. 1979).

Where does this leave us? I believe that the law suits, individual and class actions, changes in statutes, and regulations have in many aspects of our practice permanently altered the nature of the doctor-patient relationship. Patients will demand a greater role in decision making. I believe we are only seeing the beginning of the questioning of psychiatric expertise, and if I am right, judges and lawyers will preside over a greater narrowing of our authority and autonomy.

However, these conflicts have raised our consciousness about certain moral and ethical issues in our practice. It has forced us to address such matters as our social and political roles as well as the abuse of psychiatric power.

Can anyone truly object to such requirements as truly informed consent? What then are the resentments and the grumblings about? Some speak of siege mentality and see "psychiatry under siege."[48] We must ask ourselves how much of our reaction is concern for the best interest of our patient and how much the result of our perception of recent changes as assaults on our prerogatives, threats to our privileges, i.e. as narcissistic injuries, as our roles are narrowed and restricted to a more expert role. Certainly, there are better ways to cope than by becoming defensive and negativistic.

A more constructive way to cope is to demonstrate the scientific basis of our clinical practice. For example, a recent article distinguished between two groups of schizophrenic outpatients on medication: Those who stopped taking their medication and those who did not.[49] Those who *did* stop were found to develop an "ego-syntonic grandiose psychosis." They wanted to experience the feelings of grandiosity that resulted from their illness. The others— the ones who did not stop taking their medication—would, if they stopped, experience dysphoric affects, depression, anxiety. They would get depressed if they stopped, so they did not. This type of research may clarify some of the clinical issues relating to a patient's refusal of medication and thereby reinforce our clinical judgment.

---

[48]This was the theme of the Annual Meeting of the American Academy of Psychiatry and the Law, San Francisco, Oct. 21, 1976.

[49]Van Putten, T., Crumpton. E., Yale, C., *Drug Refusal in Schizophrenia and the Wish to be Crazy*, 33 ARCH. GEN. PSYCH. 1443 (Dec. 1976).

The law is a very coarse instrument. It cannot undertake the detailed regulation of our work. It cannot take into account the subtleties of the psychiatric relationship, or communications made in the context of the psychiatric relationship. So we can further cope by insisting that the lawyers who participate in or intrude themselves into issues of patient care be well trained and appreciate the complex issues of psychiatric treatment.

Finally, to cope with effects of legal activism on psychiatric practice, we must regain our roles as advocates for the patient. To do this we must ally ourselves with the consumers—our patients (and their families)—to fight for and assure for them in these days of budget cuts the best care that can be provided. We must make it unmistakably clear that our primary concern is the well-being of our patients, especially the poor and helpless.

Chapter 4

ASSESSING DANGEROUSNESS

PETER M. CRAIN, M.D.

Nowadays, clinical practice has come under increasing legal scrutiny. No longer is the psychiatrist presumed to act unilaterally in the best interests of patients and society. In many jurisdictions, involuntary confinements and treatments are subject to court adjudications of dangerousness, based upon psychiatric testimony. Serious questions have been raised, however, as to the competence of psychiatrists, indeed anyone, to identify who is dangerous.[1] A conference held on October 27, 1979, at the annual meeting of The American Academy of Psychiatry and the Law entitled "The Great Debate" brought together a number of authorities in psychiatry and the law, who expressed their opinions on whether or not psychiatrists could determine dangerousness.[2] Table 4-I presents the various viewpoints tabulated according to two dimensions: (1) prediction of dangerousness as possible or not possible and (2) whether or not psychiatric expertise pertaining to dangerousness can be demonstrable in the courtroom. These viewpoints will now be discussed in detail.

Prediction of Dangerousness Not Possible—Psychiatric Expertise Not Demonstrable in the Courtroom

This position typifies the authorities in category I.A. of Table 4-I. Eleven studies that deal with clinicians making a prediction of violent behavior are displayed in Table 4-II. The first five suggest that variables exist which are associated more often than not with violence-prone individuals. The last six, including the eleventh, which utilizes factors compiled from nine previous studies, find a high level of false positive predictions and/or no significant correlations between variables and violent behavior. The feature that consistently distinguishes the two groups of studies

TABLE 4–I

VIEWPOINTS FROM THE GREAT DEBATE

"Can Psychiatrists Determine Dangerousness?"

	I Psychiatric Expertise Not Demonstrable	II Psychiatric Expertise Not Decided Yet	III Psychiatric Expertise Demonstrable
A. Prediction Not Possible	No objective, empirical evidence exists for clinical predictions at acceptable levels of reliability and validity (Steadman, Shah, Perloff)	Dangerousness can be defined by factors other than prediction, involving a sociopolitical decision. Psychiatrists can present data, which may or may not aid the court in its essentially legal decision. (Brooks)	(1) Mental disorders manifesting certain impairments can produce a "potential for harm." (Pollock) Certain states of mind are intrinsically more "explosive" than others. (Quen) (2) The impairments of mental disorder are not in themselves dangerous, but rather their copresence with past violent behavior can be identified. "Conditions" which either facilitate or inhibit these impairments can be assessed. (Sadoff)
B. Prediction Possible	Clinicians are already intuitively identifying dangerous individuals; they do not know how to discuss the basis of their assessment. (Heller)	(1) Not all of the data is in; it has not yet been shown whether or not short-term predictions can be made. (Brooks) (2) Current studies of prediction lack validity. (Perr, Halpern)	Perimeters do not exist that can aide clinicians in identifying dangerousness. This assessment leads to a "high index of suspicion." (Lion)

from each other consists of the manner in which the outcome data is compiled—retrospectively or prospectively. Other factors, such as clinical versus statistical analysis of the data and presence or absense in the study of nonviolent control groups, fail to discriminate between the two different results. For example, a study that identifies twenty-one variables from neuropsychological tests as significant correlates of violent backgrounds uses a sophisticated statistical analysis with a matched nonviolent control group that compares favorably with the experimental designs of studies yielding

TABLE 4-II

STUDIES OF VIOLENCE PREDICTION

Investigator	Contexts of Prediction or Validation	Prospective or Retrospective	Data Analysis	Nonviolent Controls	Results
Abrahamsen[28]	Not Specified	Not Specified	Clinical	Nonindicated	14 danger signs identified
Hartogs[29]	Not Specified	Not Specified	Clinical	Nonindicated	48 predictors
Malmquist[30]	20 adolescents charged with murder, detained in jail	Retrospective	Clinical	Same danger signs found in nonviolent controls	8 danger signs identified, hours to days preceding the murder
Hellman and Blackman[31]	31 adult prisoners charged with aggressive crimes	Retrospective	Clinical	Unmatched controls	Triad of symptoms identified from childhood histories
Spellacy[3]	80 adult prison volunteers from a penitentiary	Retrospective	Statistical	Matched controls: 40 violent, 40 nonviolent	21 variables identified from neuropsychological tests
Climent, Ervin[32]	80 patients brought to an emergency room for violent behavior	Prospective	Statistical	Matched controls: 40 violent, 40 nonviolent	Triad of Hellman and Blackman fails to distinguish the two groups
Mac Donald[27]	100 patients admitted to the hospital who made threats to kill	Prospective (5–6 years)	Clinical	None	Threats to kill not carried out by 93 patients (3 homicides, 4 suicides)
Steadman[33]	967 Baxtrom patients confined in security hospitals	Prospective (4 years)	Statistical	None	80% false positive predictions. Age and legal status yield 67% false positives
Steadman and Cocozza[34]	257 C.P.L. cases evaluated by psychiatrists	Prospective (3 years)	Statistical	Controls unmatched: 59.9% judged dangerous 40.1% judged non-dangerous	No significant difference found between the two groups
Kozol[35]	49 male sexual psychopaths convicted of violent crimes, confined in a security hospital. Released by court against medical advice	Prospective (10 years)	Clinical	None	65.3% false positive predictions
Schlesinger[36]	Review of records of 122 juveniles evaluated by a court psychiatric clinic	Prospective (1 year)	Statistical	Controls unmatched: One group containing a predictor variable compared to another group without it	30 factors identified by 9 previous studies failed to distinguish the groups or predict subsequent violent behaviors.

negative findings.[3] If *predictive* validity is a crucial issue for admissibility of testimony pertaining to dangerousness in the courtroom, then psychiatric expertise must be excluded, despite the positive findings of the five retrospective studies. The viewpoint of category I.B. (Table 4-I) may actually represent the other side of I.A. Even though the claim is made that clinicians can intuitively identify dangerous individuals, while the relevant perimeters cannot be articulated, theoretically this would also call for exclusion of testimony, since the basis of the opinion is not amenable to direct and cross examination.

Prediction of Dangerousness Possible — Psychiatric Expertise Not Decided Yet

The authorities of II.B (Table 4–I) point out that existing studies of prediction do not settle the issue entirely. All of the investigations deal with long-term outcome; none are involved with the short-term prospective assessment that occurs in a hospital emergency room. Usually, the prediction is made within an institution and validated some months or years later, after release from the institution or transfer to another one.[4] As the authorities of table entry II.B.2. indicate, the making of a prediction necessitates taking precautions, which in themselves modify the risk; the true experiment, ordinarily prohibited by professional ethics and social policy, would be to set the identified violent individuals free following the assessment. One study is currently in progress which involves making short-term prospective ratings and collecting outcome data within the same institutional setting.[5]

Prediction of Dangerousness Not Possible — Psychiatric Expertise Not Decided Yet

According to position II.A. in Table 4-I, although long-term prediction appears invalid, other factors may be used to define dangerousness. In two judicial cases, Judge Bazelon ruled that a finding of dangerousness under a District of Columbia sexual psychopath statute comprised three determinations. First, "the likelihood of recurrence." Under what conditions is it probable, rather than just possible, that an individual will engage in the same conduct? Relevant to this determination is the availability of inpatient and outpatient treatment, the expected length of confinement, the seriousness of expected harm. Second, "the likely frequence of any such behavior" may distinguish between individual propensities for isolated or repetive acts. Third, "the magnitude of harm to other persons" must be substantial, not merely offensive or obnoxious.[6,7] It can be specified or defined, theoretically, in a criminallike law code.[8] The authority of table entry II.A. appears to assign to the legal profession the role of deciding what is and is not dangerous. The extent to which psychiatrists can contribute data pertinent to the legal standard has not yet been decided.

Prediction of Dangerousness Not Possible — Psychiatric Expertise Demonstrable in the Courtroom

The authorities of table entries III.A.1. and III.A.2. agree that psychiatrists are trained to assess potentialities, rather than make predictions. For example, there are trucks driving through city streets that may carry poisonous gas; a high potential for serious harm to others exists if a collision should occur. The actual probability of a collision — a prediction of a chance event — is low, given that certain safety precautions are followed. The viewpoint of III.A.1. is that mental disorders by virtue of their functional impairments can produce a potential for harm. As a result of delirium, a patient who suffers disorientation, loss of recent memory, and illusionary paranoid perceptions may very well act in self-defense when misinterpreting his environment. Such a vulnerability may be assessed even in the absence of an actually violent act. The authority of table entry III.A.2., however, does not consider the impairments of mental disorders dangerous in themselves but dangerous when conditions associated with past violent behavior coexist with those disorders. If a man engages in wife beating only when intoxicated and experiencing auditory hallucinations, then he is considered dangerous under the conditions of discontinuing antipsychotic medication, dropping out of Alcoholics Anonymous, and missing marital therapy sessions. Dangerousness may not necessarily be a violent trait intrinsic to the individual; a man who smokes on an oil tanker, while not himself violence prone, can be deemed dangerous because of the explosive potential outside of him.[9] A mental disorder can conceivably impair the judgement needed ordinarily to prevent such a risk.

Prediction of Dangerousness Possible — Psychiatric Expertise Demonstrable in the Courtroom

The viewpoint of table entry III.B. is that perimeters do exist which alert clinicians to a "high index of suspicion" concerning dangerousness. Patients do make threats, give intimidating signals, and engage in agitated behaviors that require clinical intervention. One does not have to wait for a violent act before identifying the risk for harm. This viewpoint, which is derived from clinical experience, could also overlap with the position of III.A., in that the term prediction might perhaps be equated with a reliance upon factors that pertain to conditions or potentialities.

Standards for Assessing Dangerousness

The preceding discussion of viewpoints can be consolidated into essentially three types of evaluation: actualities, unacceptable thresholds, and potentialities.

ACTUALITIES: Actualities encompass substantial threats of physical harm or violent acts that can be observed and reported as facts. The result is a rather narrow or tight definition of dangerousness, favored by the authorities of viewpoint I.A. (Table 4–I). Since the validity of prediction remains unestablished, their recommended approach takes the form of criminal legal procedure; charges of specific code violations, based upon one's past behavior, must be proven beyond a reasonable doubt, allowing the defendant various due process safeguards to ensure fairness of the determination. Judge Bazelon has applied a similar way of thinking to civil commitment hearings, considering it "cruelty beyond comprehension" to hospitalize someone involuntarily who is not mentally ill or dangerous.[10] In the absence of criminal conviction or indictment, the significant loss of liberty entailed by civil commitment, following an adjudication of dangerousness, tends to require a narrow yes or no definition. To present the pertinent facts, psychiatric experts are probably no better qualified than laymen. Assuming adherence to such a tight standard, very few individuals would probably be adjudicated as dangerous.

UNACCEPTABLE THRESHOLDS: Though not constituting violent acts, certain situations can be deemed sufficiently dangerous to justify some involuntary restrictions or treatments. From a clinical perspective, interventions designed to prevent violent behavior fall into primary, secondary, and tertiary categories. Tertiary prevention deals directly with violent behavior in order to stop it. Secondary prevention refers to early detection and treatment of the previolent phase, while the primary type means modification of underlying conditions that predispose to violence.[11] The authority of viewpoint III.B. in Table 4–I probably assumes that clinicians can identify previolent signs or underlying conditions. To verify such an assumption experimentally, as discussed before (viewpoints II.B.1. and 2.), is nearly impossible. In addition, clinical expertise in making short-term predictions has not yet been settled. With reference to primary situations, however, much has been written about increased incidences of violence related to inadequate staffing, male versus female wards, and dormitory compared with cubicle housing space in regard to body buffer zones.[12, 13, 14]

The determination of unacceptable thresholds, in a legal sense, does not necessarily require an assumed connection to future acts of violence. It may involve an arbitrary sociopolitical decision, following the viewpoint of authority II.A. (Table 4–I). For example, a legislature can decide that exposure to pornographic materials is harmful to minors, even though unsupported by scientific fact.[15] In some instances, society may regard behavior as dangerous when it occurs unpredictably, repeats sufficiently to threaten the rule of law, and induces others to do the same.[16] Supposing that the legal threshold were set at an unacceptable level of aggressiveness, psychometric tests do exist that could discriminate between high and low aggressive groups with adequate concurrent and construct validity. But, such tests, again, fail to predict which group will actually engage in violent acts.[17] At times, the legal and clinical perceptions of unacceptable thresholds may approximate, especially when the social need for restrictiveness outweighs individual liberties. This looser, situationally defined standard permits more individuals to be adjudicated dangerous than the preceding standard determined by actualities.

POTENTIALITIES: This may represent the broadest definition of dangerousness. No specific acts or unacceptable threshold situations are identified per se; instead, any conceivable risk associated with a mental dysfunction under circumstances of inadequate supervision or treatment may be considered. Such an assessment is far removed from making a prediction. It constitutes a prudent, conservative approach, applied to an individual who has already committed violent acts in the past or currently presents unsettling behavior. The viewpoints of III.A.1. and 2. (Table 4–I), discussed previously, are encompassed within this model. By far, assessment of potentialities as the court standard will lead to the greatest number of individuals adjudicated dangerous. In contrast to the standard of actualities, psychiatric expert testimony is essential for this determination.

Application of Models

CIVIL COMMITMENT: In some states, where the issue involved in involuntary hospitalization has been viewed primarily as the interest of police power in overriding individual freedoms, confinement requires an adjudication of dangerousness. The Wisconsin Supreme Court specified for this purpose, "Imminent dangerousness . . . based, at minimum, upon a recent act, attempt, or threat to do substantial harm."[18] The evidential standard of actualities would seem to apply here. Indeed, "A psychiatric opinion, however persuasive, could not prevail, absent such a showing."[19]

Was this approach practical? Probably not, because in fact over 56 percent of Wisconsin judges interpreted substantial harm as property damage, or as psychological or financial hardship to the family of a mentally ill person.[20] Rather than requiring evidential proof of violent acts, the judges would appear to be setting unacceptable thresholds as the standard of dangerousness for civil commitment. This looser approach could better enable the court to translate psychiatric testimony, as it pertained to disturbed behavior, into the legal rubric of dangerousness. Various societal needs would thereby be accomplished—reducing the visibility of disruptive behavior in public, easing the burden of caretakers in the community, and providing shelter for the homeless, mentally disabled. Depending upon the particular jurisdiction involved, dangerousness might be assessed according to actualities or by judicial precedents for unacceptable thresholds.

HOSPITAL DISCHARGE FOR MENTALLY DISORDERED OFFENDERS: In these cases, the societal need for self-protection generally outweighs the interest in preserving the freedom of such patients. "Each obstacle [to release] is justified by a single rationale: Criminally committed patients are an 'exceptional class,' in whose continued confinement the public has a 'special interest.' "[21] Besides actualities and unacceptable thresholds, the court may accept the broadest standard of dangerousness—potentialities—as justification for continued hospitalization. Even a personality disorder with some potential for violent behavior might suffice to preclude release.[22] In one jurisdiction, where civil commitment hearings were held following the verdict of acquittal by reason of insanity, judges and/or juries tended either to construe personality disorders as mental illness or else to identify dangerousness in the absence of mental illness—both determinations resulting in confinement. Then, when one patient discharged by this procedure went on to perpetrate a second homicide, the legislature amended the statute in a way to facilitate court-ordered hospitalization.[23] In a sense, this amended statute would seem to equate mental illness with dangerousness, consistent with a reliance upon assessed potentialities for harm, beyond any demonstrated violent acts or assumed tendencies.

EMERGENCY TREATMENT: One recent court decision has mandated that a hospitalized patient can only be secluded or receive psychotropic medication when a failure to so act "would result in a substantial likelihood of physical harm to that patient, other patients, or to staff members of the institution."[24] A congruence in legal and clinical perspectives would be expected in regard to overtly violent acts and certain unacceptable thresholds—threats or intimidations to do physical harm. But then, what about situations where an observed nonagressive patient behavior, such as rearranging furniture, tends to precede an unprovoked assaultive outburst? Would the court accept imposition of secondary clinical interventions here as justifiable emergency treatment? Most likely, the definition of unacceptable thresholds would vary from one jurisdiction to another, related to the interest in preserving an individual's right to refuse treatment. With patients appearing competent to give informed consent, the standard of unacceptable thresholds would probably tighten in the direction of actualities, while in the case of the grossly incompetent, it might loosen more toward approximating potentialities.

PROFESSIONAL NEGLIGENCE: At what level of dangerousness should the clinician act to protect others from a risky patient? Failure to demonstrate proper investigation of warnings and take reasonable precautions, representing unacceptable threshold situations, may constitute grounds for negligence.[25] Another case goes so far as to mandate, "When a psychotherapist, pursuant to standards of his profession, determines that his patient presents a serious danger of violence to another, he is obliged to exert reasonable care to protect the intended victim."[26] If psychiatric standards are applicable, then this might permit an assessment of potentialities. The court specifies, however, what amounts to an unacceptable threshold; the psychotherapist knew of the patient's homicidal intention, without notifying the victim. In fact, the actual homicide occurred two months later. Threats to kill, the subject of one prospective study quoted earlier, are not carried out in 93 percent of instances over a long-term period.[27] Despite the clinical evidence, the court imposes an unacceptable threshold designed to favor societal self-protection over the patient's right to privacy and professional confidentiality.

Conclusion

At the present time, it would appear that prediction hardly plays any role in assessing dangerousness for legal purposes. Even if clinicians could predict violence with adequate reliability and validity, the findings might not affect the influence of social policy. The adjudication of dangerousness seems to be essentially a resolution of competing interests, societal self-protection and individual freedom. Given a particular issue, one side may be favored over the other. In order to safeguard individual liberty, the more narrow standard of actualities may prevail. Where societal self-protection is uppermost, an assessment of broad potentialities will probably apply. The court may specify some unacceptable threshold situation that serves to take both sides into account. Overall, these factors would appear to influence the extent to which a given court might rely upon psychiatric expert testimony pertaining to dangerousness. The question is not whether psychiatrists can make a helpful contribution but rather what is the standard of assessment set by the court to suit its purpose.

BIBLIOGRAPHY

1. Cocozza, J. J. and Steadman, H. J.: Prediction in psychiatry: an example of misplaced confidence in experts. *Social Problems* 25 (February), *3*:265–276, 1978.

2. Sadoff, R. L., Steadman, H. J., Perlin, M. L., Shah, S. A., Heller, M. S., Lion, J. R., Brooks, A. D., and Pollack, S.: *The Great Debate: Determination of Dangerousness by Psychiatrists.* Tenth Annual Meeting of The American Academy of Psychiatry and the Law, October 27, 1979, Baltimore, Maryland.

3. Spellacy, F.: Neuropsychological discrimination between violent and nonviolent men. *J Clin Psychol, 34(1):*49–52, 1978.

4. Monahan, J.: Prediction research and the emergency commitment of dangerously ill persons: a reconsideration. *Am J Psychiatry, 135:*2, 198–201, 1978.

5. Crain, P. M.: *Research Protocol: Assessment of Short-Term Assault Risk.* Unpublished, June, 1980.

6. Millard v. Harris, 406 F.2d 964 (D.C. Cir. 1968).

7. Cross v. Harris, 418 F.2d 109 (D.C. Cir. 1969).

8. Schreiber, *Indeterminate Therapeutic Incarceration of Dangerous Criminals: Perspectives and Problems,* 56 VA. L. REV. 602, 628–634, 1970.

9. Scott, P. D.: Assessing dangerousness in criminals. *Br J Psychiatry, 131:*127–142, 1977.

10. *In re* John Ballay (U.S. Appeals, D.C., 1973).

11. Harrington, J. A.: Hospital violence part II. *Nursing Mirror, 135:*32–33, 1972.

12. *In re* Robert Torsney, State of New York, Court of Appeals, July 18, 1979.

13. Depp, F. C.: Violent behavior patterns on psychiatric wards. *Aggressive Behavior.* Alan R. Liss, Inc., 1976, vol. 2, pp. 295–306.

14. Kinzel, A. F.: Violent behavior in prisons. In Fawcett, J. (Ed.): *Dynamics of Violence.* Chicago, American Medical Association, 1971, pp. 157–164.

15. Ginsberg v. New York, 390 U.S. 629, 641, 88 S. Ct. 1274, 1281, 20 L. ED. 2nd 195 (1968).

16. Scott, P. D.: Assessing dangerousness in criminals, *British Journal of Psychiatry, 131:*127–142, 1977.

17. Edmunds, G., and Kendricks, D.C.: *The Measurement of Human Aggressiveness.* New York, Halsted Press, John Wiley and Sons, 1980.

18. Lessard v. Schmidt, 379 F.Supp. 1376, 1379 (E.D. Wis. 1974).

19. Brooks, A. D.: Notes on defining the "dangerousness of the mentally ill." In Frederick, C. J. (Ed.): *Dangerous Behavior: A Problem in Law and Mental Health.* Rockville, Maryland, NIMH Center for Studies of Crime and Delinquency, DHEW Publication No. (ADM) 78–563, 37–60, 1978.

20. Zander, *Civil Commitment in Wisconsin: The Impact of Lessard v. Schmidt,* WIS. L. REV. 503–526 (1976).

21. Brooks, A. D.: Note: release of persons committed after a verdict of not guilty by reason of insanity. In Brooks, A. D.: *Law, Psychiatry and the Mental Health*

System. Boston, Little, Brown and Company, 1974, pp. 456–459.

22. *In re* Robert Torsney, State of New York, Court of Appeals, July 18, 1979.

23. Benedek, E. P., and Farley, G.: The McQuillan decision: civil rights for the mentally ill offender. *Bull Am Acad Psychiatry Law, V(4):*438–449, 1977.

24. Rogers v. Okin, Civil Action 75–1610–T (D.C. Mass. Oct. 29, 1979).

25. Merchants Nat'l Bank and Trust Company of Fargo v. United States, 272 F.Supp. 409 (1967).

26. Tarasoff v. Regents of the University of California, 131 CAL. RPTR. 14, 551 P.2d 334 (Cal. 1976).

27. MacDonald, J. M.: Homicidal threats. *Am J Psychiatry, 124:*475, 1967.

28. Abrahamsen, D.: *Our Violent Society.* 1970, p. 218.

29. Hartogs, R.: Who will act violently: the predictive criteria. In Hartogs, R., and Artzt, E. (Eds.): *Violence, Causes and Solutions.* 1970, p. 332.

30. Malmquist, C. P.: Premonitory signs of homicidal aggression in juveniles. *Am J Psychiatry, 128:*461, 1971.

31. Hellman, and Blackman: Enureses, firesetting and cruelty to animals: a triad predictive of adult crime. *Am J Psychiatry, 122:*1431, 1966.

32. Climent, and Ervin: Historical data in the evaluation of violent subjects. *Arch Gen Psychiatry, 27:*621–624, 1972.

33. Steadman, J. J.: Follow-up on Baxtrom patients returned to hospitals for the criminally insane. *Am J Psychiatry, 130:*317, 1973.

34. Cocozza, J. J., and Steadman, H. J.: The failure of psychiatric predictions of dangerousness: clear and convincing evidence. *Rutgers Law Review* 29 (late summer), *5:*1084–1101, 1976.

35. Kozol, J. L., Boucher, R. J., and Garofalo, R. F.: The diagnosis and treatment of dangerousness. *Crime and Delinquency,* 371–392, October, 1972.

36. Schlesinger, S. E.: The prediction of dangerousness in juveniles: a replication. *Crime and Delinquency.* 40–48, January, 1978.

Chapter 5

THE IMPACT OF CHILD ADVOCACY ON FAMILY STRUCTURES

Henry H. Foster, LL.B., LL.M.

The phrase child advocacy is used in at least two different senses. The term currently is being used by social workers to refer to investigations of, and checks upon, the child care system and its delivery of services, and to lawyers the phrase relates to legal representation of children involved in litigation. Although we are here concerned primarily with the second meaning of child advocacy, it may be relevant to compare these two differing concepts of advocacy.

In 1969 an important report was issued by the Joint Commission on the Mental Health of Children entitled *Crisis in Child Mental Health.* The following year the White House Conference on Children urged the creation of a child advocacy system, and subsequently the Office of Child Advocacy was established within the Department of Health, Education and Welfare. This agency is to provide federal leadership in child advocacy and has sponsored demonstration programs on the state and local levels. New York, in 1971, stimulated by these developments on the federal level, established a state committee for children, which at the request of the governor issued a report and recommendations on November 30, 1971.

The governor's committee concluded that despite government's professed concern over the lot of children and substantial expenditures of public funds, "We are failing our children to some degree." The report then cited statistics. "Sixty thousand children drop out of school each year; 29,000 youths of 16–20 years of age are arrested for major crime. Twenty percent of the million children in New York State have some degree of emotional disturbance; three percent are mentally retarded; three percent have brain injury with associated learning disabilities. Licensed day care facilities are available for only 6,000 children, while 880,000 mothers with children under age six are presently working."[1]

The report of the governor's committee described the objectives of what it termed child advocacy as a strategy to reduce the discrepancies between the services that are presently available and the things we say children need. It recommended the creation of a 100 member citizens commission and a statewide network of local advocacy councils, which would serve as the mechanism for redressing grievances of children and families. The state commission would work towards reducing institutional rigidities and improving delivery of services.

A subsequent paper prepared by the New York State Committee for Children was issued December 12, 1972,[2] and after reviewing the history set forth previously, the report suggested alternative ways of constructing a child advocacy system. This report visualized the objective of child advocacy was to stimulate and utilize the energy of private citizens to represent and speak for children and to work with governmental units such as a proposed office on children and youth in the governor's office, a joint legislative committee on children and youth, and a special legal unit in the attorney general's office. However, only a portion of these ambitious proposals have been put into effect in New York.

It is obvious that the social work concept of child advocacy is mainly concerned with a checkup on the delivery of services in the child care system. This is a commendable objective due to the waste and failures of the governmental and private agency administrators involved with child care. The emphasis, however, is on the interests of consumers, not children as such, and the immediate aim is to provide another check on bureaucrats. This kind of child advocacy ordinarily will strengthen family structures rather than disturb them by improving the delivery system and perhaps ultimately providing a forum for complaints in individual cases.

Child advocacy in the legal setting traditionally has been

---

[1] New York State Commission for Children, report to Governor Rockefeller, "A Child Advocacy System in New York State," Nov. 30, 1971, p. 10.

[2] New York State Committee for Children, "Child Advocacy in New York State, Background and Recommendations for the Governor's Conference on Children," Dec. 12, 1972.

concerned with a much more limited objective and program. Essentially, the concern has been over independent counsel for children where their placement is at stake, and the rationale has been that since the legal system usually operates by means of an adversary process, all concerned and interested parties, including children, are entitled to their own spokesperson. Moreover, unless children have their own counsel, it may be gratuitously assumed that their interests are protected either by a parent's lawyer or by the court, when in fact there often is a conflict of interests involved in such a vicarious representation.

The concept that children may have a constitutional right to their own counsel, although not new, has only recently been secured by court decision. The *Gault* case,[3] and more important for this discussion, *Bartley v. Kremens*,[4] place the child's right to counsel on a constitutional basis, in terms of due process. From the perspective of history, this means that more of the relics of feudalism are being discarded, and children are coming to be regarded as persons by the law. Indeed, it has been anomalous that our law regarded corporations as legal persons but children and, formerly, wives as nonpersons.

There are two compelling reasons why children need and should want independent representation. The first is that in this century there has been a tremendous increase in governmental intervention into what formerly was regarded as family autonomy.[5] The second is that the legal process ordinarily insists upon the adversary system, and that system requires that all concerned parties have their own counsel. Functionally speaking, conflict of interests should be eliminated from the conflict that is implicit in the adversary process.

Although many of us who are nostalgic would welcome a reduction in governmental intrusion into private and family affairs, nonetheless we witness a proliferation of state and federal intervention and see an increase in public and private social agencies that affect our lives. For example, child abuse legislation has been

---

[3] *In re* Gault, 387 U.S. 1 (1967).

[4] 402 F.Supp. 1039 (E.D. Pa. 1975).

[5] *See* Katz, S., WHEN PARENTS FAIL, Chap. 2 (Beacon Press, Boston, 1971).

enacted in every state and by Congress[6] since the battered child syndrome articles first appeared in the 1960s.[7] There has been an expansion of the concept of neglect to include psychological deprivation as well as physical abuse.[8] The welfare program entails inspection, regulation, and control of homes by social workers. Juvenile delinquency, in some states, may include conduct not regarded as criminal for adults, such as truancy or disobedience, although more properly what Massachusetts formerly called the "stubborn child" is classified as a person in need of supervision.[9] However, as we shall see, the autonomy and individual rights of minors received a serious setback due to 1979 decisions by the Supreme Court of the United States.

Within the bureaucratic maze concerned with families and children the decision as to how a particular problem will be processed often is an arbitrary one. A given fact pattern may warrant its classification as a "delinquency" case, a "neglect" matter, or something that merely requires an informal adjustment. There is built in discretion and the opportunity for arbitrary decisions throughout the whole process. Although some bureaucrats may fail to see any need for a check on arbitrary discretion, most of us are aware that a system of checks and balances lies at the heart of our democratic order.

Child advocacy, meaning independent representation by counsel, is needed at every stage of governmental intrusion into the parent-child relationship. The crucial decision in the processing of children often occurs at the initial or screening stage, rather than later. The situation of the child, no matter what the administrative intent may be, is comparable to that of the accused who has been booked and placed under interrogation.[10] Where his liberty

---

[6]*See* Sussman, A., and Cohen, S., REPORTING CHILD ABUSE AND NEGLECT (Ballinger, Cambridge, Mass., 1975), for a recent study of child abuse statutes.

[7]*See* Kempe et al., *The Battered Child Syndrome*, J.A.M.A. *181:*17 (1962).

[8]*For example see,* N.Y. Fam. Ct. Act   1012 (h), which refers to "failure to thrive, control of aggressive or self-destructive impulses, ability to think and reason, or acting out or misbehavior" etc. in defining "impairment of mental or emotional condition."

[9]*See* Sidman, *The Massachusetts Stubborn Child Law: Law and Order in the Home,* FAM. L. Q. 6: 33 (1972).

[10]*Compare,* Escobedo v. Illinois, 378 U.S. 478 (1963).

is at stake and he may be removed from his home, he needs counsel.

The possibility of a serious conflict of interests, between the child and his parents or between the court staff and the child is too real to be dismissed as imaginary. Many parents are anxious to pass the responsibility and difficulty in child rearing along to others.[11] Court staffs and judges all too seldom share the child's point of view. In more basic terms, essential fairness requires that a child be treated as a person whenever his placement is in question and that he be heard through his own counsel.

Of course, there are those who feel that lawyers only complicate matters. The notion is raised that lawyers are not objective; rather, they are objectionable. One answer to that thesis is the following situation: Suppose you are arrested or your liberty is at stake; do you want impartial representation or your own advocate whose professional responsibility is to protect and serve your best interests, as you perceive them?

It is obvious that child advocacy in the legal sense may either strengthen or undermine the structure of a family. Where the interests of the child and his family coincide and they are agreed upon a course of action, the family interest is solidified. Where parent and child disagree, counsel for the child may, where warranted, effect a conciliation, or he may urge the child's point of view upon the decision maker. The point is that children should be heard as well as seen.

In addition to the delinquency and neglect problems that fall within the jurisdiction of the family or juvenile court, there also are many disputed child custody cases where a child's placement is at stake. Most often, such occurs in connection with divorce or separation proceedings and commonly is considered to be an ancillary matter. The potential for conflict of interests between the child and either or both parents is conspicuously present. Children have been used as pawns or items for parental bargaining in conjunction with the one upmanship divorce so often entails. Ideally, children should have independent representation in all

---

[11] For a bitter criticism of how the juvenile justice system may work in practice, *see* Forer, L., NO ONE WILL LISSEN (Grosset & Dunlap, New York, 1970).

contested custody cases, and there probably should be a court check on the custody arrangement even where there is parental agreement on terms.[12]

The title for this chapter, which was given to me, may imply that child advocacy is a menace to family structure. Obviously, so too is the woman's movement, no-fault divorce, and equal job opportunity. The question is, What is the order of priorities? A figurative emancipation of children so that they are regarded legally as persons may be as disconcerting as other emancipations were to those who had power and authority. But, paternalism or the *noblesse oblige* of the guardian-ward relation is demeaning to the subject who is not treated as a person. The dignity of the individual and his worth as a human being is central to Judeo-Christian philosophy, and the vestiges of feudalism are incompatible with that paramount value.

In the long run, individual autonomy will stabilize the family and make for a more meaningful relationship. We cannot expect people to behave responsibly unless we accord them responsibility. It would be naive, however, to assume that individual autonomy may be achieved without cost. Parental authority is diminished to the extent that children are emancipated. Ideally, what is taken from the parent will be diffused so that there is shared authority and responsibility, depending upon the age and maturity of those involved in the relationship.

There is a further danger. Our society, according to much evidence, is becoming increasingly oriented towards individual rights and prerogatives without regard to duties and responsibilities. In many instances, psychiatry or psychotherapy nourishes and encourages an emphasis upon individual needs and interests without regard to relational or social consequences. In a sense, psychiatrists fall into the trap imputed to lawyers, namely, they become champions of the individual patient, without regard to the consequences to other individuals.

Before making my concluding remarks there are two examples of child advocacy, in the lawyer's sense, that may make the assumed threat to family structure more specific. The first example involves

---

[12]*See* Foster, H., A "BILL OF RIGHTS" FOR CHILDREN. Chap. 3 (Thomas, Springfield, Ill., 1974).

court decisions on the voluntary or involuntary commitment of minors, and the second is the first published volume of the Juvenile Justice Standards Project.

On June 20, 1979, the Supreme Court of the United States simultaneously decided two cases involving the issue of whether due process required the consent of a minor, individually, to hospitalization in a mental facility or whether parental consent alone made such institutionalization voluntary. *Secretary of Public Welfare v. Institutionalized Juveniles* was the sequel to *Bartley v. Kremins* and involved Pennsylvania mental health law. *Parham v. J.L.* was the companion case and principal decision and involved Georgia mental health law. In each case, the Supreme Court held that parents might supply the consent for hospitalization of minor children so as to make admission voluntary.

The *Parham* case involved two minors who had been admitted as voluntary patients but under their own protests. J.L. had received outpatient care until he was about eight years old, when his mother and stepfather requested that he be admitted on an inpatient basis. The admitting physician talked with the parents and learned that he was uncontrollable in school, extremely aggressive, and had a "hyperkinetic reaction to childhood." The other minor, J.B., had been in seven foster care families since he was three months old, and the last foster parents had returned him to the Georgia child care agency, which requested his admission as a voluntary patient.

Chief Justice Burger wrote the majority opinion, and after discussing the Georgia procedure and the holdings below, started with the premise that parents generally act in the child's best interests, saying that "the statist notion that governmental power should supersede parental authority in *all* cases because *some* parents abuse and neglect children is repugnant to American tradition." He then said that "the fact that a child may balk at hospitalization or complaint about a parental refusal to provide cosmetic surgery does not diminish the parent's authority to decide what is best for the child." He concluded that absent a finding of neglect or abuse, the presumption should apply that parents act in the best interests of their children. That presumption was deemed to be reinforced by the independent role of the admitting physician at the state institution. Regarding the latter, the Chief Justice said that the Court was satisfied that the admissions officer in question had "operated in a neutral and detached fashion in making medical judgments in the best interests of the children."

In *Secretary of Public Welfare v. Institutionalized Juveniles*, the sequel to the mooted case of *Kremins v. Bartley*, the revised Pennsylvania procedure passed muster, and the same result was reached as in *Parham*, and for the same reasons. The Chief Justice, moreover, held that the interests of the children, the interests of the parents, and the interests of the state were all the same. Justices Brennan, Marshall, and Stevens dissented on the ground that the Pennsylvania procedure provided neither for representation nor for reasonably prompt admission hearings to mentally retarded children thirteen years of age or older and held that the state constitutionally was required to assign each institutionalized child counsel to ensure that the child's rights are fully protected.

The majority opinions by Chief Justice Burger constitute a major obstacle to the concept that a child should be entitled to independent representation and have standing to voice objections whenever his placement or freedom are at stake. The facile identification of the child's interests with those of parents (and the state) ignores the realities of many child-parent relationships where there is a substantial conflict of interests and perpetuates the fiction that parents know what is best. The result is that the child, the one primarily concerned, has a junior grade status before the law, and mental hospitals may become dumping grounds for difficult children whose parents are tired of their responsibilities. This is not unlike using hospital facilities as homes for the aged.

Prior to the preceding Supreme Court decisions, the case that provoked the widest comment was *Bartley v. Kremins*,[13] which had been decided by a three-judge federal court in Pennsylvania. It, too, was a class action, brought on behalf of named plaintiffs and persons of their class similarly situated, namely, children committed as voluntary patients to mental institutions in Pennsylvania. It was alleged that such children were denied due process because they were processed by procedure specified by statute in the Penn-

---

[13] 402 F.Supp. 1039 (E.D. Pa. 1975).

sylvania Mental Health and Mental Retardation Act.[14] The majority of the court, one judge dissenting, held that such children were entitled to a probable cause hearing within seventy-two hours from the date of initial detention, to a postcommitment hearing within two weeks, to written notice of the right to counsel, to the right to be present, and to confront and cross-examine witnesses and offer evidence in their own behalf and that the burden of proof was by clear and convincing evidence. The court rejected the "beyond reasonable doubt" standard of the criminal law and also held that the children were not entitled to a jury trial.

The key issue in the case was whether or not the Pennsylvania procedures "adequately assure against the mistaken commitment of children who are not mentally ill" was sufficient without regard to the consent of the children. The defendants urged that Pennsylvania's interest in protecting the child, preserving the family unit, and maintaining the rights of parents were sufficient to justify the statutory procedure and that parents or guardians could effectively waive any due process rights of the children.

The court noted that it could not find that in all instances parents act in the best interests of their children and hence might waive the constitutional rights of their children, citing the example of child abuse. The majority concluded that parents "may at times be acting against the interests of their children," and hence, they were not entitled to waive personal constitutional rights. Following the three-judge decision, the state of New Jersey, by rule of court, also adopted the position that consent of children, in addition to that of the parents, was essential for a commitment to a mental institution.

We are not here concerned with the procedural due process prescribed by the court or its workability. Rather, we stress the impact of the decision on the parent-child or family relationship. The Pennsylvania statute declared to be unconstitutional presumed a coincidence of interest between parent and child. The court, however, in an exceedingly brief discussion, assumed that such interests might be in conflict. Of course, the age of the children involved is and should be relevant to standing to object to hospi-

---

[14] 50 P.S.   4402 and 4403 (402 and 403).

talization. Moreover, presumably the mental condition of the particular child also is relevant to the capacity to consent in a particular case. The difficult problem arises where an adolescent is found to need care and treatment, the parents consent to hospitalization, but the child, "stubbornly" rejects hospitalization for whatever reason. Should involuntary commitment be imposed? Perhaps there should be no hard and fast rule with regard to parental waiver, but the answer should depend upon the age, condition, and maturity of the particular child. If this is so, a prompt hearing is essential to determine the matter on a case by case basis, and parental waiver would not be conclusive.

One of the problems implicit in the preceding decisions is that children, minors, or juveniles, all are lumped into one category despite individual differences. Neither the unconstitutional Pennsylvania statute nor the court's decision noted the differences between individual cases. It also should be noted that the doctrine of *Kremens* is both a sword and a shield. Inferentially, the child should be free to seek out therapy, counselling, or treatment on his own without regard to parental consent. In the areas of sex, drugs, and other problems, consent of the minor alone may be a blessing for the therapist, assuming he has made proper arrangements to get paid.

No doubt the last word has not been said on the sensitive issue of the rights of children to independent representation and to speak for themselves. The Supreme Court's presumption on the identity of parental and children's interests simply cannot withstand close scrutiny, and it is reckless to assume that such interests coincide and that an unrepresented minor will have other than a minor role in determining his fate.

The first volume of the Juvenile Justice Standards Project is entitled "Counsel for Private Parties." It is the first of some twenty-three volumes on the subject. A cursory glance through this tentative draft reveals that its authors seek to impose all or almost all of criminal due process upon the family court in delinquency cases. There is no room for a socialized court meting out individualized justice. The juvenile is to have a right to effective counsel at all stages of the proceedings, and the professional responsibility of such counsel is to accept the decisions of his client. The juvenile or family court, if these standards are adopted, will become a special criminal court for youthful or juvenile offenders. The due process will be the same as that accorded in adult criminal court. However, counsel, whether assigned or not, will have the responsibility of follow-up on the case in order to make sure that his juvenile client obtains treatment and has his rights respected.

For some of us who shared the dream that the juvenile court would work in a humane and effective way, it is difficult to accept that we have come full cycle. But, the ideal of treatment and rehabilitation is a cruel hoax and a rationalization for punishment and warehousing if we do not provide the program and personnel that are required for rehabilitation.

These two examples—the commitment of minors to mental facilities and the format of the juvenile court—may be taken to be examples of youth coming of age, of being treated more like adults. What young people do with enhanced autonomy and responsibility remains to be seen. Undoubtedly, increasing emphasis upon procedural due process and individual autonomy impairs the authority of both professionals and parents. It is understandable that such encroachments should be viewed as threatening. However, paternalism no longer is in vogue, and as the women's movement has demonstrated, protective measures often serve other ulterior purposes. The masters of slaves and the masters of households claimed that the welfare of those subject to their powers justified subjugation, and parents wielding the rod have been known to say "this hurts me more than it does you." Today, everybody wants some control of his life, and it should not be surprising that minors want, and will get, some of that responsibility. The rest of us will have to make adjustments accordingly.

SECTION II

THE EXPERT WITNESS

Chapter 6

MEDICAL DISABILITY COMPENSATION: A PRACTICUM

RICHARD ROSNER, M. D.

M ost physicians have few thoughts about the interface of medicine and the law. Nonetheless, there is at least one area in
which doctors often make contributions to legal determinations,
the field of medical disability compensation. This paper will offer
a series of practical comments on the history, theory, and practice
in this sector of forensic medicine.

With the onset of the industrial revolution, it became a political
and economic necessity to protect the owners of the fledgling
factories from legal liability for accidents that impaired the health
and well-being of their employees. In those early days, before
effective unionization of laborers, men were more expendable
than machines. If an industrialist were to have been held strictly
liable for the on-the-job injuries sustained by his workers, few
industries would have survived. One of the early means of protecting
the financial interests of the owners was called assumption of risk.
Under this concept, a worker was regarded as free to accept or
refuse any particular employment. If he accepted a job, he sup-
posedly did so of his own free will and knowingly accepted and
assumed the responsibility for any of the on-the-job risks and
dangers that the work entailed. For example, if a steam-boiler
engine exploded and hurt or killed the worker, the owner could
claim that the worker knew that boilers occasionally did explode
and had freely accepted the job, and the owner was not liable
because the worker had knowingly assumed the risks entailed in
working around steam engines. Another protection for the indus-

Reprinted from Richard Rosner, Medical Disability Compensation: A Practicum, *New York
University Medical Quarterly, 34(1):3–6,* Summer 1978. Courtesy of the New York University
Medical Center.

trialist was the fellow servant rule. Under this concept, an owner could claim that the party responsible for an on-the-job injury was a colleague, coworker, fellow servant of the injured worker, rather than the factory owner himself. For example, if a steam-boiler engine exploded, the responsible party might be regarded as the shop foreman, rather than the shop owner. As the foreman was usually another relatively poor employee, there was no value to be gained in suing the shop foreman for liability. If all else failed, the economic interest of the factory owner could be protected by the principle of contributory negligence. Under this concept, the injured worker was himself responsible for whatever harm had befallen him. For example, if a steam-boiler engine exploded, the fault was with the injured worker, who had not checked the machine properly before using it, whose negligence in taking reasonable precautions had contributed to the accident's occurrence. By these three legal bars to liability, the industrialists could continue to employ workers in dangerous occupations without much concern about providing compensation for medical impairments incurred on the job.

A suit by a worker against his employer, on the ground of liability for on-the-job injuries, is conducted in civil law. It is one of a large group of lawsuits relating to the concept of *tort*. Whereas the criminal law seeks to punish and deter and reform persons who have been found guilty of a crime, that is not the function of *tort* law. In a civil lawsuit, the goal is to restore a currently unfair situation to the conditions that existed before the wrong was committed or, if restoration is not possible, to compensate an injured party for the wrong that was done to him. For example, an injured worker usually does not want his employer to be sentenced to jail under criminal law; rather, the worker wants his medical and rehabilitation costs paid, wants to be given the salary he would have earned if he had been able to continue his work, and may want punitive damages assessed against the shopowner along with compensation for mental and physical anguish and impairment.

The medical doctor may become involved in a civil suit for compensation under *tort* law as an expert witness. Any time that a patient seeks treatment from a physician, after an on-the-job injury, the doctor may be called to testify in court on that case. Most physicians are unaware of that possibility and find themselves surprised when served with a subpoena to appear as a witness. It will be useful, at such times, to have a conceptual framework that will permit an intelligent organization of medical data that will be relevant to the specific legal issues under consideration.

One useful schema is built around four basic questions:

1. What is the specific medical-legal issue?
2. What are the legally defined criteria relevant to the issue?
3. What are the relevant medical findings?
4. Is there a cause-and-effect relationship between the medical findings and the legally defined criteria for deciding the issue?

Let us assume that a doctor is at his office and receives a telephone call from his patient John Smith. The doctor is told that Smith is suing his employer, the Efficient Product Company, and wants the doctor to testify on his behalf. What should the doctor do? (He may want to say, "I'm too busy." However, he must comply with a subpoena to appear, even if he refuses to do so voluntarily.)

The first step requires that the physician ask the patient to have the patient's attorney call the doctor. The doctor cannot expect the patient to understand the complexities of the law; that is the job of the attorney. Upon being contacted by the patient's lawyer, the first question for clarification is, What is the specific medical-legal issue? For example, the issue may be *tort* liability, or it may be workmen's compensation, or social security disability, or compensation under a private disability insurance plan. Each of these four types of on-the-job injury compensation cases entails different rules of law, different legally defined criteria, and may require different medical data. It is important that the doctor understand what the specific medical-legal issue is in the particular case. Lack of this understanding may waste time, cost money, and lose the lawsuit.

The second matter, which the doctor should ask the patient's attorney to explain, relates to the legally defined criteria of relevance to the specific medical-legal issue. Each of the fifty states in the U.S.A. has its own constitution; each has its own legal statutes passed by its own legislature; each has its own body of case law, i.e.

previously adjudicated lawsuits. In addition, the federal courts have their own body of statutes and case law. Thus, there are a minimum of fifty-one possible legally defined criteria on any possible medical-legal issue in the United States. What is necessary is to know which criteria apply in the specific case. For example, the doctor treated Mr. Smith in New York, but Mr. Smith resides in Connecticut, and the Efficient Product Company is incorporated in New Jersey. It is important to know in which state the suit is being made. The criteria for *tort* liability may be different in different states. Furthermore, it is vital to know what the specific criteria relevant to the issue are. What does the statute and the case law of the specific jurisdiction define as *tort* liability for medical impairments due to on-the-job injuries? The law may be vague, it may be precise, but whatever it is, the doctor must know the law to respond relevantly.

Let us assume, for the sake of exemplification, that the law is vague in the state in which the case will be tried. The law may say merely that if an employee is now (or has been) suffering from a diagnosable medical illness that substantially impairs his ability to function, and that impairment was caused by a work-related injury (undeterred by the fellow-servant rule, by the assumption of risk, or by contributory negligence), then the employee may be entitled to compensation from his employer. Actually, the law will probably be even more vague than that, referring not to employees and employers but rather to the broad class of allegedly injured parties and accused *tort-feasors*, i.e. wrong-doers. Regardless of how vague the statute may be, there will probably be myriad case law precedents, in which similar issues have been adjudicated, and which will provide ample instances of how the general statute has been interpreted by the court. It is the doctor's task to get the patient's attorney to give the physician a copy of the statutes and case law decisions that are pertinent to the specific medical-legal issue. Failing to obtain this, the doctor should ask the attorney to explain clearly what the relevant legal criteria happen to be.

The next step relates to the third question: What are the relevant medical findings? Does Mr. Smith have a diagnosable medical illness at the present time? Did he have one at the time he was examined by the doctor? What was the illness? What was the cause of the illness? Did the illness impair Mr. Smith's ability to function at all? Did it specifically impair his ability to function at his job? Is it likely to be a temporary impairment or a permanent impairment? How long will the impairment probably last? How much does it impair Mr. Smith's ability to function at all (or to function on the job): 100%, 75%, 50%, 25%, etc.?

In responding to the issue of relevant medical findings, it is important for the physician to remember that not all of his findings are relevant. There may be no need to comment about a nervous condition in a patient whose alleged on-the-job injury is an orthopedic problem. The courts do not know what to do with such extraneous information, may be distracted from the principal matter under litigation, and will not thank the doctor for providing more data than was desired.

The doctor should be careful to distinguish between relatively objective signs and symptoms, on the one hand, and his interpretation of those findings, on the other hand. The court needs to know at what point the transition is made from data that virtually all medical practitioners would agree exists to inferences and deductions from that data that may be open to disagreement among competent physicians. Usually, it is in the transition from hard medical facts to soft medical deductions that the physician may be subject to challenge when he is asked to testify as an expert witness.

The most difficult of the four steps described is the final one, the determination of whether or not there is a causal connection between the medical findings, e.g. Mr. Smith has a neurotic depressive reaction, and the specific legally defined criteria applicable to the particular medical-legal issue, e.g. *tort* liability of the Efficient Product Company. Strictly speaking, this step is the field of expertise of the specialist in forensic medicine. Most attorneys can give data about medical-legal issues and the criteria for their definition. Most doctors can give relevant medical data. Few attorneys and few doctors are trained to apply medical expertise to legal ends by legal means.

Part of the difficulty with proving a cause-and-effect linkage between a specific medical finding and an objective event that can satisfy the legally defined criteria for an action or omission on the part of an employer (for which the employer might be regarded as liable under civil law) is the fact that causation has different meanings in medicine and in law. In medicine, we are usually talking about scientific evidence sufficient to convince the majority of rational men that x caused y. In law, we are usually talking about legal evidence sufficient to convince a judge or jury that x caused y. Scientifically convincing evidence and legally convincing evidence are quite different.

In civil law, with regard to *tort* liability suits, causation refers to proximate cause. If Mr. Jones lends matches to a known (to him) pyromaniac, who then burns down a building in the Bronx, what is the proximate cause of the ruin? Is it the pyromaniac, who actually set the fire? Is it Mr. Jones, who gave the matches to the pyromaniac? Is it the manufacturer of the matches, without which the pyromaniac could never have misbehaved? Is it the owner of the building in the Bronx, who did not take adequate care that madmen should be excluded from his property? Is it the superintendent of the building, who was not watching when the fire was started? Is it the City of New York, whose fire engines came so late that the building could not be saved? As these questions serve to demonstrate, the cause of the ruin is not something open to scientific inquiry in the usual sense. The law is using cause to refer to the person (or corporate entity) that is to be regarded as responsible for a particular thing, event or condition. The proximate cause is the legally responsible action or actor.

Another source of communication problem between the medical-scientific vocabulary and methodology and that of the legal system relates to time. In science, it is quite satisfactory and usual to state that a problem, e.g. did x cause y, cannot be solved currently because there is insufficient data to make a certain judgment. The law does not have the luxury of not deciding issues. In fact, the principal function of court is to resolve disputes between contending parties. The court wants to make *the best possible* decision, *not the very best* decision. The court must decide *now*, with whatever limited data is currently available, *not in the future*, when more evidence may be handy. The court provides *an adequate trial* of the facts, *not a perfect trial*. Thus, the scientist may say, "It is not possible to state with certainty that x has caused y." Whereas the court must say, "We have come to a conclusion based upon the available data as to whether or not x was the cause of y." Science can wait, the court must decide.

Also to be considered is that scientists like to refer to *the* cause. The law is content to speak of *a* cause. It may be, to take our example of the fire in the Bronx, that the superintendent was not *the* cause of the fire, but the law wants to know if he was *a* cause, one of the contributing factors to the fire. But for his actions or omissions, would the fire have occurred or not? A particular thing, event or condition may be multiply determined; all of the antecedent actors and actions may be regarded as sharing responsibility, and all of them may be held legally liable as proximate causes under civil law.

Mr. Smith relates that, while driving through New York City, in a car owned by the Efficient Product Company, and while performing a task directly related to his employment, e.g. delivering a special report, the front tire sustained a blowout. He further states that he had repeatedly brought the poor condition of the car's tires to the attention of the garage mechanic in charge of servicing cars of the company and to his immediate supervisor, all with no effect. As a result of the accident, he ran over a pedestrian, causing her death. Since that event, he has had insomnia, has lost his appetite, has suffered from constipation, has become agitated, is easily distracted, has shortened attention span, has lost weight, has become lethargic, has lost interest in his job/family/friends/hobbies, and feels guilty to the point of having suicidal ideas. He was seen by a competent psychiatrist and is currently under treatment for what has been diagnosed as a neurotic depressive reaction. Mr. Smith is suing the Efficient Product Company, claiming that his illness was caused by the accident and that the accident is a direct consequence of negligence on the part of the company. His psychiatrist has been asked to be an expert witness on Mr. Smith's behalf.

The doctor must be aware that proof at law has different levels of certainty. In some cases, such as in murder trials in criminal law, proof requires that a judge or jury be convinced "beyond a reasonable doubt," e.g. more than 90% certain. In other cases, proof is established by "clear and convincing evidence," e.g. more than 75% certain. In still other cases, proof depends on "a prepon-

derance of the evidence," e.g. more than 50% certain. The doctor
ought to know what the statutorily defined standard of proof is so
that he can know how to present his data. Often the law is not
clear; the doctor may be asked whether his opinion is based on "a
reasonable degree of medical certainty." How high a degree of
certainty is a reasonable degree — 50+%? 75+%? 90+%?

It may be useful to summarize these differences between medicine and law in a tabulated form.

Causation in Science	*Causation in Law*
1. The first efficient cause is sought.	1. The proximate cause is sought.
2. The single cause is sought.	2. A principal cause is sought.
3. A decision about causality can be postponed until all the relevant data are in.	3. A decision about causality must be made now, with the limited data at hand.
4. The standard of proof is always the same.	4. The standard of proof varies in different legal contexts.

In all modesty, it should be noted that even proof in science is a
questionable item. The English philosopher David Hume in his
essay "An Inquiry Concerning the Human Understanding" has
noted that we can never really know that x causes y. Rather, we can
only assert that no y has ever been known to occur without the
antecedent occurrence of x. Causation is a convenient theoretical
entity that bridges x and y, but is never truly known.

Many doctors may think that issues of this sort occur rarely. In
fact, they are quite common. Health insurance forms (a special
type of medical disability compensation) have a short question
whether or not the treatment being provided by the doctor is work
related. Depending on whether the doctor checks the yes box or
the no box on the health insurance form, the patient may experience different legal consequences. A yes may support a potential
suit against an employer. A yes may invoke the special legal
mechanisms of the workmen's compensation laws of the particular
state. A yes may activate a union paid private disability insurance
policy.

If compensation for medical impairment is such an important
issue, why is it that so few doctors are aware of the procedure? The
answer to that problem moves us back to the historical develop-

ments in the field of labor relations. With the organization of labor into effective unions, the conflicting interests of workers and industrialists were less unequally represented. Furthermore, as technology became more advanced, it became possible to reduce the incidence of injuries due to inherently faulty machinery. Employers remained concerned about the possibility of being sued for large sums of money for on-the-job injuries to their workers. Employees remained concerned to get around the legal obstacles of the fellow-servant rule, the contributory negligence rule, and the concept of assumption of risk. Out of this labor-management conflict, one of the resolutions was the creation of workmen's compensation laws. Under these laws, individual workers would forego their rights to sue under *tort* law (with the risk of not winning the suit), in order to obtain a much smaller, but guaranteed benefit for medical impairments sustained in the course of their work. Through workmen's compensation, individual companies would forego their right to challenge in court any workers who sought compensation (with the risk that the company might lose the suit), thereby protecting the firm against major monetary loss at the price of a small financial commitment to aid injured employees. In most instances of on-the-job injuries, *tort* liability actions are avoided in favor of the use of workmen's compensation procedures. Only in cases of the relations between employers and employees who are not participants in the workmen's compensation programs would civil suits be utilized.

The medical doctor can be called on as an expert witness in workmen's compensation issues. Again, it is important to know that each state has its own particular legislation enacting its own specific workmen's compensation procedures. The particular criteria used to determine whether or not a specific medical impairment qualifies for compensation under any specific state's workmen's compensation procedures will be found in the guidelines established by that state's workmen's compensation board. In most states, the initial ruling of the board on any given case can be appealed to a higher administrative panel established by the board. Appeals from the higher administrative panel's decisions are made to the court system of the particular state. Thus, even in cases under the jurisdiction of the workmen's compensation laws, the physician may find himself appearing in court as an expert witness.

It is not anticipated that reading this article will immediately permit any physician to function comfortably as a medical-legal specialist. Rather, it is hoped that physicians will recognize how easily one can become enmeshed in the interface of medicine and law. In order to permit doctors to understand the complexities of forensic medical practice, the School of Medicine and the Post-Graduate Medical School, in cooperation with the department of psychiatry, have recently initiated special training programs.

In 1976, A Practicum in Psychiatry and the Criminal Law was presented by the department of psychiatry, the forensic psychiatry clinic of the New York State Criminal and Supreme courts, and the Center for Forensic Psychiatry. In 1977, under the same conjoint auspices, A Practicum in Psychiatry and the Civil Law was offered. It is planned that these two courses will alternate yearly within the curriculum of the Post-Graduate Medical School.

In 1977, the New York State section of The American Academy of Psychiatry and the Law (NYS-AAPL) cosponsored a course with the Post-Graduate Medical School on Legal Activism: Its Impact on Psychiatric Practice and Social Structures. In 1978, the same two sponsors presented The Expert Witness in Forensic Psychiatry. Plans are in process for the 1979 course on Domestic Relations, Family Law, and Forensic Psychiatry.

Most ambitiously, in 1977 New York University, through the department of psychiatry, agreed academically to credential a full-time, year-long fellowship training program in psychiatry and the law. This program pools the resources of three agencies of the government, the forensic psychiatry clinic of the Criminal and Supreme courts, the mental health services of the Family Court of New York City and the mental health section of the Prison Health Services of the City of New York, with the resources of the School of Medicine and the Law School of NYU. Designed as a fifth year of postgraduate training, the program graduated its first two physicians in the summer of 1978 and continues to recruit applicants for the future.

While these programs are directed to psychiatrists, it is anticipated that other medical specialties will begin to offer programs to assist their members in functioning better in the medical-legal arena. Until such time, it is hoped that this review of the history, theory and practice of forensic medicine as it applies to the doctor's role as expert witness in civil law suits related to *tort* liability will prove to be of practical utility.

Chapter 7

HISTORICAL DEVELOPMENT
OF THE EXPERT WITNESS

FAUST F. ROSSI, J. D.

As the first participant in this program, addressing the broad
subject of "The History of the Expert Witness," my function
will be to lay a foundation for the scholarship that will follow.[1]
Thus, my analysis will be more informational than original and
more general than specific. The intellectual fireworks should come
in the more focussed topics of the other participant authors. My
introduction offers a brief historical tour of the development of
the expert witness and the rules of evidence governing his in-
court testimony.

The expert has undergone three periods of judicial acceptance,
receiving in each era a different measure of hospitality. There is
the early common law period before 1700; a time when today's
courtroom procedure of a witness testifying in court to supply
information to uninformed jurors was coming into vogue. The
expert, when called upon in this period, operated as an advisor
without restrictions. The second period, from about 1700 until the
near present, saw acceptance of the in-court witness, the modern
jury, the growth of oral testimony, and, consequently, the development of precise rules of evidence including restrictions on
opinion and expert testimony. The third and final era is too recent
perhaps to be part of a historical discussion. I view it as including
the last three decades from about 1950 to the present. It is a period
which is liberating the expert from many of the barriers devised
during the eighteenth and nineteenth centuries. Taking these
stages together, we may say that the development of expert opin-

---

[1]This chapter is a revised version of a report read at the annual conference of the New York
State membership group of the American Academy of Psychiatry and the Law on January 28,
1978.

ion began with unrestricted use. Then it became hedged with limitations. Now it is moving back toward liberal admissibility.

EARLY DEVELOPMENT OF THE EXPERT WITNESS

In its early stage of development, the jury was selected precisely because of its knowledge of or access to the facts in dispute. No witnesses were called to the stand to supply data. Jurors were relied upon to furnish themselves both knowledge and decision. In the years before 1700, the jury trial permitted and condoned the practice of out of court jury investigation. What jurors did not themselves know about a case when they were initially selected they would find out on their own. It was the duty of jurors as soon as summoned to make inquiries about facts, talk to people in the neighborhood, and get their own information from speaking with informed persons out of court.[2] Of course, expert knowledge might be necessary. There were two modes of using the expertise then available. One way was to select the experts as jurors. Those with the special skill necessary to understand the case would investigate and decide. Another approach was to call the expert to aid the court. He would participate not as a formal witness but as an advisor.[3] Early examples involved criminal cases of mayhem. Was the wound serious enough to constitute mayhem? The court would consult the surgeon out of court and report the opinion to the jury.[4] A sixteenth century report indicated the judge's knowledge of Latin failed him in construing a phrase in a commercial contract. The grammarian gave the tribunal its meaning, without formal testimony or the status of witness.[5] These experts were aides to the court, and their status in this capacity prevented any objection or formal inquiry into the nature of the information supplied. In short, this first period saw experts functioning as either actual jurors and decision makers or as advisors to the court

---

[2] 5 J. WIGMORE, EVIDENCE. 1364, at 13–15 (rev. ed. 1974).

[3] L. Hand, *Historical and Practical Considerations Regarding Expert Testimony,* 15 HARVARD L. REV. 40 (1901).

[4] 28 Ass. pl. 5 described in 9 W. HOLDSWORTH, HISTORY OF ENGLISH LAW 212 (3d ed. 1944).

[5] Y.B. 9 Hy, VII, Hil. pl. 8 described in 9 W. HOLDSWORTH, HISTORY OF ENGLISH LAW 212 (3d ed. 1944).

operating without formal instructions.

THE GROWTH OF RESTRICTIONS ON EXPERT TESTIMONY

By the 1700s, jurors no longer acted upon their own knowledge. Facts were presented in the current fashion. Witnesses were called to testify in court. The power to compel witnesses to appear developed for the first time. Oral interrogation and cross-examination were utilized. As this kind of public testimony increased, so too did concern for the reliability of evidence. The best available evidence should be presented. So, of course, rules of evidence, meaning rules of exclusion, came to be developed with increasing precision. The first comprehensive treatises in evidence were published. The hearsay rule was defined. From 1790 to 1830, a period of forty years, there were more recorded rulings on evidence than in all the prior two centuries of reports. Out of these exclusionary rules of evidence came restrictions on opinions and expert testimony, many of which continued into the contemporary period.[6]

In the area of opinion, the most fascinating restriction was the prohibition against the giving of opinions by lay witnesses, even opinions based on matters actually observed. This is a rule that more or less hangs on in some jurisdictions even today and that provides that a lay witness, including one who has closely observed the actor over a long period of time, may not express an opinion as to the actor's sanity or mental condition.[7] The rule against lay opinion is fascinating because it was largely a historical accident. It began with the sensible principle that a witness should testify from personal knowledge. The witness should know the facts from his own perception and should not be allowed to speculate. No opinions meant no testimony without personal knowledge. But what about expert witnesses? They might lack personal knowledge of the case facts but still have useful information and opinions to convey. The expert, then, was an exception to the usual

---

[6] 1 J. WIGMORE, EVIDENCE 8 at 237–241 (3d ed. 1940); 12 W. HOLDSWORTH, HISTORY OF ENGLISH LAW 504–510 (3d ed. 1944).

[7] People v. Pekarz, 185 N.Y. 470 (1906).

prohibition and could give an opinion without personal knowledge. There was no duplication of functions between the expert and the jury. Jurors, not witnesses, are usually supposed to draw inferences from the evidence. But it was assumed that the expert had the expertise to draw conclusions that the jury lacked and needed. Out of this analysis grew the rule that the lay witness, having no special expertise, should not duplicate the jury function by giving opinions from facts. Let the lay witness give the facts alone. So, in the case of a lay witness, the rule went from no opinion, meaning no testimony without personal knowledge, to a rule of no opinion even if based on perception. In the United States, but not in England, the rationale switched from excluding an unreliable guess without personal knowledge to a rationale excluding inferences from observed facts. In about thirty years from 1800 to 1830 a large portion of previously acceptable lay witness testimony was hewed off.[8] It is this rule excluding lay opinion based on fact perception which Wigmore calls pernicious and which was the subject of Judge Doe's notable protest in the New Hampshire Supreme Court decision of *State v. Pike* in 1870.[9]

As for the expert witness, his flow of information was also circumscribed. Rules inhibiting expert testimony grew from several concerns. Among these were desires that the evidence be reliable; that it help rather than detract from the truth seeking function of the jury; that the jury be protected from misleading, confusing, or unimportant data; and that the jury's function of finding facts and applying the law not be abandoned to expert witnesses. These concerns were exacerbated by recognition that the adversary system, whatever its benefits, posed special problems in handling expert testimony, including the selection and compensation of experts by partisan parties, the direct cross-examination confrontation model for presentation of testimony, and the tendency of the trial lawyers sometimes to persuade by oversimplification. These aspects of the system suggested the need for special limitations, and they came.

It was, of course, required that the witness be formally qualified

---

[8]7 J. WIGMORE, EVIDENCE 1917 (rev. ed. 1978).

[9]State v. Pike, 49 N.H. 399, 423 (1870).

as an expert. His qualifications bear on his competency to testify at all as well as on the weight the jury should give to his evidence. Moreover, the expert, when he gives his opinion on the matter at issue, should speak with reasonable certainty or probability. Pure speculation is naturally to be avoided. Beyond these rather obvious limitations, there grew up three special barriers to expert testimony.

First, the subject matter upon which the expert sought to testify had to be appropriate for expert testimony. The subject matter was appropriate only if it dealt with complex matters beyond the ken of the ordinary lay juror. The appropriateness inquiry was not "Can the expert help?" Rather, the question was "Is the expert essential or necessary for jury understanding of the topic?" The emphasis on necessity rather than on assistance for the trier of fact limited the admissibility of many expert opinions.[10]

A second requirement limited the data upon which the expert opinion could be based. The factual data underlying the opinion had to be either facts personally known by the expert or facts that were actually supplied by the evidence at trial.[11] For example, assume the psychiatrist is to give an opinion of the patient's mental condition. His opinion may be founded upon a private examination of the patient (episodes witnessed directly by the expert and, therefore, within his personal knowledge). This presents no problem, since the witness is the treating psychiatrist giving an opinion founded on facts within his personal knowledge. However, the psychiatrist's opinion may also be based in part on episodes related to him by relatives of the patient. If so, the psychiatrist could only give his opinion if the episodes were in evidence and testified to by the relatives who witnessed them.[12] Moreover, in this latter situation, the episodes upon which the expert is relying would usually have to be identified by being included in a hypothetical question put to the psychiatrist before eliciting the opinion.

At this point the hypothetical question deserves some special

---

[10]C. McCORMICK, EVIDENCE   13 at 29–30 (2d ed. 1972).

[11]*Id*   15, at 34–36.

[12]People v. Samuels, 302 N.Y. 163 (1951); People v. Keough, 276 N.Y. 141 (1937).

attention. It is an example of the law's fear of jury dominance by the expert and is founded on theoretical logic, which has floundered in practice. The jury should know the premises for the expert's opinion in order to evaluate its weight properly. So, the factual premises must be part of the evidence heard by the jury, and the supporting facts must be identified as the underlying premises upon which the opinion is founded. Thus, to return to our example, when the psychiatrist bases his opinion on patient episodes described by relatives, we require two things. The episodes must be in evidence so the jurors can decide whether the events really occurred. The hypothetical question then seeks the expert's opinion "assuming the truth of the episode evidence." This means the episode testimony will be highlighted as one of the evidence facts upon which the opinion is based. In this way, if the jurors disbelieve the episode evidence, they will also know enough to discount the expert's opinion, since it relies upon what they regard as unworthy evidence. Indications are that the hypothetical question requirement grew out of decisions on mental condition. There are vague references to it on the issue of lunacy in a 1760 trial[13] and again on the issue of seaworthiness in 1807.[14] But, its most deliberate early reference was the judge's response to the House of Lords' questions in the 1843 McNaghten case. On the issue of insanity, could the expert who never examined the defendant but heard evidence in court give an opinion assuming the testimonial facts to be true?[15] The answer in practice came to be yes if the evidentiary premises for the opinion are identified.

The third requirement was that the expert could not testify upon the ultimate issue in the case.[16] This doctrine has been said to be more ignored than followed, but it hangs on today in some jurisdictions. At times it is applied sensibly. The psychiatrist may not testify that defendant is not criminally responsible. Nor may the structural engineer opine that defendant owner of a collapsed structure was negligent. But, no special rule is needed to prevent

---

[13]Earl Ferrers' Trial, 19 How. St. Tr. 943 (1760).

[14]Beckwith v. Sydebotham, 1 Comp. 116 (1807).

[15]10 Cl. & F. 200, 207 (1843).

[16]C. McCormick, Evidence 12 (2d ed. 1972).

such testimony about legal matters. It is enough to say the expert opinions in these situations are not helpful to the jury. They represent conclusions of law that are outside witness expertise. But, the prohibition against ultimate issues goes much further. It has prevented the psychiatrist from giving a direct opinion on sanity or the engineer from describing an observed structural condition as unsafe. The rule has proven difficult to apply, has been described as obstructive to needed expert testimony, and has been universally condemned by modern evidence scholars.

THE MODERN PERIOD OF CODIFICATION AND REFORM

What of the present? In the last thirty years, the dominant trend has been to codify evidence law into a comprehensive code of rules. Until the 1950s, evidence law consisted of a mixed bag of court decisions and scattered statutes. Hearsay, for example, was defined in the cases and judicial opinions. In most jurisdictions there were no statutes or rules defining it. Yet, exceptions, for example, the rule that business records through hearsay may be admitted, were often found in statutes. The restrictions regarding expert testimony that developed after 1700 were found in decisional law and were seldom pulled together into statutes or court rules. In the 1950s and 1960s several states, most notably California and New Jersey, enacted codes, or rules, of evidence. In 1975 the Federal Rules of Evidence became law in federal courts. Since then some twenty states have adopted codifications based upon the federal rules. New York and at least a dozen other states are now engaged in drafting codes similar to the federal rules.

Codification compels analysis of existing principles and provides at least the opportunity for reform. Specifically, Article VII of the Federal Rules treats "Opinions and Expert Testimony." It represents now, or very soon will represent, the majority view in this country. The thrust of the article is to liberalize admissibility. Most of its six short sections are concerned with removing restrictions that we have described as the product of the middle period in the history of the expert witness.

We begin with the lay witness. May he testify to inferences based upon his perception? Section 701 of the Federal Rules provides that opinions that are rationally based upon the perception of the lay witness are admissible if "helpful to a clear understanding of his testimony or the determination of a fact in issue." The formulation greatly liberalizes the admissibility of lay opinion, since the test is now one of helpfulness rather than necessity. Abandonment of the no-lay-opinion rule eliminates the former confusion, which resulted from trying to draw difficult distinctions between facts and opinions and between opinions that were necessary and those which were not.

What of the expert witness? Under prior law we said the subject matter of expert testimony was appropriate only if it dealt with matters sufficiently complex to be beyond the ken of the ordinary juror. Section 702 of the Federal Rules abandons this requirement and, as in the case of lay witnesses, substitutes a standard of helpfulness in place of necessity. If specialized knowledge "will assist the trier of fact to understand the evidence or to determine a fact in issue," the subject matter is suitable for the expert witness.

The most substantial change involves the basis for expert opinion. Traditionally, as we have seen, the facts underlying the opinion must be either those within the personal knowledge of the witness or facts that are in evidence and are identified by inclusion in the hypothetical question. Federal Rule 703 adds a third acceptable basis for expert opinion. The facts underlying the expert's opinion need not be in evidence. They need not even be theoretically admissible in evidence. The only limitation on the supporting data is that it be of a type "reasonably relied upon by experts in the particular field in forming opinions or inferences upon the subject." The emphasis has shifted from a standard of admissibility of the data that involves technical evidence concepts to a standard of reliability as demonstrated by the practice of the scientific community. Return again to the hypothetical situation of the psychiatrist who bases his opinion on patient episodes related to him by relatives. No longer need the episodes be in evidence. The history, as related by relatives of the patient is the kind of data upon which psychiatrists may reasonably rely in forming opinions, and therefore, the standard for Section 703 is met.

This willingness to receive opinions based on reliable non-evidence facts has special significance for us because it derives case support from psychiatric testimony decisions in criminal cases. In New York, for example, there are three decisions by the court of appeals on this issue, and all three involved the psychiatrist witness.

In *People v. DePiazza*[17] the prosecution psychiatrists were permitted to base their opinions as to defendant's sanity "upon certain hospital records of tests and examinations which were not produced for the jury's consideration." In affirming defendant's conviction, the court noted that this nonevidence data played a small role in the process leading to the psychiatric opinions. Next came the decision in *People v. Stone*,[18] which held that a psychiatrist, after rendering a legally competent opinion, could further support that opinion by reference to medically relevant, albeit hearsay, evidence. The hearsay in *Stone* consisted in part of interviews with four persons who did not testify at trial. The latest pronouncement was *People v. Sugden*. Again, the issue was the sanity of the defendant. The prosecution psychiatrist was allowed to express his opinion, even though it was based in part upon "a psychologist's report about defendant when aged seven, other psychiatric and medical reports, defendant's written confession, and written statements of four of the persons involved in varying degrees in the crime." The court held that the psychiatrist "may rely on material, albeit of out of court origin, if it is of a kind accepted in the profession as reliable in forming a professional opinion."[19]

The expert may now rely upon nonevidence facts if they are reliable. Do these supporting facts have to be identified by inclusion in the traditional hypothetical question? Section 705 of the Federal Rules states that "unless the court orders otherwise, questions calling for the opinion of an expert witness need not be hypothetical in form." Logical in concept, the hypothetical question proved obstructive in practice. The culprit was the adversarial construct in which testimony is given. In framing the hypothetical question, counsel is free to select evidence facts most favorable to his position. Therefore, the inquiry often presented an opportu-

---

[17]24 N.Y. 2d 342 (1969).

[18]35 N.Y. 2d 69 (1974).

[19]35 N.Y. 2d 453, 460 (1974).

nity for a one-sided summation of proponent's case. To the extent the question is partisan in scope, the expert's answer is less meaningful. In any event, the question was often so long and so structured that the jury was confused rather than aided in its comprehension of the expert's underlying premises.

The Federal Rules also put to rest the ultimate issue prohibition. Section 704 provides that testimony "is not objectionable because it embraces an ultimate issue to be decided by the trier of fact." The final section of the article provides expressly for the court appointment of impartial experts when deemed appropriate by the trial judge with compensation to be paid by the parties as the judge directs.

The full scope of these changes may not be apparent. Taking all the rules together, here is what is possible. The expert may testify in answer to just three questions on direct examination. First, what are your qualifications? Second, do you have an opinion based upon reasonable scientific probability? Third, what is that opinion? In theory that could conclude direct examination.[20] The opinion may be on the ultimate issue and may be based upon reliable nonevidence facts, but identification of those underlying facts is not a condition to receipt of the opinion. It is clear that many traditional evidentiary restrictions on the admissibility of expert testimony have disappeared during the codification movement.

I would like to think that the trend away from restricting the expert is a sign of the law's confidence in the expert, in the trial attorney who offers and explores the testimony, and in the trial judge who oversees the process of its presentation. In fact, however, the trend against exclusionary rules is a general one. It reflects, more than anything, confidence in the modern jury and its ability to weigh evidence appropriately. It relies upon the trier of fact to discard the unreliable and to accept the meaningful, without the need for prior evidentiary controls.

---

[20]3 J. WEINSTEIN & M. BERGER. EVIDENCE ¶705 [01] at 705-2 (1978).

Chapter 8

PSYCHOLOGICAL TESTING AS A BASIS FOR EXPERT TESTIMONY: USE OR ABUSE?

RALPH SLOVENKO, LL.B., Ph.D.

A psychiatric evaluation is based on interviewing, sometimes background information, and sometimes neurological or psychological tests. The information derived from interviews may, of course, consist of explicit verbal responses or nonverbal signs or body language. The evaluation thus relies upon inferences made from such derivatives as speech, nonverbal communication, actions, and behavior.

In general, opinion that is based on such "soft" information is susceptible, at least in the courtroom, to controversy and often to ridicule. The cross-examiner attacks the witness with such questions as "Doctor, isn't it true that psychiatry consists mostly of a number of theories about human behavior, none of which have been scientifically proven?" "Doctor, isn't it true that there is a substantial body of scientific and professional literature to the effect that the psychiatric interview is influenced by many factors, which affect the conclusions that are drawn but have little to do with the actual mental condition of the person being examined?" "Doctor, isn't it true that there is a substantial body of scientific and professional literature to the effect that psychiatric diagnoses are not very reliable and not very accurate?" "Doctor, isn't there a substantial body of scientific and professional literature to the effect that psychiatrists with considerable experience are no more accurate in their diagnoses than those with little or even no experience?"[1]

---

[1]Two leading books on coping with psychiatric and psychological testimony are Blinder, M., PSYCHIATRY IN THE EVERYDAY PRACTICE OF LAW (Rochester, N.Y.: Lawyers Co-operative Publishing Co., 1973), and Ziskin, J., COPING WITH PSYCHIATRIC AND PSYCHOLOGICAL TESTIMONY (Beverly Hills, Calif.: Law and Psychology Press, 2d ed. 1975). *See also* Flannery, T. A., *Meeting the Insanity Defense*, J. CRIM. LAW, Criminology & Police Science *51:* 309–316, 1960.

To the extent that the opinion of the psychiatrist (or psychologist) rests upon what the subject told the examiner, it is open to the challenge that the expert is not able to detect deception or malingering. To the extent that the opinion relies upon psychological tests, particularly the Rorschach inkblot and Bender gestalt, the argument is made that the expert is indulging in something akin to the reading of tea leaves. To the extent that other inferences are possible, the expert is open to the question, "Another conclusion is possible, isn't it?" Even assuming the tests have high validity, that is, they evaluate or predict what they are supposed to, there is the objection that none of the tests are designed specifically to answer a legal question but are used inferentially.

Under the law of evidence, a witness qualified as an expert by knowledge, skill, experience, training, or education may give opinion testimony in his area of expertise. The ordinary witness, on the other hand, can only testify as to what he has himself seen or done; he may report on what he has heard subject to the limitations of the hearsay rule. The facts or data upon which an expert bases an opinion or belief need not be independently admissible as long as they are the "type reasonably relied upon by experts in the particular field."[2] Thus, a psychiatrist's reliance on the results of psychological testing performed by a psychologist would be acceptable, whether or not the tests themselves are admissible evidence.[3] Similarly, an expert may use a lie detector or amobarbital sodium to support his opinion, though they are not independently admissible as evidence. The jury, though, may be cautioned that the basis of an opinion is a factor in weighing that opinion.[4] When, on cross-examination, it is shown there are no facts to support the opinion, there may be a motion to strike the testimony.

Under the law of evidence, facts or data upon which expert opinions are based may be derived from three possible sources. One source is the firsthand observation of the witness; a treating physician affords an example. A second source is presentation at the trial; the technique may be the familiar hypothetical question

---

[2] Federal Rules of Evidence, Rule 703.

[3] *See, e.g.*, Doherty v. Dean, 337 S.W.2d 153 (Tex. Civ. App. 1960) (child custody).

[4] Jenkins v. United States, 113 U.S. App. D.C. 300, 307 F.2d 637 (1962).

or having the expert attend the trial and hear the testimony establishing the facts. The third source consists of presentation of data to the expert outside of court and other than by his own perception. This is similar to the daily practice of the experts themselves; thus, a physician in his practice bases his diagnosis on information from numerous sources and of considerable variety, including statements by patients and relatives, reports and opinions from nurses, technicians and other doctors, hospital records, and x-rays. As noted, to pass muster at trial, the facts or data underlying the opinion must be of a type reasonably relied upon by experts in the particular field.[5]

Under the new Federal Rules of Evidence applicable to trials in all federal courts but not under the prevailing law of most state courts, the bases of an expert's opinion need not be adduced by the examining counsel unless it is required by the trial judge.[6] In effect, the Federal Rules place the burden of drawing out any missing data with the cross-examiner; the direct-examiner is not required to substantiate the opinion of his expert. In practice, however, for the sake of persuasiveness, the direct-examiner usually asks the expert to make disclosure of the underlying facts or data of his opinion. Usually, the interest of the direct-examiner will operate to place the basis of the opinion before the trier of fact. Conclusory labels standing alone are not very convincing, even from a highly touted expert. In any event, the new Federal Rules make the direct-examiner less apprehensive about the need for use of hypothetical questions, since it is no longer essential to include every bit of arguably pertinent data to support every expert opinion on penalty of a successful objection or of reversal.

Given that a psychiatric evaluation may have several bases, the expert is asked, "Have you performed the *full* battery of tests?" "Have you done a *complete* physical and neurological examination, an electroencephalogram test, as well as the other modern methods of examination?" Failure to test fully, of course, gives rise to the inference of incompleteness of data usually relied upon by others in the field. Thus, where the psychiatrist does not utilize the results of psychological tests, the adversary argues, "His exam-

---

[5]Advisory Committee's Note, Federal Rules of Evidence, Rule 703.

[6]Federal Rules of Evidence, Rule 703.

ination was *woefully* inadequate." When a test is not done, or does not square with the opinion that is tendered, the expert says that it was not necessary for his testimony. In that event, the lawyer's argument is that the test is not probative and ought to be ignored at those times when it is relied upon by the expert. In logic, the claim is that only that which is necessary warrants consideration. The problem is partly resolved by treating the unessential as corroborating, but the argument has weakened the foundation of the opinion.

The problem sketched so far is troublesome but not nearly so substantial as that of avoiding ridicule. Psychiatric interviewing and, particularly, psychological testing are uniquely vulnerable to mockery.[7] The lawyer's technique is to fragment and then to ridicule. Sometimes the trial judge takes over the questioning of the witness and resorts to the same type of questioning. By requiring the witness to describe in isolation the most minute symptoms on which the diagnosis rests—for example, the subject's answer to a particular question or his reaction to a particular inkblot—the trial lawyer or judge (when he takes over the cross questioning) may succeed in making these trivial or commonplace.

It often requires little or no expertise to ridicule the testimony of a psychiatrist or psychologist. It is a common occurrence (one need only look at the cartoons of any issue of the *New Yorker* or indeed of a daily newspaper); it is no more difficult in the courtroom. Indeed, one who knows little or nothing (or pretends to know nothing) about psychological testing is often the most effective in demolishing the testimony. And who does not have the urge to mock the psychiatrist or psychologist? He is the avowed expert on the mind, the great mystery of the ages. He is the wizard who reads minds. To try to deflate that claim of authority is indeed tempting.

ILLUSTRATIONS

Just about any case where a psychiatrist or psychologist has appeared as a witness would illustrate the process of fractioning a

---

[7]Becker, L. E., *Obstacles to the Presentation of Psychiatric Testimony Remain,* in Bonnie, R. J. (ed.), PSYCHIATRISTS AND THE LEGAL PROCESS: DIAGNOSIS AND DEBATE (New York: Insight Communications, 1977), p. 53.

diagnosis and deflating it piece by piece. Several illustrations are here presented.

One notable example appears in *United States v. Leazer.*[8] In this case, involving a person convicted of selling narcotic drugs to a juvenile, a psychologist testifying on behalf of the defense offered the following testimony in explanation of his opinion that the defendant "was suffering from a passive-aggressive personality":

> *Witness:* . . . This [referring to Defendant's Exhibit] is a popular kind of card on the Rorschach, where people see human figures, commonly. If they see it anywhere, they generally would see them here. [The accused] does not see them here. He sees animals there. Just an example . . .
>
> *Court:* Well now, let's take this one, Doctor. You say that most people see human figures, by which I take it some people see animals?
>
> *Witness:* That is correct.
>
> *Court:* This defendant is a man who saw animals. What kind of animals did he see?
>
> *Witness:* Animals—he said dogs eventually. He said animals, and he said dogs when we asked him what kind of animals.
>
> *Court:* Very well. What did you conclude from that?
>
> *Witness:* Nothing in isolation . . .

The problem is by no means limited to the cross-examination of psychologists. Defending his conclusion that the accused "was suffering from a passive-aggressive personality," one of the defense psychiatrists testified as follows:

> . . . I think you can see on the interview, for example, a kind of composure, a sparsity of feeling tone. When people talk, they usually communicate a certain amount of feeling or by bodily movement, gesturing and so forth. There is also a kind of presenting himself in a kind of compliant, docile manner. In my interview, there seemed a lack of spontaneity of people when they talk. . . . [The accused] gave me the impression that in his early life a lot of stress was on control and limitation and structure rather than on spontaneity, feeling, being able to just be with people.

That testimony was followed by a colloquy between the witness and the trial judge:

> *Court:* You are saying, Doctor, he had trouble making friends. Is that what you are saying?
>
> *Witness:* I am saying not trouble making friends, having trouble sustaining any friendship.

---

[8]148 U.S. App. D.C. 356, 460 F.2d 864 (1972).

> *Court:* Having trouble sustaining friends, and he has a feeling of a need for attention, is that right?
>
> *Witness:* Attention, interest from someone.
>
> *Court:* Now, what were the facts that led you to that conclusion?
>
> *Witness:* As I said, a certain history of needing to get involved constantly in protective types of situations.
>
> *Court:* That is a conclusion. Give us some facts.

A particularly striking example is *United States v. McNeil,*[9] involving the commitment to a mental hospital of a sixty-one-year-old man who had been acquitted by reason of insanity of a charge of taking indecent liberties with a minor child. The respondent, opposing commitment, produced two witnesses to testify on his behalf, a clinical psychologist and a psychiatrist. The psychologist had administered a battery of psychological tests twice in a six-month period. In addition, he was also familiar with the results of an earlier series of tests administered by another psychologist. It appears that the substance of his testimony, as he sought to present it, was that his opinion of the respondent's condition rested primarily upon Rorschach inkblot tests that he had administered. In the first testing, the respondent had exhibited "a number of rather crass sexual responses" to the blots, chiefly female genitalia. Perhaps along with other of the respondent's responses, this indicated that the respondent at that time was too much preoccupied "with his own sexual adequacy." When six months later the tests were again administered, these responses no longer appeared. The psychologist still found "a type of sexual response on there," but this time he did not consider it inappropriate. It was, he said, "a nurturing kind of response, female breasts, things of this kind."

The trial judge constantly intruded into the psychologist's presentation of his testimony, as follows:

> *Court:* What is the test you gave him, the Rorschach test?
>
> *Witness:* It is a standard psychological inkblot test.
>
> *Court:* I am very familiar with it. How does it happen that anybody has sexual feelings in the Rorschach test?
>
> *Witness:* The cards themselves are not pictures of anything.
>
> *Court:* I know.
>
> *Witness:* They are ambiguous—

---

[9] 140 U.S. App. D.C. 228, 434 F.2d 502 (1970).

Court: I have seen them. I can't figure out what they are either. . . . What are his responses to the Rorschach test?

Witness: In 1969—no, in 1968, there were four—as I recall, four—responses which were explicitly related to female genitalia.

Court: What are they? I don't know what they are. What were the responses from the Rorschach test? What were the four? . . . Are you telling me from the cards you showed him in the Rorschach test he said that it was a woman's genitalia?

Witness: Yes, sir. That was in 1968 and again in 1969.

Court: Don't you think he is a little mentally sick, then, if he picks out something from a Rorschach test like that? Do you think that is normal? Can you pick out a woman's genitalia in the Rorschach test? . . .

Witness: . . . I did not finish in regard to the Rorschach test in which I indicated that both in the original testing and again in the testing late last summer these female genitalia responses were there and he was making no effort to hide them. Also, as well as these, there were also—

Court: When you looked at the Rorschach test, did you get any idea it represented female genitalia? . . . You still think he is sick, don't you?

Witness: No. As I am trying to say, on the present testing there was no evidence of this type of response, although there was a type of sexual response on there. But it was a nurturing kind of response, female breasts, things of that kind.

Court: Is there anything in the Rorschach test that would indicate to a normal person female breasts?

Witness: Yes, there is . . .

Court: Is there anything in the Rorschach test that will lead a normal person to determine that there was a female organ involved?

Witness: Yes, Your Honor.

Court: There is?

Witness: Yes. A female breast is a good, plus response.

Court: There is nothing about a female breast in the Rorschach test. You are a Clinical Psychologist and you are telling me that as a result of looking at these ink spots there is a female breast in there?

Witness: I didn't say there was a female breast there. I said it is not abnormal to see a female breast.

Court: There isn't?

Witness: A female breast by standard, statistical analysis has been shown to be a frequent response of normal people and it is a good, plus response.

Court: A normal person looks at a Rorschach test and sees a female breast, right?

Witness: Not every normal person, but it is not abnormal to do it. Many normal people do it.

Court: That's all. Step down.

Immediately thereafter, the respondent called his second witness, a psychiatrist. The trial court promptly returned to the same point:

Court: Do you agree with the Clinical Psychologist that as a result of the Rorschach test that a normal person gets the idea that there is some female organ there?

Witness: I would agree that —

Court: No. I didn't ask you that. Are you familiar with the Rorschach test?

Witness: Yes, sir.

Court: As I am. Are you going to tell me that a normal person looking at that Rorschach test is going to find anything resembling a female organ?

Witness: Your Honor, the only way I can answer is to say that some normal people will and some won't.

Court: You don't know then. You are the psychiatrist and you don't know. Right?

Witness: I can't answer your question.

Court: That is pretty good. You can't answer the question. . . .

Witness: May I elaborate an answer, Your Honor?

Court: Certainly.

Witness: I think what [the psychologist] was saying is that if you show a stimulus to a large number of people —

Court: You are talking now about a stimulus. I am asking if you show the Rorschach cards —

Witness: O.K.

Court: Is there anything in there that shows a stimulus?

Witness: There are many stimuli.

Court: Is there anything in those ink spots that shows a stimulus as to female genitalia?

Witness: Your Honor, that depends on what is in the person's head who is looking at them.

Court: If a person's head is looking at it and he concludes there is something like that, isn't there something wrong with him? . . . The man was acquitted of taking indecent liberties with a female, because he was insane. Now you are testing him. And you give him the Rorschach test and he still sees a female organ. That means nothing to you?

Witness: Oh, yes, sir. It means something to me.

Court: What does it mean?

Witness: It makes me think that—

Court: —he is sound?

Another example appears in the prosecutor's closing argument in *United States v. Brawner.*[10] In this case the accused, after a morning and afternoon of wine drinking, went to a party at the home of acquaintances that evening; several fights broke out. The accused, mouth bleeding, went home and within a half-hour returned with a gun, and killed one of the people at the party. The expert witnesses called by both defense and prosecution agreed that the accused "was suffering from an abnormality of a psychiatric or neurological nature." The diagnosis was given as "epileptic personality disorder," "psychologic brain syndrome associated with a convulsive disorder," "personality disorder associated with epilepsy," and, more simply, "an explosive personality." Where the experts disagreed was on the connection that the condition had played in the killing. The opinion of the expert witnesses called by the government was that he was just angry. The experts called by the defense, however, maintained that there was a cause and effect relationship between the act and his mental abnormality. The prosecutor, speaking of the testimony of a psychologist who, on the basis of Rorschach, Bender gestalt, and intelligence tests, had suggested that the accused suffered some organic brain damage, and an "explosive personality disorder," that is, "an explosive response to threats and a tendency to perseverate," argued before the jury as follows:

> Now, another one, you remember on the same test, that drawing test, the [psychologist] said he had ten of those little things and they had squiggles and lines and angles, and he was asked to draw those, ten of them separately. And the [psychologist] said he rotated one. And I said, well, what was the significance of that? Well, the significance, he says, is that it shows there is organic brain damage. That, he says, is a very hard indicator of organic brain damage! Why organic brain damage? He said he meant structural damage, something physically wrong with the brain, a part missing, a dead cell, something like that, a lesion in the brain.
>
> And I asked the [psychologist] how many of them did he rotate, how

---

[10]471 F.2d 969 (D.C. Cir. 1972).

many of them did he turn the picture a little bit. I asked him how many did he rotate 90 degrees, and I think he said it was—how many out of those ten?—one. That is a hard indicator of organic brain damage!

Ladies and gentlemen, then we came to that ink blot, and the [psychologist] said, well, the usual thing about that was those anatomical things. How many of them were there? Well, let's see, and he counts, and there are four. How many responses? Fourteen. Fourteen responses, and four of them turn out to be anatomical things—hearts or whatever it happened to be.

Is there something unusual about that? Is a man crazy when he sees a heart or something else four times, four different anatomical things or maybe the same things in those little drawings, these little inkblots. After all, they are just blots of ink. Is a man crazy when he sees them? And how about that last one, that rocket one? He says he sees a rocket going off.

I asked [the psychologist], was there any rocket fired during that period of time that might stick in a man's brain and might suggest it to him? [The psychologist] doesn't know. But there is something explosive about a personality if he sees a rocket on a little inkblot.

Well, ladies and gentlemen, there is not much I can say about that. I am not an expert. You heard the expert on the stand and he testified about that. But I can say one thing . . . It is your function to take that evidence and weigh that evidence and decide whether what that [psychologist] said as far as you are concerned made any sense at all.

In a number of opinions and articles, Judge Bazelon of the D.C. Court of Appeals has been critical of "conclusory expert testimony" on the issue of mental illness and criminal responsibility. How can trial judges remedy that state of affairs? In *United States v. Alexander & Murdock,*[11] the trial judge apparently believed that an opinion based on the results of a battery of psychological tests could be supported only by testimony reciting specific test questions and answers. The psychologist indicated, however, that individual responses would be meaningless or even misleading and that the defendant's answers should be interpreted by comparing his total pattern of responses with accepted diagnostic standards. On the basis of the tests, the psychologist found that Murdock, the accused, was alienated and sullen, with "paranoid and sociopathic trends almost ingrained and severe enough to be diagnosed as a character disorder." When the trial judge asked the psychologist to support his opinion with fact, the following dialogue ensued:

---

[11]471 F.2d 923 (D.C. Cir. 1972).

Witness: On the Minnesota Multiphasic Personality Inventory, it is a series of 500 or so true and false statements which have been standardized against people with known mental symptoms and complaints. There are various patterns, profiles we call them, based on the way an individual responds to 500 some odd items. Mr. Murdock's pattern of responses is very similar to standardized groups of people who are known to be sullen, known to be alienated, known to be a kind of loner, not being identified with any of the establishment's kinds of views.

Court: That is an opinion.

Witness: No, I am telling you a fact.

Court: I beg your pardon, Doctor. That is an opinion. Give us the facts on which you reached that opinion. What answers did he give that led you to that opinion? Give us some examples of sullen answers to questions. . . .

Witness: I don't have the raw [data]. I have the summary sheet. I don't have the actual 568 questions. I have his responses, but I don't know what the actual questions were. I just have a summary sheet here which essentially is just comparing the results of that, not breaking down to the various parts. I do have the results of other tests which I perhaps can go into to justify the sullen quality, the idea of being alone and against the system, and things of that sort.

Murdock's counsel then attempted to elicit from the witness the specific test responses that the trial court clearly wanted.

Defense Counsel: What test do you have the actual questions or raw materials on?

Witness: Well, I have responses, for example, to the sentence completion test which is a series of beginning sentences and the individual is supposed to then follow through and put the answers. Like, "I like — — —" and then the individual is supposed to add to this.

Defense Counsel: Is there any such thing as a representative sampling of those questions?

Witness: Yes.

Defense Counsel: Would you read several representative questions?

Witness: O.K. Back home everybody is well. At bedtime I go to sleep. Men will be men. A mother should love her family. I need freedom. The future is not — — —

Defense Counsel: Don't read the whole test.

Witness: This is just a sample. I am showing the fact that he is not — You know, this manner of questioning is most difficult for me. It is so difficult. These tests are looked at and combined, I mean, in their totality. Individually we can come up with some conclusions based on each test, but they only make sense when they are compared to other tests and the relationships between them comparing to what we know about the individual totally. I can't isolate and on the basis of a few responses say he is this or that. There is consistent evidence in various tests to show that he basically harbors a good deal of resentment, that he does seem to have a tendency to blame others for things he is very inadequate in. I have evidence which shows he does seem to feel basically inadequate and things of that sort.

Court: Mr. Witness, you are entitled to those opinions, but you are not the judge. The jury is the judge of the facts and, therefore, you are required to explain to the jury in factual terms in whatever manner you wish to do it what the underlying material is from which you reach your opinion, because the jury is not required to accept the opinion of any expert and they have to weigh the testimony of experts and to do that they need to know what it is that the expert relied on to reach his conclusions.

Defense counsel asked no further questions of his witness, apparently in the belief that he would be unable to elicit the kind of information the trial judge was demanding. It is easy to understand how under these circumstances a lawyer might abandon in frustration the effort to examine his witness, especially if, as here, the lawyer was inexperienced in examining experts in psychiatry and psychology. Concluding that the witness's answers were unsatisfactory, the trial court ruled that his testimony was entitled to no weight and instructed the jury to disregard it. Murdock's counsel moved for a mistrial. On appeal, the court of appeals did not rule squarely on the propriety of the judge's questioning or on his instruction to the jury to disregard the psychologist's testimony but affirmed the conviction and described the situation as a "failure of communication ending in evident mutual exasperation."

Judge Bazelon, however, dissented. In that dissent he observed, "By asking exclusively for specific test responses, which would add little to the jury's understanding of the expert's opinion, the trial judge may have inadvertently cut off the flow of information about the statistical nature of the tests, information without which the jury could not evaluate [the psychologist's] opinion testimony." The issue in the case was whether the accused, when called a "black bastard," had an irresistible impulse to shoot. Judge Bazelon suggested that "since his emotional difficulties were closely tied to his sense of racial oppression," it is probable that he "had an irresistible impulse to shoot." As a consequence, Judge Bazelon said, the jury should have been instructed to consider whether

Murdock's "rotten social background," and the resulting impairment of mental or emotional processes and behavior controls, ruled his violent reaction in the same manner that the behavior of a paranoid schizophrenic may be ruled by his "mental condition."[12]

In *Simpson v. United States*,[13] the accused was indicted for cutting his estranged wife's throat. The defense was insanity, based primarily on his own testimony that he often has blackouts and has no memory of what he does at such times. In rebuttal, the prosecution introduced testimony of the supervisory psychiatrist of the maximum security division of the mental hospital where he had seen the defendant at a staff conference. He reported that it was the consensus of this conference that the defendant was "without mental disorder." On cross-examination he indicated that a variety of tests had been conducted to determine whether the defendant was suffering from "epilepsy equivalent" and that they did not indicate that he was. He explained "epilepsy equivalent" in the following terms:

> In certain types of patients instead of having the conventional epilepsy seizure which most people have heard about, people falling down and losing control of their bowels and bladder, in certain types of individuals they have periods when they become extremely disturbed. They don't fall down but they become extremely disturbed, very aggressive, very violent and perhaps destructive. This might last for five minutes and it might last for ten minutes or fifteen minutes. They come on rather abruptly and maybe over a period of a minute and they disappear in pretty much the same way and the patient is completely unaware of such an episode, completely unaware of what happened in that period of time.

When asked what methods are used by psychiatrists to determine epileptic equivalent, the doctor replied:

> One of the most important, of course, is the history. Almost invariably when an individual presents himself with this kind of problem he has a history of such episodes in the past and the history, of course, has to be confirmed by relatives, neighbors, friends, doctors who have examined him or other agencies or institutions or other witnesses of such episodes.

He proceeded to state that, although an electroencephalogram may sometimes be useful in detecting this disease, "It is possible

---

[12]471 F.2d at 957 *et seq.*

[13]116 U.S. App. D.C. 81, 320 F.2d 803 (1963).

that it might not reflect it," especially if its source was "deep seated in the brain or if it was between seizures."

The doctor was then asked whether epileptic equivalent was difficult to diagnose.

> No, I don't think so. If they are well documented and if there had been several episodes and the description is given and they are fairly accurate, there is confirmatory evidence, they are pretty reliable, but in the absence of that, you either have to make an assumption that it might be such an episode or wait until further development and keep the individual under close observation.

Later in his testimony he reiterated this theme as follows:

> One [episode] certainly would not be an adequate basis for making such a diagnosis because in a period of five or ten or fifteen minutes when a person becomes extremely disturbed and assaultive and destructive, it could occur on the basis of anything. An individual could be drunk, he can be irritated, toxic and he can be angry about something and it could occur for numerous reasons but when there are series of such episodes and no basis for them and other factors are ruled out, then there is strong presumptive evidence that he is suffering from an epileptic equivalent. One can never be absolutely one hundred per cent certain unless there is a long recorded history, unless these occurred many times and reliable witnesses have seen them and perhaps you have confirmatory evidence . . . or a well recorded history. . . ,and in the absence of anything like that, the best you can do is make a presumption.

Simpson was convicted, and on appeal the conviction was affirmed, but Judge Bazelon, dissenting in part, maintained that no trustworthy conclusions regarding the presence or absence of epileptic equivalent could be reached on the basis of the testimony presented. He said that a thoroughgoing investigation should have been conducted either by court-appointed counsel, by the hospital, or by the prosecution to determine whether the defendant had, as he claimed, a history of blackouts with loss of memory. Judge Bazelon cited Justice Brennan's article in the *American Bar Association Journal*, the title of which speaks for itself, "Law and Psychiatry Must Join in Defending Mentally Ill Criminals."[14]

Testimony based on body language has fared little better than

---

[14]Brennan, W., *Law and Psychiatry Must Join in Defending Mentally Ill Criminals*, A.B.A.J. *49*:239, 1963. *See also* Shaw, B., *The Indigent's Right to Psychiatric Assistance at Trial*, WAYNE L. REV. *20*:1365, 1974.

the Rorschach, Bender gestalt, MMPI, and intelligence tests, notwithstanding the acclaim and publicity given the emerging science of kinesics and paralinguistics. According to this science, body language—body movement, facial expressions, gestures, posture, vocal intonations, pauses, and the like—tells us things, if we are only willing to listen and observe. We are told that the essence of one's personality is discovered largely by the study of one's body language. The way a person opens and shuts the door, how one walks, takes a chair, turns the pages of a book—all these gestures paint the portrait of one's personality. The Latin *gerere*, from which the word gesture comes, means to show oneself.

One may deceive by verbal language as it is under the control of consciousness, but not, we are told, by the involuntary language of the body. If you know what to look for, said Freud, "no mortal can keep a secret. If his lips are silent, he chatters with his fingertips; betrayal oozes out of him at every pore."[15] This leakage by our bodies reveals to the experienced observer whether or not we are speaking the truth.[16] Dr. George Sheehan in his book, *Running and Being*, puts it this way: "Who I am is no mystery. There is no need to tap my phone or open my mail. No necessity to submit me to psychoanalysis. No call to investigate my credit rating. Nothing to be gained by invading my privacy. There is, in fact, no privacy to invade. Because like all human beings I have no privacy. Who I am is visible for all to see. My body tells all. Tells my character, my temperment, my personality. My body tells my strengths and weaknesses, tells what I can and can't do."[17]

In a recent child custody case, the science of interpreting the nonverbal in verbal terms was put to an acid test in a courtroom.[18] In custody disputes, as a practical matter, the husband must carry the burden of proving the mother is unfit to be named the custodial parent. Allegations and proof are tuned to result; judges often frown on beer-drinking and lesbian mothers; so, a husband seek-

---

[15]FREUD, COLLECTED PAPERS (1905), quoted in *Time*, March 20, 1978, p. 56.

[16]NICHOLSON, J., HABITS (London: Macmillan, 1977), p. 143.

[17]SHEEHAN, G., RUNNING & BEING/THE TOTAL EXPERIENCE (New York: Simon & Schuster, 1978), p. 32.

[18]Civil Action No. 42926, Superior Court for the County of Cobb, State of Georgia. I am grateful to Lawrence B. Custer, Esq., of Marietta, Ga., for bringing this case to my attention.

ing child custody would consider himself lucky to have that kind of evidence about his spouse.

In this case, the husband one day came home early from work to discover his wife in bed, not with a man, but with another woman. They were both lying there naked. The wife claimed that they were just resting. When the husband came into the room the "paramour" jumped under the bed, had a nervous breakdown, was hospitalized, and was unavailable as a witness. To counter the husband's eyeball testimony, the wife's attorney decided to have his client undergo psychiatric and psychological testing. The evaluation was that she was not a lesbian. Having this favorable report, the attorney put the doctor on the stand. On direct examination he testified categorically that his client was not a lesbian. On cross-examination the expert witness was tested by an almost ingenious questioning of his credentials, and then of his science:

> Q. What sort of certificates do you have?
> A. I have a letter to the effect that I am a recognized Gestalt therapist.
> Q. And where is the writer of the letter?
> A. He is deceased, he died about three years ago.
> Q. And where is his organization now?
> A. All over the world.
> Q. Oh, it's got a mailing address all over the world?
> A. No, There are centers of Gestalt therapy in various parts of the country.
> Q. There is no central organization?
> A. No, there is no central organization as such.
> Q. Where was Dr. Gestalt located when he died?
> A. Where was *he* located?

The expert was stunned by the question, and for the rest of his testimony he did not recover his prescience of mind. To this day, observers of the trial wonder whether the cross-examiner acted deceptively or actually took "Gestalt" to refer to a person. The chief tenet of the gestalt approach, of course, is that analysis of parts, however thorough, cannot provide an understanding of the whole; it is necessary to look at the whole. Following is the cross-examining of the expert's science:

> Q. Do you believe everything that [the wife] said was the truth?
> A. I have no reason to believe that it was not the truth. See, the way I determine the truth, when I listen to someone, I note discrepancies

between what someone says with his words and what someone says with the rest of his body, with his tone of voice, with his physiological responses, with his facial movements—with everything that goes on.

And when all of these messages are integrated and all say the same thing—just as a polygraph test indicates whether someone is falsifying, making his words say one thing while his body says something else—I am able to determine whether someone is telling me the truth.

Q. You mean you are sort of a walking polygraph?

A. Everyone is, if they are willing to pay attention to the messages that are put out. There is no such thing as telling a lie, when someone is really listening.

Q. How do you mean there is no such thing as telling a lie, Doctor?

A. Well, what I mean by that is if you listen to what someone says with their words, and you also pay attention to the other messages that are communicated by the rest of the body, you will be able to appreciate the fact that you can check out what one portion of the body says by what the other portion of the body says, so that it's impossible for somebody to tell a lie and get away with it, if the respondent is willing to pay attention.

Q. You mean I talk with my feet?

A. You may be talking with your feet, you may be talking with your eyebrows, you may be talking with your forehead.

Q. Well, what did my foot say?

A. I could infer what it was saying, but you would have to verify that for me.

Q. What did it say?

A. When?

Q. Just then.

A. Could you tell me what it was saying?

Q. You heard the communication. I just wonder what it said.

A. Okay. This foot?

Q. My left foot.

A. Your left foot said to me, "I am feeling some discomfort and I want some relief, and I will raise myself, and I will put myself back down." That is what your left foot said.

Q. It said all that to me?

A. Yes.

Q. What did it say to you?

A. That is what it told me.

Q. It told you that it was tired?

A. That's right.

Q. What did my right foot say?

A. I don't know. It didn't move. It didn't say anything.

Q. It has to move to say something?

A. That is correct. You have to put the whole picture together.

Following all of this, for whatever impact it may have had, the father was awarded custody—even though his most valuable witness, the cross-examiner's left foot, was never sworn in.

In the spectacular Alger Hiss trial of the early 1950s, Dr. Carl Binger, psychiatrist, testified that Whittaker Chambers, the key prosecution witness, was a "psychopath with a tendency toward making false accusations." Chambers claimed that Alger Hiss, Chairman of the Carnegie Foundation for Peace and the fair-haired boy of the Democratic party, had passed secrets to Communists in the 1930s. On retrial of the case, Binger testified that his opinion was based on "personal observation of Chambers at the first trial for five days and one day at this trial" and that "he had read plays, poems, articles, and book reviews by Chambers and books he had translated from German." On cross-examination, Binger's testimony was discredited. Binger on direct examination had pointed out Chambers' untidiness, and on cross-examination he was made to acknowledge that the trait was found in such persons as Albert Einstein, Heywood Broun, Will Rogers, Owen D. Young, Bing Crosby, and Thomas A. Edison. Ridiculing the symptoms Binger had used in defining his key concept, the prosecutor, Thomas F. Murphy, began with the notion of lying. The courtroom audience laughed at one point when he asked if telling children that the stork brought babies constituted "a symptom of psychopathic personality." Binger replied, "Well, if the parents believed it I would think it might." At another point Murphy caught Binger in an amusing trap of his own making. Binger had testified on direct examination that there existed "certain confirmatory things" by which to detect a psychopathic personality and mentioned, as one of them, Chamber's tendency on the witness stand to gaze up at the ceiling frequently. In a cross-examination that is still talked about, the prosecutor said to Binger, "We have made a count of the number of times you looked at the ceiling. We counted a total of fifty times that you looked at the ceiling in fifty-nine minutes. Now I was wondering whether that was any symptom of a psychopathic personality?" Binger shifted uneasily in his chair. Hiss, we well know, was convicted.[19]

---

[19]United States v. Hiss, 88 F. Supp. 559 (S.D.N.Y. 1950).

There is a great reluctance on the part of professional persons, especially psychiatrists, to become involved in the presentation of expert testimony. Part of this reluctance is based on lack of knowledge of the legal system and the role of the adversary in it, but much of this reluctance relates to the unfortunate experiences and encounters of the expert witness with attorneys who attempt allegedly to embarrass, belittle, or anger them either in pretrial conferences or the courtroom. Thus, after such an encounter, a specialist or expert refuses to subject himself to any further harrassment, with resulting loss of such experience and training in the courtroom. Binger, still bitter from his experience years later, had the following to say in correspondence with the author:

> The prosecutor, Mr. Murphy, who looked like a dumb cop, turned out to be highly astute and tricky. He resorted to all kinds of subterfuges to trip me up. He tried to turn words around in my mouth and forced me to answer yes and no to questions framed by him in such a manner that the answers did not convey the meaning that I wished to present. I know that this is all part of the game, but it seemed to me shocking and preposterous. I had only one wish and that was to tell the truth and not lose my temper. I think I did both. Mr. Murphy, on the other hand, was determined to try to have me lose my temper and to distort the truth.[20]

DISCUSSION

One school of thought says that the psychiatrists do not belong in the courtroom, that they cannot function effectively there, that it is not their proper sphere of action, and that they do not understand the language addressed to them nor convey what they intend to.[21] Another school of thought holds that psychiatrists have much to offer in the tribunal, as both are concerned with human behavior, if only they would not cling to conclusory labels. In substituting in the criminal trial the _Durham_ rule (the accused is not responsible for his act if it "was the product of a mental disease or defect")[22] for the _M'Naghten_ rule (the accused is not responsible if he lacked understanding of the "nature and quality"

---

[20]SLOVENKO, R., PSYCHIATRY AND LAW (Boston: Little, Brown, 1973), p. 46.

[21]MENNINGER, K. A., THE CRIME OF PUNISHMENT (New York: Viking, 1968), p. 139.

[22]Durham v. United States, 214 F.2d 862 (D.C. Cir. 1954).

of his act or did not know that his act was wrong),[23] Judge Bazelon sought, he said, to open the inquiry beyond cognitive functioning to encompass modern theories of personality. His goal, he said, was to allow the jury a more complete picture of why the accused acted as he did, in order to render the judgment of blame as informed as current knowledge of human behavior would permit.

Notwithstanding the broadened formulation of the test of criminal responsibility, Judge Bazelon found that "psychiatrists continued to use conclusory labels without explaining the origin, development, or manifestations of a disease in terms meaningful to the jury."[24] He was obviously irritated and humiliated by the path he had taken the law.

> Psychiatry, I suppose, is the ultimate wizardry. My experience has shown that in no case is it more difficult to elicit productive and reliable testimony than in cases that call on the knowledge and practice of psychiatry. . . . One might hope that psychiatrists would open up their reservoirs of knowledge in the courtroom. Unfortunately in my experience they try to limit their testimony to conclusory statements couched in psychiatric terminology. Thereafter they take shelter in a defensive resistance to questions about the facts that are or ought to be in their possession. They thus refuse to submit their opinions to the scrutiny that the adversary process demands.[25]

Judge Bazelon says he wants psychiatrists, as he put it, to "let it all hang out."[26] Judge Bazelon is opposed to conclusory labels, but at the same time he is critical of the fragmentation of the testimony by cross-examiners. He is thus between the Scylla of conclusory labels and the Charybdis of fragmentation, and that is where he has placed the trial judge. Trial judges, fearing reversal of their decisions on appeal, have sought desperately (at least in the District of Columbia, where Judge Bazelon has appellate jurisdiction)

---

[23]Daniel M'Naughten's Case, 10 Clark & Fin. 200, 8 Eng. Rep. 718 (1843). There is no agreement on the spelling of the defendant's name. Diamond, B. G., *On the Spelling of Daniel M'Naghten's Name*, Ohio S.L.J. 25:84, 1964.

[24]Bazelon, D. L., *The Role of Psychiatry in Society*/A Jurist's Viewpoint, in Kriegman, G., Gardner, R. D., and Abse, D. W. (eds.), AMERICAN PSYCHIATRY/PAST, PRESENT, AND FUTURE (Charlottesville: University Press of Virginia, 1975), p. 157.

[25]Bazelon, D. L., *Psychiatrists and the Adversary Process*, SCIENTIFIC AMERICAN 230: 17, 1974.

[26]Bazelon, D. L., *The Psychiatrist in Court*, in Brady, J. P., and Brodie, K. K. H. (eds.), CONTROVERSY IN PSYCHIATRY (Philadelphia: Saunders, 1978), p. 909.

to draw out the bases of the expert's opinion. In an apparent mood of resignation, Judge Bazelon concluded his dissent in *Murdock* with this appraisal of psychological testimony:

> The problem of dealing effectively with testimony based on psychological tests is not a new one for this court. We have frequently seen attorneys and judges elicit from a psychologist a series of test questions and answers, thereby setting up an easy target for ridicule. It would be inappropriate to shield these tests from scrutiny by prohibiting such questions, especially in light of the fact that the validity of psychological tests is subject to considerable question within the mental health profession. Indeed, it may be that the validity of the tests is so doubtful that they should be excluded from evidence as a matter of law. But if courts are willing to accept the tests as legitimate diagnostic tools, it is troublesome to see counsel or the court attempting to discredit them in a particular case by ridicule, rather than exploring their acknowledged strengths and weaknesses.[27]

The lawyer, too, is put in a dilemma, as he is an advocate hired to pull apart the adversary's case. Admittedly, the whole is greater than the sum of its parts, a person is more than a set of biological or psychological functions, but in the nature of cross-examination, the parts must be made to seem greater than the whole. The lawyer is taught that cross-examination is the great engine for the discovery of truth. As cross-examination dissects, it focuses on the fragment. The limitation on this type of cross-examination is at most one of discretion, turning upon how the judge thinks the truth may best be extracted from the particular witness who chances to be on the stand.[28] Fragmentation of testimony, to be sure, is not necessarily an abuse. Indeed, in retrospect, Murphy's cross questioning of Binger in the Hiss trial may prove more commendable today even to Hiss's sympathizers, following the publication of

---

[27]*Supra* note 11, at 955.

[28]United States v. Petrone, 185 F.2d 334 (2d Cir. 1950). In personal injury cases, a disputed technique of counsel for the plaintiff in arguing damages to the jury has been to break physical and mental suffering down into days, hours, or even minutes, set a value on each unit, and multiply it by the total number of such units that pain and suffering has lasted and may be expected to last. There is, or can be, a certain element of trickery in this, since it first poses an apparently reasonable and even insignificant figure, and then multiplies it by a concealed factor to accomplish a possibly enormous result. Thus, ten cents a minute becomes $52,560 a year, and one dollar a minute becomes ten times as much. Prosser, W. L., Wade, J. W., and Schwartz, V. E., CASES AND MATERIALS ON TORTS (Mineola, N.Y.: Foundation Press, 6th ed. 1976), p. 543.

Allen Weinstein's book *Perjury* than it did at the time of trial.[29]

The objection to conclusory labels is, of course, a variation of the opinion objection. That objection was relaxed in the law of evidence when it became apparent that, at root, every perception is a conclusion. The statement, "I see an automobile," for example, is not literally true unless automobile is adequately and completely defined as a lot of things put together — bolts, tires, and so forth. As a practical matter, the court would run into trouble expecting a witness to reproduce the sensory impressions received when observing an event. Long ago Bishop Berkeley said, "We should speak with the vulgar but think with the learned." By this, Berkeley suggested that we should use the kind of language that our listeners can understand, for language is for the purpose of communication, but that we should know the meaning of our language even though our listeners do not. The question reduces to whether or not the witness can, with reasonable facility, describe more basically the facts upon which his conclusion is based.[30]

The testimony must not only be understandable and trustworthy but also relevant to an issue at hand. Usually in the case of psychiatric testimony, the issue is an excusing condition. What excusing conditions are acceptable and which are not? That is the crucial question. The *Durham* test, now abandoned,[31] was bewildering. Judge Bazelon in 1972 in *Murdock* suggested "rotten social background" as an excusing condition.[32] Actually, investigation might reveal that tight shoes causes one to be irritable and to explode.

That year Judge Bazelon in his concurring in part and dissenting in part opinion in *United States v. Brawner* suggested a "justly responsible test," which proposes that "a defendant is not responsible if at the time of his unlawful conduct his mental or emotional processes or behavior controls were impaired to such an extent

---

[29]WEINSTEIN, A., PERJURY/THE HISS-CHAMBERS CASE (New York: Knopf, 1978).

[30]Slovenko, R., *The Opinion Rule and Wittgenstein's Tractatus*, ETC.: A REVIEW OF GENERAL SEMANTICS *23*:289, 1967.

[31]United States v. Brawner, *supra* note 10.

[32]*Supra* note 11.

that he cannot justly be held responsible for his act."[33] The majority, rejecting Bazelon's proposal, expressed "substantial concern that an instruction overtly cast in terms of 'justice'... will splash with unconfinable and malign consequences."[34] The prosecutor in the case warned that "explicit appeals to 'justice' will result in litigation of extraneous issues and will encourage improper arguments to the jury phrased solely in terms of 'sympathy' and 'prejudice.'"[35] The American Law Institute rejected the formulation because it was deemed "unwise to present questions of justice to the jury."[36]

The psychiatrist is one among others who is cast as one of society's excuse providers and then is blamed for the behavior for which the individual is excused.[37] The psychiatrist offering excusing testimony is often called "the big con" or "the snow man,"[38] but the fundamental and controlling question is what type of excuse is allowable by the judge or jury. A defendant to a criminal charge who pleads not guilty on the basis of some excuse might claim accident, mistake, duress, necessity, or insanity, the most familiar and controversial of all excuses. Excuses that fail to exculpate, or nullify responsibility, may yet warrant mitigation of punishment. Also, what would otherwise be criminal behavior is sometimes justifiable rather than excusable. The killing committed by the police in the course of trying to apprehend an armed felon or by the ordinary citizen in self-defense are well-known examples of legally justified harm. In justification, "we accept responsibility but deny that it is bad," while by an excuse, "we admit that it was bad but don't accept full, or even any, responsibility."[39]

To be sure, life is replete with excusing conditions—some are acceptable, others not. Thus, in the wake of being insulting, a

---

[33]United States v. Brawner, *supra* note 10, at 1010 (D.C. Cir. 1972).

[34]United States v. Brawner, *supra* note 10, at 987.

[35]Brief of prosecutor in United States v. Brawner, *supra* note 10.

[36]Model Penal Code, Tentative Draft No. 4 (Philadelphia: American Law Institute, 1955).

[37]HALLECT, S. L., THE POLITICS OF THERAPY (New York: Science House, 1971).

[38]STERN, G. M. THE BUFFALO CREEK DISASTER (New York: Vintage Books, 1976), p. 292; Tanay, E., *Psychic Trauma and the Law,* WAYNE L. REV. *15*:1033, at 1041, 1969.

[39]Bedau, H. A., *Rough Justice: The Limits of Novel Defenses,* HASTINGS CENTER REPORT *8:* 8, 1978.

woman asks to be excused because of her premenstrual depression. "Harry, you know how I get." Wallach and Rubin vigorously urge that there be a new "insanity" defense based on impairment resulting from the "premenstrual syndrome."[40] Horney, on the other hand, argues that an insanity defense based on menstrual symptomatology would be inappropriate.[41] Is the excuse acceptable? What excuses are acceptable? Is compassion or condemnation in order? In one case psychiatrists testified that the accused had two different personalities—with different IQs, memories, and voices—and that each personality would take control of the accused's body and mind. The judge, on sentencing, said to the defendant, "The testimony presented on your behalf was very interesting. I will send *both* of you to prison." That judge did not consider a split personality a sufficient excusing condition.

What weight actually is given the psychiatric testimony? Does it really sway judge or jury? Or, do judge and jury accept the testimony only when, in the words of famous singer Bing Crosby, it is already "going my way"? "Jurymen seldom convict a person they like, or acquit one they dislike." This remark, made some forty years ago by Clarence Darrow, the famous trial lawyer, may not be far from the truth. Based on simulated trials, University of Michigan researchers found that physical attractiveness of individuals on trial "appears to have a significant impact on juror decisions."[42]

---

[40] Wallach, A., and Rubin, L., *The Premenstrual Syndrome and Criminal Responsibility*, U.C.L.A. L. Rev. *19*:210, 1971.

[41] Horney, J., *Menstrual Cycles and Criminal Responsibility*, Law & Human Behavior 2: 25, 1978.

[42] *Law Quadrangle Notes* (University of Michigan), Winter 1974, p. 2; *see also* Simon, R. J., The Jury and the Defense of Insanity (Boston: Little, Brown, 1967). In a survey (by the author) of jurors who had found the accused guilty of first degree murder, the following questions were asked: (1) Was your original opinion changed during the trial or deliberations, and if so, what facts caused you to change your mind? (2) What facts influenced your returning a verdict of guilty? (3) What circumstances or symptoms do you feel must exist to require a verdict of not guilty by reason of insanity? (4) Do you at this time remember any of the judge's charges given at the close of the trial? (5) Do you feel there should be a criminal insanity defense? (6) Would you have liked to have had more information at trial, and if so, what? (7) What do you think would have happened to the defendant if he had been found not guilty by reason of insanity? In this case the defendant went to collect his paycheck and carried a gun when he heard he was being discharged from his employment. An argument

The scale is the symbol of justice, but who in law wants measurement? A number of law review articles have suggested ways in which jurors might use certain mathematical techniques of decision theory or probability analysis as aids in the evaluation of circumstantial evidence, but except for the use of mortality tables to prove length of life when that is in issue, statistical data is rejected in the administration of the law. The public is enamored of statistics when they relate to batting averages or to major political or social issues, but they have no influence on the judgments of courts. The courts say the accused is not a statistic. Charlie Chaplin was held to be the father of Miss Berry's child notwithstanding the contrary indication of blood tests.[43] In another case, the court put it thus: "Under our jury system, it is traditional that in criminal cases juries can, and sometimes do, make findings which are not

---

ensued, and he shot his supervisor. A number of psychiatrists testified on behalf of the defendant. As to what facts influenced one juror, a sixty-nine-year-old housewife, she stated that more people testified about what really happened, and that these people testified against the defendant. The testimony of the witnesses who witnessed the actual occurrence was in her words what "really happened." She considered the number of eye witnesses highly important. Another juror, a forty-six-year-old housewife, stated that she changed her mind back and forth during the trial and finally decided on the final verdict during the deliberations—what most influenced her verdict was that the defendant took a gun to pick up his paycheck. She did not remember any of the judge's instructions. She expressed concern that the NGRI (not guilty by reason of insanity verdict) would result in the defendant's being back on the streets in a couple of months. Another juror, a thirty-year-old business graduate, indicated that he believed the "original testimony" over that of the psychiatrists, whose observations did not take place until months after the shooting. The judge's instructions, he added, had no effect on his deliberations and verdict. Another juror, a forty-year-old housewife and a former business executive, said that the insanity test was completely confusing to her. She concluded that the things the accused did in the office indicated that he knew what he was doing and what was going on around him. Another juror, a forty-eight-year-old housewife married to a vice-president of a manufacturing firm, stated that her original impression was not changed during the trial. She felt there should be no insanity defense. Another juror, a fifty-five-year-old widow, felt that the accused should not be allowed out on the streets to commit another crime. Another juror, a fifty-four-year-old utility company supervisor, made up his mind prior to the closing arguments and gave little or no weight to the psychiatric examination because it occurred months after the event. The observations of the other jurors were similar. In some states, upon defendant's request, a jury must be instructed on the consequences of a NGRI verdict. People v. Cole, 382 Mich. 695, 172 N.W.2d 354 (1969). *See also* Morris, G. H., Bozzetti, L. P., Rusk, T. N., and Read, R. A., *Whither Thou Goest? An Inquiry into Jurors' Perceptions of the Consequences of a Successful Insanity Defense,* SAN DIEGO L. REV. *14:*1058, 1977.

[43]Berry v. Chaplin, 74 Cal. App.2d 562, 169 P.2d 442 (1946).

based on logic, nor even common sense."[44] The jury has the power to nullify the instructions of the court and to acquit in the face of all the evidence against the accused. As the U.S. Supreme Court put it, "The jury has the power to bring in a verdict in the teeth of both law and facts."[45]

Dickens, when placing the famous words in Mr. Bumble's mouth that the law is an ass, wished to point out that the law reflected mythical attitudes or desiderata that the public wished it to reflect, even if those values are unrealistic or outdated. In Mr. Bumble's case, the particular value was that a married man is the head of the household and could be expected to control the actions and behavior of his wife.[46]

Psychiatric evidence is probably more prized for its entertainment value than for its probative worth. Whatever else might be said about it, psychiatric testimony is imaginative and anything but dull—and that cannot be said for most of the mundane and monotonous day-to-day court proceedings. The testimony enlivens the court, often making the proceedings newsworthy. Because of this, psychiatrists merit an Oscar for their performance. The courtroom is not much drama without psychiatric testimony; the trial as morality play is very much the point in cases where the psychiatrist is called in as witness.[47] In particular, the insanity defense is a suspension of the rules of evidence, allowing character evidence. Alfred North Whitehead said that "the basic quality of any proposition is not that it be true [whatever that means] but that it be interesting and exciting."[48]

---

[44]State v. Lawrence, 120 Utah 323, 234 P.2d 600 (1951).

[45]Horning v. District of Columbia, 254 U.S. 135, at 138 (1920). The jury has the power, but not the right, to disregard the judge's instructions, so the defendant has no right to have the jury instructed that it may ignore the facts and the instructions. Sparf and Hansen v. United States, 156 U.S. 51 (1895). *See* SLOVENKO, R., HANDBOOK OF CRIMINAL PROCEDURE AND FORMS (Baton Rouge: Claitor, 1967), p. 671; *see also* Halpern, A. L., "Uncloseting the Conscience of the Jury—A Justly Acquitted Doctrine" (address presented on January 31, 1979, at Department of Psychiatry, Cornell University Medical College.

[46]DICKENS, C., THE ADVENTURES OF OLIVER TWIST (1838).

[47]Younger, I., *Psychological Testing that Might Invade the Province of the Jury,* in Holmes, G. W. (ed.), NEW FRONTIERS IN LITIGATION (Ann Arbor: Institute of Continuing Legal Education, 1979), p. 37.

[48]Quoted in Aring, C. D., *The Freudian Influence,* JAMA 237:651, 1977. *See also* Slovenko, R., *Reflections on the Criticisms of Psychiatric Expert Testimony,* WAYNE L. REV. 25:37, 1978.

One reason given for the rejection of mathematical techniques of decision theory or probability analysis in the administration of the law is the potential dehumanization of the trial. It would subvert the nature of a trial as a morality play. Actually, the major impact of psychiatric testimony in the courtroom is its impact *outside* the courtroom on educating the public on the dynamics of behavior, however one may feel about the merits of such education. Diamond, a keen student of psychiatric testimony, has the following to say in connection with the famous trial in 1924 of Leopold and Loeb, where the most prominent names in psychiatry testified in behalf of the defense:

> The psychiatric testimony in the case lasted over a month and the transcripts reached tens of thousands of pages . . . Healy, Glueck, White, Bowman and others attempted with all of their rhetoric, ingenuity, and ability to teach and lecture over a period of a month from the witness stand in the courtroom. At the end the judge sentenced the boys to life imprisonment without possibility of parole. Judge Calvary stated: "The court is willing to recognize that the careful analysis made of the life history of the defendants and of the present mental, emotional, and ethical condition, has been of extreme interest and is a valuable contribution to criminology." But then he went on to say, "In choosing imprisonment instead of death the court is ruled chiefly by the consideration of the age of the defendants." It was very clear that this exhaustive application of psychoanalysis to the courtroom had relatively little effect on the legal decision. The impact of this case outside the courtroom, however, was very great. Although Freud and psychoanalysis were well known to psychiatric professions, I think the average man in the street had never heard of Freud and had never heard the word *psychoanalysis* until it was screamed at them from the newspaper headlines.[49]

The publicity, however, of an alleged nexus between a certain condition and behavior is not without its peril in the community. When epileptic seizure, for example, is claimed as an excuse, individuals with an epileptic condition may become concerned about their committing a criminal act. Doctors treating epileptics hear such concerns whenever epilepsy is raised as a defense in a trial. Indeed, the urging of the excuse in the courtroom may be considered an insult to epileptics. Likewise, it may be stigmatizing

---

[49]Diamond, B., *Psychoanalysis in the Courtroom*, Dialogue/J. PSYCHOANALYTIC PERSPECTIVE, Spring 1978, p. 3.

the poor to say that poverty causes crime.[50] Add to this peril that of the self-fulfilling prophecy. The claim of epilepsy or poverty, or whatever, may be used as rationalization of antisocial behavior.

CONCLUSION

Psychiatric testimony, whether or not acceptable, opens options to judge and jury. It brings flexibility and an element of humanity into the law. What is accepted as an excuse, or as proof, depends on whether one is sympathetic to it. The tendency is to find a causal nexus between one horrible condition or incident and another, although they may have little or nothing to do with each other. Whether a judge or jury accepts or declines excusing testimony is for them to decide—but without some testimony they may not be able to rationalize a decision they would like to return. The scale is the symbol of justice, but the court does not want measurement or empirical evidence. Empirical evidence is too boring, too dehumanizing, and would not fulfill the function of the trial as a morality play.

[50]Pines, M., Superkids, *Psychology Today,* Jan. 1979, p. 53; *see also* WILSON, J. Q., THINKING ABOUT CRIME (New York: Random House, 1975).

Chapter 9

EXPERTISE IN PSYCHIATRY AND CIVIL LAW

Robert L. Sadoff, M.D.

Training in forensic psychiatry has emphasized expertise in psychiatry and the criminal law and has not focused as clearly on training in civil legal procedures. Most forensic psychiatric training programs had been funded by and supported by agencies working within the criminal justice system. Most people not entirely familiar with the field consider a forensic psychiatrist to be one who is primarily concerned with criminal law including such issues as competency to stand trial and criminal responsibility. Thus, training in civil-legal matters for psychiatrists has been sporadic; most psychiatrists develop expertise through experience or on-the-job-training. Much of the practice of civil-legal psychiatry involves private evaluations and examinations not amenable to clinic training programs. Very little training has been offered in the field of civil law and psychiatry, either in medical schools, in psychiatric residency programs, or in special fellowship programs in forensic psychiatry.

Most forensic psychiatrists indicate that they work more frequently in matters of civil law than they do in criminal law. The private practice of forensic psychiatry especially requires expertise in such areas as competency procedures, domestic relations matters, and personal injury problems.

The field of forensic psychiatry is broad enough to include expertise in criminal law, administrative procedures, regulations, and legislation in addition to the several areas of civil law that involve psychiatric expertise. These areas include the following:

1. Civil competency procedures including but not limited to—
   a. competency to manage one's own affairs
   b. testamentary capacity (competency to write a will)
   c. competency to enter into contracts
   d. competency to make decisions about one's own treatment
   e. testimonial capacity (competency to testify in court hearing)
2. Domestic relations matters including but not limited to—
   a. marriage
   b. divorce
   c. annulment
   d. child custody issues
   e. visitation procedures
   f. child abuse and neglect
3. Personal Injury Matters including—
   a. workmen's compensation law
   b. tort law
   c. negligence and professional malpractice law
4. Involuntary Hospitalization including but not limited to—
   a. emergency involuntary commitment
   b. civil commitment procedures
   c. Patients' right to treatment
   d. Patients' right to refuse treatment
   e. Guardianship procedures

CIVIL COMPETENCY PROCEDURES

The test of competency in civil law is different for each purpose for which competency is sought, e.g. the specific criteria of competency to manage one's own affairs are different from those necessary to be competent to write a will. Generally, a person must have sufficient mental ability at the time of the evaluation for the purpose of competency to know the nature of the proceedings in which he is involved and the consequences thereof. He must know what he is doing, what his purpose is, and what goal he hopes to achieve. He must also know what will happen as a result of his decision making. If he is not able to know these two basic requirements, then he may not be competent to proceed in the civil matter in which he is involved. However, the psychiatrist gives an opinion regarding only the mental competency to proceed in a legal situation. It is the judge who determines whether the person has legal competency to proceed. The psychiatrist becomes a consultant to the court and gives an opinion that the judge may accept, modify, or reject, depending on other evidence he has before him.

In assessing a person's competency, the psychiatrist must ascertain from independent sources the answers to the questions he asks the patient. For example, when assessing a person's competency to write a will, the psychiatrist must ask whether the patient knows that he is writing a will and how much money the patient believes he has to give in his will, and to whom he may leave the money if he chooses. That is, he must know the nature of his act and the natural objects of his bounty and affection. He must know, for example, that he has two daughters and one son (though he does not need to know how old they are precisely, he should know their names), but he need not give his money to them. He must only be able to show that he is aware that they exist and could leave his money to them if he chose. This is one reason lawyers instruct their clients to leave a dollar to a natural heir if the person preparing the will does not wish to leave him anything. By leaving a son or daughter one dollar, the patient acknowledges that he knows that he has a son or daughter and could leave him/her money if he chose but decided to leave only one dollar. Also, the people or organizations to whom the patient leaves the money must be real and not fantasied or delusional. Thus, the psychiatrist must verify from independent sources the information he receives from the patient about the names of the children and other potential heirs. He must also determine whether the people or institutions to whom the patient leaves money are, in fact, real, not fantasied. The last factor involved in determining competency to write a will or the validity of the will is whether the patient was improperly influenced by the desires of designing persons, that is, persons who wish to influence him unduly to leave them his money. This may be ascertained in part by assessing whether the person writing the will is of weak mind, is infirm, or is overly dependent upon those who are taking care of him and may be exploited by them.

When determining whether a person is competent to manage his own affairs, the psychiatrist must ask questions and verify through independent sources the answers he receives. Thus, in order for a person to be competent to manage his or her own affairs, that person must know how much money he or she has, in what form the money exists, where it currently is deposited or kept, and how it may be spent in a relevant and rational manner. Also, the person evaluated must not be deemed a spendthrift, an alcoholic, or a drug addict who may be unable to conserve his money because he must spend it on the object of his addiction or freely without good judgment on other frivolous items. It appears that in this particular evaluation a person must have a higher level of mental ability to manage his or her own affairs than to write a will. The person needs to know not only how much money he has but where it is and in what form it is and how he may spend it within reasonable judgment. Typical questions that may be asked of the person being evaluated are the following:

How much money do you have?
Where is it?
How much would you pay for a loaf of bread?
How much change would you receive from a five dollar bill if you bought a loaf of bread, a quart of milk, and a dozen eggs?

One must also be fairly well oriented to time, place, and person to be deemed competent in a civil sense. It is not uncommon to find, when examining an elderly woman in a nursing home, for example, that she has testamentary capacity because she knows approximately how much money she has and to whom she could leave her money if she chose but that she does not have competency to manage her own affairs because she does not know in what form her assets exist or how she may spend the money without being exploited.

Determination of competency to enter into a contract is similar in that the psychiatrist must ascertain whether the patient knows that he is entering into a contract and what the results of that contract would be for him. Some have even included the contract of marriage as requiring competency. That is, a person who is of sufficiently unsound mind not to know that he is getting married and what obligations and responsibilities the marriage entails for him may not be competent to marry.

Evaluations for competency to testify in court have increased in frequency for forensic psychiatrists. Witnesses testifying in criminal cases may be challenged on their competency to testify. In other civil cases, witnesses may also be challenged as to their competency to give testimony on the basis of mental illness, mental retardation, or confusion.

One of the more recent tests of competency has arisen from the patients' rights movement, i.e. the right to refuse medication. In these cases judges have determined that a patient has the right to refuse medication unless there is an emergency or unless the patient is incompetent to so refuse. Often that determination is made in court as a judicial, legal decision. However, in at least one recent case, *Rennie v. Klein,* the judge indicated that the treating psychiatrist could make a determination of functional competency to decide on giving medication.[1]

One final form of competency is related to competency to determine one's own medical treatment, and that is the competency one may have to agree or consent to a surgical procedure. Often psychiatrists are called by surgeons or other physicians to evaluate patients in a hospital who have refused life-saving surgery. The psychiatrist needs to determine whether the patient is competent to make that decision or whether the patient is incompetent and may need a guardian appointed in order to make the decision for him or her. One recent case involved an elderly woman who was told that she had gangrene of her right foot and required surgery to save her life. She refused surgery and agreed to have medical treatment to determine whether the gangrene would spread or become worse. She was treated conservatively and noted that the gangrene had not become worse and she was willing to wait until it did before having her surgery. She was not clear in her communi-

---

[1]462 F.Supp. 1131 (1978).

cation to the surgeon; however, upon careful examination by a forsensic psychiatrist, she clearly stated that did not wish to lose her foot, and she would keep it as long as she could, until an operation was absolutely necessary. She clearly revealed that she would have her foot taken off before she lost her life. On that basis she was determined to be competent to continue to treat her foot conservatively under careful medical supervision. She was released from the hospital and continued to care for her foot for several months until the operation did become necessary.

In all cases involving competency, then, the psychiatrist conducting the evaluation must have evidence from outside sources to support or negate the allegations or statements of the individual examined. He also must know the questions to ask regarding the particular form of competency that is in question. Finally, he must remember that the testimony he gives regarding competency must be within reasonable medical certainty and not absolute.

DOMESTIC RELATIONS MATTERS

Perhaps one of the most important civil-legal functions of the forensic psychiatrist involves evaluations of domestic relations crises. The importance is reflected in the effect these crises have on children whose mental and emotional lives may be affected by disruption of the family. Newer divorce laws may require divorce counseling with no-fault options, rather than putting the family through the battle of a divorce based on fault of one party to the innocent, injured spouse. Often children suffer when parents battle or the courts insist on an adversary procedure and not on a collusion that both parents wish to divorce. Under the fault system, where both parents wish to divorce, the court will not grant the divorce. However, under the no-fault option, most states have built-in divorce counseling procedures. It is during this counseling time that the therapist has an opportunity to alert the divorcing parents to the difficulties their children will have and to instruct the parents how to prevent further emotional damage to the children.

Perhaps the most frequent area of involvement for the forensic psychiatrist in the domestic relations matters is in child custody and visitation issues. The forensic psychiatrist is often called by one side to present an adversarial approach to help the lawyer help his client achieve custody for or increased visitation with the children. Most often the psychiatrist is able to see only one side, but sometimes he can achieve the goal of evaluating all sides in order to advise the judge properly.

It behooves the forensic psychiatrist who is limited in his evaluation to one side of the family only not to make unwarranted comparative statements without having the opportunity to examine the other side. He must limit his comments to the information that he has received in the examination he was allowed to conduct. Thus, it may be perfectly appropriate for a forensic psychiatrist who is limited in his examination to make statements about the relationship of that parent to his or her children and the relation-. ship of the children to each other and to that parent. However, without examining the other parent and observing the children in the company of the other parent, it would not be wise to make comparative statements such as which parent would be superior. If, however, there is ample evidence to indicate the brutality of one parent over the other or the extremely negative effect one parent has on the children, as learned through examination of the children, some opinions may be made. However, it must be kept in mind that children are easily influenced by one parent or another, and it would only be fair to corroborate the statement of the parent examined and the children's statements by data from independent sources or by comparing those statements with the allegations made by the other parent. Whenever possible, it is best to request a comprehensive examination of all parties concerned.

Depending on the age of the children involved, it may be wise to have a child psychiatrist or child psychologist conduct testing and further evaluation of the children. Sometimes the battle is not between the parents but between one parent and the state or between both parents and the state because of alleged child abuse or neglect. As in all other areas of civil law, the examining psychiatrist must make every effort to obtain independent verification of the allegations made.

The forensic psychiatrist working in domestic relations law must be familiar with the marriage, divorce, and custody laws of the particular jurisdiction in which he works. He must also be familiar with the child abuse statutes and be able to consult with other agencies involved in the case. He must have some familiarity with child psychiatry, developmental psychiatry, and the best interests of the children.

Should children make a decision or testify in court or in chambers in such matters? Should child custody procedures be an adversary matter, or should the judge appoint a blue ribbon panel to make the decision from a behaviorist standpoint? Can a lesbian mother be a proper mother to a latency age daughter, or should the daughter go to another parent or a foster home? These are some of the difficult questions that face the forensic psychiatrist working in domestic relations law.

A recent case that challenged the expertise of the forensic psychiatrist working in domestic relations law involved the examination of a twelve-year-old girl who had been living with her mother but whose custody was challenged by the father who lived in a different state. It was the opinion of the forensic psychiatrist that the daughter should maintain her custody with her mother and that she ought to continue in treatment that had started about six months previously. The daughter was concerned about her father and was afraid to visit with him or to be with him. The mother and the child's psychiatrist had raised child abuse charges against the father for his brutality to the daughter. She was therefore frightened of him and his parents, who spent time taking care of her in the past. She did not wish to spend time with her father or to see her paternal grandparents. Following testimony in court, the forensic psychiatrist was then asked by the judge to comment on the judge's decision to place the child with the mother but allow the paternal grandparents to visit. The daughter was very anxious about the judge's decision, and the judge agreed that the forensic psychiatrist could discuss the matter with the child first, to determine whether she was ready for the decision and how it might best be implemented. Furthermore, the judge ordered the child's psychiatrist to withdraw from the case because he had expressed bias toward the father in joining with the mother in raising child abuse charges that were not substantiated. The examining psychiatrist was put in a position of interpreting and explaining the judge's decision to the child, to the mother, and subsequently to the father and the paternal grandparents.

Thus, the expertise of the forensic psychiatrist working in domestic relations matters does not end with the evaluation or even with the courtroom testimony. These matters may be very complex, highly emotionally charged, and very difficult procedures. The future of the child may be at stake, and careful, thoughtful opinion must be presented after comprehensive and thorough evaluation of all parties involved.

Sometimes it is better to advise a settlement out of court to avoid further difficulties with the child, and at other times the child needs to be involved in the procedure. Sometimes it is best to allow the children to participate in the decision making by discussing their preferences with the judge in chambers. At other times it is best to prevent the children from such involvement because of their ambivalence and their conflicting attitudes about both parents.

In sum, the forensic psychiatrist working in this area must be a consultant to the judge as well as to the attorney who calls him. He must be the advocate for the child and not for either parent.

PERSONAL INJURY LAW

Personal injury matters usually involve workmen's compensation injuries or automobile accidents or negligence. Evaluation of individuals may also include those who are disabled and are applying for social security disability. One of the most important factors for a forensic psychiatrist working in personal injury law to be aware of is the ability of the plaintiff to fake or exaggerate his symptoms. The forensic psychiatrist must be available to evaluate for either plaintiff or defense and to arrive at the same opinion irrespective of which side that hires him. He must also be aware of the phenomenon known as the rule out syndrome. A patient may have been thoroughly evaluated by physicians of other specialties and no organic or physical etiology to the symptoms are found. The patient is then sent to the psychiatrist to rule out psychiatric etiology or causation of the symptoms. The psychiatrist must be comprehensive and thorough in his evaluation and must not automatically ascribe all symptoms to psychiatric causes because no physical etiology was ascertained. Rather, there must be a positive correlation between emotional conflict and physical symptoms in order to arrive at a positive correlation opinion. The psychiatrist must also look for other areas of a person's life that might cause the psychiatric symptoms noted. It is quite easy to ascribe all symptoms to a trauma that one has experienced, but the patient has other aspects of his life that may just as readily cause the symptoms involved.

An example of such an evaluation is the nineteen-year-old woman who had been evaluated one year after she was hit over the head by the leg of a wooden chair in a barroom fight. She sustained a concussion and was hospitalized for one week with periods of amnesia. At the time of the examination, one year later, she was depressed and tearful, with poor appetite and sleep disturbance. The plaintiff's attorney wished to ascribe her current depressive symptoms to the blow on the head the year earlier. However, careful history taking revealed that the woman's mother had suffered a heart attack six months before the examination, causing the patient to drop out of school to stay home and take care of her three younger siblings. Subsequently, she lost her boyfriend and became more socially withdrawn. It is much more reasonable to ascribe her depressive symptoms to the illness of her mother, which affected her significantly, than it is to the trauma she sustained one year before.

The forensic psychiatrist must be aware of the various labels given to traumatic neurosis, compensation neurosis, triggered neurosis, and all other forms of illness that may be caused by and related to traumatic experiences. Robitscher has listed these labels in his book *Pursuit of Agreement: Psychiatry and the Law,* and has developed a three-part category that simplifies the complexities.[2]

---

[2]J. B. ROBITSCHER, PURSUIT OF AGREEMENT: PSYCHIATRY AND THE LAW (1966).

1. *Traumatic neurosis.* A healthy individual became mentally ill as the result of an overwhelming stress.
2. *Compensation or triggered neurosis.* The individual had a latent illness triggered or precipitated by the trauma and held onto by the patient for largely unconscious reasons.
3. *Malingering.* The individual consciously deceives.

It behooves the psychiatrist to be able to determine whether a patient who emerges with a number of symptoms is consciously malingering or whether the patient has psychosomatic or conversion symptoms, or whether the symptoms are totally reflective of physical pathology. The psychiatrist must also be aware of concepts in law that relate to aggravation of preexisting conditions or the so-called egg shell skull in which the individual appears to be perfectly healthy but has a significant vulnerability in the area affected. Often the psychiatrist is not the one who is able to determine malingering, but he may recommend the use of private investigators to determine whether a patient sustains or maintains the symptoms he or she brought into the office at the time of the examination. Psychological testing is often very helpful in the determination of etiology of illness. One may also require the use of a neurological examination, CAT scan, skull x-ray, or EEG to help rule out physical or organic etiology.

Perhaps the most complicated injury for the forensic psychiatrist is the back or neck injury, which has few symptoms or observable signs noted by the orthopedic surgeon or the neurosurgeon. The functional components in back and neck injuries are high and may be related to internal conflicts or may be due primarily to physical pathology.

In at least two cases examined by the author, the referral was made as a rule out psychiatric etiology to neck and back injury. In each case there did not seem to be a positive correlation of emotional conflict with the symptomatology presented. The patient was referred to another orthopedic surgeon, who examined the patient more intensively, found organic pathology, and operated successfully. In two years at follow-up, the patient was symptom free. One case involved the neck and the other the lower back.

These examples are revealed primarily to demonstrate the need for positive correlation between emotional conflict and physical symptoms. The psychiatrist should not jump to the conclusion that because an orthopedic surgeon or neurologist did not find significant physical pathology the symptoms must be, therefore, of psychiatric origin. The symptoms may also be consciously malingered rather than psychiatrically determined.

The forensic psychiatrist working in the area of personal injury law must be aware of the effect of the system upon the patient and the stress the plaintiff experiences each time he is reexamined and he faces the legal considerations. As in other cases of psychiatric expertise in civil law, the psychiatrist working in this particular area must be available for examination of plaintiffs, either by plaintiff's attorneys or for the defense counsel. He must not be labeled as biased toward plaintiff or defense, as a number of psychiatrists are labeled in criminal law as prosecution or defense oriented.

The principles outlined herein are applicable in workmen's compensation matters as well. In these cases the psychiatrist must be familiar with workmen's compensation laws and procedures and must be able to testify before workmen's compensation referees as well as before judges in tort issues.

INVOLUNTARY HOSPITALIZATION

Perhaps one of the most rapidly growing areas in civil law has been the changes made in patients' rights and commitment laws. The forensic psychiatrist working in this field must be able to keep up with the changing laws and be able to communicate these changes to his colleagues as well as to be able to apply them when evaluating patients and testifying in court. The changes have been so rapid that the area is in a state of flux. Newer changes occur for both adults and children in the area of commitment, patients' rights, and involuntary hospitalization.

Perhaps the most important current issue is the patient's right to refuse medication. Most psychiatrists have accepted the newer regulations on patient's rights and have advocated the availability of adequate psychiatric treatment. However, there is conflict among psychiatrists about the issue of patients' rights to refuse medication. Courts have determined that all patients have a right to refuse medication, unless there is an emergency or unless the patient is incompetent to make the decision about his own treatment. In those cases a psychiatrist may be called to interpret the law in each case. For the most part, the forensic psychiatrist in this area must be able to advise his colleagues about their obligations and responsibilities within the patient's rights issue.

Finally, the forensic psychiatrist working in the area of civil law must be in a position to work on regulatory boards and commissions to help interpret laws as they affect the mentally ill and also be able to testify before legislators about changes in laws that involve mental illness.

Developing expertise in civil law for psychiatrists is a very complicated matter, which requires years of training and experience in several diverse matters. It appears to be more complex than criminal law and offers a greater challenge and opportunity for the comprehensive practice of forensic psychiatry.

Chapter 10

NEW DIMENSIONS OF EXPERTISE IN PSYCHIATRY AND CRIMINAL LAW: THE DETERMINATION OF THREE UNUSUAL FORMS OF COMPETENCY

ROBERT LLOYD GOLDSTEIN, M.D.

Like the *Man Who Came to Dinner,* the psychiatrist who elects to work at the interface between psychiatry and criminal law is in the position of being an invited guest who has overstayed his original welcome.[1] In addition to refusing to leave, he adds insult to injury by taking *new liberties* in the legal arena at the very time when critics are warning that he has gone much too far already. Menninger pointed out that "the psychiatrist is not self-invited to these parties. He is not a trespasser. He is called, then he is questioned, criticized, disputed, attacked, suspected, discarded, and ridiculed."[2] Menninger himself, as well as Szasz and other distinguished observers of the *Forensic Psychiatry Scene,* has long argued that society should exclude *all* psychiatrists from the courtroom.

> "The proposed elimination of the psychiatrist from the courtroom is not just because we do not like to be disputed by our colleagues, badgered by opposing attorneys, suspected of being purchasable and discredited as scientists. I oppose courtroom appearances because I consider guilt, competence and responsibility to be moral questions, not medical ones. The judge and the jury are the community's representatives in this area. It is for them to make the judgment and apply the sanctions deemed appropriate, not us psychiatrists. Society decides—through them—what crime is and what proof it requires in any particular instance and what penalty applies.[3]

---

[1]Kaufman, G. S., and Hart, M.: *The Man Who Came to Dinner.* New York, Random House, Inc., 1939.

[2]Menninger, K.: *The Crime of Punishment.* New York, The Viking Press, 1968, p. 140.

[3]Menninger, *The Crime of Punishment,* p. 139.

Others are more vehement in their criticism. Arens wrote the following: "Like the picture of Dorian Gray, the picture of judicial psychiatry and psychiatric justice, viewed over a period of more than a decade . . . emerges as a study in horror."[4]

Yet, despite these claims that psychiatry has been exploited and burdened with the responsibilities of the legal system and that psychiatry has become a tool of the police powers of the state in order to control and incarcerate deviants, many psychiatrists have continued to take an active role in the legal process, believing, as I do, that their expertise can be critically helpful in assisting judges and juries to reach more informed and intelligent decisions.[5-7] Much of this controversy has focused on the insanity defense.[8-11] Admittedly a rare event, rarely raised as a defense and even more rarely successful, the insanity defense has, nonetheless, drawn a disproportionate amount of attention and notoriety. It is certainly a political issue that inflames the imaginations of the professions of psychiatry and law and the public alike. Stone wrote the following: "Rejection of the insanity defense comes from all sectors of the political spectrum. It is attacked on one side because it excuses too many and on the other because it excuses too few. One [side] claims it is unfair because it is only available to the rich. Another claims it is applied only to the poor and minorities as a stigmatizing weapon of oppression. Former President Nixon is concerned that the insanity defense allows dangerous criminals to go free

[4]Arens, R.: *Make Mad the Guilty.* Springfield, Charles C Thomas, Publisher, 1969, p. 257.

[5]Goldstein, R. L.: The Fitness Factory. Part I: The Psychiatrist's Role in Determining Competency. *Am J Psychiatry, 130:*1144–1147, 1973.

[6]Robey, A., and Bogard, W. J.: The Compleat Forensic Psychiatrist. *Am J Psychiatry, 126:* 519–525, 1969.

[7]Bromberg, W.: Psychiatrists in Court: The Psychiatrist's View. *Am J Psychiatry, 125:*1343–1347, 1969.

[8]Fingarette, H.: *The Meaning of Criminal Insanity.* Berkeley and Los Angeles, University of California Press, Ltd., 1972.

[9]Goldstein, A. S.: *The Insanity Defense.* New Haven and London, Yale University Press, 1967.

[10]Smith, R. J.: The Criminal Insanity Defense Is Placed on Trial in New York. *Science, 10:*1048–1052, 1978.

[11]Halpern, A. L.: The Insanity Defense: A Juridical Anachronism. *Psychiatric Annals, 7:* 41–63, 1977.

while others argue that the blameless mentally ill are confined longer than criminals."[12]

The insanity defense will probably continue to claim the limelight in both public and scholarly debate because it does touch on "ultimate social values and beliefs,"[13] and it does possess a certain cachet that fascinates us on many levels. Nevertheless, the most significant mental health inquiry is *not* the insanity defense; it is the issue of *competency to stand trial.* Nowhere is the power and influence of psychiatry more evident in the psycholegal arena than when the psychiatrist is called upon to advise the court as to who is competent to stand trial and who shall be deprived of personal liberty until such time as he becomes competent. The import of psychiatric hegemony in this aspect of the criminal justice system is clear when one realizes that the majority of persons now held in institutions for the criminally insane are not there because they have been found not guilty by reason of insanity, but rather because they were judged incompetent to participate in a trial and therefore have never been tried on the question of guilt or innocence.[14] The crucial import of the *competency to stand trial* issue stems from the large numbers of defendants to which it is applied and to the far-reaching consequences it holds in store for defendants in terms of regaining their liberty and having their day in court.

The many complex aspects of the competency to stand trial issue have been described and analyzed exhaustively in a vast literature on the subject. This literature has traced the historical development of legal standards for competency, discussed current standards, clarified the nature and goals of competency determinations, elucidated the problems raised by the incorporation of psychiatric information into competency standards, proposed an array of competency examination clinical guidelines, checklists, questionnaires, and psychological tests, which can be useful to the

---

[12]Stone, A. A.: The Insanity Defense. In *Mental Health and the Law: A System in Transition.* New York, Jason Aronson, Inc., 1976, pp. 218–219.

[13]Ibid.

[14]Goldstein, R. L., and Stone, M.: When Doctors Disagree: Differing Views on Competency. *Bull Am Acad Psychiatry Law, V*:90–97, 1977.

examining psychiatrist.[15-19] It has expounded on special problems of both a psychiatric and a legal nature, e.g. why doctors disagree, psychoactive drugs and competency, "hypercompetency," the Jackson decision, competency and dangerousness.[20-24] Education of both the psychiatric and the legal profession as to the niceties of *competency to stand trial*, the theory, practice, technique, the interrelated legal, psychiatric, and social implications, and its relationship to other forensic issues, namely, the insanity defense, has helped to correct the abuses and misunderstandings that have led to "considerable wasting of human lives and unnecessary deprivations of freedom."[25-26]

Yet, even while the controversy rages on about whether or not (or to what extent) psychiatrists should involve themselves in criminal proceedings in the areas of competency to stand trial and the insanity defense, in recent years psychiatrists in the courtroom have begun taking *new liberties*. Their knowledge, skills and expertise have been tapped by attorneys in areas hitherto unexplored or obscure. This chapter will elucidate three such new dimensions in psychiatry and criminal law — the determination of three unusual

[15]Misuse of Psychiatry in the Criminal Courts: Competency to Stand Trial. GAP report No. 89. New York, Group for the Advancement of Psychiatry, 1974.

[16]Goldstein, The Fitness Factory, 1973.

[17]Robey, A.: Criteria for Competency to Stand Trial: A Checklist for Psychiatrists. *Am J Psychiatry, 122:*616–623, 1965.

[18]Lipsitt, P. D., Lelos, D., and McGarry, A. L.: Competency for Trial: A Screening Instrument. *Am J Psychiatry, 128:*105–109, 1971.

[19]Rosenberg, A. H., and McGarry, A. L.: Competency for Trial: The Making of an Expert. *Am J Psychiatry, 128:*1092–1096, 1972.

[20]Goldstein and Stone, When Doctors Disagree, 1977.

[21]Winick, B. J.: Psychotropic Medication and Competence to Stand Trial. *Am Bar Foundation Res J, 3:*769–816, 1977.

[22]Marshall, M. H., and Resnik, H. L. P.: The Diagnostic Clue of "Hypercompetency." *Am J Psychiatry, 125:*570–572, 1968.

[23]Jackson v. Indiana, 406 U.S. 715 (1972).

[24]Forst, M. L.: The Psychiatric Evaluation of Dangerousness in Two Trial Court Jurisdictions. *Bull Am Acad Psychiatry Law, V:*98–110, 1977.

[25]McGarry, A. L.: The Fate of Psychotic Offenders Returned for Trial. *Am J Psychiatry, 127:*1181–1184, 1971.

[26]McGarry, A. L.: Competency for Trial and Due Process via the State Hospital. *Am J Psychiatry, 122:*623–631, 1965.

forms of competency: (1) the *competency* (or *credibility*) of the complaining witness, (2) the *competency* of a juror, and (3) the *competency* to consent to sexual relations. These new psycholegal collaborations will predictably meet with a fresh torrent of criticism and invective from those who fear further encroachments by the psychiatrist within the legal arena. I continue to believe that psychiatry has established itself as an "inextricable cog in the machinery of the law"[27] and that the system is far better off availing itself of psychiatric expertise when the alternative may be leaving the judge and jury to their own devices and the pitfalls of uninformed ignorance and common sense myths and misconceptions.

THE COMPETENCY (OR CREDIBILITY) OF THE COMPLAINING WITNESS

In 1906, in one of his rare ventures into the area of forensic psychiatry, Sigmund Freud delivered a lecture before a University of Vienna Law class entitled "Psycho-analysis and the Ascertaining of Truth in Courts of Law,"[28] in which he suggested that the psychiatrist may have at his disposal scientific means by which the testimony of witnesses can be tested for truthfulness and reliability. He cautioned that these scientific methods were of a highly experimental nature and for research purposes only. They were not intended to influence the verdict of the court. In later writings he deprecated any half-baked application of psychoanalytic theories in legal proceedings.[29-30] He thus anticipated a controversy that has raged on for three-quarters of a century in regard to the psychiatrist's special ability to evaluate the competency or credi-

[27]Goldstein, The Fitness Factory, 1973, p. 1144.

A portion of this section, in somewhat modified form, is from R. L. Goldstein, Credibility and Incredibility: The Psychiatric Examination of the Complaining Witness, *The American Journal of Psychiatry,* vol. *137*:10 pp. 1238–1240, October 1980. Copyright 1980, the American Psychiatric Association. Reprinted by permission.

[28]Freud, S.: Psycho-analysis and the Ascertaining of Truth in Courts of Law. In the standard edition of the *Complete Psychological Works of Sigmund Freud.* London, Hogarth Press, vol. IX, 1961, pp. 99–114.

[29]Freud, S.: The Expert Opinion in the Halsmann Case, *Complete Psychological Works,* 1961, pp. 251–253.

[30]Freud, S.: Memorandum for the Defense Prepared in 1922 (not extant).

bility of the complaining witness in a legal proceeding. Davidson contends that the psychiatric appraisal of the witness represents a new field of forensic psychiatry and describes nine clinical conditions that only the psychiatrist is uniquely qualified to discern and to relate to the credibility issue (the conditions are schizophrenia, senile psychoses, manic states, paranoid states, drug addiction, mental deficiency, alcoholism, psychoneurosis, and psychopathic personality).[31-32] He states: "If the psychiatrist were given all the facts about the witness' background; if he were given time to do a thorough physical and mental examination; if he could take a psychiatric history on the witness, he could give the trial lawyer a solid opinion about testimonial capacity." The most well-known use of psychiatric evaluation of a complaining witness' credibility came in the second Alger Hiss perjury trial in 1949. The judge ruled that "it is apparent that the outcome of this trial is dependent, to a great extent, upon the testimony of one man—Whittaker Chambers. Mr. Chambers' credibility is one of the major issues upon which the jury must pass. The opinion of the jury—formed upon their evaluation of all the evidence laid before them—is the decisive authority on this question, as on all questions of fact. The existence of insanity or mental derangement is admissible for the purpose of discrediting a witness."[33] The judge therefore allowed a psychiatrist, Dr. Carl A. L. Binger, to testify that, in his expert opinion, Chambers was a "psychopath with a tendency toward making false accusations."[34] This opinion was based on personal observation of Chambers on the witness stand and on a reading of some of Chambers' poems, plays, and book reviews. There was no psychiatric examination, per se, carried out. The jury chose to disregard the psychiatric testimony and found Hiss guilty as charged.

In some jurisdictions, in sex offender cases when the credibility of the complaining witness is in doubt, a psychiatric examination is ordered "not to determine whether the witness is telling the truth, but to determine whether the emotional or mental condi-

[31] Davidson, H. A.: *Forensic Psychiatry,* 2nd ed. New York, Ronald Press Co., 1965, p. 258.

[32] Davidson, H. A.: *Testimonial Capacity.* BOSTON U. LAW REV. *172:*39, 1959.

[33] Slovenko, R.: *Psychiatry and Law* Boston, Little, Brown and Co., 1973, p. 45.

[34] Ibid.

tion of the witness *may* affect his or her ability to tell the truth."[35] A report of the American Bar Association Committee on the Improvement of the Law of Evidence recommended psychiatric examination of all complainant women in sex offense cases to ascertain the presence of a psychiatric disturbance.[36]

Critics of psychiatric involvement raise serious questions in regard to the desirability, accuracy, and effectiveness of psychiatric evaluations of credibility. In 1980, Wigmore asked, "[W]here are the exact and precise experimental and psychological methods of ascertaining and measuring the testimonial certitude of witnesses . . . "[37] In a famous rape case, the judge ruled that the jury alone would best decide the issue of the complaining witness' credibility. He refused to allow the introduction of psychiatric testimony: "We are not convinced that the time-honored and well settled and undefined rule of impeachment of the veracity of a witness should thus be innovated upon. It is yet to be demonstrated that psychological and medical tests are practical and will detect a lie on the witness stand."[38] Other courts have been even more skeptical: "The divergence of psychiatric opinion and its frequent inexactness render its value minimal in enabling the jury to decide the issue of credibility . . . the jury after being subjected to several conflicting, equivocating and highly technical psychiatric opinions may actually be more confused than before."[39] Another court failed to see the benefit to be gained from "an amateur's voyage on the fog-enshrouded sea of psychiatry."[40]

There is considerable concern about reducing the prerogatives of the jury and giving the psychiatric expert the power to decide the issue of credibility (transferring power from the "crucible of the community" to the "couch of the psychiatrist");[41] about the

---

[35] California v. Francis, 5 Cal. App. 3d. 414, 85 CAL. RPTR. 61(1970).

[36]Report, ABA Committee on the Improvement of the Law of Evidence. In Brooks, A. D.: *Law, Psychiatry and the Mental Health System.* Boston, Little, Brown and Co., 1974, p. 1006.

[37]Wigmore, J.: *Professor Munsterberg and the Psychology of Testimony.* ILLINOIS L. REV., *3:* 999, 1909.

[38]Slovenko, *Psychiatry and Law,* 1973, p. 49.

[39]Slovenko, *Psychiatry and Law,* 1973, p. 59.

[40]Slovenko, *Psychiatry and Law,* 1973, p. 59.

[41]Falknor, J. F., and Steffen, D. T.: *Evidence of character: From the "Crucible of the Community" to the "Couch of the Psychiatrist."* U. PENN. L. REV. *102:*980, 1954.

competing interests of witness credibility and privacy; and about the possible misuse of psychiatry by calling for psychiatric opinions based on questionable practices that are not firmly grounded in good clinical evaluation methods. Slovenko concludes that "to obtain an ideal climate for an effective psychiatric evaluation, a number of legal reforms would be necessary that might be unwise either from a social or legal point of view. If this is the case, then psychiatrists and jurists should realize the limitations that the legal procedure places on the accuracy and effectiveness of the psychiatric examination and, in turn, on the psychiatric opinion."[42]

Following are two case reports wherein the court permitted my testimony on the mental state of the complaining witnesses. In these cases it was the contention of the defense that the mental disorder of the complaining witness and not reality was the source of the complaint. In these cases, application was made to perform a direct psychiatric examination of the complainant, an approach that was promoted as being the most accurate and rewarding approach to be followed. The court denied permission but did allow for psychiatric testimony based on a review of the complainant's previous psychiatric hospitalization records. This might be viewed as a compromise between the competing issues of a need to evaluate credibility and a desire to infringe on the privacy of the complainant as little as possible. Such testimony, once in evidence, proved to have decisive consequences in these cases.

Case Report 1

A seventy-four-year-old woman, living alone, claimed that the son of her building superintendent had assaulted and robbed her. He was arrested the same day. He had known the complaining witness over ten years and lived in the same building. He emphatically denied the charges against him but had no solid alibi, was unemployed, and had a criminal record and a history of drug abuse (he was currently attending a methadone program). Shortly before the trial, it came to light that the complainant had a history

---

[41]Falknor, J. F., and Steffen, D. T.: *Evidence of character: From the "Crucible of the Community" to the "Couch of the Psychiatrist."* U. PENN. L. REV. *102*:980, 1954.

[42]Slovenko, *Psychiatry and Law,* 1973, p. 56.

of several psychiatric hospitalizations since age forty-five for paranoid schizophrenia, characterized by delusions, hallucinations, confusion, memory lapses, and antagonistic behavior towards friends and family. During these episodes she had delusional ideas of being robbed of cherished possessions. She even accused her relatives of stealing from her. As a result of these disclosures, the court ruled that a psychiatrist retained by the defense could review the psychiatric records and testify about the possible influence of her mental condition on her credibility. The psychiatrist testified that in view of her documented psychiatric history and the particular nature of her disorder, there was a *substantial index of suspicion* that her testimony represented another example of delusional thinking. He conceded that his opinion would be more cogent if it were based on a direct psychiatric examination of the woman. The jury acquitted the defendant. It appeared that the critical impact of psychiatric testimony was facilitated by the overall weakness of the people's case, which was based on the complainant's word without any other corroboration.

Case Report 2

A forty-year-old woman charged that her boyfriend had raped her. She stated that he visited her in order to inform her that their liaison could not continue, since his estranged wife was returning to live with him. He allegedly forcibly raped her after they quarrelled. She made no outcry about this until three days later. At a gynecological examination two days after the alleged rape, she made no mention of a sexual assault. It was learned that she had been hospitalized twice in recent years for depressive illness with hysterical features. One month prior to the alleged rape, she underwent a hysterectomy. The court allowed a defense psychiatrist to review her hospital records but not to examine her directly. The court stated that a direct psychiatric examination was an unacceptable invasion of her privacy. The psychiatrist testified to the possible effects of narcissistic blows to the complainant as a result of her hysterectomy and being jilted by her boyfriend. The possible relationships between narcissistic injuries of this nature, a personality make-up including depressive and hysterical traits, attempting to maintain a shaken feminine self-image and allegations of rape were aired at length before the jury. The jury could not find the defendant guilty of rape "beyond a reasonable doubt," and he was acquitted.

Discussion

A psychiatric evaluation of the complaining witness in a criminal proceeding may be necessary to allow for informed deliberation by the jury in the case. In cases where doubt exists whether the complainant may be psychiatrically impaired, information regarding the mental state of the complainant is germane and should be made fully clear to the jury if that jury is to function meaningfully. The determination of the effect of any psychiatric condition on the credibility of the complaining witness remains the sole province of the jury; nonetheless, information provided by an expert witness permits the jury to make an informed decision as to that witness's worth. In order to enhance the *truth-finding* function of the jury, courts have ruled that they have an *inherent power* to order the complainant to cooperate. Not only is such testimony admissible, but the court of appeals in New York State has reversed conviction where such information was *not* put before the jury![43-44] The court held that the inability of the jury to appreciate the nature of the psychiatric infirmity was sufficient grounds to overturn the conviction. The purpose underlying the testimony of an expert is not to substitute his estimation of credibility for that of the jury. Rather, it is to provide a scientific perspective for the jury by which it can then evaluate the complainant's testimony for itself.

Scrutiny of the psychiatric condition of the complaining witness is an area of forensic psychiatry that warrants continuing study. Is the psychiatrist invading the usual province of the jury? Is he really determining the credibility of the complaining witness, or is he being used to discredit the complainant improperly? Slovenko asks, "Is psychiatry here being used more for its prestige value than for its probative value?"[45] Is the privacy of the complainant

---

[43]People v. Rensing, 14 N. Y. 2d 211 (1964).

[44]People v. Parks, 41 N. Y. 2d 36, 46–49 (1976).

[45]Slovenko, *Psychiatry and Law,* 1973, p. 56.

being invaded to an unacceptable extent? A New York court has ruled that although the right to psychiatric testimony clearly exists, the defendant must make a clear showing that it is warranted in view of the infringement on the complainant's right to privacy.[46] Is it the complainant who will be tried instead of the defendant? Will this serve to discourage victims of crime from pressing charges, lest they be exposed themselves to humiliation and vilification? Proponents of this trend have already tried to expand it further. It has been argued that the presentation of critical scientific data on the psychiatric condition of a complainant should not be left to depend on the chance that he or she has a history of psychiatric illness that warrants a closer scrutiny. Where such a history is not preexistent, some have contended that there exists an a priori right to launch such an inquiry before trial in any case whatsoever. This would certainly place all complaining witnesses on trial with or without a psychiatric history.

I have suggested the term *incredibility* to describe that quality in a witness which renders his evidence unworthy of belief. Although the invention of a technical term may help to clarify an issue and avoid confusion and distortion, it can also give the appearance of creating *facts* for the social sciences.[47] Psychiatry is already replete with such *facts* in the form of technical terms, and these are reified and often misused in the courtroom and other places to overawe those who are not used to scrutinize authorities. The danger is that determination of *incredibility* might be overused and misused to harass and stigmatize complaining witnesses if not managed judiciously and vigilantly. It remains to be seen what impact this direction in psychiatry's involvement in court proceedings will have, what specific guidelines and safeguards will evolve for its application, and what will result from renewed conflicts between the individual's right to privacy and the jury's right to know in order to insure a fair trial and protect the accused. This is but one further example of the constant need of the law to adjust two conflicting ideals so that one is not sacrificed to the other. Last, just as Freud

---

[46]People v. Sandra Lowe, N.Y.L.J. 12/22/78.

[47]Cohen, M. R.: Reason in Social Science. In Feigl, H., and Brodbeck, M. (Eds.): *Readings in the Philosophy of Science.* New York, Appleton-Century-Crofts, 1953, p. 667.

cautioned against "wild analysis" as a reckless and blind misuse of psychoanalysis, so must the forensic psychiatrist avoid introducing any testimony based on incomplete, inadequate, or questionable methods of clinical evaluation in order to aid the legal process to reach more informed and intelligent decisions.

THE COMPETENCY OF A JUROR

A constant preoccupation of the law is mediating the clash between equally valid and worthy alternative principles or ideologies. In the preceding section, we discussed the conflict between the individual's right to privacy (in the case of the complaining witness) and the jury's right to know in order to insure a fair trial and to protect the accused. In this section we will learn that there is great judicial reluctance to inquire into the state of mind of any juror during his deliberation, even when evidence is brought forward that raises doubts about the competence of that juror.* This is so despite the unchallenged cornerstone of our system that says the accused in a criminal proceeding has the right to have his case heard by a panel of twelve competent jurors. This could be viewed as the need to protect the sanctity of the jury room and the privacy of individual jurors versus the right to a fair trial. With respect to posttrial evidence of possible juror incompetence during the trial, courts have been willing to set aside a verdict or at least make further inquiry only under the most stringent conditions. Only when there is clear and incontrovertible evidence of

---

*Juror competence has not been adequately defined. U.S.C. 1865, which is part of the Jury Selection and Service Act of 1968, P.L. 90–274, 82 Stat. 53, provides in relevant part as follows: [The] judge ... shall deem any person qualified to serve on grand and petit juries ... unless he ... is incapable, by reason of mental or physical infirmity, to render satisfactory jury service.

I have suggested the following criteria or standards for measuring juror competence. To be a competent juror, one must possess the following qualities:

1. the ability to exercise rational judgment
2. the ability to concentrate on and follow the proceedings without serious distractions that interfere with comprehension
3. the ability to be objective, detached, and impartial
4. the ability to convey the appearance of rationality, impartiality, and so forth in order to maintain the dignity and meaningfulness of the judicial process itself

incompetence shortly before, during, or after jury service,[48] clear evidence of some criminal act (e.g. bribery), or clear evidence of some objective fact of internal impropriety in the jury (e.g. a blood relationship between juror and defendant or extraneous material brought to a juror's attention during deliberations) will, in "the gravest and most important cases only," judicial reluctance about further inquiry be overcome.[49] As one court expressed it, "Cases might arise in which it would be impossible to refuse evidence of impropriety (or incompetence) without violating the plainest principles of justice. But, unquestionably (even in those cases), such evidence ought to be *received with great caution* [italics mine]."[50]

This strong policy against any postverdict inquiry into a juror's state of mind and conduct during deliberations rests on sound reasons. To make what was intended to be a private deliberation the constant subject of public investigation would seriously compromise the frankness and freedom of discussion that is the heart of a jury's work. Jury room deliberations would become inhibited and self-conscious. The jurors themselves ought not to be subjected to harassment, intimidation, and invasion of their privacy. Courts ought not to be burdened with large numbers of worthless applications, and verdicts ought not to be made so uncertain.[51] Thus, only strong evidence that it is *likely* that a particular juror suffered from incompetence to understand the issues or to deliberate at the time of service will justify inquiry into whether such incompetence did in fact exist.[52]

Following are two case reports in which the issue of juror incompetence was raised (by the defense in case 1, by the prosecution in case 2). Both cases illustrate the court's resistance to dealing with this issue. This appears to be a sensitive area, where psychiatric expertise (again, like *The Man Who Came to Dinner*) is

---

[48]Mattox v. United States, 146 U.S. 140, 149–150, 13 S. Ct. 50, 36 L.Ed. 917 (1892). 18 U.S.C. §§ 245 (b), 1503, 1504. 28 U.S.C. § 1867 (f).

[49]McDonald v. Pless, 238 U.S. 264, 269, 35 S. Ct. 783, 59 L.Ed. 1300 (1915).

[50]United States v. Reid, 53 U.S. 361, 366, 13 L.Ed. 1023 (1851).

[51]Miller v. United States, 403 F.2d 77 (2d Cir. 1968).

[52]Anderson v. State, 54 Ariz. 387, 96 P.2d 281 (1939). Grand Lodge A.O.U.W. of Ark. v. Wood, 113 Ark. 502, 168 S.W. 1070 (1914).

an unwelcome guest who will not take the hint and depart gracefully. In both cases it is alleged that the juror's psychiatric condition (which inadvertently came to light *after* the trial) specifically interfered with his ability to function as a competent juror.

Case Report 1:
United States v. Dioguardi

Dioguardi and his codefendant were convicted of violations of the federal securities laws after a three week trial in 1973.[53] Prior to sentencing, they moved for a new trial, or at least for an evidentiary hearing. The basis for this motion was a bizarre and unsolicited letter from one of the jurors, which alleged to establish that juror's incompetence. The trial judge denied the motion, noted that his observations of that juror were within the normal range both during the trial and during the deliberations, and sentenced the defendants to an extended prison term. One year later, the United States Court of Appeals (Second Circuit) heard the appeal and found the defendants' arguments not persuasive. They accordingly affirmed the convictions and let the sentences stand.

About ten days after trial, one of the two defendants received a letter from one of the jurors. The letter was written on stationary bearing the zodiac sign of Libra and a picture of a woman with scales. Under the picture, on the last page of the letter, the juror wrote, "The sign *Libra* is the heavenly sign of the zodiac under which I was born." The letter reads as follows:

February 8, 1973

Dear Mr. Dioguardi,

Under the situation and such circumstances I hope that I have made the right decision. I talk to my friends Bertha and her husband Olive about this, Olive agree that I write to you. Bertha, however, was against it. Nevertheless, I felt I had to write to you. I cannot omit what I have seen. When I saw the good within you and how hard your wife was trying; I prayed about it. One word appear before me: *repent.* If you repent and run a clean business it is the good within you that will save you, and you will gain what you have lost. Before I continue I must explain something to you. I have eyes and ears that I can see things before it happen. I can tell

---

[53]United States v. Dioguardi, 492 F.2d 70 (1974).

you about other and what they are thinking and doing. If I am wrong about this it is the first time.

I would like to visit you. I would like to talk to you about what appear before me. I would like to do so when my eyes fully open. They are only partly open. I don't know at the present when they will open. Unfortunate, a curse was put upon them some years ago. I have some people working on them. Everything is being done that can be done. So we will have to wait. As I stated I cannot omit what appear before me, when I was on the jury bench. You feel that this is the end for you. However, it is not. Something appear before me that I must do. It is the good within you that I must use and within that good, you will gain what you have lost. If, however, I am wrong it is the first time . . .

Mr. Dioguardi, I want to ask a favor of you please.

I want you to look upon me as a woman and I look upon you as a man and not white man and black woman. Olive agree with me.

Let's leave color out, O.K.?

I was told you will only have to serve one third of the time given. So relax, this is not the end. Soon you will be free. . . .

Sincerely,
Genena (signed)

Attorneys for the defense had this letter examined by *seven* forensic psychiatrists, all of whom responded to the effect that the juror appeared to be mentally ill, possibly psychotic, with hallucinations, grandiose delusions and an inability to distinguish reality from fantasy. They further pointed out that this was a preliminary impression and that further psychiatric examination and testing (of the juror) was necessary to establish the precise diagnosis and to determine whether or not her infirmities might have rendered her incompetent to serve as a juror at the time of the trial.

Excerpts from the psychiatric reports of two of the seven psychiatrists who were consulted are as follows:

April 2, 1973

[T]he letter makes a positive presumptive showing that . . . the juror suffered from a chronic psychotic thought disorder which so severed her relationship with reality that she was unable to exercise critical judgment or to function in an unbiased manner in the evaluation of evidence produced at the trial. Indeed, it would appear that her unsoundness of mind was so overwhelming that she was subject to auditory and visual hallucinations, delusions and a belief in her own omnipotence.

The exact nature of the type of psychosis with which the juror is afflicted can be further investigated ... Such an investigation would entail clinical psychiatric interviews and, of particular importance, psychological testing.[54]

February 28, 1973

[T]his letter was written consciously with every good intention on the part of Mrs. Rush in an effort to be helpful to Mr. Dioguardi. However ... the writer was here showing evidence of being hallucinated, delusional and would prove to be suffering from a Paranoid Condition.

Taking it in a far less literal fashion, allowing the greatest degree of latitude interpreting what she wrote, so that it can be taken as a somewhat picturesque, idiosyncratic expression of her ideas, influenced by educational, cultural, and religious factors, I still would find important grounds for believing that the letter shows that she was involved in this situation in a very unreal and unusual way.

In my opinion it is most likely that she is, in fact, suffering from a Paranoid Condition in which she has hallucinatory experiences and delusional thinking.

Whatever the court may consider the proper steps to take in regard to any other aspect of the case, it would be my hope that further psychiatric examination would be gently encouraged upon her, and that she would be willing to cooperate.[55]

All seven of the psychiatrists rendered expert opinions that the juror who wrote the letter suffered from severe mental illness. They agreed that direct psychiatric examination of the juror would be required to reach a precise diagnosis but nonetheless felt on the basis of what they already knew that she was probably incompetent to function as a juror. They were enjoined, however, from carrying out any such direct examination (the district judge stated in open court that she was not to be contacted by anybody or communicated with by anybody in any possible way, directly or indirectly).

After considering these facts, the court of appeals wrote the following: "Only strong evidence that it is likely that the juror suffered from such incompetence during jury service will justify an inquiry into whether such incompetence did in fact exist. In our view the juror's letter and the *essentially horseback uninformed*

---

[54]Affidavit of April 2, 1973 of Dr. Stanley L. Portnow.

[55]Letter of February 28, 1973 of Dr. Donald M. Brough.

opinions of the psychiatrists [italics mine] regarding the letter fall considerably short of justifying any further inquiry."[56] They go on to say that no evidence was offered of any history of mental instability on the juror's part, much less any evidence of an independent adjudication of insanity or incompetence. She had been steadily employed for a number of years, had performed satisfactorily at *voir dire,* during the trial per se and at the time of deliberations. The trial judge had noted nothing peculiar or disturbed about her countenance or behavior. In regard to the psychiatric testimony itself, they commented, "Although the opinions of experts are not to be dismissed altogether, they were here of necessity formed in a vacuum, based on one piece of evidence and fall far short of constituting the sort of 'objective fact' which can justify inquiry into the internal workings of the jury."[57]

Judge Feinberg, one of the court of appeals judges, did not agree. In his dissenting opinion he noted the following:

> The letter is staggering in its implications. No special training is needed to appreciate that this juror seems to believe that she is clairvoyant and could see things that could not be apparent to others such as what people think or an event before it happens. If she did believe she was clairvoyant in this way, is it really necessary to point out why she could not fairly try the guilt of innocence of any man? It seems obvious that a "clairvoyant" juror might honestly "see" a defendant's guilt despite the lack of evidence because she can see into the defendant's mind. Or conversely, she might for the same reason divine a defendant's innocence in the face of overwhelming proof of guilt. In fact, a person who was known, before trial, to regard herself as clairvoyant would certainly not be allowed on a jury in the first place.[58]

> He concluded his opinion as follows: Although it is true that once a trial is over there is great judicial reluctance to inquire into the state of mind of a juror during his deliberations, *reluctance to inquire is not the same as obdurate refusal to face facts* [italics mine], especially such "objective" facts as a rambling unsolicited letter sent 13 days after verdict that strongly suggests mental illness.[59]

---

[56] *Supra* note 53, at 78.

[57] *Supra* note 53, at 81.

[58] *Supra* note 53, at 85. *See also* United States v. Silverman, 449 F.2d 1341, 1344 (2d Cir. 1971).

[59] Ibid.

The Dioguardi case is a striking example of the enormous resistance of the courts to look into the mind of a juror under almost any circumstances. Even when psychiatric expertise of the highest caliber is utilized to elucidate the issues before the court (and even when these expert views stand uncontradicted on the record), it can still be lightly dismissed as *essentially horseback uninformed* when a court is determined to protect a competing issue such as the sanctity of the jury.

Case Report 2:
Sullivan v. Fogg

Sullivan was convicted in 1973 after a jury trial of two counts of murder.[60] One month after trial, one of the jurors complained to the district attorney of harassment by "voices." At the District Attorney's request, the juror came before the trial court in order for the court to inquire further as to his competence. He stated that he heard voices and vibrations throughout the trial, that these voices and vibrations were transmitted or powered by overflying airplanes, steam pipes, and hidden electronic devices, and that the defendant and his confederates were behind all of this. He saw it as some sort of sinister plot aimed at influencing his vote during the trial. After trial, the voices berated him and called him an assassin because he had convicted an innocent man. In a previous case in 1969 in which he had served as juror, he had experienced similar hallucinations but had not brought it to anyone's attention. Like the juror in the Dioguardi case, he had appeared quite normal during the proceedings and had made a stable occupational and social adjustment. The trial judge appointed a psychiatrist to examine the juror (who readily agreed to such an examination) and to submit a written report, which would be made part of the record.

The psychiatrist reported that the juror suffered from a "schizoid personality with paranoid features" and concluded that he had been a competent juror: "He heard the voices but they did not influence him and his logic in evaluating the factors in the trial and coming to the conclusion that he did was quite sound. Although

---

[60]Sullivan v. Fogg, U.S. Court of Appeals (2d Cir.) Decision (1980).

he heard the voices, he had not formulated them into a systematized delusion . . . [H]e was competent to make a rational judgment on the merits of the case presented to him in Court."[61]

The judge in this case had already gone much further than in Dioguardi by pursuing an inquiry into the juror's competence and then having him undergo a psychiatric examination. The court accepted the psychiatric report, incorporated it into the record, and concluded there was no necessity for further inquiry. The defendant appealed, contending that he was denied due process when the trial court failed to conduct a full and fair hearing on the issue of juror competence. The defendant had had no opportunity to cross-examine the court's psychiatrist about his conclusions or to present his own psychiatric expert witness. Although the court might have decided not to grant any hearing at all, once an inquiry was ordered, the defendant claimed that it was then not sufficient for the judge to obtain one written psychiatric report and nothing more. The conviction was affirmed by the New York State Supreme Court Appellate Division and the New York Court of Appeals. Sullivan then applied for a writ of *habeas corpus* in federal district court, which was denied. In January 1980 (*seven years after trial!*) the United States Court of Appeals (Second Circuit) reversed the decision of the district court and ordered a reopening of the hearing. They wrote, "In light of the serious question as to the juror's competence, we think that due process requires at least the opportunity to test [the doctor's] opinion on cross examination."[62]

On May 28, 1980, the court psychiatrist was cross-examined at length before the original trial judge. The adequacy of his examination, the accuracy of his diagnosis, and the basis of his conclusion that the juror was competent were called into question. Although the defense was prepared to offer the testimony of its own psychiatric expert (who had reviewed all relevant reports and written materials and whose testimony, it contended, would have been a prerequisite to a fair assessment of the issue before the court), the judge declined to accept such testimony and limited the

---

[61]Psychiatric Report of June 27, 1973, of Dr. Martin I. Lubin.

[62]*Supra* note 60, at 988.

reopened hearing merely to cross-examining the original psychiatrist. The defense contended that their own expert would have provided testimony that was highly relevant and that would have assisted the court in properly assessing the original psychiatrist's methodology, diagnosis, and conclusions. For example, the defense alleged that the original examination had been too brief and superficial in its scope, that the diagnosis of a *personality disorder* rather than of a *psychosis* was clearly at odds with accepted medical opinion (and represented the doctor's penchant for labelling patients in as favorable a light as possible), and finally, that by accepting at face value the juror's statements that he was not influenced at all by his own hallucinations and delusions (which were intimately intertwined with the case itself) in reaching a verdict, the doctor had grossly underestimated the irrational forces that were obviously at work in the juror's mind. The defense charged that the psychiatrist showed a lack of concern for his own decision making process, i.e. an inability to link up data with conclusions in such a way that the data substantiated the conclusions and that the decision making process itself could easily be understood and scrutinized. Judge Bazelon has severely criticized psychiatrists for woolly reporting[63] and for the deliberate or unintentional concealment of what goes on between *input* and *output* in their thinking (what Jonas and Jonas have termed *throughput*).[64] Additional testimony of this sort would have been proper from both a legal and a psychiatric point of view. A psychiatric expert may testify about another psychiatrist's methodology and may offer interpretation of stated data such as symptoms and the effect on a person of a defined mental disorder.[65] This sort of testimony provides something more than cross examination can by itself, namely, a separate expert perspective on the crucial psychiatric issues before the court.

A decision has not been handed down in this case as of this writing. In any event, further appeals seem likely. As in Dioguardi,

[63]Bazelon, D. L.: The Perils of Wizardry. *Am J Psychiatry, 131:*1317–1322, 1974.

[64]Jonas, A. D., and Jonas, D. F.: The Evolutionary Mechanisms of Neurotic Behavior. *Am J Psychiatry, 131:*636–640, 1974.

[65]Suggs v. LaVallee, 570 F.2d 1092 (1978).

but to a lesser extent, there appears to be an active resistance to the intrusion of psychiatric expertise when the sanctum sanctorum of the jury is under seige.

THE COMPETENCY TO CONSENT TO SEXUAL RELATIONS

When sexual acts occur without the consent of the victim, lack of consent results from (1) forcible compulsion, (2) incapacity to consent, or (3) any circumstances, in addition to forcible compulsion or incapacity to consent, in which the victim does not expressly or implicitly acquiesce in the actor's conduct. In general, a person is deemed incapable of consent when he is less than seventeen years old, mentally defective, mentally incapacitated, or physically helpless. We define *mentally defective* to mean that a person suffers from a mental disease or defect, which renders him incapable of appraising the nature of his conduct. *Mentally incapacitated* means that a person is rendered *temporarily* incapable of appraising or controlling his conduct owing to the influence of a narcotic or intoxicating substance administered to him without his knowledge or consent.[66] We will focus on the *competency* (or *capacity*) to consent to a sexual act in the case of the allegedly *mentally defective* individual.

Mental illness or mental retardation per se does not automatically render an individual incapable of consenting to sexual relations. People who are severely mentally ill or of very limited intellect still may have the requisite intactness to function in society and to give (or withhold) consent for sexual relations. The courts have emphasized the parameter of the individual's "awareness of prevailing moral code(s)" as a guideline for competence.[67] Her understanding of how coitus would be regarded in the framework of her social milieu, how it would relate to the taboos and prohibitions of her family, friends, and peers, and what would be the social costs to her in terms of how others regard her (social status, reputation, etc.) would be important issues to determine in

---

[66]*McKinney's Consolidated Laws of New York: Penal Law,* Book 39. St. Paul, West Publishing Co., 1970, p. 269–295.

[67]People v. Boggs, 107 Cal. App. 492, 290 p. 618. People v. Palvino, 216 App. Div. 319, 214 N.Y.S. 577.

evaluating her competency or capacity to appraise her conduct. This has been regarded as an emphasis on the *moral quality* of the sexual act as it is measured by society and as the victim is able to assess and appreciate this "social" aspect of the question. This is different from assessing the victim's own moral code or sense of values: "Whether her character is exemplary or depraved is besides the point. The object is not to probe the degree of her conformity or nonconformity to the norms of society. A knowing defiance of social mores, a mere yielding to temptation or to passion, or even an inclination to vice [is not the law's concern.] . . . But to flout society or to arraign oneself against its views is entirely different from having an understanding of, or the capacity to understand, that one is doing so."[68] Understanding within the social context, then, is the law's concern and not merely whether she is mentally ill, mentally deficient, immoral, or even lacking in knowledge of the physiological nature of coitus.[69]

Following are two case reports in which the issue of competency to consent to sexual relations was raised. In the first case the defendant was charged with sexual misconduct because the victim was allegedly incompetent due to mental deficiency. In the second case, the defendant was charged with rape because the victim was allegedly incompetent as a result of a psychotic state.

Case Report 1

It was conceded that the act of sexual intercourse on which the prosecution was based took place. It happened at the home of Donna's mother, where she also resided. Gibson, the defendant, was a family friend for years who was almost a member of the household; he was aware that Donna was "retarded" at the time of the incident. On the night in question, Donna and Gibson were left alone in the apartment. She invited him to rub her neck, which was sore. She related that "it felt good" and that it progressed to kissing, petting, undressing, and finally to coitus. She states that the defendant never hit her, threatened to hit her, or in any way verbally or physically coerced her. She states that she "told him

---

[68]People v. Easley, 396 N.Y.S. 2d 635.

[69]*Supra* note 67.

not to do it" and also that she hit him. It was difficult to assess how much actual resistance she offered or whether she was attempting to rationalize or conceal her own part in the incident out of fear, shame, or guilt. Donna's mother was enraged when she learned what had happened shortly thereafter and vigorously involved herself in the proceedings that followed. Gibson was charged with *sexual misconduct* because Donna was allegedly incapable of consent (although nineteen years old) because of her *mental defective status.*

Donna had been identified early as a retarded child and placed in a facility for the mentally deficient at age four. She returned to live with her mother at age six and had been enrolled in special classes since. In her most recent reevaluation by the Bureau of Child Guidance, she was directed to continue in a program for the trainable mentally retarded. (The "trainable" child is one who may not become literate but who can develop reasonably adequate language skills, self-help skills and a degree of economic usefulness. These children attain an acceptable level of *social adjustment* to home and neighborhood and can learn an income-producing skill via the home, residential facility, or sheltered workshop.)[70] At the time of the incident, Donna attended classes at a special school and worked at school as a messenger. She functioned at a first grade level at school and demonstrated visual, coordination and speech articulation problems. Her full scale I.Q. was 61, placing her in the mildly retarded rage. Nonetheless, she functioned well within her own social environment despite her limitations. She attended school, had many friends there, took very good care of her personal appearance and grooming, and displayed excellent self-control and deportment. She noted that her mother, teachers, and friends had all impressed on her the need to be well-behaved. "They taught me the differences between right and wrong," she said. She stated that when she was "bad" her mother punished her by restricting her to the house. Specifically in regard to her understanding of "prevailing moral codes," she stated that she had some boyfriends at school, held hands with them or kissed them,

---

[70]Report of the American Medical Association Conference on Mental Retardation. *JAMA, 191:*10–244, 1965.

but did not become more intimate because she "knows it is wrong." She stated it is "bad" to have sex if unmarried. She knew her teachers, friends, and mother would be "upset and angry" if she had sex with boys and that she might "be thrown out of school." Thus, although she was mildly mentally retarded, the examining psychiatrist felt that she appreciated and understood the attitudes, sanctions, taboos, mores, and moral codes of society (and more specifically of her friends, teachers, and parents) in regard to whether or not (or under what conditions) she should have sexual relations. She understood the possible and probable consequences, "social cost," and attitudes toward such conduct. In view of this, he concluded that she *was* competent to give or withhold consent and that she was *not* mentally defective in this legal sense.

After prolonged pretrial negotiations, the defendant elected to plead guilty to a lesser offense and was granted probation.

Case Report 2

Marietta was a forty-six-year-old woman with a long-standing history of mental illness, which necessitated frequent and prolonged stays at various mental institutions in the New York City area. For several months prior to the incident in question, she lived either "on the streets" or at the home of a sixty-three-year-old "boyfriend" who kept his refrigerator locked and only fed her in exchange for sexual favors. Marietta was known to wander up to strange men in the neighborhood and offer to have sexual relations with them if they would buy her "a cup of coffee and a doughnut." She would then accompany them to the nearest available rooftop to consummate these arrangements. On the day in question, Marietta met the defendant, Spencer, and made her usual proposal. They repaired to the roof, but before they could complete sexual relations, they were spotted by a group of onlookers in a neighboring building, and the police were summoned. Eventually, Spencer was charged with a sexual offense. Marietta was an attractive woman who looked younger than her stated age. On psychiatric examination it was found she had a severe thinking disorder and was rambling, disorganized, and "loose" throughout the interview. There were no hallucinations present. Her affect was superficial and inappropriately mischievous or silly. She evinced no concern or uneasiness about her life-style in general, about her sexual behavior, or about the particular case before the court. She noted that "men are all interested in nothing but sex. You may not want to go with them for sex, but when you see 'that certain look' in their eyes, there is nothing you can do. You have to submit." Aside from this delusional material, she seemed blithely unaware that there was anything amiss about her coffee and doughnut for sex routine or that society at large might not condone such behavior even if she herself did. She noted that "it would be better, more secure, to be on birth control when you have sex," but that was her only concession to or acknowledgement of any social standard of appropriate or proper behavior.

In view of her apparent inability to form an intelligent opinion on the subject with an understanding of the act, its nature, and its possible social consequences or to appraise "the nature of the stigma, the ostracism or other noncriminal sanctions which society levies for conduct it labels only as immoral,"[71] the psychiatric examiner was unequivocal in his conclusion that she was *incompetent* to consent to sexual relations and was *mentally defective,* (that is, suffering from a mental disease (schizophrenia) that rendered her incapable of appraising the nature of her conduct).

At the time of this writing, the case has yet to come to trial.

CONCLUSION

As this chapter has demonstrated, the evolution of psychiatric expertise as it relates to the criminal law has resulted in an expansion (sometimes unwelcome by the law itself or by the antipsychiatry establishment) of the psychiatrist's role in the legal arena, a taking of *new liberties* by the psychiatrist. Although this has occurred to the dismay of some, I believe that it serves the best interests of justice in the broadest sense when psychiatric information and insight, however imperfect, are made available to the legal decision maker.

Three unusual forms of competency determination have been discussed and illustrated with relevant case reports.

---

[71]*Supra* note 68, at 640.

SECTION III

FAMILY LAW, DOMESTIC RELATIONS, AND FORENSIC PSYCHIATRY

Chapter 11

MISGUIDED LOYALTY, THERAPEUTIC GRANDIOSITY, AND SCIENTIFIC IGNORANCE: LIMITATIONS ON PSYCHIATRIC CONTRIBUTIONS TO FAMILY LAW AND JUVENILE JUSTICE

RICHARD ROSNER, M.D.

The problems that face the practioner of child and adolescent psychiatry, upon being asked to assist in a psychiatric-legal matter, are myriad. Generally, they can be considered to fall into four types. In the first instance, the child and adolescent psychiatrist is not well versed in the legal issue that he is called upon to address. Second, he is faced with vaguely formulated legal criteria that are alleged to determine the psychiatric-legal issue. Third, he is bereft of adequately demonstrable clinical data (as opposed to metapsychological theories) to offer the court. Finally, given any one or all of these initial problems, he is hard pressed to reason cogently from the available facts, to apply them to the criteria, and to provide an expert opinion on the legal issue. All of these problems are further compounded when a general psychiatrist is called upon to provide forensic services in the area of child and adolescent psychiatry.

It is important for the psychiatrist to clarify the legal issue because that data is essential to determining his role, his ethical commitment of loyalty, and the data he will require. Among the various issues are those which relate to child custody, to determinations of whether a child is a person in need of supervision, to before-disposition evaluations of alleged juvenile delinquents, to determinations of child abuse, to abrogation of parental rights. Traditionally trained general psychiatrists often feel that their primary loyalty should be to their patient (the child) or to his parents. Child and adolescent psychiatrists may be more inclined to favor loyalty to the child over loyalty to the parents. Forensic psychiatrists realize that their ethical commitment and professional loyalty is a context-dependent matter.

If the case entails functioning as a friend of the court, as *amicus curiae*, many forensic psychiatrists believe that the ethical commitment is to the family law/juvenile justice system rather than to the individual child or adolescent. This may entail advising the court about data that will lead to an outcome inconsistent with the wishes of the child, the adolescent, and his parents. The forensic psychiatrist in that setting has a loyalty to society as a whole as embodied in the judicial system rather than to the person he has examined. In such settings, a doctor-patient relationship does not exist. It is essential for the forensic psychiatrist to understand this nontherapeutic role from the beginning and to advise the child, the adolescent, and the parents that the materials that they provide will *not* be held in confidence, that the doctor is functioning as a consultant to the court, that he hopes that the outcome will be beneficial to the child and the family, but that the wishes and goals of the child and the family are secondary to the doctor's duty to the court. Failure to advise the child, the adolescent, and the parents adequately of these facts may, in some instances, lead to invalidation of the psychiatric report on the grounds that it was obtained under false pretenses and in the absence of voluntary, competent, informed consent from the parties who permitted the psychiatric evaluation.

There is often an understandable, but lamentable, tendency on the part of psychiatrists, generalists, or specialists in child and adolescent psychiatry to be advocates of faith, hope, and charity in dealing with youngsters. They may confuse the ideal and the actual. *If* the best possible psychotherapeutic resources, *if* the best residential treatment facilities, and *if* the best educational and vocational services were to be made available to a child or adolescent or family, then such optimism might be appropriate in a substantial number of instances. However, in the real world, the social service network, the mental health services to the poor, and the public school systems are woefully inadequate to the needs of disturbed clients of the family law and juvenile justice systems. In many instances, parents who abuse their children are the products of abuse themselves. Long-standing maladaptive patterns of thought, feeling, and behavior are recalcitrant to minimally funded, short-term service programs. In other instances, children and adolescents come from impoverished families, have been subjected to prejudice as members of ethnic minorities, have received inadequate education, have no marketable skills, are the products of broken homes, have long-standing untreated medical conditions (e.g. malnutrition, dental caries), and have never experienced a nonexploitative human relationship. For many such children, teenagers, and families, *in reality* there are no psychotherapeutic resources, no residential treatment centers, no educational or vocational programs except in juvenile justice detention facilities or in prison. Psychiatrists who plead that abusing fathers and mothers, and violently delinquent children and adolescents, should be spared the stigma of incarceration and should be permitted to participate in community-based rehabilitation programs and probationary supervision often reveal more of their ignorance of public resources than they reveal of their psychiatric skills.

In situations where the issue of abrogation of parental rights is concerned, psychiatrists may confuse legal issues. They may think that the criteria to be considered is what is in the best interest of the child and may not recognize that parental competence is the issue that must be addressed first. There are many children who might benefit by being raised by persons who are not their natural parents; however, the law has set up a protective hedge around the integrity of the family — a barrier that may not be breached unless specific legal criteria demonstrating parental abuse, neglect, or incompetence have been demonstrated. The psychiatrist who has been hired to provide a report to the court regarding criteria for abrogation of parental rights must be clear on the nature of his task. It is thoroughly correct to assist a parent in resisting charges of neglect, abandonment, and unfitness — to place loyalty with the parent's interest first — if that is the psychiatric-legal issue under consideration. Every parent has the right to be idiosyncratic, to be mistaken, to be less than ideal, without having to fear that a psychiatrist will testify that it would be better for the child to have that parent's rights terminated.

Some people in this world are bad. They are not mentally ill;

they are wicked. This is an unfashionable viewpoint in psychiatric circles. However, to understand all is *not* to condone all. Many psychiatrists, especially child and adolescent psychiatrists who are committed to a developmental perspective on the genesis of behavior, have great difficulty in distinguishing between understanding and exculpation. The goal of the family law and juvenile justice system is not therapeutic. To the extent that *civil law* is at issue, the goal may be restoration of damages to the injured; it may be the protection of minors. To the extent that *criminal law* is at issue (even the quasi-criminal procedures that prevail in the juvenile justice system), the goal may be to protect society, to deter others from similar misdeeds, and (if funding permits) to attempt some sort of rehabilitation. However, these are not therapeutic goals in the way that medical doctors and psychiatrists are accustomed to discuss therapeutics. In many instances, children, adolescents, and parents *deserve* to be punished. In the same manner that socially praiseworthy acts *deserve* to be rewarded, socially blameworthy acts *deserve* punishment. This must be understood by the psychiatrist who functions in the area of family law and the juvenile justice system. Insisting on the medical-therapeutic value system while working within the judicial system is as fruitless as insisting that baseball rules be obeyed by players in a game of soccer.

Even when the psychiatrist has addressed the consideration of the specific psychiatric-legal issue and has determined the focus of his ethical commitment and professional loyalty, he has merely passed the first hurdle. The legal criteria that determine an issue are often vague and imprecise. For example, what does it mean that a parent is morally unfit or what are the best interests of the child? It is possible to read the statutes carefully in a given state, to review the pertinent case law carefully, to examine the administrative codes, and still to be left with ambiguous terminology. Some claim that this nonspecificity of criteria provides for judicial discretion, provides for the evolution of mores and knowledge, gives flexibility to decision makers, and avoids premature closure in areas that remain in flux. Whatever the reasons, it is extremely difficult to obtain relevant clinical material in any psychiatric-legal case in family law and the juvenile justice system in the absence of a clear, consistent, and coherent body of legally determined criteria on which an issue must be settled.

To use an obvious example, surely there are as many definitions of the best interests of the child as there are theories of human personality. If one believes in the model society that Plato described in *The Republic*, then it is in the best interest of a child to be raised to obey the rulers of his nation, to serve unquestioningly as a soldier in the armed forces of his nation, and to work at maximum efficiency to enhance the wealth of the nation. Of course, one might reply that there is no empirical evidence to demonstrate that this model of human personality and this type of citizen *really* is in the best interests of the child. However, at least the model is clearly defined. In many courts, the psychiatrist is not routinely called upon to state the theoretical model of human personality and the related theories of human growth, development, and adjustment to which he subscribes. Nor is he required to show that empirical studies prove that one model is clearly superior to another model or that the predictions derived from one model are demonstrably more accurate than the predictions drawn from a rival model.

Theories of human personality abound: One can enter any college bookstore and find texts that explain four, twelve, twenty, or thirty-six such theories. What are the empirical supports for a Freudian model, as opposed to a neo-Freudian model, as opposed to a Rogerian model, an x model, a y model or a z model? With few exceptions, it is difficult to find an atheoretical description of human growth and behavior. More often, the observers of children look through theory-colored lenses. Piagetians find data that support Piaget's theories. Freudians find data that support Freudian theories. Behaviorists find that infant behavior is understandable in Skinnerian terms. But man, according to Freud, Sullivan, Jung, Cattell, Eysenck, and dozens of other personality theorists, varies considerably. What is in the best interest of the child must correspondingly vary with the theoretical model of man that the psychiatrist employs. To say that one does not subscribe to any theory is, very often, merely to admit that one does not know which theory has influenced one, that one does not know any of the rival theories well, that one has not considered the matter carefully, or that one does not know what is in the best interest of the child.

Here we touch on the issue of vanity. For many reasons, psychiatrists are often reluctant to admit, especially on a witness stand, that they do not know the answer to a question. Perhaps some psychiatrists do not know that they do not know. More often, there is something coercive and accusatory about the questions that are posed to the psychiatrist, as though implying that there may be something wrong or inadequate about him if he admits to innocence or ignorance. "What kind of an expert can *you* be, doctor, if you don't know the answer to a simple question like that?" says the hostile attorney, with his eyes wide in mock dismay. In such a setting, many a physician is conned and set up to claim a degree of knowledge that no physician can realistically possess.

In fact, one of the major problems of the forensic psychiatrist, whether trained in general psychiatry or in child and adolescent psychiatry, is that he is often asked to respond to questions he cannot possibly answer or cannot know definitely. Every custody dispute about the best interests of the child invariably entails a prediction about the future. How can anyone know whether Johnny will be better off in the future with his mother or with his father, especially if (as is usually the case) both of the parents suffer from the customary mixture of assets and frailties? After all, if one of the parents was actually a saint and the other a depraved sinner, the court would not have need for psychiatric expert testimony; it would be obvious which parent should have custody of Johnny. Rather, the psychiatrist is called in uncertain cases rather than clear-cut disputes. In a substantial number of instances, all the psychiatrist can say after carefully interviewing the parents and the child, after reviewing psychodiagnostic testing, and after reading the testimony of witnesses, is that he *does not know* which parent will be better for Johnny.

Generally psychiatrists have some skill in describing current ideas, feelings, and behaviors. It is often contested whether they are able to reconstruct past thoughts, affects, and actions. However, their record as predictors of future behavior, future emotions, and future ideas has rarely been outstanding. They dispute whether or not they can offer valid short-term predictions of violently dangerous behaviors, as in cases of involuntary hospitalization. If psychiatrists doubt their skills in such a brief time span and on such a specific action, how can they have the presumption to predict what is in the best interest of the child five, ten, or fifteen years in the future?

There is no lack of psychiatrists who are willing to provide such testimony. In some instances, books have been written that purport to tell the court when it is appropriate to set aside the legal protections that surround the integrity of family units, advising the court uniformly to place the alleged psychological needs of children ahead of the legal interests of their parents. Close inspection of such texts will frequently demonstrate that the predictions are based on psychiatric or psychological *theories* rather than based on well-designed longitudinal studies of the growth and development of statistically significant numbers of children recorded by atheoretical measures. Two highly influential, and highly biased, examples are the twin books *Beyond the Best Interests of the Child* and *Before the Best Interests of the Child* by Goldstein, Freud, and Solnit. In these books, psychoanalytic theory is applied to family court issues and numerous specific recommendations are presented for consideration and implementation. As demonstrations of how thought provoking psychoanalytic theory may be, the books are valuable. As serious research or as reports of serious research, they are worse than valueless—they are dangerous. The firm beliefs of the authors color their interpretations of their clinical data, and their convictions overpower their critical judgement. A far more useful book, more modest in its aspirations and based on more varied and atheoretical observations of human development is *Maternal Deprivation Re-Assessed* by Michael Rutter. In it, Rutter clarifies the complexities of time, age, person, and locale that are required in the most elementary description and potential prediction. The simple truth is that we really do not know enough about human beings to forecast their development and cannot provide reliable predictions about the best interest of the child in custody cases, except in the most obvious instances.

It is perhaps appropriate to note that the majority of psychiatrists in the United States are trained in general psychiatry, not in child and adolescent psychiatry. It is not farfetched to estimate that the majority of psychiatrists who testify in family law and juvenile justice cases, or who prepare reports on such issues for the court, are also general psychiatrists rather than specialists in child and adolescent psychiatry. Notwithstanding the June 1979 revision by the Liaison Committee on Graduate Medical Education (L.C.G.M.E.) to Section 20 of *Essentials of Accredited Residencies*, "Training Programs in Psychiatry," the exact amount of "the clinical portion of the curriculum" that "must provide experience in . . . psychiatric care of . . . children and adolescents in both inpatient and outpatient settings" varies substantially among different residency training programs in general psychiatry. It is relatively clear that general psychiatrists are less experienced in evaluating children and adolescents than are graduates of specialty programs in child and adolescent psychiatry. Exactly how many generalists are sensitive to the limitations of their expertise and express reality-based and appropriate modesty about their skills in the courtroom is matter open to conjecture.

It need hardly be noted that the same L.C.G.M.E. document also notes that "the clinical portion of the curriculum must provide experience in . . . forensic psychiatry." Both general psychiatrists and specialists in child and adolescent psychiatry tend to be willing to admit that they lack adequate training in forensic psychiatry. However, in the majority of instances, this encourages avoidance rather than continuing relevant education.

The task of the forensic psychiatrist, whether trained as a generalist or as a specialist in child and adolescent psychiatry, is undoubtedly difficult in family law and juvenile justice problems. However, the tribulations of the practicioner will be fewer if he can pursue his task with conceptual clarity and scientific honesty. Failure to know the precise issue under judicial consideration, failure to understand the criteria that determine the resolution of the issue, failure to understand the scope and limitations of existing clinical knowledge (as contrasted to metapsychological theories), and failure to reason clearly and cogently from relevant facts (as opposed to fancies) undermine much psychiatric-legal testimony. A willingness to admit honest ignorance, derived from gaps in scientific knowledge, a therapeutic modesty based upon the real resources available to the clients of the family law and juvenile justice systems, and an effort to explain (rather than to pontificate) will go a long way towards improving the image of forensic psychiatry in areas that affect children, adolescents, and families. More importantly, it will raise the value of psychiatric contributions to the court.

SUGGESTED READINGS

1. Arieti, S. (Ed.): *American Handbook of Psychiatry, Volume Two: Child and Adolescent Psychiatry,* 2nd ed. New York, Basic Books, Inc., 1975.
2. Arkes, H., and Garske, J.: *Psychological Theories of Motivation.* Monterey, Brooks/Cole Publishing Co., 1977.
3. Barker, P.: *Basic Child Psychiatry.* New York, Science House Inc., 1971.
4. Freud, A.: *Normality and Pathology in Childhood.* New York, International Universities Press, 1965.
5. Goldstein, J., Freud, A., and Solnit, A.: *Before the Best Interests of the Child.* New York, The Free Press, 1979.
6. Goldstein, J., Freud, A., and Solnit, A.: *Beyond the Best Interests of the Child.* New York, The Free Press, 1973.
7. Hall, C., and Lindzey, G.: *Theories of Personality.* New York, John Wiley & Sons, Inc., 1957.
8. Heacock, D. (Ed.): *A Psychodynamic Approach to Adolescent Psychiatry.* New York, Marcel Dekker, Inc., 1980.
9. Josephson, M., and Porter, R. (Eds.): *Clinician's Handbook of Child Psychopathology.* New York, Jason Aronson, 1979.
10. Josselyn, I.: *Adolescence.* New York, Harper & Row, 1971.
11. Kessler, J.: *Psychopathology of Childhood.* Englewood Cliffs, Prentice-Hall Inc., 1966.
12. Marohn, R. (Ed.): Legal and Psychiatric Perspectives on Delinquency and Acting Out. In *Adolescent Psychiatry.* Chicago, University of Chicago Press, 1979, vol. VII.
13. Mussen, P.: *The Psychological Development of the Child.* Englewood Cliffs, Prentice-Hall Inc., 1963.
14. Noshpitz, J. (Ed.): *Basic Handbook of Child Psychiatry.* New York, Basic Books Inc., 1979.
15. Office of Children's Services, Judicial Conference of the State of New York: *Desperate Situation — Disparate Services: Psychiatric Hospital Care for Court Related Children in the City of New York.* New York, July 1973.
16. Office of Children's Services, Judicial Conference of the State of New York: *Juvenile Injustice.* New York, Oct. 1973.
17. Office of Children's Services, Judicial Conference of the State of New York: *The P.I.N.S. Child: A Plethora of Problems.* New York, Nov. 1973.
18. Patterson, C.: *Theories of Counselling and Psychotherapy.* New York, Harper and Row, 1966.
19. Piaget, J., and Inhelder, B.: *The Psychology of the Child.* New York, Basic Books Inc., 1969.
20. Rice, P.: *The Adolescent.* Boston, Allyn and Bacon, 1975.
21. Rosner, R.: The Adolescent Day Care Program. In Heacock, D. (Ed.): *A Psychodynamic Approach to Adolescent Psychiatry.* New York, Marcel Dekker, Inc., 1980.

22. Rosner, R.: Long-Term Versus Short-Term Hospitalization. In Heacock, D. (Ed.): *A Psychodynamic Approach to Adolescent Psychiatry.* New York, Marcel Dekker, Inc., 1980.

23. Rosner, R.: Psychiatric Medications with Adolescents. In Heacock, D. (Ed.): *A Psychodynamic Approach to Adolescent Psychiatry.* New York, Marcel Dekker, Inc., 1980.

24. Rosner, R., Wiederlight, M., Rosner, M., and Wieczorek, R.: An Analysis of Demographic Variables in Adolescent Defendants Evaluated in a Forensic Psychiatry Clinic. *Bull Am Acad Psychiatry Law, 4(3):*251–257, 1977.

25. Rosner, R., Wiederlight, M., Rosner, M., and Wieczorek, R.: *A Comparison of Violent and Non-Violent Adolescents Evaluated in a Forensic Psychiatry Clinic.* Oral presentation at the annual convention of The American Academy of Psychiatry and the Law, New Orleans, October 1977.

26. Rosner, R. Wiederlight, M., Rosner, M., and Wieczorek, R.: Adolescents Accused of Murder and Manslaughter: A Five-Year Descriptive Study. *Bull Am Acad Psychiatry Law, 7(4),* 1980.

27. Rutter, M.: *Maternal Deprivation Reassessed.* New York, Penguin Books, 1972.

Chapter 12

THE HISTORICAL ROOTS
AND DEVELOPMENT
OF PSYCHIATRIC INVOLVEMENT
IN DOMESTIC RELATIONS

Michael G. Kalogerakis, M.D.

It is generally recognized that, among jurists, domestic relations are an unpopular career choice. The judge who likes to deal with neatly defined legal issues in which the weight of the evidence alone determines the decision of the court, the judge who views his role as strictly judicial, to be distinguished clearly from that of the social scientist or mental health worker, the judge who remains a skeptic with regard to the value of psychiatric testimony in the court—that judge, if he has the choice and his wits have not left him, will steer clear of any involvement in domestic affairs.

The psychiatrist, for his part, however accustomed to working in a clinical setting with the intricacies of family relations, has a natural aversion to adversary procedure and little interest in exposing his judgments to the legal system's probing analysis.

Omnipotent strivings, an occupational disease known to both the bench and the couch, do not stand up well in courtrooms dealing with family disputes. The arena of domestic relations is clearly neither for the meek nor the arrogant, for neither fares well under the demands of an ugly divorce case or a difficult custody battle.

At the same time, there is a need for interested, competent individuals from both the law and psychiatry to serve the disturbed and distraught children and families whose problems bring them into court. There is also a need to reexamine the place of the psychiatric consultant in domestic relations and juvenile matters,

171

in the light of increasing criticism of that role and unfolding constitutional and other judicial developments.

This chapter will review selected aspects of the history of family law and its relationship to psychiatry and examine some of these in depth. A major focus throughout will be on the child and his rights, particularly as they interface with the rights of parents and the interventions of the state. As a psychiatrist, I shall attempt to delineate some of the difficult developmental and clinical issues that confront the clinician working in this area, while dealing only in passing with the many complex and important legal questions that we face.

Interest in the child by the court has evolved *pari passu* with society's own interest. Aries has pointed out that the notion of a child as a person in his own right did not enter social awareness until very recently in man's history. [1] Not until the 16th Century were children generally regarded as having physical or emotional needs specific to their stage of development. Kroll, however, details medieval laws regarding children, which make it apparent that Aries was only partly correct.[2] In modern times, the court's early concern can be traced through two rather distinct lines of development—the child in divorce, where custody is the issue, and the child who is abused or neglected by his parents or who runs afoul of the law. Later, the emotionally disturbed child in need of hospitalization often required involvement of the court. More recently, examination of minors' rights in a global sense has come to the fore and is being actively debated on many fronts.

In a review of the history of custody disputes, Derdeyn has pointed out that, whereas the father in eighteenth century England had a virtually unchallenged right to custody (since the child was essentially property), the mother in the nineteenth century gradually assumed greater importance until, in this century, she came to replace the father as the appropriate guardian, particularly of the younger child.[3] This occurred as women gained in-

---

[1] Aries, P.: *Centuries of Childhood.* New York, Knopf, 1962.

[2] Kroll, J.: The Concept of Childhood in the Middle Ages. *J Hist Behav Sci, 13:*384–393, 1973.

[3] Derdeyn, A.: Child Custody Contests in Historical Perspective. *Am J Psychiatry, 133:* 1369–1376, 1976.

creasing rights and as greater awareness developed of the needs of the child, leading to the formulation of the doctrine known as the tender years presumption.

At about the same time as the tender years doctrine was emerging, the notion of the best interests of the child began to appear in court decisions on custody. A direct outgrowth of the *parens patriae* function of the court (which had been crystallized in 1839 in Talfourd's Act and gave the court the power to determine custody of infants under seven), the principle was laid down in two decisions made nearly a half century apart:

1. In Chapsky v. Wood in 1881, a judge chose to award custody of a five-year-old girl to the maternal grandmother who had raised her, rather than to her father, saying that the paramount concern was the welfare of the child.[4]
2. In Finlay v. Finlay in 1925, New York's great jurist, Judge Benjamin Cardozo, specified in a classic decision that the court's role is to serve as *parens patriae* and do "what is best for the interests of the child."[5]

Though both of these doctrines, the tender years and the best interests, arose out of a growing concern to give the mother her due rather than as a developing interest in the specific needs of the child, it is apparent that they also represent the opening wedges that were to lead ultimately to major involvement of psychiatrists in custody matters, for it was but a short step from the tender years doctrine to questions of developmental stages and age-related needs. Similarly, best interests raised the question of the *range* of interests, from economic to emotional. Once custody decisions were no longer automatic, an expert was soon needed to make determinations that the court itself could not, except in a very general way. As the supremacy of the mother has come to be questioned more often now than earlier in the century, the need for data and testimony has become critical in contested cases to help decide with whom the child would be best off.

Turning now to the second early concern of the court with

---

[4] Chapsky v. Wood, 26 Kan. 650 (Kan. 1881).

[5] Finlay v. Finlay, 148 N.E. 624 (N.Y. 1925).

family matters, the ungovernable and delinquent child, a number of historical events preceded the founding of the juvenile court. With the exception of children under seven, who were protected under English common law, child offenders had always been held criminally liable and were jailed with adults. In 1756, the Marine Society in England established a school for the reception and reform of younger criminals, followed in 1788 by a similar effort in London. True reform did not take place until the nineteenth century, however, with the establishment in New York City in 1825 of the House of Refuge for child offenders and, later, training schools and reformatories in England as well as the United States. Even prior to the establishment of the juvenile court, Massachusetts, in 1869, made it a law that courts must give written notice to the visiting agent of the State Board of Charities before committing children. The agent was to attend the hearing on behalf of the child and arrange placement in a family home if possible. This was probably the first time in Anglo-Saxon legal history that a social worker was officially introduced into court proceedings.

July 1, 1899, marks the event that Harvard's great legalist Roscoe Pound was to call "the greatest advance in judicial history since the Magna Carta." On that date, the state of Illinois established in Chicago the world's first juvenile court. Coming in the wake of a rise in delinquency related to the serious social conditions in the poorer wards of Chicago, it was recommended in a report of the committee of the bar, which said the following: "The fundamental idea of [juvenile court] law is that the state must step in and exercise guardianship over a child found under such adverse social or individual conditions as develop crime ... It purposes a plan whereby he may be treated, not as a criminal, or legally charged with a crime, but as a ward of the state."[6] From the start, it sought to replace the punitive approach to the offender with a compassionate approach, whose purpose was rehabilitation.

Here, in contrast to custody matters, the child was clearly the focus of the court's concern. The juvenile court shortly became a true *family* court in the hands of Judge Ben Lindsey of Colorado,

---

[6]Chute, C. L. : The Juvenile Court in Retrospect. In Vedder, C. B. (Ed.): *The Juvenile Offender.* New York, Doubleday, 1954.

who, in 1903, extended the court's jurisdiction to parents and others contributing to delinquency. Open hearings were replaced by private sessions in chambers, and families were encouraged to bring their problems into court. In the course of time, the concept of probation was introduced, and separate staffs having a distinctly social service function became a regular feature of the juvenile court. Adversary procedure, which is the essential ingredient of Anglo-Saxon jurisprudence and is ubiquitous in our other courts, virtually disappeared from the juvenile court.

Despite Dean Pound's assertion (he later changed his mind) and the hopes of the early idealists, the juvenile court has had a rocky course. Recently, the American Civil Liberties Union has asked for its abolition. The court came into bad times on a number of accounts:

1. The original concept, which called not only for a particular approach but sufficient, properly trained personnel in the court to implement the idea and a network of service outside the court, was realized all too rarely.
2. The results, which were supposed, as a consequence of introducing the treatment or rehabilitation model, to reduce recidivism, failed, thereby laying open to question the value of the social worker and psychiatrist in delinquency matters.
3. Due process considerations began slowly to eat away at the informality of the original model and, starting with the landmark Supreme Court decision *In re Gault* in 1967, introduced procedures that have narrowed the gap between the adult criminal court and the juvenile court. Today, only trial by jury remains as a major point of distinction between these courts.
4. Related to the concern with due process, more and more advocates have questioned the justification for maintaining court jurisdiction over non criminal offenses, i.e. the so-called status offenses such as truancy and running away. This is an area where the view of the clinician, who may be more concerned with status offenses as early warning signs that are harbingers of delinquency, comes into direct conflict with the civil libertarian's preoccupation with deprivation of liberty and intervention by the state.

Although under heavy attack for these and other reasons (the public has been increasingly vocal about the juvenile court's failure to provide sufficient protection against the violent offender and the recidivist), the court is likely to survive, albeit with significant changes. New York State has been in the vanguard of some of these changes, with its Juvenile Justice Reform Act of 1976 and the Omnibus Anti-Crime Bill of 1978, both of which introduced harsher penalties for juveniles committing specified crimes. The latter law now permits the state to try even a thirteen-year-old in the adult criminal court and to impose the same sentence that would be imposed on a mature adult convicted of a crime.

In another of its jurisdictions, the juvenile or family court is concerned with child abuse and neglect. In such cases, it is of course the parents or guardians who are being scrutinized, not the child. The role of the court here is *parens patriae* in the true sense, in that the child is felt to need the intervention of the court in its behalf in order to survive and prosper. Once an abusive family is identified, it will be evaluated and assisted by Child Protective Services. In those instances in which the parents do not cooperate and the neglect or abuse is severe enough to endanger the child, the matter is turned over to the court. At that point, the issue faced by the court is whether the child should be placed out of the home. Ultimately, the serious question of possible termination of parental rights may have to be confronted, and the input of the psychiatrist may be crucial to such a determination.

A totally different area is the problem of commitment of mentally ill minors to a psychiatric hospital. This, too, has been an area of intense activity on the part of libertarian forces and grew naturally out of the concern for the protection of the rights of the adult mentally ill. In part, the issues are the same as with adults, e.g. involuntary hospitalization should be reserved for those adjudged incompetent or mentally ill and dangerous to themselves or others. Differences arise with regard to voluntary admission; it has been affirmed that the so-called minor voluntary admission by which the parent agrees to have his or her child admitted to a hospital is a denial of the rights of the child, since the child's opinion is neither sought nor considered. What procedures are necessary to assure due process? How old must the child be before wishes concerning himself outweigh his parents'? What about traditional parental prerogatives in decisions that concern the child's welfare?

In June, 1979, the U.S. Supreme Court handed down its long-awaited decision in *Parham v. J. L.* and *Secretary of Public Welfare v. Institutionalized Minors.*[7] It dealt with these questions and, at least temporarily, laid to rest much of the controversy.

This overview has touched on issues of concern to the child and adolescent psychiatrist and other mental health professionals. In what follows, I should like to consider each of these major areas in greater detail. The emphasis will be on the role of the psychiatrist serving as consultant to the court, with some thought given to the further evolution of this role as it applies to domestic relations.

CUSTODY

Uncontested divorces seldom require psychiatric consultation, since the issue of custody is usually resolved before the court appearance, and action by the court is not needed. Contested cases, on the other hand, generally end with the children becoming pawns in the struggle between the parents and getting trapped in a loyalty conflict. In these cases, the court typically needs the help of experts in arriving at a decision on who should get custody and will frequently turn to the psychiatrist experienced in custody matters.

The psychiatrist in this situation may be called upon to do the following:

1. Evaluate the parents as to suitability and fitness
2. Evaluate the child developmentally with regard to ability to comprehend the events
3. Interpret the child's stated wishes
4. Render an opinion on how the child's best interests may be assured

In order to have access to all parties, maintain objectivity, and contribute most meaningfully, it is best that the consultant be

---

[7]Parham v. J. R., 99 S. Ct. 2493 (1979); Secretary of Public Welfare v. Institutionalized Juveniles, 99 S. Ct. 2523 (1979).

appointed by the court rather than one of the parties to the dispute. Even with such an arrangement, the task of the consultant can be inordinately difficult. What criteria determine fitness in a parent? When one is clearly destructive and the other reasonably healthy, there is, of course, little to decide. Much more likely is the situation in which there is psychopathology in both and one must weigh the potential impact of each on the child.

What of the child's wishes? Can they be taken at face value, regardless of age? What weight should they be given against other considerations? How does one evaluate the reality of the child's perceptions of the parents? At what point in development should the child have the right to choose between his parents?

From the legal standpoint, given the history of supremacy of parental rights, is it not time to mandate a lawyer to represent the children in custody battles? The guardian *ad litem*, who is sometimes appointed to represent the child's interests, is likely to be a comparatively weak advocate at a time when the most vigorous representation may be needed. In an era of emerging and widespread concern for minors' rights, this would seem a most appropriate next step in the evolution of the court's involvement with custody matters.

The primacy of the interests of the child is given strong support in an influential volume authored by Goldstein, Freud, and Solnit.[8] They state, "A child's placement should rest entirely on consideration for the child's own inner situation and developmental needs."

Elsewhere in their book, they develop another important concept, the notion of the *psychological parent.* After pointing out that biological parents have mistakenly (in a more romantic era) been "credited with an invariable, instinctively based positive tie to the child," a notion belied by such things as child abuse and abandonment, they go on to say the following:

> For the child, the physical realities of his conception and birth are not the direct cause of his emotional attachment. This attachment results from day-to-day attention to his needs for physical care, nourishment, comfort,

---

[8] Goldstein, J., Freud, A., and Solnit, A.: Beyond the Best Interests of the Child. New York, The Free Press, 1973.

affection, and stimulation. Only a parent who provides for these needs will build a psychological relationship to the child on the basis of the biological one and will become his "psychological parent" in whose care the child can feel valued and "wanted". An absent biological parent will remain, or tend to become, a stranger.

Concerned with the basic need for continuity in a child's life, these authors have also taken two more controversial positions with regard to custody: first, that all custody decrees should be final (they are at present subject to continuous litigation), second, that the custodial parent should have the right to decide whether the noncustodial parent may visit. The latter seems an unnecessarily extreme position, which ignores both the basic rights and needs of both the child and the noncustodial parent and the well-established fact that vindictiveness, even on the part of usually reasonable people, is all too common in divorce. The former, though undoubtedly born of bitter experience with endless, destructive litigation in custody matters, also seems to this writer to be too rigid. In the area of human relations, particularly in the light of our limited capacity to predict and the never-ending potential of human error, it is risky indeed to preclude reconsideration of a custody decision regardless of changing events (which may, for example, involve diminished capacity of the custodial parent to care for the child). A more reasonable position would be to attempt to develop strict criteria for permitting relitigation of a custody decree, which should include a preliminary evaluation by a court-appointed psychiatrist.

JUVENILE DELINQUENCY AND CHILDREN IN NEED OF SUPERVISION

The psychiatric consultant to the court is called upon for two major purposes in delinquency-related matters:

1. A determination of competence
2. Recommendations for placement/treatment

Interspersed among these basic concerns are a variety of issues to which the psychiatrist may be able to make a contribution. They include evaluation of the parents with regard to their role in

the child's delinquency and, in general, of the pathogenic qualities of the home; predictions about the future behavior of the
child, particularly when violence is a potential; the degree of
security that must be provided in the placement contemplated;
the readiness of a child for return to the community, and so forth.

Competency determinations have not figured prominently in
the requests of the Family Court in New York State, but with the
recent furor over delinquents' being returned to the community
while still posing a threat, legislation is being introduced that will
mandate competency examinations.

Judges who view the juvenile court as a court of law in the strict
sense, i.e. as designed solely to establish guilt or innocence, are
not inclined to seek recommendations from mental health professionals prior to adjudication. Competence is their only concern.
Others, however, would rather have help in deciding how best to
plan for a child from the start and are not so concerned with the
question of guilt.

As the juvenile court has moved closer and closer to the criminal court model, adversarial procedures have been insinuated,
which sometimes cause serious problems for the psychiatric clinic
or the individual consultant. The post-Gault era ushers in the law
guardian as counsel to the child. Though this has contributed
greatly to the removal of abuses in many sections of the country
which have complied with the Supreme Court's decision, it has in
some notable instances redounded to the detriment of the child, at
least as seen from the psychiatrist's corner. In these cases, overly
zealous advocacy by the law guardian leads to his interpreting his
role as doing what his client wants, irrespective of age or mental
condition.[9]

The dangers in this interpretation should be evident to anyone
with even a superficial knowledge of developmental psychology
and psychopathology. The oppositional child will, as a matter of
course, assume a posture diametrically opposed to what may be
obviously in his best interests, e.g. placement, or to what his
parents want for him. Adolescents are characteristically so dis-
posed. As to psychopathology, the child psychiatrist knows that a

---

[9]Wizner, S.: The Defense Counsel. *Trial, 7(5):*30–31, Sept.–Oct. 1971.

child's judgment may be affected by many conditions, which would not in themselves be sufficient to have him declared incompetent. Yet, he is unable, even if cognitively mature, to speak for his own best interests because of intrapsychic conflicts with a self-destructive component.

When placement is at issue, the question of mandating it when the child or family will not cooperate may arise. Many in the mental health field maintain that coerced treatment will not work. Others prefer to argue that, often, leaving a child free in the community merely insures that he will continue on a destructive antisocial path and that in such cases it is incumbent on the state to intervene forcibly. They would apply this to the status offender as well, whom others, as mentioned earlier, would remove from the jurisdiction of the court altogether.

The psychiatrist who is concerned about the genesis and evolution of delinquent patterns will wish to intervene early, before any serious crime has been committed, in the hope of preventing such a course. Once again, the concerns of civil liberties proponents and the clinician may be in direct conflict.

What emerges clearly from this controversy between clinician and law guardian is that, as long as the law guardian eschews the role of advocate for the best interests in favor of a doing what the client wants position, there is no one but the judge (who must maintain a position of neutrality) to represent the best interests of the child. This has led this author to recommend introduction into juvenile proceedings of a *clinician-advocate* who could effectively execute this responsibility.[10]

Another familiar battleground where these two forces are apt to collide involves the prediction of dangerousness. A considerable literature supports the contention that psychiatrists and other mental health professionals are unable to predict with any accuracy whether a given individual will commit violence. Yet, the court (and placement facilities) need such predictions to plan appropriately, and it is likely that in the foreseeable future the psychiatrist will still be asked to make them. Clearly, such prog-

---

[10] Kalogerakis, M. G.: Developmental Issues and their Relationship to Due Process in the Family Courts. *J Psychiatry Law, 3:*493–499, 1975.

nostication is needed each time a child is released from placement, when it is not so much a matter of predicting that violence will be committed but that it will not.

Despite the pessimism widely expressed about our ability to predict violent behavior, it is my experience that, with careful evaluations, it is possible to do so for a segment of those adolescents who have already been involved in violent activity. In any event, placement for this group is invariably necessary to prevent more general psychosocial deterioration.

In making recommendations for placement of a delinquent child, the psychiatrist must weigh first the degree to which the antisocial activity was under the conscious control of the individual and second the degree to which anxiety (or other psychopathology) was a feature of the child's behavior. It is worth noting that, after years of minimizing the significance of psychiatric disturbance in these youngsters, careful evaluations have established the presence of significant psychopathology in many delinquent youths.[11]

CHILD ABUSE

What has happened in the area of delinquency has its counterpart in child abuse. Social service agencies, which have been mandated by law to identify and assist child-abusing families, have discovered after the first few years of effort that a much more significant input from mental health forces than was ever anticipated is needed to help families involved in abuse. The consequence is that a major effort is now being launched to integrate the expertise of protective services and mental health services in behalf of families in which abuse is a pattern.

Generally, only the most refractory cases are likely to come before the court. Parents who have failed to cooperate with protective services may have to be coerced and, in the extreme situation, threatened with removal of custody. Clinicians are aware that such an approach often backfires, since it increases guilt and fuels the cycle that may lead to further abuse. Perhaps more than in any

---

[11] Lewis, D. O., and Balla, D. A.: *Delinquency and Psychopathology.* New York, Grune & Stratton, 1976.

other situation he is likely to encounter, the judge handling an abuse case is called upon to be more than jurist, for the most sensitive of clinicians would be taxed in trying to maintain objectivity and compassion with such seriously troubled families.

Ultimately, of course, the court may have to deal with the awesome question of termination of parental rights. It has been my experience that this decision, always painful, is hardest for the best judges—those who are sensitive to the complexities of family life, aware of the importance to child development of adequate parenting, and genuinely compassionate. Lucid, thoughtful testimony from a psychiatrist in such cases is valuable, even necessary. Here again, prediction is involved, in that the psychiatrist recommending termination of rights is in effect saying that no manner of intervention is likely to alter the parents' destructiveness and that the child's growth and development will suffer significantly if he is not removed. One can never be too humble in dealing with such cases.

A related and in some ways more hazardous problem for the court, also requiring expert opinion, is the question of *emotional maltreatment.* Difficult enough for clinicians to define (how does one distinguish it from ordinary pathogenesis, in which parents are contributing agents but for which they cannot be held legally liable?), it is virtually impossible for the judge. New York's Family Court Act ventures a fairly acceptable statement.[12] Still, it is a long way from defining emotional maltreatment, to establishing its presence, to the imposition of legal sanctions. Despite these inherent difficulties, most authorities working in the area of child abuse feel it is essential not to limit the definition of abuse to physical assault, since all have seen serious psychological trauma inflicted by other means, and the impact on the child's life has often been more disastrous.

A word should be said about abuse of children in placement. In such cases, the institution or agency is operating *in loco parentis* and has a serious responsibility to protect its wards against neglect or abuse. Despite the best efforts, however, abuse occurs and is often the bane of an institution's existence. Controlling it and

---

[12] Family Court Act, State of New York, Sec. 1012.

dealing with staff who are prone to be being abusive are major problems, most severe when the institution is large, the children most disturbed, and recruitment of competent staff most difficult.

Though not domestic violence in the strict sense, and unlikely to lead to involvement of the family court, institutional child abuse can and often does lead to litigation against a voluntary agency or the state.

CIVIL COMMITMENT

Dissatisfaction with institutions has of course led to a series of judicial decisions and legislative changes that have revolutionized hospital practices and strengthened due process in commitment procedures. Some of the activity in this area has addressed hospitalization of children and, as described previously, has focused on use of the so-called minor voluntary admission.

In 1979, thirty-seven states had statutes that permitted parents or guardians to commit minors voluntarily to mental institutions. Most of these were passed in the years following publication in 1951 of a National Institute of Mental Health draft act on hospitalization,[13] which outlined procedures for voluntary admissions of adults and juveniles. Almost none of these laws provided for judicial due process prior to admission. Adults who voluntarily admitted themselves were, of course, able to sign themselves out. Minors, however, could only be released by the staff of the hospital or by those who volunteered their admission, their parents, or guardians. In addition, provisions for periodic review of hospitalization existed only in a few states. By and large, the liberty interest of minors in need of psychiatric hospitalization received scant attention, leading inevitably to court challenges:

In *Bartley v. Kremens,*[14] the plaintiffs, all minors over thirteen years of age, in a class action, attacked as unconstitutional the provisions of the Pennsylvania Mental Health and Mental Retardation Act of 1966 governing voluntary commitment and admission

---

[13]National Institute of Mental Health: A Draft Act Governing Hospitalization of the Mentally Ill. Public Health Service Publication No. 51.

[14]Kremens v. Bartley, 431 U.S. 119 (1977).

to mental health facilities. Before the matter could be heard by the Supreme Court, the Pennsylvania Legislature passed a new law, the Mental Health Procedures Act of 1976, which gave those fourteen or over the same rights as adults and by creating new distinctions between mentally ill and mentally retarded altered the original class action, which was then declared moot.

The lawyers for the plaintiffs subsequently modified their action to include minors under fourteen ("Institutionalized Minors"), and the matter was again brought to the Supreme Court.

In *J.L. & J.R. v. Parham*,[15] the plaintiffs, two children aged twelve and thirteen hospitalized in a state facility in Georgia, sued on the grounds that the Georgia law denied them due process in permitting hospitalization without providing them with a "meaningful and complete opportunity to be heard" or "initial and periodic consideration of placement in the least drastic environment." The U.S. District Court for the region invalidated the state law, and the state took the matter to the U.S. Supreme Court on appeal.

In an amicus brief on behalf of the State of Georgia, the American Psychiatric Association, the American Society for Adolescent Psychiatry, the American Academy of Child Psychiatry, and the American Association of Psychiatric Services for Children took a stand that the basic constitutional right and responsibility of parents to raise their children must be preserved except in "extraordinary circumstances" and that adversary procedures "in the context of the delicate emotional problems presented by these parent-child conflicts, will prove therapeutically counterproductive for the child."[16]

The A.P.A. brief goes on to say, "Amici contend that balancing the important competing interests at issue should lead this Court to except from formal hearing requirements those cases in which (1) parents in an intact family wish to admit (2) a pre-adolescent child (3) to an accredited institution (4) for a short-term period (e.g., less than 45 days)."

---

[15] J.L. & J.R. v. Parham, 412 F.Supp. 112 (1976).

[16] Amicus brief, Parham v. J.L. & J.R., by American Psychiatric Association, American Society for Adolescent Psychiatry, American Academy of Child Psychiatry, and American Association of Psychiatric Services for Children (October, 1977). No. 75-1690.

Thus, there was acknowledgment, first on the part of the State of Pennsylvania in its 1976 act, second by official psychiatry, that increased due process guarantees for minors being volunteered for psychiatric hospitalization were necessary. At the same time, however, the psychiatric profession sought to introduce distinctions relating to the child's age, the accreditation status of the institution, and the length of hospitalization.

In June, 1979, the Supreme Court decided as follows:

1. Due process at the point of admission is satisfied by an independent *medical* evaluation of the need for hospitalization and does not require a judicial hearing.
2. It affirmed the right of parents to admit their children for psychiatric hospitalization.
3. It rejected the notion that neither parents nor doctors can be trusted to act in the best interests of children in making medical decisions.
4. It underlined that the expertise for making such decisions lies with physicians and is "not the business of judges."
5. The Supreme Court also recognized the danger that "formalized fact finding hearings" may be significantly intruding into family relationships, as well as jeopardizing the treatment of a youngster, which generally requires parental cooperation.
6. While holding that periodic review of hospitalization was essential to meet due process requirements for initial admission, it did not address what procedures might be necessary to justify continuing a minor's confinement. It chose to remand this matter to the lower court for its consideration.

The Court failed to address the question of the age of a minor as an important factor in decisions about entering or leaving a psychiatric hospital. This is a matter that has concerned both clinicians and advocates. This and other unanswered questions led to the establishment by A.P.A. of a task force to develop a model statute on hospitalization of minors. (The work of this task force was not completed at this writing.)

SUMMARY

The history of the juvenile court and domestic relations has been reviewed from the standpoint of the psychiatrist's role. The four major aspects of a court's work that directly involve children and adolescents have been examined and the clinical conclusions facing the expert that emerge in each area have been discussed. Particular attention has been paid to minors rights issues, which are judged to be as important from the perspective of the psychiatrist as they are to the lawyer.

Chapter 13

FORENSIC PSYCHIATRY AND FAMILY LAW

THE HON. JUSTINE WISE POLIER

It is only possible to discuss the contribution of forensic psychiatry to family court law within a framework of diverse definitions of what one means by forensic psychiatry. As I read the excellent recent *Bulletin of the American Academy of Psychiatry and Law,* entitled "The Isaac Ray Award Symposium," I rediscovered the wide range of definitions and attitudes of psychiatrists toward forensic psychiatry. They ranged from the neat use of such formulas as "the application of psychiatry to legal issues for legal ends," which caused me as a Yale trained lawyer to exclaim "How many weasel words can be packed into one short phrase!"

Then there was also the rather defensive stance that "the forensic psychiatrist looks upon himself not as an excuse-giver but as a fact-finding or opinion offerer" who, nevertheless, is "criticized for performing according to rules dictated by society itself." From this vantage point, psychiatrists are described as seeking to be "objective, dispassionate, non-adversarial, unemotional and non-speculative." The latter description is exactly how judges and other professionals would like to see themselves and be seen. Can forensic psychiatrists really claim exemption from criticism on the ground that "they play no part in the making of the rules?" They may not draft the laws, though they may have been consulted, but theirs is a more direct responsibility as evidenced in the writings of Dr. Andrew Watson "On the Preparation and Use of Expert Testimony." He renders practical advice on the ways, after compensation has been determined, that clinical data are to be related to the legal questions that will be put by counsel and says that it will then be for counsel to decide "if it would be advantageous to proceed with their [clinical data] use." This can hardly be described as the passive, nonadversarial or objective role of expert testimony.

My own experience in regard to both expert testimony by physicians and psychiatrists in the field of workmen's compensation many years ago may add to my sensitivity toward the use and abuse of expert testimony. In a study done in the 1930s, I found that in controverted cases where the medical or psychiatric experts were paid by the insurance companies, they found no disability due to an accident in 80 percent of the cases, while experts paid by the union in the same cases found 100 percent disability due to the accident. It was only when impartial experts were introduced that testimony established substantial disability due to the accident in 60 percent of the cases.

To get back to definitions, I can find no better goals for forensic psychiatry than those summarized by Dr. Naomi Goldstein as the concerns of Isaac Ray:

1. Concern with the rights as well as the medical treatment of the mentally ill
2. Concern with the laws of commitment and with the moral right to treatment
3. Concern with the relationship between criminal actions and insànity, with alcoholism as an illness, *and* with social issues such as the proper care and rights of the indigent

These are but introductory remarks to my assigned task—a discussion of some memorable contributions by forensic psychiatry to family law, as I saw it operate in the court.

It is nearly forty years since I began my work on the bench. At that time, there was a remarkable woman, Dr. Helen Montague, as Director of Psychiatry for the Court. She had two or three assistants who worked in counties other than Manhattan. The clinic saw only those children and parents referred by a judge for diagnostic study or for advice as to hospitalization. There was a remarkable personal concern for individuals, unimpeded by constraints of due process or confidentiality in those days. What was most important was that her presence was a constant teaching experience that slowly stretched the understanding and gave insights into human behavior. There was also humor that allowed probation officers and judges to move from accustomed postures and long-held moralistic prejudices and pretensions.

An example, vividly recalled, is the frequent visits by Dr. Montague, who came from her office to confer with the judge in chambers about some perplexing problems that she felt would injure the child or parent if discussed in court or included in her formal written report to the court. She was concerned that any mention of sexual experience, family immorality, poor IQ testing, or emotional problems would bar a child from admission for treatment by voluntary agencies or widen the tensions between parent and child. I must add, parenthetically and out of chronological order, that as the years passed, the diminution of such concerns, and later the requirements of due process, combined to form barriers between court psychiatrists and court staff in personal efforts on behalf of individual children and families. Outward directed accountability often replaced inner directed responsibility.

At a later period, it was the clinic that supported the idea that it could provide short treatment to children and parents when they were accessible to treatment and so prevent unnecessary removal of a child from his or her family. In this program a team was developed to help the sparse clinic staff. It included advanced students from the Columbia University School of Social Work, a supervisor of case work, and some secretarial help to form an early interdisciplinary group. The student workers, with light case loads, were able to work closely with children and families. This, too, led to greater understanding by the court of the real conditions of life and of interpersonal conflicts within families. There was also an active advisory council that included men and women from the fields of mental health, criminology, what would today be called urbanology, and the court. They were the active fund raisers, as well as advocates for mental health services in the family court.

In recent years some proposals for reform in juvenile justice and social welfare have sounded as though the discovery of the importance of the relationship between parent and child, like the discovery of childhood, were new achievements in human history. However, the work with parents and children stemming from and developed by the mental health clinic long anticipated these so-called discoveries. Dr. Montague, after six years of work with parents and children, reported in 1945 that placement had been prevented in some 75 percent of the cases treated.

With the war, the city administration turned away from the development of treatment services in the court, as the mayor announced that Sheffield-Borden (milk) was more important than Stanford-Binet. Other factors contributed to a downhill slide of mental health services in the family court besides the lack of funds. Psychiatrists and psychologists appointed to public agencies, including the courts, became largely composed of young people seeking a steady income until they were established in private practice or older professionals no longer able to compete adequately in the growing marketplace of mental health professionals.

At the same time, more mental health professionals were employed by private agencies to select those children for whom care and treatment promised the most likely success. The dull-normal child, the child severely scarred by family disorganization, the child who was a runaway, the child with sexual experience, the child who had no cooperative family with whom to work, and the child of minority groups had little hope of acceptance by facilities that provided treatment.

Yet, from the beginnings in the 1930s, leaders in the mental health field and in law continued to show active concern about the absence of mental health services or for its discriminatory use in the courts and in agencies where children were placed by the court. Several important projects were developed by joint ventures between court and psychiatry in a time when the costs of such projects were not astronomical and when the best legal and psychiatric consultants were available without fee. Courses were given without charge to probation officers and child guidance workers after working hours. Recently I reviewed the budget for the continuation of the treatment clinic submitted by Dr. Montague to Dr. Marion Kenworthy, an active leader in the development of that clinic and the use of it for training social work students. The annual budget for 1945, including one psychiatrist, one supervisor, one social worker and two stenographers, was $12,800.

Other contributions from forensic psychiatry and law showed concern for social issues such as the proper care and rights of the indigent in the light of present problems or old problems perceived in new ways, two of which follow:

There was a joint project in 1943 to study three schools in Harlem that provided the highest concentration of delinquency cases. Dr. Max Winsor and Dr. Viola W. Bernard were on the first team. It sought answers to why the intelligence and educational achievement of children attending these schools began to decline in the third grade and continued to decline. It examined educational, social work, and court procedures as they affected the lives of these children. It challenged corporal punishment, school suspensions, and discrimination as practiced under law in all three areas. Long delayed, its findings were ultimately allowed very limited publication.

One of the most interesting projects that grew out of the experience of some forensic psychiatrists was made possible by private funding and the support of the presiding Justice. Under the direction of Dr. Harris Peck, aided by an interdisciplinary team, children and parents charged with delinquency or neglect were interviewed separately while awaiting an adjudicatory hearing. Then, after a finding was made, the clinic team made a recommendation on whether a child should be temporarily removed from the home, returned home pending a fuller study, or hospitalized for full study without further delay. As a result of this screening, there was a sharp decline in hospitalizations, and more careful planning of both temporary and long-term placement. The court now received some guidance from experts before acting, following an adjudication.

Unhappily, this project, like the old treatment clinic, was scrapped, not only due to lack of funding. It was sacrificed in the name of administrative efficiency, the promise of economies through greater centralization of forensic psychiatry for all the courts. There was little concern for the difference in needs for forensic psychiatry in a family court and the criminal court. In fairness, the quality of forensic psychiatry within the courts had been lowered so much as to leave it with few ardent protagonists. Besides, an older generation of psychiatrists dedicated to making their skills available to those who needed them most had become a generation of unfashionable elders.

In recent years, the onslaught against "the medical model"

intensified, and civil libertarians joined in attacks against governmental intervention or the imposition of treatment, except when a child wished it. Opposition to the failed medical model and due process protections were also reflected in the ever more stringent admission policies for children to mental hospitals beginning in the 1960s. They now accepted patients only if "homicidal, suicidal, or dangerous to themselves or others." Having battled against treating mental illness as a stigma, the drive now was directed to restricting admission for treatment to those regarded as psychotic. Hospitals were no longer seen as places to help people to get well or become better adjusted, unless the people were critically ill or dangerous. Like many other reforms in this recent period, new exclusionary policies and policing of mental hospitals were in large part a response to widespread abuses in law and poor quality services by psychiatry for the poor and minority groups as well as to fiscal restraints.

I would like to return for a moment to the concerns of Isaac Ray to ask some questions of forensic psychiatry today. My first question is, How many of those engaged in forensic psychiatry today have shown concerns as broad or deep as those of Ray 140 years ago? My second question is addressed to lawyers, judges, and civil libertarians. How far have they selectively chosen to be concerned in only one-half of important concerns outlined by Ray?

Have they become enamoured with and concentrated on concepts of due process for the mentally ill with too little regard for the need of or right to treatment? Have they become more actively involved in laws for commitment than in the moral right to quality treatment and the duty of the state to provide it? To what extent have they been actively engaged in or involved in such social issues as the proper and adequate care of the indigent?

Finally, my question for both forensic psychiatry and law is whether the time is ripe or approaching to move from concentrating in defensive fashion on past abuses in mental health services to a more positive concept of both law and psychiatry in helping human beings. I do not believe we must forever live in the shadow of Watergate or fears engendered by past abuses. There is urgent need to explore, with at least equal concern, past negligence and the denial of mental health services when and where needed in the light of what we know. Meaningful progress will depend on changes in our society that make possible, not only procedural safeguards, but a steady increase in substantive support for those who need assistance. The current notion that government or the doctrine of *parens patriae* must forever be viewed as the enemy is surely not the last word.

The true enemy of forensic psychiatry lies in the lack of imagination, the absence of commitment to extending or improving services, and the failure to develop the impartial objectivity, which Dr. Perr attributes to forensic psychiatrists. Forensic psychiatrists are not a breed apart from the human race. They, like lawyers, professors, and judges, are heirs to all human errors. But, they also have much to contribute in the future as they have contributed in the past.

This is especially important to the work of the family court, where interpersonal relationships are so important in every case, where inadequate homes, neighborhoods, abuse, delinquency, and emotional problems abound amid dire poverty. Yet, the role of forensic psychiatry will continue in the future, as in the past, to depend on many factors. It will depend on the quality and commitment of psychiatrists who choose to serve children and families involved in legal issues, and it will depend on how those in power value such services and select professionals. As ever, it will depend on funding, largely by the public sector, but funding will depend in part on the extent to which forensic psychiatry draws on experience and expertise to demand and help develop more effective ways of providing mental health services. Once again, this will require lonely digging, imaginative concepts, cooperative efforts, often without either compensation or glory.

Finally, forensic psychiatry can no longer claim immunity from criticism on the ground that law or society make the rules. It is responsible in a very special way for how the rules are implemented. From its vast expertise on the basis of professional observation and work, it is in a unique place to draw upon fact finding and knowledge as the basis for social change in policies and law affecting human welfare. As in other professions, it, too, needs a fair share of conscientious objectors who refuse to be used for purposes of which they disapprove or to answer questions that are inappropriate and invite misleading responses. It must also refuse to provide false certainties despite popular clamor, as in the area of prediction, when the data are lacking.

In summing up the heavy responsibilities and potential of forensic psychiatry, I recall the description by Heywood Broun in 1922 of psychoanalysis as a "science which deals with things which cannot be seen, or heard or touched."[1] Whether we accept or reject this definition, what I would hope is that forensic psychiatry, by its work, will enhance the ability of courts and the powerful who shape the laws affecting courts to see, hear, or touch beneficently those who need help, who need personal concern, who need mental health services, and who need far more than either custodial control or community neglect.

---

[1]"The Young Pessimists," reprinted, *New York Times*, Op Ed 1/1/79.

Chapter 14

FOCUS OF CLINICAL PRACTICE IN A FAMILY COURT MENTAL HEALTH SERVICE

RICHARD SCHUSTER, Ph.D., and PETER D. GUGGENHEIM, M.D.

INTRODUCTION

Clinicians in a forensic setting are typically asked to make assessments that essentially are predictions regarding future behavior. In a family court setting, mental health professionals usually become involved with cases in the dispositional phase, after fact finding, where the court is interested in appropriate dispositional alternatives. For instance, should a delinquent be given probation or placed in a secure or nonsecure facility; should a parent on a neglect-abuse case have his or her children returned at this time? These are questions that require astute clinical judgement as well as an understanding of the total situation, including the legal setting in which it occurs.

It has been suggested that psychiatrists and psychologists are inherently incapable of predicting future behavior, especially the future behavior of children and adolescents. Nonetheless, it is the responsibility of court-related mental health services to provide such predictive data to the judges, in so far as it is possible to do so. It is important to understand that the court does not expect the impossible, it merely expects an honest and thorough effort to provide what can realistically be given by psychiatrists and psychologists who examine children, adolescents, and their families.

This chapter is designed to provide clinicians with an orientation for clinical practice in family court. Its aim is to highlight the

The authors acknowledge gratefully the encouragement and assistance provided by Justice Joseph B. Williams, Administrative Judge of the Family Court of New York City, without whose support this chapter could not have been written.

196

issues and perplexities found in a family court setting in a large urban center. Hopefully this chapter will help clinicians gear their assessments to the court's purposes and the patient's needs. It is no way meant to be a comprehensive and/or complete delineation of clinical practice in a forensic setting. Many of the legal as well as clinical issues that are encountered are not explored. However, it is hoped that such an exposition will provide those clinicians who are unfamiliar with this unique setting with orientation and perspective. Through such an orientation and focus, mental health clinicians can begin to be a valuable asset in the decision-making process.

This material is based upon clinical methods and experience in the Family Court Mental Health Service. The case load of approximately 8,000 individuals yearly is referred to the service by the Family Court Judges.

THE FAMILY COURT SETTING

The New York City Family Court deals with a multitude of cases. Both children and adults are seen before this court. The family court handles juvenile delinquency, persons in need of supervision (status offenders), designated felonies, and juvenile offenders. Such cases involve juveniles sixteen years of age or under. In addition, the family court has jurisdiction and is concerned with custody and/or visitation, neglect and/or abuse, termination of parental rights, and adoption cases. Adults are the main focus of the court's attention in these cases, while children are evaluated when pertinent and necessary. Other types of cases before the family court involve family offense, paternity, and support. Patients in such cases are seen in the clinic for evaluations, frequently on an emergency basis to ascertain the need for immediate hospitalization.

Competency is another area in which the clinic becomes involved. More recently, the New York state legislature has mandated formal competency evaluation for juvenile delinquents.

Court procedures vary. In general, cases are first seen in the intake part. The intake judge decides basic questions regarding remand, parole, and so forth. In addition, the intake judge sets the hearing date. The case is then assigned to a hearing part. In the hearing part evidence is brought forth. After a hearing the judge makes a finding, i.e. a decision. When a finding has been made, the case moves into a dispositional phase. It is usually during the dispositional phase that the clinic becomes involved. (The judge has already ascertained that the respondent has violated the law. However, the judge has not decided what should be done. The clinic is therefore asked for clinical assessment and recommendations.)

On special occasions the clinic becomes involved prior to finding. For example, in cases where competency is unclear, determination must be reached prior to adjudication. In those cases posing potential danger to children in the home, the parent or surrogate is examined prior to finding to determine the necessity for removing a child from a dangerous situation. The majority of cases, however, are referred after findings and during the dispositional phase. It should be added that emergency evaluation for immediate hospitalization can occur at any time, as soon as a petition is drawn and ordered by a judge.

Although the necessity for clinical evaluation is raised by many sources, no patient can be seen unless ordered by the family court judge. Reports are prepared for the use of the court. The clinic serves as an arm of the court; reports are written at the judge's request to answer questions posed by the court.

BACKGROUND MATERIAL

In order for clinicians to evaluate the patient in respect to the judge's questions, pertinent background information is always helpful, if not essential, in understanding the issues surrounding the case. Background data is needed to provide a framework in which the clinicians can examine the patient. The gathering of pertinent background information is the job of the social work staff. Ideally, before a patient is seen by the clinician, the social worker has gathered pertinent information from a variety of sources (such as Department of Probation, Bureau of Child Welfare, mental health agencies, hospitals, and clinics.) A written summary of this information is provided for clinical use. If time does not permit the provision of a written report, a conference is scheduled to share gathered information. Single or multiple interviews are scheduled as clinical practice demands. A comprehensive report of the social worker's investigation is forwarded to the court in conjunction with the clinical evaluations. This provides a framework for the court; it fosters a longitudinal and cross-sectional assay.

JUVENILE CASES INVOLVING DELINQUENCY, PERSONS IN NEED OF SUPERVISION, AND DESIGNATED FELONS

Juvenile cases involve juveniles up to the age of sixteen as the primary focus. A child is adjudicated a delinquent if he has committed acts that would be labeled as crimes if he or she were an adult. A persons in need of supervision (PINS) child, or status offender, is a youngster who is found to be beyond parental control, i.e. who runs away from home or does not attend school, but who has not committed a criminal act. A designated felon is a thirteen–, fourteen–, or fifteen-year-old adolescent who has committed one of eleven designated felonies, all of a very serious nature, e.g. murder or rape. A juvenile offender is a newly legislated category of delinquent who because of the seriousness of the crime is first seen in criminal court. Removal to family court can occur at various junctures during criminal court proceedings.

The clinic is asked for recommendations regarding feasible dispositional alternatives. Such possibilities usually include probation, placement in a nonsecure facility, or placement in a secure facility. The fundamental criteria for such recommendations take into consideration both what is best for the patient and what is best for the community. The likelihood of continued delinquent activities and uncontrollable behavior must be evaluated. Recommendations are geared towards the least restrictive setting that will foster appropriate behavior for the juvenile and/or opt for rehabilitation. A recommendation for probation, therefore, indicates that the clinician believes the juvenile is capable of making an adequate adjustment in the community. The clinician believes the juvenile will not get into further delinquent activity, will attend school regularly, will behave appropriately at home, and so forth.

A recommendation for placement in a nonsecure facility indicates that the clinician believes the juvenile cannot make an adequate adjustment in the community—that if he remains in the home he will continue to behave in delinquent and/or uncontrollable ways. Therefore, it is felt that if he is removed to a more supervised environment in another community away from the usual community and peer influences, an appropriate adjustment can develop. A recommendation for placement in a secure facility indicates that the clinician feels the juvenile cannot make an adequate adjustment if he continues to live either in an open setting or in his home community. Such recommendations are typically for juveniles who are felt to be entrenched in their delinquent behavior, usually of a violent nature. The likelihood of continued antisocial acts of a markedly aggressive fashion is high. Thus, there is a strong need for a restrictive enclosed setting. (Persons in need of supervision cannot be placed in a secure setting. They have technically not committed a crime; they cannot be detained for extended periods of time in a restrictive setting. If it is felt that such a child needs to be removed from the community, recommendations can be made for a nonsecure, supervised facility outside of New York City, making the possibility of elopement and/or involvement with the home community more unlikely.)

The clinical interview focuses not only on the patient's past history but also on his present mental status. The clinician attempts to ascertain if the patient's acting-out behavior is isolated in nature or entrenched. The clinician keeps many facets in mind while assessing the juvenile. For example, does the juvenile impress the clinician as being very street oriented; does the youngster manifest an underlying aggressivity or manipulative tendencies? Does the juvenile tend to have a psychopathic orientation indicative of characterological problems, or is his or her acting out a factor arising from neurotic intrapsychic conflict? The possible presence of retardation and/or minimal brain dysfunction is also explored. Such factors may contribute to impulsivity, poor judgement, poor planning ability, and little frustration tolerance—propensities that could easily foster delinquent acting-out behavior. The presence or absence of brain damage is assessed carefully.

In general, a good way to begin the interview is by asking for basic information. The ability to delineate innocuous information such as age and place in sibling order not only helps provide an assessment of intellectual capacities but also provides an understanding of attitudes. In this respect is he or she guarded, suspicious, belligerent, negativistic, friendly, or superficially glib? The interviewer may then focus on school involvement. It is particularly important to examine the early school history. Retention in an early grade suggests the possible presence of learning difficulties and/or hyperkinetic behavior that may have inadvertently fostered acting out in the classroom. Is the patient a truant? Has he been suspended often? If he does become suspended, is this due to fights, lateness, or failure to attend school? Is he failing his courses? Not only is the patient questioned about such areas, but his explanations for his actions are also examined. In this way the clinician gathers information regarding the patient's understanding of his problems. The examiner is cognizant of the patient's quality of thinking and defensiveness. Is the patient very concrete and nonintrospective; does he tend to minimize, externalize and/or rationalize his problems? Does he show some degree of insight into his difficulties? The patient is also questioned about his delinquent record as well as the allegations regarding the current delinquency petition. Important issues to examine in this area are whether the patient initiated such actions by himself or with others. Is he part of a gang? Are his actions well planned or impulsive? How long has he been engaging in delinquent activities? Does he show remorse for his actions? In this way the clinician not only obtains a history but tries to elicit from the juvenile his understanding of what causes such behavior. Further areas of inquiry involve the juvenile's behavior at home. Areas of investigation include the juvenile's perception of any problems in the household. Does he keep curfews? Is he respectful to his parents? Does he fight with other family members? His understanding of the family situation is important. Previous psychiatric history is mandatory. The clinician explores the reason for referral for any psychiatric treatment. Finally, the juvenile is asked for his feelings regarding proper dispositional plans. Surprisingly, some juveniles ask to be removed from the home and the community, believing that if they remain at home they will just get into further difficulties. Whatever the juvenile's feelings regarding proper dispositional plans, the patient's reasons for such requests are elicited. If the juvenile says that he feels probation is proper, the clinician then explores how he expects to live his life differently in order to make an adequate adjustment in the community.

Reports sent to court vary; they must include, however, the patient's basic appearance as well as clinical impressions regarding his demeanor, attitude, and so forth. Appropriate quotes to convey the essence of the interview are extremely useful. A completed mental status is mandatory. This section contains an estimate of the patient's intelligence. Any peculiarities in speech, manner, or affect are noted. Feelings about the juvenile's capacity for judgement, impulse control, frustration tolerance, and insight are needed. Questions regarding suicidal and/or homicidal ideation and intent, as well as evidence of psychotic processes are mentioned. In addition, any other pertinent information such as the possibility of organic factors, memory defects, drug abuse, or marked mood states are also stated. A diagnostic impression is indicated as well. In addition, it is suggested that a conclusion or summary section be included after the diagnostic impression. This helps to integrate all pertinent information for the court's use. The recommendation section follows. The recommendation section is congruent with the information stated in the report. It is geared to answer the judge's question, usually regarding proper dispositional alternatives. Reasons for the recommendation are succinctly stated.

In the evaluation of children involved in delinquency or status offenses, collateral interviews with parents or parent surrogates are needed. Such interviews are almost always with the juvenile's mother but occasionally an interview with another parental figure such as a father, aunt, or grandmother may also be necessary. Interviews entail the gathering of basic background information from the parental figure (i.e. age, work status, education, and psychiatric history). Information regarding the juvenile's perinatal history, developmental history, educational background, psychiatric history, delinquent records, and behavior at home is helpful. The parent's understanding and attitude regarding the juvenile's acting out is also needed. The parental figure is questioned regarding his or her feelings for a proper dispositional plan. It is not unusual for the parental figure to state that placement of the child is needed to forestall further delinquent acts. The focus of collateral interviews is not only for the clinician to gather basic background information but also for the clinician to assess the parental figure as an adequate supervising influence for the juvenile in the community. Such an assessment includes a descriptive evaluation of the parental figure's current mental condition, child-parent interaction, and parental attitudes as well as the parent's concern regarding disposition. In this respect the clinician not only examines the parental figure's desires and feelings regarding the child but also gives his or her evaluation of the parental figure as a good resource for this child in the community. Reasons for such statements are delineated.

PSYCHOLOGICAL EVALUATION IN PINS, DELINQUENCY, AND DESIGNATED FELONY CASES

Psychological evaluations are needed in order to aid placement of juveniles; in designated felony cases they are mandated by law. Testing includes an intelligence test (usually a WISC-R), a word recognition test (WRAT reading), Bender gestalt, and projectives. The initial focus of evaluations is on the patient's current level of intellectual functioning as well as the juvenile's educational capacities and potential. Evidence of minimal brain dysfunction and the presence of learning disabilities are examined. Psychodynamics regarding the patient's acting out are also explored. In this respect the clinician tries to formulate the etiological factors fostering the patient's maladaptive behavior, as well as to provide the court with an understanding of the patient's experience of his or her world. Particular emphasis on possible characterological problems is helpful. If intrapsychic dilemmas are contributing to the child's behavior, this is also delineated. Evidence of psychopathology, particularly psychosis, is mentioned; its ramifications regarding acting out, as well as placement alternatives, are also explored. Conclusions, integrating material from the test protocol, are drawn with emphasis on proper dispositional alternatives.

CUSTODY VISITATION DISPUTES

Custody and visitation disputes arise usually as a result of antagonism between warring parents. The petitioner in such cases is that parental figure who does not have custody of the child or who does not have adequate visitation with the child. The court may request a mental health study to assess the situation. The study is used by the judge as one of the factors in making a decision. The recommendations take into consideration the child's best interest as well as the rights of the parents. The clinician evaluates the circumstances and background surrounding the case, the parental figure's current mental status, the child's psychiatric condition, and the child's wishes. Although most cases involve both custody and visitation, occasionally only one or the other may be an issue. Visitation should not be granted if the clinician feels that visits can be detrimental to the child. This is particularly the case if it is felt that physical harm to the child or marked emotional turmoil is a potential. If visitation is beneficial (or at least neutral to the child's well-being) but the parents sabotage such visitation arrangements, visitation in a supervised neutral setting where the parents avoid contact is recommended. It should be noted that statements made by parental figures involved in such cases are often bitter and full of resentment. Typically they accuse each other of being violent, abusive, alcoholic, psychotic, irresponsible, etc. Each parental figure often accuses the other of wrongdoing. Consequently, it is up to the clinician to ferret out the reasonableness of such accusations by looking for inconsistencies in the history as well as incongruities made by parties when viewed in light of the current mental status. In this way negative statements made by parental figures must be internally consistent with the history and congruent with the present mental condition of the other party. For example, if a wife describes her husband as violent or explosive, her statements are given more credence if her husband impresses as agitated, impulsive, and negative during the interview or if other parties, particularly neutral collaterals and children, corroborate crucial statements.

Interviews with primary parental figures entail an assessment of their current mental status, the petitioner's and respondent's understanding of the history regarding the current case, and their feelings about the most appropriate dispositional plan. Chronological information presents the initial point of departure. The client's basic demeanor and way of relating can be assessed when questioned about benign material in a structured interview. A marital history is gathered. Information relating to the patient's first meeting, difficulties in their relationship at early periods, their understanding of what caused marital problems, and so forth are explored. Current visitation schedules are assessed; any difficulties arising from such a schedule need to be noted and delineated. Psychiatric histories, if present, are pertinent. A history of psychiatric treatment, the reason for referral, type of treatment, medication given, and similar factors are examined. If the allegations describe assaultive behaviors and/or drug abuse, these assertions are particularly crucial. The interview is concluded by stating the patient's feelings about a proper plan for the child. In this way the clinician not only gathers the patient's perspective attitudes and wishes regarding the custody visitation dispute but also garners an understanding of the patient's basic way of relating and possible psychiatric symptomatology. In a court situation particularly, actual quotations form the basis of subsequent clinical impressions and recommendations.

Interviews with children are geared towards an assessment of the child's current mental status as well as the child's understanding of the circumstances involved. The clinician must be certain that the child understands what the case is about. Basic background information is gathered from the child. The child is questioned about his or her feelings regarding the custody-visitation dispute. Explanations of the child's statements are examined. The clinician must be aware of possible coaxing or coercion by parental figures to influence the child to make statements against the child's true wishes. If the child suddenly uses phrases that are beyond his age, intelligence, or typical manner of speaking and/or appears very fearful of expressing his or her ideas frankly, this may indicate that the child has been coached, coerced, or influenced. As a rule children are reluctant to take sides in parental disputes. The child's perception of parental figures is investigated. Incongruities in the child's statement are noted and explored. For example, if the child states that he does not want to visit a parent but cannot provide an explanation for such a wish nor can he describe any substantial problem or dislike for such a figure, such incongruities need further examination. Asking the child what he particularly likes or dislikes about parental figures is often helpful. The clinician must be particularly alert to transient situational disturbances arising from the current family tensions. If such tensions are contributing to psychopathology, the type of symptoms and possible etiological factors are discussed.

Collateral interviews often are helpful in custody-visitation disputes, including grandparents, babysitters, paramours, etc. These people are knowledgeable in the case and may contribute pertinent information; they are often parental surrogates. Basic chronological information is gathered including a psychiatric history. Any pertinent background information regarding their understanding of the case is elicited and explored. If such a figure is to be utilized as a primary parental caretaker (such as when the father goes to work), the ability to function in such a role is evaluated.

NEGLECT AND ABUSE CASES

Neglect and abuse cases constitute perhaps the most fascinating and certainly the most sensitive cases seen. Cases may involve allegations of parental neglect or lack of responsible behavior. Typically such charges include leaving a small child unattended, failing to feed the child regularly, failing to take the child for proper medical treatment, etc. Willful or malicious intent alternates with poor judgement, intellectual limitations, or psychiatric disorders. Abuse allegations involve excessive corporal punishment, malicious physical beatings, impulsive violent acts, and so forth, as well as severely traumatizing the child by markedly destructive and willful acts (such as locking the child in a closet for

.extended periods of time as a punishment). Neglect implies a more passive failure to behave responsibly as a parental figure, thus causing the child harm. Abuse implies a more active willful destructive action. Both may be conscious and purposeful; however, there are some cases of neglect that are strictly involuntary. In such cases the parent (usually due to intellectual and/or psychiatric deficits) is unable, despite a manifest desire, to act responsibly. The child is thus neglected because the parent lacks sufficient psychological or intellectual resources to act appropriately.

Cases involving neglect and abuse are referred to the clinic after a judicial finding. The judge is interested in a feasible explanation and dispositional recommendations. The clinic's recommendation is geared towards the child's best interest. Ideally the clinician tries to formulate a recommendation that enables parental figures to maintain contact with their child, develop a more productive family relationship, and (most importantly) protect the child from future neglect or abuse. The child can be returned to the family only if potential danger can be ruled out. However, this is usually not the case. More frequently children cannot be returned home, since it is felt that the potential for abuse or neglect is still high. Suggestions to intervene therapeutically are provided. The possibility of visitation at an agency or home visits is also explored. Recommendations are thus geared to help the family develop a healthier way of interacting, hopefully without severing present parent-child ties. Nevertheless, if continued parent-child contact is viewed as detrimental to the child or currently unrealistic, then the clinician does not jeopardize the safety of the child to help assuage the parent or child's sense of loss or the family's desire for a swift family reunion.

Background material is particularly important, especially if the data reveals a previous history of neglect and/or abuse as well as consistent failure to follow through on appropriate treatment and preventive plans. This not only provides a framework to understand the respondent's current problems and behavior but aids in formulating recommendations. The clinician explores the patient's action as an isolated impulsive act or part of an entrenched pattern of neglect and/or abuse. In addition, the clinician attempts to investigate whether the respondent's actions arose from poor judgement, intellectual limitations, psychiatric disorders, or maliciousness. Markedly abused children may be used as scapegoats by abusive parents. Such parents are not psychotic or intellectually limited; they appear to be entrenched character disorders who utilize their children as outlets to alleviate tensions or aggressivity in themselves.

Occasionally children are abused as a means to coerce. A prime consideration is whether such coercion is likely to continue if the child is returned to the patient. In other cases the clinician may feel the parent is fundamentally benign but may still opt to keep the child in placement. The child cannot be returned home due to the parent's mental condition or intellectual limitations. If intellectual limitations and/or psychiatric disorders mitigate against the return of the child, then recommendations emphasize the need for appropriate support systems or treatment.

Interviews with respondents in such cases focus on the respondent's current mental status, his history, his understanding of the allegations regarding the current petition, and his wishes regarding the return of the child. Basic chronological information is gathered first. The interview then focuses on the patient's understanding of the allegations, as well as other related history. Any abnormalities, peculiarities, incongruities, or rationalizations by the respondent are explored. Inconsistencies in the respondent's statements are particularly suggestive of confusion, minimization, externalization, or lying. Inconsistencies are thus explored in great detail. Suggestions by the respondent regarding the return of the child are also examined. Reasons for the neglect and/or abuse are postulated and tied in with the history, interview, and current mental status.

The neglected or abused child is seen whenever possible. The child's current mental status is important. A question uppermost in the clinician's mind is whether any psychopathology that the child exhibits is a result of the abusive or neglectful situation. Does the child appear to be severely traumatized; has consistent parental neglect fostered substantial intellectual and/or emotional blunting? Is the child developing significant psychiatric disturbance due to a long-standing history of abuse and/or neglect? Basic information from the child is gathered, such as what the child's grade in school is and who the child lives with. The child's statements regarding the allegations need to be explored. Again, the clinician pays special attention to incongruities or inconsistencies in the child's statements. The child's wishes regarding disposition are noted. Does the child want to return home or remain in placement? Whatever the child's response, explanations regarding such statements are elucidated.

Collateral interviews on neglect/abuse cases are often done. Such parties typically include parents of the respondents, foster parents taking care of the children, etc. The focus is on the history and pertinent background information, as well as the patient's basic mental status, particularly if they are to be used as a resource for the child.

PSYCHOLOGICAL EVALUATIONS FOR NEGLECT-ABUSE AND CUSTODY-VISITATION CASES

When situations arise where a psychiatric or clinical evaluation needs to be amplified, particularly in cases of mental retardation, psychological testing is administered. If the patient is retarded, the presence of organic factors is examined. Are the patient's intellectual capacities limited by organic/neurological deficits? In other cases there is a long history of psychiatric illness. The patient may show periods of lucidity followed by periods of disorganization to a varying degree. A psychological evaluation may thus be helpful in clarifying the patient's current mental status and degree of stability. In other cases the patient's basic adjustment is obscure; the history, clinical impressions, and interview do not mesh into a coherent picture. Psychological testing may clarify ambiguities, integrating diverse material into an understandable pattern. All such psychological evaluations are specifically geared to the referral question. They are used as adjuncts to the clinical or psychiatric evaluations. Information from psychological assessments are combined in the mental status, diagnostic impression, and conclusion section of the respective clinical or psychiatric report.

TERMINATION OF PARENTAL RIGHTS
OR PERMANENT NEGLECT

In order to adopt a child that has been adjudicated neglected, the parental rights of the natural parent must be abrogated judicially. If parents are felt by placement agencies to lack a real interest in their children for an extended period or are permanently impaired (either due to mental retardation and/or psychiatric disturbance), the agency will institute a termination of parental rights or permanent neglect proceeding. Although both types of cases are designated to end parental rights, they arise for different reasons. In termination of parental rights the agency attempts to prove that the parent (due to impairment) cannot be an adequate parental figure in the foreseeable future, even if the parent earnestly desires to be reunited with his or her progeny. With permanent neglect there is no indication of marked impairment; rather, the parent has apparently opted to avoid keeping contact with the child in spite of diligent efforts by the agency to maintain parent-child contact over an extended period of time.

In abrogation proceedings the agency attempts to make a case that despite their diligent efforts the parent is unable or unwilling to establish ongoing contact with their child and it appears that they will be unable or unwilling to establish contact or assume a parental role with their child in the foreseeable future. Consequently, there is no reason to continue the natural parent's rights, especially if there is a chance for the child to be adopted (often by the foster parents with whom the child has been residing for many years). For the clinician in termination of parental rights cases, two main issues are mental retardation and/or chronic psychiatric disturbance. The clinician must make an assessment whether the patient's mental capacity is such that the patient can assume parental obligations and responsibilities; if he or she can, then it must be determined under what circumstances this is possible. If retardation is a factor, then psychological testing is needed. The presence of organic factors is explored. If there is a long history of psychiatric illness, the patient's prognosis is important as well as his or her current mental status. Interviews contain basic chronological information, psychiatric history, the patient's explanation of circumstances surrounding the allegations (as well as other related history), and the patient's plans and wishes regarding the children. The clinician is atuned to inconsistencies and glib excuses. Confusion regarding plans, child rearing practices, and history are noted and explored. If termination is not recommended, the report emphasizes that the patient does not exhibit current mental disorder or intellectual limitation that will intrude on his or her ability to function as an adequate parental figure.

Where possible, the children are interviewed as well. In some cases children show marked psychiatric problems and retardation. If this is the case, then the parent's ability to take care of children with marked handicaps demanding special attention is also considered. Occasionally the judge will ask specific questions in such a case; the focus of the report is always geared to answer the judge's specific questions, as well as more general issues. Ultimately the child's best interests need be considered.

Background information is essential. This is particularly true regarding a patient with chronic psychiatric hospitalizations. A history of continued psychiatric hospitalization with short lapses of reconstitution is examined closely. In cases of retardation the primary question is whether the patient's ability to function as a parental figure can be improved with appropriate remediation or education. The focus of the evaluation is thus on the etiology of the patient's retardation. If there is clear evidence of marked neurological/organic impairment, this augurs poorly for the patient's capacities to be rehabilitated substantially with remediation. However, if retardation is due to psychosocial deprivation, lack of education, and/or psychiatric disturbance (that could be mitigated with appropriate treatment), the prognosis is more favorable for the eventual return of the children.

Evaluations may entail both psychiatric and psychological assessments. Reports attempt to combine pertinent background information with the patient's current mental status to develop a clear assessment of the patient's ability to function in a parental role in the foreseeable future. A child can remain in placement even if parental rights are not terminated. Presumably the patient shows a capacity to function as a parent in the future. He or she appears willing to maintain contact with his or her children but is unable to take the children home at the present time; the recommendation then can be for continued placement without terminating parental rights.

FAMILY OFFENSE

Family offense involves an allegation by one family member (petitioner) that another family member (respondent) is harassing the petitioner in some way. This can be a physical way such as beating the other party or destroying property in the household or it can be a nonassaultive but harrassing manner such as threats, continual yelling, screaming, drunken behavior, banging on the door at night, and threatening telephone calls. The party that feels threatened (petitioner) comes to court for an order of protection. This allows the petitioner to have the respondent arrested if the respondent violates the stipulations in the order of protection. The clinic rarely becomes involved in these cases for long studies, since there is no need for a dispositional plan. However, the clinic is frequently involved in such cases on an emergency basis. At those times the court is asking if there is a need for immediate hospitalization of one or both parties. If there is no need for hospitalization, a referral to an appropriate outpatient community mental health center may be instituted.

EMERGENCY EVALUATIONS

As previously mentioned, at any time during a patient's court involvement the judge can order an emergency evaluation to ascertain whether there is a need for immediate hospitalization. Such requests are made by the judge if there are indications either from the allegations, assertions made by involved parties, and/or the patient's behavior in the courtroom to indicate that there is evidence of marked mental disturbance. If the judge feels that there may be a need for immediate psychiatric hospitalization, the patient (as well as other parties involved in the case) is referred for an emergency evaluation. This entails reviewing the court folder and related material, speaking to pertinent parties (such as parents, BCW workers, or agency workers), and then interviewing the patient. A clinical assessment is provided to ascertain the degree of mental illness and the potential for violence. (The law states that the patient can be remanded to a city hospital if there are signs of mental derangement in addition to indications that the patient is a danger to himself or others.)

The clinician attempts to formulate a current mental status with diagnosis if possible. The clinician is faced with two problems: (1) can a diagnosis be made on an outpatient basis or is inpatient observation necessary? (2) is necessary treatment in a hospital setting mandatory? In either case immediate hospitalization is recommended to the court. It is the court then who remands the patient to the hospital. The judge decides to take the clinician's suggestions and recommendations regarding hospitalization, as is almost always done, or for legal reasons, does not.

Ideally, the clinician who makes the referral for hospitalization remains in liaison with appropriate hospital staff. In this way the hospital coordinates their efforts with the court to provide the quickest and most comprehensive assessment of the case. The clinician helps clarify the hospital's questions so that the hospital can expeditiously provide an answer to the judge's concerns regarding this patient. The mental health service attempts to maintain close communication with the appropriate city hospital.

Questions of competency may arise during an emergency evaluation. If competency cannot be ascertained fully on an outpatient basis, hospitalization is requested. Referral questions are forwarded to the hospital, as well as initial impressions, pertinent background information, and possible resource persons for the hospital to contact in order to aid their study.

COMPETENCY

Recently, a law was passed in New York State regarding competency for juveniles. This law states that a person must be assessed when the issue arises to determine his ability to stand trial. If due to mental illness, mental retardation, or developmental disability his capacity is limited, he cannot proceed. Competency evaluations require that two psychiatrists examine the respondent for mental illness. If there are indications of retardation or defect, one or two qualified psychiatrists and one certified psychologist are necessary to evaluate competency. The focus is the respondent's "capacity to understand the proceedings against him or assist in his own defense." Basically the patient must show an understanding of court proceedings; he should understand the charges against him; he should be able to delineate circumstances surrounding the allegations in the petition. If due to mental illness or retardation he is unable to provide such information or understand the proceedings, then the patient is designated incompetent. The adjudication of incompetence is a court function based on clinical input.

There is no statute at this time that directly relates to patients who may be incompetent in PINS, custody-visitation, or neglect-abuse proceedings. In general, such patients are either evaluated for competency according to the preceding guidelines by the clinic staff or are remanded to the hospital for an extensive evaluation.

CONCLUSION

This monograph is a short overview of the fundamental issues involved in a family court forensic setting. As previously mentioned, it is by no means exhaustive. Each case has its idiosyncratic complexities. Of crucial importance is that reports are geared to the court's purposes. Clinicians must be responsive to the judge's questions; reports are combined to provide a coherent assessment regarding pertinent issues. All conclusions and recommendations are based on the background data, clinical impression, and interview. This material is combined into a well-integrated whole, without any internal inconsistencies. If inconsistencies arise or ambiguities are present, then the clinic has failed to clarify recommendations adequately for the court. The clinician is then likely to experience a more difficult time on the witness stand, since lawyers very often astutely pick out inconsistencies in the evaluation. It should be added that clinicians are often asked to testify regarding their reports. If the report has been well thought through and formulated, the clinician is able to present and defend his or her explanation of why such conclusions were drawn and recommendations made.

It is hoped that this chapter has provided a basic orientation for clinicians unfamiliar with workings of family court. However, it must again be stressed that this is a foundation that needs considerable elucidation and delineation before it can begin to approach a comprehensive understanding of the complexity of forensic work. Such work requires not only a good understanding of psychopathology but also an intuitive sense for predictive assessments regarding the patient's abilities and capacities. Consequently, in order for a clinician to function effectively a thorough understanding of legal issues, family court procedures, sociological-cultural factors, and psychiatric disorders is mandatory.

BIBLIOGRAPHY

Bellak L., and Sheehy, M.: The broad role of ego functions assessment. *Am. J. Psychiatry*, 1976, *133(11)*, 1259–1264.

Benedek, E.: Forensic psychiatry training for child psychiatrists. *Bull. Am. Acad. Psychiatry Law*, 1974, *2(4)*, 262–265.

Danto, B. L.: Writing psychiatric reports for the court. *Int. J. Offender Therapy Comparative Criminology*, 1973, *17(2)*, 123–128.

Fenster, C., Litwick, T., and Symondo, M.: The making of a forensic psychologist: Needs and goals for doctoral training. *Professional Psychology*, 1975, *6(4)*, 457–467.

Gordon, R. *Forensic Psychology: A guide for Lawyers and the Mental Health Professions.* Tucson, Arizona: Lawyers and Judges, 1975.

Gordon, Robert: The application of psychology to the law. *Law Psychol Rev*, 1976, *2*, 1–8.

Kaslow, F., and Abrams, J.: Forensic psychology and criminal justice: An evolving subspeciality at Hahnamann Medical College. *Professional Psychology*, 1976, *7(4)*, 445–452.

Quen, J. M.: Historical reflection of American legal psychiatry. *Bull Am. Acad Psychiatry Law*, 1974, *2(4)*, 242–245.

Slovenko, R.: *Psychiatry and Law.* Boston, Mass.: Little, Brown, 1973.

Sturup, G. K.: Forensic psychiatry and abnormal dangerous offenders. *Int. J. of Offender Therapy and Comparative Criminology*, 1976, *20(2)*, 134–143.

Svendsen, B. et al.: Present functions of forensic psychiatry in Scandinavia. *Acta Psychiatrica Scandinavica*, 1977, *55(3)*, 165–175.

Chapter 15

PSYCHIATRIC CONTRIBUTIONS TO CHILD CUSTODY DETERMINATION

EMANUEL TANAY, M.D.

In this age of transience, marriage is often shorter than the phase of life known as childhood. Thus, we have a temporal discrepancy between two mutually dependent social institutions — marriage and child rearing. Psychosocial factors have shortened the life expectancy of marriage without corresponding change in the duration of childhood. The nuclear family has become a modular relationship, the only permanent members of which appear to be the children. I have encountered in my clinical practice what I call third order custody disputes. By that I mean a situation where the remarried partners fight for the custody of children from previous marriages. Relationships are often thicker than blood, and I have at times recommended custody to be given to the "unnatural" parent. The ever-increasing divorce rate is accompanied by an ever-increasing need to make a judicial determination as to which parent shall have custody of a child in the postdivorce period.

There is a multiplicity of reasons for the high divorce rate in our society. One of them is the stress of geographical mobility of Americans. I recall an eight-year-old boy who told me that he wanted to live with mother even though he said he loved both of his parents equally. He explained, "I am used to being away from Dad, he is always on the road." It would seem that once parents get used to being away from each other it is easier to separate and divorce. The travelling salesman and the itinerant worker are

This chapter was originally presented at the American Academy of Psychiatry and the Law, "Family Law, Domestic Relations, and Forensic Psychiatry," January 27, 1979, New York, New York.

symbols of people whose involvements are superficial. We have become a nation of itinerant workers constantly on the move. "Commitment [emotional], however, appears to correlate with duration of relationship. Armed with a culturally conditioned set of durational expectancies, we have all learned to invest with emotional content those relationships that appear to us to be 'permanent' or relatively long-lasting, while withholding emotion, as much as possible, from short-term relationships."[1]

It would appear that many marriages begin with a prenuptial agreement limiting emotional involvement. Transient marital partners would do well to avoid having a child. The controlling factor in the decision to have a child should not be the intensity of romantic love but the durational expectancy of the marital union. This is an area where a great deal of preventive work could be done by psychiatry.

Romantic love gives rise to the wish for a child as a symbol of mutual devotion. It would be more prudent to demonstrate eternal love by flowers, diamonds, and similar concrete expressions of affection rather than the creation of another human being.

Romantic love as a condition of marriage is relatively new in the history of mankind, and its track record as a child rearing basis has not been very good.

Romantic love does not endure, it is a perishable commodity; thus, we run the risk of a temporal discrepancy between the duration of romantic love and the dependency of the child upon the parents.

Romantic love is often accompanied by a sadomasochistic relationship, which creates an environment detrimental to child rearing. The arrival of the baby is frequently quite damaging to the romantic relationship and leads to disruption of marriage based upon romantic love alone. Therefore, it would appear advisable to delay having a child until such time when romantic love has been transformed into a stable and somewhat desexualized relationship.[2]

---

[1]Toffler, A.: *Future Shock.* Des Plaines, Illinois, Bantam Books, Inc., 1970, p. 93.

[2]Benedek, T., and Anthony, E. J.: *Parenthood: Its Psychology and Psychopathology.* Boston, Little, Brown and Company, 1970, p. 112.

Parental love and care is often viewed as a necessity in the philosophical sense, a phenomenon virtually independent of environmental factors. In reality, parental functioning, like all other psychosocial capacities, is contingent upon a variety of conditions. In many cases, the essential factor for the preservation of parental capacity is the existence of marriage. Thus, many a parent loses a quality of motherliness or fatherliness with the dissolution of marriage. To be a real parent in the sense of having the quality of motherliness or fatherliness is not a matter of choice but psychosocial destiny.[3] A person is not at liberty to be an adequate or inadequate parent. Hume writes, "By liberty we can only mean a power of acting or not acting according to the determination of the will . . . ."[4]

To be an adequate parent is not an act of will, which can be induced by legal pronouncement. Thus, courts are very often powerless to bring about significant changes in parental functioning. Judges accustomed to changing reality by orders of the court have difficulty in accepting this simple truism.

A child custody dispute is the second stage of an ongoing process dealing with the fate of the child. The first and most important decision, namely, that the child will live with one parent, has already been made by the decision to bring about termination of the marriage.

The greatest challenge to judicial child custody decisions is to enhance shared parenting between the divorced parents. By that I do not mean shared custody, but the presence of cooperative interactions between divorced parents in the service of providing the child with a relationship with both parents after the divorce. The law in the recent past was actively preventing shared parenting in the postdivorce period by requiring fault as a basis for divorce. In most jurisdictions, at least in principle, the fault requirement is no longer the law. Nevertheless, there is far too little attention paid to the need to preserve parental cooperation in the postdivorce period.

---

[3] Benedek and Anthony, p. 459.

[4] Britannica Great Books. Chicago, Encyclopaedia Britannica, Inc., vol. 3, p. 252.

The final decree of divorce is a legal misnomer, there is nothing final, nor should there be, about divorce. The divorce of the parents is merely a restructuring of an ongoing relationship. Divorce is an end and a beginning. New York Assemblyman Robert C. Wert introduced legislation requiring family impact statement to accompany various legislative proposals.[5] This is particularly relevant to all the procedures that involve restructuring of family relationships.

Custody, like compensatory judgment in personal litigation, is granted, given, or awarded to a parent. A sentence in criminal proceedings, on the other hand, is imposed or pronounced upon a defendant. I propose that we cease awarding child custody and instead impose the responsibility for care of a child upon a particular parent. Whenever something is given or awarded, our competitive sense of justice is aroused. The infantile demand, "I want more or at least the same as my sibling is getting," often dominates the child custody struggle. By imposing custody, the issue would shift from who is more deserving of being given the award of custody to who is more capable of carrying the burden of child care. If the term "imposing custody" sounds too ominous, perhaps the phrase "granted approval to assume custody" would be better.

The decision as to which parent should have child custody is a psycholegal determination. It involves the use of legal criteria and utilization of knowledge about human behavior. The decision is made after some scrutiny of the competing parties as to which is more appropriate as custodian of the child. The inquiry might be formal, utilizing professional expertise, or the judge might rely simply upon his own knowledge of relevant human factors.

King Solomon devised a test of his own to determine parental love and then made an appropriate custodial decision. Historically, judges have used their own life experience to make this awesome decision. The custody determination affects profoundly at least three lives, namely, those of the child and each of the parents. Various other people are often deeply touched by such a decision. In spite of the far-reaching consequences of the custodial decision,

---

[5]*American Family*, Report No. 1, A Continuing Education Service. Smith, Kline and French Laboratories, June 1978.

this judicial activity has little legal glamour. It is, therefore, rarely the subject of law review articles or learned appellate decisions.

Child custody determination is an area where experts often play a significant role, and yet, one rarely hears protests from the legal profession of usurpation of judicial function. In criminal law, psychiatric experts play an insignificant role, and yet, judges and lawyers often express concern about the expert's dominance of the criminal process. In child custody matters, judges attempt at times to place the expert in the role of a decision maker, which is not his function. In some cases, judges attempt to assume the role of an expert in psychiatric matters, which is not their role.

The well-known case of *Painter v. Bannister* provides a good illustration of misuse of expert testimony to achieve a judicially desired result.[6] I will review that case briefly. Mark Painter's mother was killed in an automobile accident on December 6, 1962. From December to July of 1963 the father tried to look after the little boy by himself, which proved unsatisfactory. In July, he asked the grandparents to take care of Mark. They came to California, where Mark and his father lived and took Mark to their farm in Iowa. In November of 1964 the father remarried and at that point he wanted to take Mark back, but the grandparents refused to let him go. Legal action was filed in June of 1965.

Mark was five years old when he first went to live with his grandparents. There was no adverse information about the father. He was artistic, in the words of the Supreme Court "bohemian." A psychiatric examination conducted of him at the request of the grandparents showed him to be normal. His second wife was described by the Supreme Court in a favorable fashion. The grandparents were described as stable, reliable, a middle-class family. They were sixty years old at the time of the decision. A trial judge granted custody to the father. The grandparents appealed the decision to the Supreme Court of Iowa, which granted the custody to the grandparents. The Supreme Court stated, "Legal training and experience are of little practical help in solving the complex problems of human relations." This pronouncement, however, did not interfere with the court's relying primarily upon legal training

---

[6] Painter v. Bannister, 258 Iowa 1390, 140 N.W. 152 (1966).

and experience in deciding the case. The court then went on to say, "It is not our prerogative to determine custody upon our choice of one of two ways of life within normal and proper limits and we will not do so." It is apparent, however, from the reading of the opinion that this is exactly what they have done. Their protestation is merely a confession. A trial court determined upon factual information that the expert offered by the grandparents, a psychologist, was not acceptable. The trial judge said, "The court has given full consideration to the good doctor's testimony, but cannot accept it at full face value because of exaggerated statements and the witness's attitude on the stand."

The Supreme Court, on the other hand, stated, "We place a great deal of reliance upon the testimony of Dr. Glenn R. Hochs, a child psychologist."

The grandfather, as the Supreme Court informs us, was an "agricultural information editor for the Iowa State University Extension Service... Dr. Hochs [the expert upon whom they placed so much reliance] is head of the Department of Child Development at Iowa State University, however, there is nothing in the record which suggests that his relationship with the Bannisters [the grandparents] is such that his professional opinion would be influenced thereby."

One certainly could take issue with this statement. An appellate court is in no position to evaluate such a relationship. The court took cognizance of the fact that Dr. Hochs had no contact whatsoever with the child's father and determined the child's best interest without acquiring any information about the alternative selection available to the court. It is highly unusual for an appellate court to disregard a trial judge's determination of the credibility of a witness. The appellate judges relied upon their own common sense knowledge of human behavior to determine what was in the best interest of Mark Painter. This is often done on trial court level.

In this age of antiprofessionalism, many judges rely upon their own common sense in arriving at the relevant data for custody determination. Judicial inquiry, like exploratory surgery, does not provide information without trauma. Anyone who has observed judicial data collection in child custody cannot help but be troubled by the emotional stress associated with the procedure. Furthermore, judges are not skilled in interviewing techniques, and above all, the setting itself is not suitable for an interview of adults or children. The judicial system is designed to scrutinize past events. It has little utility in assessing emotions or in determining future conduct of the parents.

Psychiatrists are reluctant to become involved in the decision-making process, professing ignorance in predicting the future. There are those who believe it does not matter who makes the assessment—a psychiatrist, a lawyer, a social worker, or an educational psychologist. After all, we know so little. It is my view that the assessment of the quality of motherliness and fatherliness is the proper task of a psychiatrist. He can carry it out with more reliability and validity than laymen and other professionals. This by no means indicates that psychiatric assessments are absolutely reliable or valid. Scientific knowledge is never absolute, it merely offers a relative improvement over common sense in accomplishing a given task.

Psychiatric child custody evaluation requires familiarity with legal process, clinical competence necessary for evaluation of the parents, and knowledge of child psychiatry sufficient to make an assessment of the functioning of the child.

In child custody evaluation, we offer a clinical foresight or, loosely speaking, a prediction about parental functioning. The word prediction has recently fallen into disrepute when used in connection with psychiatry. The source of this misunderstanding has been the claim that psychiatrists predict dangerous behavior when commitment is recommended.[7] Clinical foresight is not a prediction of an event and cannot be measured as to its accuracy by the occurrence or nonoccurrence of some situation; it is a contingent statement about probabilities of child development.

Child custody evaluation is not only an assessment but also a crisis intervention, as are most forensic evaluations. Therefore, robots, mechanical or human, should not be entrusted with this particular activity.[8] Neither psychological tests nor legal formulas

---

[7] Tanay, E.: The Baxstrom Affair and Psychiatry. *J Forensic Sci,* July 1979.

[8] Freud, A. quoted in Goldstein, J., and Katz, J.: *The Family and the Law* New York, The Free Press, 1965, p. 959.

can provide us with answers in these difficult situations. There is no substitute for a painful soul-searching interaction with the troubled family.

In arriving at a child custody recommendation, a psychiatrist must gain knowledge about the following factors:

1. Nature of the relationship between parents at the present time and in the postdivorce period
2. Presence and extent of parental psychopathology
3. The relationship of each of the parents to the child or children
4. The relative impact of custodial decision upon each parent
5. Socioeconomic and logistic factors involved in daily living, school attendance, etc.

As I reflect about the many cases of child custody I have examined, I believe they could be divided into five distinct categories:

1. *The obvious case.* One parent is grossly psychotic, abusive, or entirely disinterested in the child's welfare or custody.
2. *The ambiguous case.* Both parents are adequate, equally interested in the well-being of the child, and able to provide love and care.
3. *The third party case.* Neither one of the parents is adequate. The inquiry demands that a third party be given custody of the child.
4. *The pseudocustody case.* The moving party is interested in something other than child custody and utilizes this method as a means of communication or negotiation.
5. *The symbolic case.* This refers to a situation where the well-being of the child is overshadowed by a bigger issue. One of the parents is notorious because of wealth, political power, criminality, or some unique psychosocial characteristic.

The overt dispute about who should have custody does at times hide the fact that there is a covert agreement between the parents on this issue. The decision maker has to make this implicit agreement between the parties explicit. The parties profess intense disagreement; however, various logistic arrangements have been made that convey the information that an understanding has been reached as to who should have custody. A father who insisted on having custody when asked how he would carry out his custodial functions answered, "My mother, who lives on the west coast, is willing to come to Michigan to look after the kids when I am working." Further inquiry revealed that the mother was in her sixties and had been rather sickly.

Parents involved in a custody dispute often accuse each other of mere pretense of loving child care in order to gain custody. The examiner is urged to disregard loving behavior that is depicted merely as a ploy to gain custody. It has been my experience that the opposite merits special attention, namely, the incapacity of both or one of the parents to be his or her usual loving self due to pending divorce. At the time of divorce parents are often engulfed by intense conflict, which impairs their parental functioning. Thus, the consultant might be seeing the parents at their worst and not at their best.

The legal presumption in favor of the mother as a child custodian has been applied in the past with a bureaucratic rigidity leading to many undesirable custodial decisions. At the same time, it should not be overlooked that there are valid reasons to prefer the mother as a child custodian in many custody disputes. Given the choice between a good mother and a good father, the custody of a small child should, in my opinion, go to the mother. Fathers are not able to provide the same extent of care that can be rendered by mothers. There are many reasons for this fact. There are biological, psychic, and social reasons for the superiority of a mother as a child custodian.[9] Furthermore, the noncustodial father can maintain more easily a positive relationship to the children than the noncustodial mother.

Yet, given the choice between the mother who suffers from an incapacity to be a mother and a father who has the necessary qualities to be a custodial parent, the custody should go to the father. The qualifications required to achieve the status of a father are minimal and almost universal. In contrast to becoming a father, being a father is difficult, and the qualifications are not easily achieved. Not all fathers are fatherly, and not all mothers

---

[9]Bowlby, J.: *Attachment and Loss, Vol. II: Separation.* New York, Basic Books, Inc., 1973, p. 22.

are motherly. However, motherhood is a phase of life, fatherhood is a sudden event. Mothers establish a relationship to the child long before fathers have any experiences with it. Pregnancy is not only a period of gestation for the fetus but a developmental phase for the woman. Pregnancy is a psychobiological process; expectant fatherhood is at best a vicarious experience. Pregnancy for most men is like football, something you watch but do not participate in. Even after delivery, biology and culture separate fathers and their newborn child. The child-caring practices that prevail in our culture during the infancy further contribute to the unequal bond between parents and their child.

There are many disturbances of motherhood that are often denied or overlooked. Motherhood is often intensely desired. There are, however, many realistic and unconscious thoughts that arouse ambivalence about becoming or being a mother. To become a mother is a highly stressful event, it reawakens many regressive phantasies and at times leads to psychotic breakdown (postpartum psychosis). The prevailing mythology portrays children as blessings that unite the parents. Many a good marriage has been ruined by the arrival of a wanted child. Parenthood, like Christmas, often arouses dormant feelings of rejection and hostility towards one's own parents, displaced onto the child. Our culture does not accept incapacity to be motherly or fatherly and subjects all individuals to strong pressure to become parents. "Parent-child relations have been idealized in Western culture. The prevailing mythology portrays the relations between children and parents as a picture of love and care. The suffering, frustration and anger involved in childrearing have been minimized in the collective awareness."[10]

To be designated the noncustodial parent is resisted frequently with passionate intensity. The reasons for such reactions are many, only a few can be mentioned here.

There is little doubt that becoming the noncustodial parent is experienced by a great many parents as a threat and a narcissistic blow. Separation is perceived by parent and/or child as rejection. The more ambivalent the parent-child relationship, the more

---

[10] Tanay, E.: Reactive Parricide. *J Forensic Sci, 21(1):*81, 1976.

anxiety provoking will the separation become.

Realistically, separation does constitute a trauma, thus, the noncustodial parent not only loses the child but is also placed in the role of being the traumatizer. Separation reactivates in the parents fears or experiences of abandonment. Being alone arouses atavistic fears. "Throughout man's earlier history, in many circumstances still today, it is as appropriate to avoid being alone as it is to avoid any of the other natural clues to potential danger. That we should be so constructed that we find comfort in companionship and seek it, and that we experience greater or less degrees of anxiety when alone, is therefore, in no way surprising."[11] Becoming the noncustodial parent creates the occurrence of a premature empty nest syndrome.

The capacity of a parent to tolerate separation from the child should be considered in the child custody determination process.

The postdivorce family continues to be a child caring unit after the custody has been granted to one or the other parent. The affective bond holding the postdivorce family undergoes a shift towards aggressive investments in each other. These ambivalent ties are strong and create the atmosphere in which the child will live after the divorce. The capacity of a parent to be a parent can become irreparably damaged by the custodial decision. The noncustodial parent at times ceases to function in a parental role, a development that is often welcomed by the custodial parent.

During the divorce process, the parents take pleasure in discovering in each other evidence of inadequate parental functioning. Not only is such evidence useful in the custody litigation, but it also represents emotional ammunition for the ongoing struggle between the divorced couple. Prior to divorce such statements as "you don't love me" or "you don't care for me" constituted powerful indictments useful in the battle between the marital partners. They would arouse anxiety and mobilize defensive responses. During and after the divorce, such accusations lose their incriminating power. At this point, accusations involving parental functioning become the only vehicle of aggressive communication. The legal dissolution of the marital bond does not abolish the

---

[11] Bowlby, p. 143.

sadomasochistic relationship between the marital partners, it merely shifts the focus of sadomasochistic interactions.

The dangers facing a child whose parents are getting a divorce are many. I will name only three that appear to be significant.

1. Being abandoned by both parents
2. Having one or both parents become unable to function in a significant psychosocial role
3. Losing contact with the noncustodial parent

The child has virtually no means of protecting itself against these dangers. It is, therefore, a responsibility of the society to minimize the trauma associated with divorce.

The dangers facing the parents are those associated with the loss of a loved one. These are separation anxiety, loneliness, and depression. Divorce at times leads to permanent impairment of the functional capacity and is associated with inability to earn an adequate living or continue to perform the parental role.

The pathogenic impact of divorce should be evaluated in every child custody determination. The predivorce performance of parents will not necessarily correlate with their postdivorce adjustment. The divorce has a selective impact upon the parents. One marital partner may regress as the result of the divorce, whereas the other might progress as a consequence of it.

At the time of divorce, both parents and children need support and protection. All too often the law and society impose instead additional stress upon the divorce-seeking parents. Our society provides assistance to a variety of disaster victims. We give aid to victims of natural and man-made calamities such as floods, fires, and airplane crashes. We provide help for those who lose their loved ones by death and become orphaned or widowed. When the loss or injury is the result of divorce, there are very few helping hands and many pointing fingers. The best interests of the child requires that the postdivorce family be restructured with a minimum of emotional damage to all concerned.

I once had a young automotive executive in psychotherapy, which extended for many years. His parents were divorced when he was seven years old. The mother identified herself after the divorce as a widow. She demanded that her son tell friends that his father was dead. The father, a professional man, after the divorce moved to Florida, gave up working, and subsisted on a disability pension. My patient, on my advice, visited the father after twenty years of no contact. The psychotherapy of this young man was significantly promoted by the reunion with the living-dead father.

Child custody determination represents a complex psychosocial intervention, which is likely to have far-reaching impact upon many lives. Psychiatric participation in this process is essential in order to minimize the pathogenic impact of disrupted family life.

SECTION IV

PSYCHIATRIC TREATMENT
AND THE LAW

Chapter 16

THE ROOTS OF THE CONTROVERSY BETWEEN PSYCHIATRY AND THE LAW: AN ESSAY IN SPECULATIVE IDEOLOGICAL ARCHEOLOGY

RICHARD ROSNER, M.D.

W hen two professions of great authority and long history have substantial conflicts, it is reasonable to believe that each has worthy aims and is defending its conception of truth or good. Such appears to be the case in the disagreements between medicine, as represented by psychiatry, and the law. It is the contention of this chapter that many of the current difficulties can be traced to fundamentally different conceptions of the nature of man and the human mind.

If one asks lawyers to articulate the theoretical model of man and mind to which the law, as a profession, ascribes, it may be difficult to obtain a clear response. Such a question moves to the very axioms upon which law is based. It is not articulated within the law in an explicit manner. In an analogous fashion, we do not usually begin each statement of conversation by clarifying that we intend to communicate in English (unless we are communicating with a foreigner). Similarly, attorneys do not usually begin their statements on man by clarifying their model of the human mind when communicating with each other; the model is assumed to be understood by all parties—it is an unarticulated axiom of arguments being made. The exception, as with the foreigners who need to be told that English will be spoken, is when lawyers try to communicate with persons who adhere to another version of man and the human mind, e.g. physicians in general and psychiatrists in particular.

To trace out the unspoken model of man's mind inherent in law and legal processes is to engage in a somewhat speculative, and clearly arduous, venture into history and philosophy. Some of the steps in this essay in ideological archeology will be generally accepted, some will be controversial. This is an exercise in the history of ideas that is fraught with some risk, but which promises much gain.

A radical approach to the legal concept of the human mind entails literally going to the historical roots of that profession. Law in the United States of America is, in the main, derived from the law of the English colonies in North America. The law of those English colonies was based, largely, on the laws of England itself. English law had several sources, some being the unwritten Common Law, based on judicial decisions that drew on local custom and precedent, some based on canon law as preserved by the Roman church in England, some based directly on Roman law (particularly as Roman law was often used by early monarchs as the basis for the extension of power, as grounds for the formation of national states). In so far as the church, through canon law, was preserving that portion of Roman law to survive the fall of the Western Roman Empire, one must assume that the best organized body of legal thought behind the formation of the legal concept of man and the human mind drew heavily on Roman sources, at the time of the formation of English law.

Thus, a search for the roots of the current law in America takes us back to Roman law. The laws of Rome were formed slowly over centuries and codified many times, perhaps the best known codification being *The Digest of Roman Laws* compiled under the authority of the emperor Justinian. Here, too, the fundamental nature of man's mind is assumed to be understood for all practical purposes, rather than explicated neatly. Many of the contemporary issues of forensic psychiatry were first discussed in Roman times, issues such as civil incompetence to manage one's property due to lunacy or idiocy (as well as restoration of that competence), the need for the appointment of a guardian for the incompetent, the issue of competence to form a legally valid contract. While various courses of mental illness and differences of kind were recognized, the theory of mind to explain these illnesses was not stated in the legal codices.

Our next step in this historical process is to distinguish between those theories of man which are externally descriptive and those which address intrapsychic processes. The former may view man's mind as a black box out of which observable behavior comes, whereas the latter attempts to understand the internal structures and processes of that mental black box. While the moral philosophers of Rome, notably the Stoics and the Epicureans, might be regarded as members of the former school of thought, we must venture yet further into the past to find the major student of intrapsychic processes, back to Hellas, specifically, to Athens.

It is our view that the root model of mind that has been the foundation of the legal view of man throughout these intervening centuries is Plato's psychodynamic view of human personality. This view is perhaps best stated in his book the *Republic*. In that book, Plato addresses the issue of why any person should be just. The answer, anachronistically condensed, is that it is in the interest of man to be just, because the just man is a mentally balanced (healthy) man. This requires Plato to draw out his model of man's mind and its internal processes. He uses an ingenious literary device, suggesting that the ways in which persons organize their city states, their political units of government, stand in an analogous relationship to the structures within their minds and the interactions between those structures. The city state is, as it were, a projective test revealing the contents of the mind to the beholder.

The Platonic model has three basic components. On the level of the city state, there are the mass of the people. They represent the fundamental passions within the mind. The soldiers of the city state, who enforce the laws, represent the mental faculty of temperance or self-restraint. The rulers of the city state, who make the laws, represent the reasoning faculty of the mind. All behavior and all character, for Plato, can be understood in terms of the relationships between these three inner psychological entities. In the just man, reason is supreme in the mind, using temperance to control the passions, while permitting lawful satisfaction of human needs and constructive relations with other persons.

The key to the legal view of man is in Plato. It is assumed that all men will act justly, as it is in each man's self-interest to act justly. Any man who does not act justly either is in error, i.e. he does not understand the nature of his true best interests, or is bad. For the former, an educational-rehabilitational program might be appropriate. For the latter, punishment is appropriate.

Using Plato's psychodynamic model of mind, we can understand how a man might not be responsible for his behaviors, if his mind were disordered. A person might have a defect of reason, due to lunacy or idiocy, so that he could not use temperance to control his passions. A person might have such an overwhelming passion that, for the moment, his reason was incapable of resisting his impulses. A person might have an inadequate fund of temperance, so he could not control his normal passions, albeit his reason knew restraint was better.

It should be immediately noted that this is the same model of mind that is unarticulated in our own day. The Model Penal Code of the American Law Institute does not state its model of man's mind. However, its proposed revision of the insanity defense law is understandable in this Platonic framework:

1. A person is not responsible for criminal conduct if at the time of such conduct as a result of mental disease or defect he lacks substantial capacity either to appreciate the criminality (wrongfulness) of his conduct or to conform his conduct to the requirements of law.
2. As used in this article, the terms mental disease or defect do not include an abnormality manifested only by repeated criminal or otherwise antisocial conduct.

The reference to capacity to appreciate is an assessment of the relative functional ability of reason. The phrase capacity to conform his conduct is a reformulation of the possibility of an irresistible impulse, which addresses the strength of passion. The exclusion of illnesses manifested by repeated antisocial conduct is a refusal to let intemperance be counted as an exculpatory ground.

It is our contention that an analysis of legal formulations at the interface of mental health and the law can always be shown to revolve about these three Platonic concepts: passion, reason and temperance, with one exception. That exception involves another theoretical concept, which was of great interest to Christian thinkers, but not to Plato. The exception is the concept of will or volition.

This is a hypothetical entity that links the incorporeal Christian soul to the physical apparatus of the body. Much was made of the will by the Roman church, and much of that has entered the law.

For those mental health professionals who are dismayed to find that the Platonic model and the subsequently added will are at the root of contemporary legal thinking, a bit of humility is called for. If we substitute for Plato's passions, Freud's id, and substitute for Plato's reason, Freud's ego, and substitute for Plato's temperance, Freud's superego, we find this model shockingly modern and entirely familiar. One principal difference between Plato's intrapsychic structures and Freud's (from the law's vantage point) is that all of Plato's psychodynamics are conscious, whereas almost all of Freud's psychodynamics are unconscious. It is perhaps for this reason, along with the rules of evidence, that it is so difficult for psychiatrists and lawyers to communicate about the mental bases for individual human conduct.

Our admittedly speculative effort in the history of ideas, ideological archeology, has led us to the Platonic roots of contemporary theories of man's mind. It has found two major conceptual differences in the medical model, as presented by psychiatry, and the legal model. Psychiatric models often assume the existence of unconscious psychodynamics, which is not an assumption shared by the legal model of mind. On the other hand, the legal model of mind includes a theoretical structure, the will, from which emanates the volitions that cause physical actions, which does not exist in the leading contemporary psychiatric theories of mental processes.

It is our suggestion that many of the difficulties in communication and cooperation exist between physician-psychiatrists and attorneys because the psychiatric models of man's mind are intrinsically different from the legal model of the human mind. It is not that law has *no* model of mind; rather, the model is implicit in the law, built into the axioms of legal thought, often unrecognized because almost never articulated, but powerfully influencing the law and members of the legal profession. Because this model of the mind exists in an unwritten form in our time, having been incorporated into legal thinking before the laws were made in modern Europe and transmitted to America as part of its English patrimony, it has been difficult to perceive and has required our present archeological effort to uncover.

The practical result of this effort, we hope, will be more effective communication between lawyers and psychiatrists at the interface of the two fields. To return to our earlier example, if two persons agree to communicate but do not know that each will use a different language, no communication will occur. It will be especially disturbing if they do not know that they are speaking in different tongues. Psychiatrists can be understood better by attorneys if they recognize that just as Freudians, Jungians, and Adlerians have somewhat different models of mind, so psychiatrists and attorneys have different models of mind. That knowledge will not immediately solve the disagreements, but it will assist in making the parties clearer on the roots and issues about which they are disagreeing.

BIBLIOGRAPHY

Allen, R. C., Ferster, E. Z., and Rubin, J. G. (Eds.): *Readings in Law and Psychiatry*, revised and expanded edition, Johns Hopkins University Press, Baltimore, Maryland, 1975.

American Law Institute: *Model Penal Code* (Proposed Official Draft), Section 4.01, Mental Disease or Defect Excluding Responsibility. Quoted in Allen, Ferster, and Rubin, p. 689.

Aristotle, *The Nicomachean Ethics*, trans. J. Thomson. Penguin Books, Baltimore, Maryland, 1965.

Arlow, J. and Brenner, C.: *Psychoanalytic Concepts and the Structural Theory.* International Universities Press, New York, 1964.

Ayer, A. J.: *Hume.* Hill and Wang, New York, 1980.

Berlin, I.: *The Age of Enlightenment: The 18th Century Philosophers.* The New American Library, New York, 1956.

Berofsky, B. (Ed.): *Free Will and Determinism.* Harper and Row, New York, 1966.

Brackel, S., and Rock, R.: *The Mentally Disabled and the Law,* revised edition. University of Chicago Press, Chicago, 1971.

Brenner, C.: *An Elementary Textbook of Psychoanalysis.* Doubleday and Company, Garden City, New York, 1955.

Brooks, A.: *Law, Psychiatry and the Mental Health System.* Little, Brown and Company, Boston, 1974.

Cicero: *On the Good Life,* trans. M. Grant. Penguin Books, Baltimore, Maryland, 1971.

Cicero: *Selected Works*, trans. M. Grant. Penguin Books, Baltimore, Maryland, 1960.

Dworkin, G. (Ed.): *Determinism, Free Will and Moral Responsibility*. Prentice-Hall, Englewood Cliffs, New Jersey, 1970.

Dworkin, R.: *Taking Rights Seriously*. Harvard University Press, Cambridge, Massachusetts, 1978.

Freud, S.: *An Outline of Psychoanalysis*, trans. J. Strachey. W. W. Norton and Company, New York, 1949.

Freud, S.: *The Ego and the Id*, trans. J. Riviere, revised by J. Strachey. W. W. Norton and Company, New York, 1962.

Golding, M.: *Philosophy of Law*. Prentice-Hall, Englewood Cliffs, New Jersey, 1975.

Hadas, M.: *The Stoic Philosophy of Seneca*. Doubleday and Company, Garden City, New York, 1958.

Hampshire, S.: *Thought and Action: A New Approach to Moral Philosophy and to the Problem of Freedom of the Will*. The Viking Press, New York, 1967.

Hart, H. L. A.: *Punishment and Responsibility: Essays in the Philosophy of Law*. Oxford University Press, New York, 1968.

Hempel, C. G.: *Philosophy of Natural Science*. Prentice-Hall, Englewood Cliffs, New Jersey, 1966.

Hook, S. (Ed.): *Psychoanalysis, Scientific Method and Philosophy*. New York University Press, New York, 1959.

Hume, D.: *On Human Nature and the Understanding*, ed. A. Flew. Collier Books, New York, 1962.

Justinian: *The Digest of Roman Law: Theft, Rapine, Damage and Insult*, trans. C. Kalbert. Penguin Books, New York, 1979.

Katz, J., Goldstein, J., and Dershowitz, A.: *Psychoanalysis, Psychiatry and Law*. The Free Press, New York, 1967.

Lazarus, R.: *Personality and Adjustment*. Prentice-Hall, Englewood Cliffs, New Jersey, 1963.

MacIntyre, A. C.: *The Unconscious: A Conceptual Study*. Routledge and Kegan Paul, London, 1958.

Melden, A. I.: *Free Action*. Routledge and Kegan Paul, London, 1961.

Miller, F., Dawson, R., Dix, G., and Parnas, R.: *The Mental Health Process*, second edition. The Foundation Press, Mineola, New York, 1976.

Munroe, R. L.: *Schools of Psychoanalytic Thought*. Holt, Rinehart and Winston, New York, 1955.

Myers, G. E.: *Self: An Introduction to Philosophical Psychology*. Pegasus, New York, 1969.

Nozick, R.: *Anarchy, State and Utopia*. Basic Books, New York, 1974.

Peters, R. S.: *The Concept of Motivation*. Routledge and Kegan Paul, London, 1960.

Plato: *Gorgias*, trans. W. Hamilton. Penguin Books, New York, 1971.

Plato: *Republic*, trans. F. M. Cornford. Oxford University Press, New York, 1945.

Plutarch: *Makers of Rome: Nine Roman Lives*, trans. I. Scott-Kilvert. Penguin Books, Baltimore, Maryland, 1965.

Plutarch: *The Rise and Fall of Athens: Nine Greek Lives,* trans. I. Scott-Kilvert. Penguin Books, Baltimore, Maryland, 1960.

Rawls, J.: *A Theory of Justice.* Harvard University Press, Cambridge, Massachusetts, 1971.

Roazen, P.: *Freud: Political and Social Thought.* Vintage Books, Random House, New York, 1970.

Rosner, R.: Medical Disability Compensation: A Practicum. *New York University Medical Quarterly, 34(1),* 1978.

Ryle, G.: *The Concept of Mind.* Hutchinson, London, 1949.

Seneca: *Letters from a Stoic: Epistulae Morales ad Lucilium,* trans. R. Campbell. Penguin Books, New York, 1969.

Strawson, P. L.: *Individuals: An Essay in Descriptive Metaphysics.* Doubleday and Company, Garden City, New York, 1963.

Whyte, L. L.: *The Unconscious Before Freud.* Doubleday and Company, Garden City, New York, 1962.

Chapter 17

PSYCHIATRIC HOSPITALIZATION:
SOME PREDICTIONS FOR THE EIGHTIES

MICHAEL L. PERLIN, J. D.

When Dick Rosner wrote to me last July asking me to speak on psychiatric hospitalization—a topic assignment not unlike a request to discuss the legal process with an audience of lawyers— I immediately sketched out some preliminary notes. When I picked my file up again in October in an attempt to outline my talk, I noted how many changes I would have to make based on significant legal developments in the interim. When I finally sat down to write the speech over the Christmas holidays, I was shocked at the number of truly major decisions that had been handed down in the preceding two months (including, but not limited to, Judge Johnson's receivership order in the neverending *Wyatt* litigation,[1] the Massachusetts right-to-refuse case,[2] and the Third Circuit's substantial affirmance of Judge Broderick's decision in the Pennhurst case).[3] There is no question in my mind that I will have had to amend this paper yet one final time before its final oral delivery; if it is published, as Dr. Rosner hinted in one of his letters to me, parts of it will appear hopelessly dated by the time it finally appears in print.

This, of course, should come as no surprise to anyone in the audience with even the most casual acquaintance with the subject matter. About four and one-half years ago, in speaking to a seminar of the full New Jersey judiciary, I made the following observations,

---

Prepared for the New York Chapter of the American Academy of Psychiatry and the Law, annual meeting, January 1980.

[1] Wyatt v. Ireland, No. 3195-N (M.D. Ala. Oct. 25, 1979).

[2] Rogers v. Okin, 478 F.Supp. (1342 D. Mass. 1979).

[3] Halderman v. Pennhurst State School and Hospital, 612 F.2d (384 Cir. 1979).

which appear to me to have lost none of their applicability over the years: "Perhaps the most significant point that can be made in discussing the 'Rights of the Mentally Handicapped' is to analogize the development of the area to the 'census clock' in the United States Census Bureau which reflects the nation's population at any given time: during the time it takes you to read the entire clock, the figures change substantially. So it is with the rights of the mentally handicapped."[4]

And, so it is with the entire subject of psychiatric hospitalization. In all of the relevant areas—admission to hospitals, treatment while hospitalized, release from hospitals, and issues arising following release from hospitalization—recent court decisions (and, in some cases, legislation) have created a climate in which the substance of this paper is, indeed, very different from what it would have been six months or a year ago. This state of flux should not provoke anxiety but should be a reminder that none of us can afford to take very much for granted in the entire field.

Since this talk is being given at the dawn of a new decade and on the eve of the Super Bowl, I thought it might be most effective if I were to try to highlight some of those *aspects* of psychiatric hospitalization that will most likely be the topic of further, significant test case litigation in the 1980s and if I were to predict, à la Jimmy the Greek, which way the courts will be headed over the next several years.

It seems to me that there are at least half a dozen aspects of psychiatric hospitalization worthy of some extended discussion: first, the twin impacts on the day-to-day operations of the commitment process of the Supreme Court's *Parham/Institutionalized Juveniles*[5] and *Addington*[6] decisions and the new State court attempts to define more precisely dangerousness;[7] second, the effect of cases such as *Rennie*[8] and *Rogers*[9] on the practice of administering medi-

---

[4] Perlin, M. L.: Rights of the Mentally Handicapped. *Bull Am Acad Psychiatry Law,* 4:77, 1976.

[5] Parham v. J. L., U.S., 99 S.Ct. 2493 (1979); Sec'y of Public Welfare of Pennsylvania v. Institutionalized Juveniles, U.S., 99 S.Ct. 2523 (1979).

[6] Addington v. Texas, U.S., 99 S.Ct. 1804 (1979).

[7] *See e.g.,* State v. Krol, 68 N.J. 236, 344 A.2d 289 (1975).

[8] Rennie v. Klein, 462 F.Supp. 1131 (D.N.J. 1978), *supplemented* 476 F.Supp. 1294 (D.N.J. 1979).

[9] *Supra* note 2.

cation to patients against their will; third, the implication of cases such as *Davis v. Balson*[10] on the whole issue of substantive civil rights of institutionalized patients; fourth, the effect—if any—of this whole new body of case law on the rights of the mentally ill in the criminal process; fifth, the meaning of the embryonic creation of a new bundle of rights that can vaguely be characterized as "rights of ex-patients in the community," with special attention to be paid to the recent *Pennhurst*[11] case, and finally, the effect of these decisions (and the climate that spawned them) on the quality of representation afforded to persons subjected to psychiatric hospitalization. Each of these areas is, I think, worthy of greater scrutiny.

At the outset, it is necessary to examine the Supreme Court's recent pronouncements in the mental health area with an eye towards gauging their long-term effect on the commitment process. Although the *Parham/Institutionalized Juveniles*[12] cases are generally seen as a defeat for the patients' bar and although *Addington*[13] can be viewed as the ultimate application of the King-Solomon-and-the-baby parable to the legal process (resulting in both sides simultaneously claiming victory in public and conceding defeat in private), it is likely that their net effect on the adult commitment process will be negligible.

Parham, which held that a neutral fact finder—not necessarily a judicial officer—must review a parent's decision to commit a child to a psychiatric hospital,[14] also held that commitment constituted a deprivation of a protected "substantial liberty interest"[15] and that that protectible interest extended to the question of "being labeled erroneously . . . because of an improper decision by the state hospital superintendent."[16] It has thus been cited by Judge Brotman in *Rennie II*[17] as "strengthen[ing]" the due process holding of

---

[10] 461 F.Supp. 842 (N.D. Ohio 1978).

[11] *Supra* note 3.

[12] *Supra* note 5.

[13] *Supra* note 6.

[14] Parham v. J.L., U.S., 99 S.Ct. 2506 (1979).

[15] *Id.*, at 2503.

[16] *Id.*, at 2504.

[17] Rennie v. Klein, 476 F.Supp. 1307 (D.N.J. 1979).

Rennie I[18] (decided pre-*Parham*) that due process be provided *prior* to the forced administration of drugs, and by the Third Circuit in the Pennhurst case[19] for the proposition that "constitutional law developments incline in [the] direction of [deinstitutionalization as the favored approach to habilitation];" its holding, then, should not give much succor to those who see it as a major judicial retrenchment. Perhaps even more significantly, its holding is limited to cases involving juveniles—of the roughly twenty states that via court rule, legislation, or a state constitutional decision, provide greater than *Parham*-level due process protections for juveniles in peril of commitment,[20] I know of none that has abrogated its procedures in the seven months since the *Parham* decision was issued.

Similarly, the remarkably ambiguous reasoning process of *Addington*—that "given the lack of certainty and the fallibility of psychiatric diagnosis, there is a serious question as to whether a state could ever prove beyond a reasonable doubt that an individual is both mentally ill and likely to be dangerous,"[21] and "the reasonable doubt standard is [therefore] inappropriate"[22]—should not mask the fact that the court held that the appropriate burden, to be decided on a state-by-state basis, was "equal to *or greater than* the 'clear and convincing' standard [held] required to meet due process guarantees."[23] Again, I know of none of the thirteen-odd states that had previously legislatively or judicially imposed the "reasonable doubt" standard[24] which have subsequently modified it in the nine months since *Addington* was decided. On the contrary, in the recently reported New Jersey case of *In re Scelfo*,[25] that state

---

[18] Rennie v. Klein, 462 F.Supp. 1145–1147 (D.N.J. 1978).

[19] Halderman v. Pennhurst State School and Hospital, F.2d (3d Cir. Dec. 13, 1979), slip op., at 64, n. 38.

[20] *See* Ferleger, Special Problems in the Commitment of Children, in 1 Friedman, ed., LEGAL RIGHTS OF MENTALLY DISABLED PERSON 397, 399 (P.L.I. ed. 1979); hereinafter LEGAL RIGHTS.

[21] Addington v. Texas, U.S., 99 S.Ct. 1811 (1979).

[22] *Id*, at 1812.

[23] *Id*, at 1813.

[24] *Id*, at 1812, n. 5.

[25] 170 N. J. Super. 394, 406 A.2d 973 (App. Div. 1979).

held that *Addington* was to be applied retrospectively and ordered new hearings for all persons in appellant's classification — persons committed following a finding of "not guilty by reason of insanity" —who might have been previously committed improperly under a *less than* "clear and convincing" standard.[27]

Thus, it appears that there will be no general post-*Addington* retrenchment. In fact, if anything, we might expect that state courts will eschew the federal constitution and turn to parallel provisions of state constitutions in support of expanded due process protections for patients in the same way that such courts came to rely on similar sections as the basis for criminal procedure decisions, which have expanded Warren court–won victories to criminal defendants on state grounds in the face of the Burger court's refusal to broaden such rights under the rubric of the United States Constitution.[28]

Yet, what *is* of substantial significance, I think, is the effort on the part of state courts to define more precisely dangerousness and to underscore that the phrase is a legal rather than medical one. The famous *Krol* decision in New Jersey defines dangerous conduct as involving "not merely violation of social norms enforced by criminal sanctions, but significant physical or psychological injury to persons or substantial destruction of property,"[29] noting that "the risk of danger, a product of the likelihood of such conduct and the degree of harm which may ensue, must be substantial within the reasonably foreseeable future,"[30] and pointing out that "a defendant may be dangerous in only certain types of situations or in connection with certain individuals, ... [a]n evaluation of dangerousness in such cases [thus] must take into account the likelihood that defendant will be exposed to such situations or come into contact with such individuals."[31]

---

[26] *Id*, at 397.

[27] *Id*

[28] *See* generally, Brennan, State Constitution and the Protection of Individual Rights, 90 HARV. L. REV. 489 (1977). For specific applications in the criminal law field, *see, e.g.,* State v. Deatore, 70 N.J. 100, 112, 358 A.2d 163 (1976) (self-incrimination); State v. Johnson, 68 N.J. 349, 353, 346 A.2d 66 (1975) (searches and seizures).

[29] Krol, 68 N.J., *Supra,* at 259.

[30] *Id*, at 260.

[31] *Id*

Thus, in a subsequent case, in reversing a commitment order based on testimony on potential danger based on observed mood swings, the New Jersey courts elaborated on *Krol,* ruling that *that* evidence did not meet the requisite standard where it was based on "a single interview without any factual support founded in the past actions of the patient or in prior manifestations of her mental illness and without any prognostication, whether or not based on factual data, of the character, imminence or likelihood of dangerous conduct which either society or the patient must be guarded against."[32] It can be expected that other state courts will make similar attempts at more meaningfully defining dangerousness in the future.

Perhaps more important, however, is *Krol's* further observation that, while courts "should take full advantage of expert testimony presented by the State and by defendant, the decision is not one that can be left wholly to the technical expertise of the psychiatrists and psychologists."[33] This admonition was underlined in a 1978 case extending *Krol* to provide periodic review protections for NGRI patients:

> Judges considering the [patient's] likely dangerousness for the purpose of assessing the appropriate level of restraints upon his liberty to be initially imposed and subsequently modified or terminated too often accord undue deference to the presumed expertise underlying psychiatric opinion on that issue. While such psychiatric opinion certainly possesses probative significance, it is no more conclusive on the dangerousness issue than is evidence from lay sources concerning particular instances where the [patient] has manifested actual or potential harmful behavior. The final decision on the need for and appropriate restrictions on the [patient's] liberty is for the court, not the psychiatrists.[34]

In an even more forceful opinion, a New York court remanded an NGRI release hearing for the taking of additional testimony with the following observations:

> Without disparaging or denigrating the profession of psychiatry, we suggest that the witnesses summoned to the new hearings should include hospital employees such as nurses, orderlies, housekeepers and others who have had daily or frequent contact with petitioner. They will be able to

---

[32]*In re* R.B., 158 N.J. Super. 542, 547, 386 A.2d 893 (App. Div. 1978).

[33]Krol, 68 N.J., *Supra,* at 261.

[34]State v. Fields, 77 N.J. 282, 308–309, 390 A.2d 574 (1978).

relate to the court petitioner's actions and reactions to the stresses and strains which are experienced in the usual happenings of each day . . . It is suggested that a display of ungovernable temper when one has been inconvenienced by a housekeeper having just washed the floor may be more revealing and indicative of future conduct than the impression one gives when he sits across the desk or lies on the couch of a psychiatrist.[35]

Cases such as these are, I think, the wave of the future; courts will look more critically at psychiatric opinion testimony, especially on questions involving a patient's dangerousness. It is not insignificant that, in holding that a criminal defendant cannot be compelled to speak to a psychiatrist who could use his statement against him at the sentencing phase of a death-penalty criminal trial, the sixth circuit specifically adopted the arguments of *amicus curiae* the American Psychiatric Association that "the psychiatrist's medical training and experience do not qualify him to provide reliable testimony about the likelihood of long-term future harmful acts."[36] This entire area, then, is most likely to be a growth area in the 1980s.

Next to consider is the impact of the right to refuse treatment decisions such as *Rennie v. Klein*[37] and *Rogers v. Okin*[38] on hospital practice. I see by the remainder of today's program that a significant portion of the other papers you will hear will deal with the various substantive issues raised by refusal-of-treatment questions — consent, intrusiveness of treatment, access to treatment, and the like — so I will speak only briefly on this topic. It is essential, however, that several points be made.

First, the concept of a "right to refuse treatment" can no longer be seen as aberrant, radical, or fleeting. The doctrines of freedom from harm, right to privacy, and right to control one's thought processes — tentatively relied on in such earlier cases as *Mackey v. Procunier*,[39] *Knecht v. Gillman*,[40] and *Kaimowitz v. Michigan Dep't*

---

[35] Application of Miller, 46 App. Div.2d 177, 362 N.Y.S.2d 628, 633–634 (App. Div. 1974).

[36] Smith v. Estelle, 602 F.2d 694, 699–700, n. 7 (6 Cir. 1979); *see* Brief of *Amicus Curiae* in *id.*, at 10–12.

[37] *Supra* note 8.

[38] *Supra* note 2.

[39] Mackey v. Procunier, 477 F.2d 877 (9 Cir. 1973).

[40] Knecht v. Gillman, 488 F.2d 1136 (8 Cir. 1973).

of Mental Health[41]—are firmly and clearly established in both *Rennie*[42] and *Rogers*.[43] The language of the *Rogers* court is instructive in this regard:

> At final argument, the Commonwealth conceded that a committed patient would have the right to sell his home, but maintained that the patient has no rights with respect to what treatment to receive, if any, in a non-emergency situation. Common sense dictates a contrary conclusion, however. Certainly the right to dispose of one's property, and the corollary right to protect and hold such property, are fundamental to any concept of ordered liberty. See *Lynch v. Household Finance Corp.*, 405 U.S. 538, 552 (1972). But, such rights pale in comparison to the intimate decision as to whether to accept or refuse psychotropic medication—medication that may or may not make the patient better, and that may or may not cause unpleasant and unwanted side effects. The right to make such a decision is basic to any right of privacy.

* * *

> The validity of psychotropic drugs as a reasonable course of medical treatment is not the core issue here. At stake is the more fundamental question as to whether the state may impose once again on the privacy of a person, already deprived of freedom through commitment, by forcibly injecting mind-altering drugs into his system in a non-emergency situation.
>
> The right to produce a thought—or refuse to do so—is as important as the right protected in *Roe v. Wade* to give birth or abort.
>
> The First Amendment protects the communication of ideas. That protected right of communication presupposes a capacity to produce ideas. As a practical matter, therefore, the power to produce ideas is fundamental to our cherished right to communicate and is entitled to comparable constitutional protection. Whatever powers the Constitution has granted our government, involuntary mind control is not one of them, absent extraordinary circumstances. The fact that mind control takes place in a mental institution in the form of medically sound treatment of mental disease is not, itself, an extraordinary circumstance warranting an unsanctioned intrusion on the integrity of a human being.[44]

Perhaps the most meaningful legal aspects of these cases are, first, the incorporation of the least restrictive alternative doctrine

---

[41] Kaimowitz v. Michigan Dep't. of Mental Health, Civ. No. 73-19434 (Mich. Cir. Ct. 1973).

[42] Rennie v. Klein, 462 F.Supp. 1144–1145 (D.N.J. 1978).

[43] Rogers v. Okin, F.Supp. (D.Mass., Oct. 29, 1979), slip op., at 60–70.

[44] *Id*, at 1366–1367.

to substantive treatment doctrines, *Rennie I* specifically extending the concept to the choice of medications so that "a patient 'may challenge the forced administration of drugs on the basis that alternative treatment methods should be tried before a more intrusive technique like psychotropic medication is used;' "[45] second, as alluded to before, the extension in *Rennie II* of the *Parham* doctrine of the protected liberty interest theory to refusal cases on the theory that "forced drugging can be as intrusive as the involuntary confinement resulting from commitment;"[46] and finally, the extension of the protected liberty interest theory in *Rogers* so as to include seclusion within the scope of its order.[47] All of these doctrinal expansions will be, it seems to me, the subject of further, discrete court actions.

Beyond these theories, of course, are two practical points that must be emphasized. First, Alan Stone is—bluntly—dead wrong when he suggests that mental health case law has developed as it has because of the intervention and support of a few "radical antipsychiatrists"[48] who deny the existence of mental illness; on the contrary, the witnesses in *Rennie* were mainstream psychiatrists —both researchers and clinicians (including, among others, George Crane, Will Carpenter, Loren Mosher, Dick Limoges, Steve Simring, and Bert Pepper)—whose very presence and testimony helped shape that section of the court's decree that ordered that the informal hearings be conducted by psychiatrists rather than by judicial officers.[49] The significance of this strong testimony cannot be minimized.

Also, the specific, virtually uncontested fact-findings of *Rennie* must be considered as a reflection of the type of institution that spawns such litigation:

> ... One expert testified that drugs are the "be all and end all" at the hospitals ... The medical director of Marlboro [a defendant hospital] states

---

[45] Rennie v. Klein, 462 F.Supp. 1146; quoting, in part, Winick, Psychotropic Medication and Competence to Stand Trial, *Am B Found Res J*, 769, 813, 1977.

[46] Rennie v. Klein, 476 F.Supp. 1307 (D.N.J. 1979).

[47] Rogers v. Okin. F.Supp. (D. Mass., Oct. 29, 1979), slip op., at 100–105.

[48] Stone. The Myth of Advocacy, 30 HOSP COMMUN PSYCH 819, 820 (1979).

[49] Rennie v. Klein, 476 F.Supp. 1312, 1313 (D.N.J. 1979).

in an office memorandum that the hospital "uses medication as a form of control and as a substitute for treatment.". . . The medical director of the Gardner Geriatric Center [another defendant hospital] estimated that 35 to 50 percent of his patients—all transferred from Trenton Hospital wards— have tardive dyskenisia . . .[50]

Finally, Judge Brotman further made a specific fact finding that patients are subjected to excessive and unwarranted doses of forced medication as reprisals for complaining about drug side effects or for contacting counsel.[51]

It is facts like these—part of a "pattern of drug usage [which] appears to be no different than that of other large state institutions"[52] —that should be taken into serious consideration. The recommendation of the President's Commission on Mental Health that a patients' bill of rights be enacted to include a right to refuse treatment,[53] echoing the more detailed recommendations of its Task Force on Legal and Ethical Issues,[54] is currently under consideration as Congress weighs amendments to S.1177, the Federal Mental Health Systems Act.[55] Fact patterns such as those faced by the *Rennie* court will not be ignored by Congress in its effort to draft appropriate, prophylactic legislation.

The third area to be considered can best be categorized as all other rights of hospitalized patients, excluding the rights to treatment, to refuse treatment, to freedom from harm, and to the least restrictive alternative. The history of cases such as the *Wyatt*[56] litigation has clarified to attorneys representing patients that omnibus treatment/conditions suits are not necessarily a sufficient palliative for dealing with the day-to-day problems of institutional life[57] and that, in order to remedy these conditions, individual

---

[50] *Id,* at 1299–1300.

[51] *Id,* at 1300–1303.

[52] *Id,* at 1299.

[53] President's Commission on Mental Health, *Report* 44 (1978).

[54] 4 App., Task Panel Reports Submitted to the President's Commission on Mental Health 1359, 1464, 1466 (1978); hereinafter Task Panel Reports.

[55] *See, e.g., Mental Health Reports,* vol. 3, #24 (Dec. 12, 1979), pp. 5, 6.

[56] Wyatt v. Stickney, 325 F.Supp. 781 (M.D. Ala. 1971), 344 F.Supp. 1341 (M.D. Ala. 1971), 344 F.Supp. 373 (M.D. Ala. 1972), 344 F.Supp. 387 (M.D. Ala. 1972), *aff'd sub nom.* Wyatt v. Aderholt, 503 F.2d 1305 (5 Cir. 1974).

[57] *See* generally, Perlin, Other Rights of Residents in Institutions, in 2 Legal Rights, *supra* note 20, at 1009, discussing, *inter alia,* the material in the text accompanying notes 58–80. *infra.*

actions will be brought urging courts to hold that institutionalized patients have the same social, civil, economic, and constitutional rights as all other citizens.

Litigation has begun on behalf of hospitalized persons in at least a dozen different areas, dealing with such issues as visitation,[58] due process in disciplinary hearings,[59] access to counsel,[60] freedom from forced labor,[61] access to the mails,[62] access to telephones,[63] use of one's own clothing,[64] the right to vote,[65] the right to be free from reprisals for exercising constitutional rights,[66] the right to exercise,[67] the right to exercise control over one's own assets,[68] and the right to have a newsletter distributed.[69] Significantly, in virtually all of the cases heretofore decided, patients have won either partial or total victories.

Of importance in this regard is the Ohio case of *Davis v. Balson*,[70] which dealt with at least half of the previously listed issues, as well as such diverse areas as the legality of fingerprinting patients, the constitutionality of hospital security measures, and the applicability of the right to counsel doctrine at hospital staffings. Although it remained unpersuaded as to several issues,[71] the *Davis* court took

---

[58]*See, e.g.,* Wyatt v. Stickney, 344 F.Supp. 379 (M.D. Ala. 1972).

[59]*See, e.g.,* Davis v. Balson, 461 F.Supp. 875–876 (N.D. Ohio 1978).

[60]*See, e.g.,* Wyatt v. Stickney, 344 F.Supp. 379 (M.D. Ala. 1972); Gerrard v. Blackmun, 401 F.Supp. 1189, 1193 (N.D. Ill. 1975).

[61]*See, e.g.,* Jobson v. Henne, 355 F.2d 129, 132, n. 3 (2 Cir. 1966); Downs v. Dep't. of Public Welfare, 368 F.Supp. 454, 465 (E.D. Pa. 1973).

[62]*See, e.g.,* Brown v. Schubert, 347 F.Supp. 1232, 1234 (E.D. Wis. 1972), supplemented 389 F.Supp. 281, 283–284 (E.D. Wis. 1975).

[63]*See, e.g.,* Rutherford v. Pitchess, 457 F.Supp. 104, 115 (C.D. Cal. 1978) (jail case).

[64]*See, e.g.,* Wyatt v. Stickney, 344 F.Supp. 380–381 (M.D. Ala. 1972).

[65]*See, e.g.,* Carroll v. Cobb, 139 N.J. Super. 439, 450, 455, 354 A.2d 355 (App. Div. 1976).

[66]*See, e.g.,* Brown v. Schubert, 347 F.Supp. 1233 (E.D. Wis. 1972); Rennie v. Klein, 476 F.Supp. 1300–1303 (D.N.J. 1979).

[67]*See, e.g.,* Wyatt v. Stickney, 344 F.Supp. (M.D. Ala. 1972).

[68]*See, e.g.,* Vecchione v. Wohlgemuth, 377 F.Supp. 1361, 1369 (E.D. Pa. 1974), further proceedings 426 F.Supp. 1297 (E.D. Pa. 1977), *aff'd* 558 F.2d 150 (3 Cir. 1977), *cert den.* 434 U.S. 943 (1977).

[69]*See, e.g.,* B.P. v. Martin, Civil Action No. H-78-104 (D. Conn. 1978).

[70]*Supra* note 10.

[71]*See, e.g.,* Davis v. Balson, 461 F.Supp. 859–862, 868–870 (N.D. Ohio 1978).

plaintiffs' allegations seriously and served as a signal to other federal courts and to potential litigants that virtually all matters dealing with the everyday fabric of institutional life will be subject to scrutiny. The subsequent Missouri case, for example, of *Eckerhart v. Hensley*,[72] applies the *Wyatt* minimally adequate treatment standard to deal with such diverse issues as climate control, lavatory conditions, and safety of patient dormitories.

My sense is that further major case law development in this area will come in litigation dealing with (1) communication rights, including such matters as patients' rights to visit other patients,[73] ex-patients' rights to communicate with patients,[74] the rights of outsiders (including patients' lawyers) to visit patients without having to submit to lengthy interrogation by staff as to the purpose of their visit,[75] and the right to contact counsel without fear of reprisal,[76] (2) labor rights, including the right to avoid participation in a nontherapeutic work program,[77] as well as the right to participate in a voluntary, therapeutic, compensated work program,[78] and (3) economic rights, including the right to control one's own assets[79] and use one's own funds.[80] Also, it can be expected that new citadels will be the subject of such actions; for example, veterans hospitals[81] and private facilities.[82] As it appears more and more that *Wyatt*-esque cases often result in little more than paper victories,[83] it can be expected that litigation in this

---

[72] Eckerhart v. Hensley, 475 F.Supp. 908 (W.D. Mo. 1979).

[73] *See, e.g.*, Falter v. Veterans Administration, No. 79-2284 (D.N.J. 1979) (pending trial); discussed in Perlin, *supra* note 57, at 1012.

[74] *See, e.g.*, Alliance for the Liberation of Mental Patients v. Fong, No. 79-1432 (E.D. Pa. 1979) (pending trial).

[75] *See, e.g.*, Falter v. Veterans Administration, *supra* note 73.

[76] *See, e.g.*, Rennie v. Klein, *supra* note 8.

[77] *See, e.g.*, Davis v. Balson, 461 F.Supp. 852 (N.D. Ohio 1978).

[78] *See, e.g.*, Schindenwolf v. Klein, Docket No. L41293-75 P.W. (N.J. Super. Ct., Law Div. 1976) (pending trial) reprinted at 2 LEGAL RIGHTS, *supra* note 20, at 1061.

[79] *See, e.g.*, Vecchione v. Wohlgemuth, *supra* note 68.

[80] *See, e.g.*, Falter v. Veterans Administration, *supra* note 73.

[81] *Id.*

[82] *See, e.g.*, Ruffler v. Phelps Memorial Hospital, 453 F.Supp. 1062 (S.D.N.Y. 1978).

[83] *See* Lottman, Paper Victories and Hard Realities, in Bradley and Clarke eds., PAPER VICTORIES AND HARD REALITIES 93 (1976).

area will increase dramatically.

A fourth area in which further litigation (and legislation) can be reasonably expected can best be characterized as rights of the mentally handicapped in the criminal process. Although this is hardly a new area in terms of legal developments, the general application of due process considerations to both procedural[84] and substantive[85] issues affecting the mentally ill criminal defendant will probably spawn important test cases and law reform actions in at least half a dozen separate areas.[86]

First, it can be expected that more and more courts will follow the lead of the District of Columbia and the Ninth Circuits and begin to deal with the question of whether the standard for incompetence to plead guilty should be the same (or more stringent than) the standard for incompetence to stand trial.[87] On the same question, it is likely that certain real life problems — Can a defendant be medicated against his will to be made competent to stand trial?[88] Can a defendant be selectively incompetent (that is, competent while represented by one lawyer but incompetent while represented by a second)?[89] Should different incompetency to stand trial criteria apply to defendants who are physically, rather than mentally disordered?[90] — will be the focal point of greater attention in the future, and, in addition, that legislatures will begin to codify some of the specific objective criteria set out in the case law

---

[84] *See, e.g.,* State v. Krol, 68 N.J. 236, 344 A.2d 289 (1975).

[85] The plaintiff class in Davis v. Balson, *e.g.,* was housed in Lima State Hospital, a "maximum security institution for the criminally insane" 461 F.Supp. 849 (N.D. Ohio 1978).

[86] *See* generally, Perlin, Overview of Rights in the Criminal Process, in 3 LEGAL RIGHTS, *supra* note 20, at 1879.

[87] *See, e.g.,* United States v. Masthers, 539 F.2d 721, 725 (D.C. Cir. 1976); Seiling v. Eyman, 478 F.2d 211, 215 (9 Cir. 1973); but *cf.* State v. Norton, 167 N.J. Super. 229, 232, 400 A.2d 810 (App. Div. 1979).

[88] *Cf., e.g.,* State v. Hampton, 253 La. 399, 218 So.2d 311 (Sup. Ct. 1969); State v. Hayes, 389 A.2d 1379 (N.H. Sup. Ct. 1978) (finding defendant competent) to Whitehead v. Wainwright, 447 F.Supp. 898 (M.D. Fla. 1978) (finding defendant so drugged that he was incompetent to stand trial).

[89] *See, e.g.,* Perlin, Psychiatric Testimony in a Criminal Setting, 3 BULL AM ACAD PSYCHIATRY LAW, 143, 149, n. 20 (1975).

[90] *See, e.g.,* Fox, Physical Disorder, Consciousness, and Criminal Liability, 63 COLUM L. REV. 645, 646–647 (1963).

as a prerequisite to a finding of competency.[91]

Second, while the insanity defense abolition rages on fruitlessly, it is likely that more states will be turning to the Michigan categorization of "guilty but mentally ill"[92]—recently upheld as constitutional[93]—in an attempt to effectuate a compromise between abolition (probably unconstitutional)[94] and the status quo (seen, incorrectly in my view, as an incubator of judicial abuse),[95] or, alternately, to a bifurcated trial process (an approach that has been both upheld and struck down in various states).[96] My sense (as those of you who have heard me speak before know) is that *none* of this matters very much and that the folkways of the insanity defense—how and why we treat the mentally ill criminal with such abject fear and loathing—are still the most (if not the only) important issue in this area.[97]

Third, as case law has developed that due process applies to commitment procedures following an NGRI verdict[98] and to periodic reviews of committed NGRIs,[99] new attention is being paid to the *treatment* of NGRIs while hospitalized,[100] i.e. are they being, or can they be, treated differently from all other patients?[101] and to the legality of the types of quasi-criminal conditions often placed on released NGRI patients (often approaching parolelike status).[102]

---

[91] *See, e.g.,* N.J.S.A. 2C:4-4(b) (effective Sept. 1, 1979).

[92] MICH. COMP. LAW ANN. § 768.209 (1)-(3).

[93] People v. Sorna, 276 N.W.2d 892 (Mich. Ct. App. 1979).

[94] *See* cases discussed in Wales, An Analysis of the Proposal to "Abolish" the Insanity Defense in S-1: Squeezing a Lemon, 124 U. PA. L. REV. 687, 702–703, notes 86–90 (1976).

[95] *See* Perlin, *supra* note 85, in 3 LEGAL RIGHTS, *supra* note 20, at 1889–1890.

[96] *Cf.* State v. Hebard, 50 Wis.2d 408, 184 N.W.2d 156 (Sup. Ct. 1971) (upholding Wisconsin's system) to State *ex rel.* Boyd v. Green, 355 So.2d 789 (Fla. Sup. Ct. 1978) (striking down the Florida scheme).

[97] *See* Perlin, *supra* note 85, in 3 LEGAL RIGHTS, *supra* note 20, at 1893, citing, in part, Perlin and Sadoff, The Adversary System, in Kutash et al. eds., VIOLENCE: PERSPECTIVES ON MURDER AND AGGRESSION 394, 401–403 (1978).

[98] State v. Krol, 68 N.J. 250–251.

[99] State v. Fields, 77 N.J. 293.

[100] *See* generally, German and Singer, Punishing the Not Guilty: Hospitalization of Persons Acquitted by Reason of Insanity, 29 RUTGERS L. REV. 1011, 1074 (1976).

[101] *Id,* at 1075.

[102] *See, e.g.,* Zion v. Xanthopoulos, 585 P.2d 1984 (Mont. Sup. Ct. 1978).

More developments can be expected here as well.

Fourth, more attention will be paid to the way mentally ill criminal defendants are being represented in the legal process. The President's Commission's Task Force made several explicit recommendations in this area, based on its undisputed findings that "those charged with criminal activity and those either detained awaiting trial or incarcerated following conviction are even more underserved and underrepresented than others mentally handicapped persons."[103] As of the preparation of this paper, none of these recommendations has been acted upon. Specific questions to be dealt with more comprehensively in this field include the basic issue of whether or not a competent defendant's refusal to plead the insanity defense can be overridden by his lawyer or the judge,[104] and, on the other hand, whether failure to plead the insanity defense in a specific case is merely a tactical decision[105] or an indication of ineffectiveness of counsel.[106] Recent case law in this area is rapidly proliferating, and more decisions can reasonably be expected in the near future.

Fifth, it is likely that litigation will increase in matters involving both procedural and substantive aspects of criminal law in mental health settings. Thus, the issue of what sort of a hearing is due when a prisoner is transferred to a maximum security psychiatric hospital—answered by several federal district courts in recent years[107]—is currently before the United States Supreme Court in the case of *Vitek v. Miller*,[108] and a decision is expected this term. Substantively, recent decisions have dealt with the inapplicability of escape statutes to walkaways from civil hospitals[109] and with the applicability of the eighth amendment's cruel and unusual pun-

---

[103] 4 App., TASK PANEL REPORTS, *supra* note 54, at 1373.

[104] *See, e.g.,* cases cited in Perlin, *supra* note 85, in 3 LEGAL RIGHTS, *supra* note 20, at 1896, and Frendak v. United States, 408 A.2d, 364 26 (D.C. Ct. App., 1979).

[105] Osborne v. Commonwealth, 389 N.E.2d 981 (Mass. Sup. Jud. Ct. 1979).

[106] Davis v. State of Alabama, 596 F.2d 1214 (5 Cir. 1979).

[107] *See, e.g.,* Evans v. Paderick, 443 F.Supp. 583 (E.D. Va. 1977); Mathews v. Hardy, 420 F.2d 607 (D.C. Cir. 1970), *cert. den.* 397 U.S. 1010 (1970); Sites v. McKenzie, 423 F.Supp. 1190 (N.D. W.Va. 1976).

[108] Vitek v. Miller, U.S., 99 S.Ct. 2029(1979).

[109] State v. Kyles, 166 N.J. Super. 343, 399 A.2d 1027 (App. Div. 1979).

ishment clause to disorderly persons offense charges brought against hospitalized patients due to their ward behavior.[110] Cases such as these reflect a growing awareness on the part of appellate courts that the issues raised by the presence of a psychiatrically hospitalized person in the criminal justice process go far beyond insanity defense and incompetency to stand trial issues.

Finally, it is my feeling that more attention will be paid to the very troubling issue of the role of the psychiatrist in providing testimony in death penalty cases. The sixth circuit case that I mentioned earlier—in which the APA filed an *amicus* brief on the low reliability of dangerousness predictions[111]—carefully scrutinizes the psychiatric testimony before it, citing over a dozen other cases in which the witness in question proferred virtually verbatim testimony as to other criminal defendants' alleged "sociopathy."[112] This careful and thoughtful analysis of canned testimony may well be a harbinger for future similar legal developments.

The fifth area of expected major growth deals with the formerly psychiatrically hospitalized and their rights as expatients in the community.[113] This group of cases, based primarily on the right to treatment and least restrictive alternative doctrines, involves at least two bundles of issues that must be looked at through slightly different filters—issues that arise directly involving an individual's status as expatient (or as one still receiving psychiatric services), and those which arise as a corollary to such a status.

In the first category are cases that have arisen under the general (if somewhat overbroad and imprecise) rubric of right to aftercare, such as *Dixon v. Weinberger,*[114] which construed a District of Columbia statute so as to obligate district officials to place patients "determined suitable for placement in alternative facilities in proper facilities that are less restrictive alternatives to the hospital . . . such

---

[110]State v. Cummins, 168 N.J. Super. 429, 403 A.2d 67 (Law Div. 1979).

[111]Smith v. Estelle, *supra* note 36.

[112]Smith v. Estelle, 602 F.2d 700–701, n. 7 (6 Cir. 1979).

[113]The issues discussed in the text accompanying nn. 112–139, *infra,* are generally dealt with in Perlin, Rights of Ex-Patients in the Community: The Next Frontier? *Bull Am Acad Psychiatry Law,* 8: 33, 1980; hereinafter Rights of Ex-Patients.

[114]Dixon v. Weinberger, 405 F.Supp. 974 (D.D.C. 1975).

alternatives including but not limited to nursing homes, foster homes, personal care homes, and halfway houses."[115] Although not specifically articulated either in *Dixon* or in consent decrees entered in similar litigation in Maine[116] and Massachusetts,[117] it appears that the decisions were premised, to some extent at least, on the legal theory that suggests that in situations where further inpatient confinement is "predictably antitherapeutic, further confinement must be deemed to effect a continuing violation of due process."[118]

Of even more importance, however, will most likely be the Pennsylvania case of *Halderman v. Pennhurst State School and Hospital*,[119] in which the third circuit has just substantially affirmed a broad district court decision ordering the deinstitutionalization of virtually all Pennhurst residents and the creation of alternative, less restrictive community facilities.[120] Whereas the lower court had held that the equal protection clause supported a right to nondiscriminatory habilitation "prohibit[ing] the segregation of the retarded in an isolated institution such as Pennhurst where habilitation does not measure up to minimally adequate standards,"[121] the circuit eschewed the Constitution and based its holding instead on the Developmentally Disabled Assistance and Bill of Rights Act,[122] ruling that, as part of the law's guarantee of treatment in the least restrictive environment, "the clear preference of the Act . . . is deinstitutionalization,"[123] and that institutionalization of the retarded would be appropriate only in those "probably compara-

---

[115] *Id.*, at 979.

[116] Wuori v. Zitnay, Civil No. 75–80–SD (D. Me. 1978), consent order reprinted, in part, in 1 LEGAL RIGHTS, *supra* note 20, at 677.

[117] Brewster v. Dukakis, Civil Action No. 76–4423F (D. Mass. 1977).

[118] Saphire, The Civilly-Committed Mental Patient and the Right to Aftercare, 4 FLA. ST. U. L. REV. 232, 286 (1976).

[119] Halderman v. Pennhurst State School and Hospital, 446 F.Supp. 1295 (E.D. Pa. 1977), *stay den.* 451 F.Supp. 233 (E.D. Pa. 1978), *aff'd and mod.* 612 F.2d 84 (3 Cir. Dec. 13, 1979).

[120] Halderman v. Pennhurst State School and Hospital, F.2d (3 Cir. Dec. 13, 1979), *slip op.*, at 67.

[121] Halderman v. Pennhurst State School and Hospital, 446 F.Supp. 1322 (E.D. Pa. 1977).

[122] 42 U.S.C.A. 6000 *et seq.*

[123] Halderman v. Pennhurst State School and Hospital, F.2d (3 Cir. Dec. 13, 1979), *slip op.*, at 48.

tively rare [cases where] adequate habilitation could not be accomplished in *any* setting less restrictive than an institution."[124]

The circuit's only major modification of the district court's decision reversed that portion of the lower court's order which ruled that Pennhurst must be entirely closed,[125] reasoning that, as "there may be some individual patients who because of advanced age, profound degree of retardation, special needs or for some other reason, will not be able to adjust to life outside of an institution and thus will be harmed by such a change,"[126] and ordered a remand for "individual determinations as to the appropriateness of an improved Pennhurst for each such patient,"[127] noting that, on remand the court "should engage a presumption in favor of placing individuals in [community facilities]."[128] It simultaneously warned that, if the facility is to remain open, "it must be dramatically improved so as to provide adequate habilitation,"[129] and cautioned that, before transfers could be made to community facilities, there must be "assurances that the sanitary, staffings and program deficiencies which were found at Pennhurst [will not be] duplicated on a smaller scale in [the community facilities]...Mere changes in the size of buildings and their location are not enough to meet the statutory requirements."[130]

As the circuit's decision is less than a month old, it is still too early to assess meaningfully its potential impact. Some aspects, however, are clear. It is by far the strongest deinstitutionalization statement ever handed down by a federal court, and because it is statutory rather than constitutional, it is probably nearly impregnable on further appeal. Although it deals with the mentally retarded rather than the mentally ill, recent amendments to the Developmentally Disabled Assistance Act have expanded the definition of "developmentally disabled person" to include a substan-

---

[124] *Supra* note 123, at 47 (emphasis added).

[125] *Supra* note 123, at 60.

[126] *Supra* note 123, at 62.

[127] *Id.*

[128] *Supra* note 123, at 64.

[129] *Supra* note 123, at 66.

[130] *Id.*

tial percentage of the institutionalized mentally ill.[131] This expanded definition—as yet relatively unnoticed—will likely have a major impact on future institutional litigation, and the *Halderman* opinion will most likely have a similar impact on the entire concept of hospitalization and institutionalization as we know it.

Other questions dealing with the rights of former patients are still in their embryonic stages. Do community-based patients, for example, have the right to minimally adequate treatment in such facilities? Do they have the right to refuse treatment? If they do receive treatment, can the facility exert the sanction of expulsion (or, in the increasingly common fact pattern through which a person is diverted to a community mental health center as a probationary term in lieu of jail for a petty offense or misdemeanor, if he/she refuses treatment, can he/she be sent to jail on the theory that he/she has violated a term of probation)? Are community facilities governed by state enacted patients' bills of rights, which establish rights to due process hearings prior to the involuntary imposition of electroshock? Can first amendment rights of freedom of speech and expression be abrogated by such centers? If a therapist feels it is detrimental to the patient's best interest, can he/she contact the local welfare or unemployment office and sug-

---

[131] Under 42 U.S.C.A. 6001(7):

The term developmental disability means a severe, chronic disability of a person which—

A. is attributable to a mental or physical impairment or combination of mental and physical impairments

B. is manifested before the person attains age twenty-two

C. is likely to continue indefinitely

D. results in substantial functional limitations in three or more of the following areas of major life activity:

    1. self-care

    2. receptive and expressive language

    3. learning

    4. mobility

    5. self-direction

    6. capacity for independent living

    7. economic self-sufficiency

E. reflects the person's need for a combination and sequence of special, interdisciplinary, or generic care, treatment, or other services that are of lifelong or extended duration and are individually planned and coordinated.

gest the patient be denied benefits? Although these questions are all couched hypothetically, it is clear that all of these circumstances have arisen in the recent past. It is not a particularly radical prediction to suggest that many of them will be the subject of litigation in the ensuing years.[132]

In addition, there remains the entire bundle of rights in the community that arise as a *corollary* to a citizen's status as an expatient in context in which the expatient's lawyer seeks to maximize the gains of otherwise qualified persons in demanding their rights to welfare entitlements.[133] Thus, courts have outlawed status discrimination against former patients in such areas as voting rights,[134] drivers' license suspensions,[135] zoning,[136] employment,[137] and welfare[138] and SSI benefits.[139] Although these decisions have been mostly idiosyncratic and reactive, they are likely the first step on a new legal path, which will eventually see litigation on behalf of former patients in all areas of community living, including such unchartered areas as professional licensure, admission to institutions of higher education, and availability of adequate housing.[140] Again, we can expect a proliferation of legal developments on these fronts as well.

The final issue to be considered is perhaps the most elusive and the least tangible: What effect will all of these decisions (and the

---

[132] *See* generally, Perlin, Rights of Ex-Patients, *supra* note 112, at 38.

[133] *See* generally, Van Ness and Perlin, Mental Health Advocacy: The New Jersey Experience, in Kopolow and Bloom eds., MENTAL HEALTH ADVOCACY: AN EMERGING FORCE IN CONSUMERS' RIGHTS 62, 65 (1977); hereinafter Mental Health Advocacy.

[134] *See, e.g.,* Carroll v. Cobb, 139 N.J. Super. 439, 450, 455, 354 A.2d 355 (App. Div. 1976).

[135] *See, e.g.,* Jones v. Penny, 387 F.Supp. 383 (M.D.N.C. 1974); Freitag v. Carter, 489 F.2d 1377 (7 Cir. 1973).

[136] *See, e.g.,* Tp. of Washington v. Central Bergen Comm. Health Center, 156 N.J. Super. 388, 383 A.2d 1194 (Law Div. 1978).

[137] Although the plaintiff in Gurmankin v. Costanzo, 411 F.Supp. 982 (E.D. Pa. 1976), *aff'd* 556 F.2d 184 (3 Cir. 1977), was blind, rather than mentally disabled, the same principles would apply under 29 U.S.C.A. 794.

[138] *See, e.g., In re* Mason, Docket No. 146–26–6397 (H.E.W., Soc. Sec. Admin., Bur Hrgs. and Appls. 1977).

[139] *See, e.g., In re* Minus, Docket No. 142–24–5334 (H.E.W., Soc. Sec. Admin. Bur. Hrgs. and Appls. 1979).

[140] *See, e.g.,* Opinion letter by Joseph Burstein, Assistant Gen'l Counsel for Public Housing, HUD (Nov. 8, 1976), reprinted in 2 LEGAL RIGHTS, *supra* note 20, at 1755.

legal-social-political climate that helped spawn these decisions) have on the quality of legal representation afforded to psychiatrically hospitalized persons?

We know that the record of the legal profession in provision of services to the mentally ill has been characterized without contradiction as "superficial and totally inadequate," "passive," and "perfunctory."[141] Until 1975 at least, all surveys were unanimous— traditional, sporadically appointed counsel in mental health cases had been unwilling to pursue necessary investigations, lacked expertise in dealing with mental health problems, and suffered from "rolelessness," stemming from near total capitulation to experts, hazily defined concepts of success/failure, inability to generate professional or personal interest in patient's dilemma, and lack of clear definition of proper advocacy function. As a result, counsel has functioned "as no more than a clerk, ratifying the events that transpire[d], rather than influencing them."[142]

Thus, George Dix's St. Louis study from the 1960s showed that only 2 of 1700 "contested cases" resulted in the patient's release,"[143] and a lengthy study of counsel in three geographically noncontiguous, politically dissimilar states found counsel *so* inadequate as to perhaps *worsen* the patient's chances for release at a commitment hearing.[144] Although this situation is not so extreme now because, in large part, of the creation of special advocacy agencies whose sole job is to provide legal representation to patients[145]— deference to the "unquestioned assumption of expert infallibility by the courts"[146] continues; thus, four years *after* the *Lessard* de-

---

[141] Perlin, Representing Individuals in the Commitment and Guardianship Process, in 1 LEGAL RIGHTS, *supra* note 20, at 497, 500, and sources cited at *id*, hereinafter Representing Individuals.

[142] *Id*, at 501; *see generally*, Van Ness and Perlin, Mental Health Advocacy, *supra* note 132, at 63, 68–69, and articles cited at *id*, nn. 31–39.

[143] Dix, Acute Psychiatric Hospitalization of the Mentally Ill in the Metropolis: An Empirical Study, (1965) WASH U. L. REV. 485, 540.

[144] Andalman and Chambers, Effective Counsel for Persons Facing Civil Commitment: A Survey, A Polemic, and a Proposal, 45 MISS. L. J. 43, 72 (1974).

[145] *See, e.g.*, N.J.S.A. 52:27E–21 *et seq.* (creating Division of Mental Health Advocacy in the New Jersey Department of the Public Advocate).

[146] Albers, Pasework, and Meyer, Involuntary Hospitalization and Psychiatric Testimony: The Fallibility of the Doctrine of Immaculate Perception, 6 CAPITAL L. REV. 11, 31 (1976).

cision[147] in Wisconsin, trial courts still accepted hospital psychiatric testimony in *94 percent* of cases in a sample studied.[148]

Thus, we should be able to place, in somewhat better perspective, Alan Stone's crocodile tears in his recent article "The Myth of Advocacy" in last month's *Hospital and Community Psychiatry* journal.[149] Stone posits a "one-sided" advocacy system[150] in which all patients are represented by zealous, conscientious lawyers and in which there is a "lack of any real adversary"[151] representing the state, the hospital, or the psychiatrist. To solve this problem, he recommends that the American Psychiatric Association hire lawyers to, so to speak, beat the patients' lawyers at their own game.[152]

Stone's analysis, unfortunately, egregiously distorts the facts. Although a few advocacy agencies such as the New Jersey Division of Mental Health Advocacy[153] do exist, the assignment of counsel to represent psychiatric patients still remains sporadic (at best). In only two or three states are there state-funded advocacy programs,[154] and only in New Jersey does the program have individual and general class action jurisdiction.[155] Nationally, the problem of meaningful access to counsel is still a critical one for most institutionalized patients.

Beyond this, Stone is right, of course, when he points out that the hospitals and doctors have not had particularly vigorous counsel (witness Chief Justice Burger's pointed comments on the adequacy of Florida's representation in the Supreme Court in *O'Connor v. Donaldson*),[156] although the recent *Parham*[157] and *Adding-*

---

[147] Lessard v. Schmidt, 349 F.Supp. 1078 (E.D. Wis. 1972), vacated on other procedural grounds 414 U.S. 473 (1974), on remand 379 F.Supp. 1376 (E.D. Wis. 1974), vacated and remanded on other grounds 421 U.S. 957 (1975), reinstated 413 F.Supp. 1318 (E.D. Wis. 1976).

[148] Zander, Civil Commitment in Wisconsin: The Impact of *Lessard v. Schmidt,* (1976) WISC. L. REV. 503, 555.

[149] Stone, The Myth of Advocacy, 30 HOSP & COMMUN PSYCHIATRY, 819 (1979).

[150] *Id,* at 821.

[151] *Id*

[152] *Id,* at 822.

[153] *See* N.J.S.A. 52:27E–21 *et seq.*

[154] *See* statutes cited at Perlin, Representing Individuals, *supra* note 140, at 516.

[155] *See* N.J.S.A. 52:27E–24, 25.

[156] 422 U.S. 563, 578, n. 1 (Burger, C.J., concurring).

[157] *Supra* note 5.

ton[158] decisions certainly reflect—almost verbatim in some particulars—the APA *amicus* briefs.[159]

This observation, however, misses a critical point: I know of no jurisdiction in which counsel is not generally provided in support of a commitment petition by either the state attorney general or the county counsel,[160] with the usual proviso that a private party can "prosecute" if it is so desired. The relevant fact is that, until recently, few jurisdictions paid much attention to this statutory assignment and attached little importance to its enforcement. While states would be sure that top-notch, experienced, savvy lawyers would be assigned to the Department of Transportation (for multi-million dollar condemnation actions) or to the Division of Criminal Justice (for organized crime prosecutions), the Division of Human Services or Mental Hospitals traditionally was the least favored assignment, a reflection of a political decision by the state executive agencies as to the relevant importance of the area. This is now changing—and I join Stone in applauding the change—but its history reflects a social attitude on the part of the citizenry that cannot be dropped at the feet of Stone's favorite scapegoats: the "zealous legal advocate" and "the radical antipsychiatrists."[161]

The issue, then, is still the same—advocacy services are still grossly inadequate, in large part because the attitudes of assigned lawyers remain paternalistic as a result of the severe role conflict they feel in representing psychiatric patients.[162] There is, to be sure, little dispute that counsel to patients can best be provided through a regularized, organized system of legal service delivery established in independent offices staffed with full-time advocates whose sole job is to provide legal representation to the institutionalized.[163]

---

[158]*Supra* note 6.

[159]*See, e.g.,* the excerpts from the APA *amicus* briefs in Addington, reprinted in 1 LEGAL RIGHTS, *supra* note 20, at 295, and in Parham, reprinted in 1 LEGAL RIGHTS, *supra* note 20, at 477.

[160]*See, e.g.,* N.J. CT. R. 4:74–7(e).

[161]Stone, The Myth of Advocacy, 30 HOSP & COMMUN PSYCHIATRY, at 820 (1979).

[162]*See, e.g.,* Perlin, Representing Individuals, *supra* note 140, at 503, 515; Poythress, Psychiatric Expertise in Civil Commitment: Training Attorneys to Cope with Expert Testimony, 2 L. & HUMAN BEHAV. 1, 15 (1978).

[163]Perlin, Representing Individuals, *supra* note 140, at 515; 4 App., TASK PANEL REPORTS, *supra* note 54, at 1368.

What this all means is that there will likely be further legal actions arguing that the *quality* of assigned counsel is inadequate and that, if right to counsel is to be given any real meaning, it must be provided through an organized, regularized advocacy system. A case currently being litigated in Michigan on this same point—*Siebert v. Wayne County Court*[164]—urges the court to order the creation of such an advocacy system; although it is too early to speculate on how the court will rule, its decision will be disseminated widely and scrutinized carefully.

In addition to litigation, it is likely that there will be accelerated legislative activity in this area as well; S.1177—the Federal Mental Health Systems Act I mentioned earlier—may be amended to include a specific advocacy title,[165] which would help provide funds for such organized advocacy programs. Again, it is too early to speculate on the ultimate fate of this bill.

In summary, then, it should be clear that in my view the case law developments of the 1970s will continue, that new areas will be explored, that new solutions will be offered, considered, rejected, accepted, and altered, and that the census clock, which I discussed in my opening remarks, will continue to tick away. My closing request is that you invite me to be a member of the audience in ten years when some *other* speaker discusses psychiatric hospitalization in the 1990s.

---

[164]No. 79–912758CZ, 13 Clearinghouse Rev. 405 (Mich. Cir. Ct., Wayne Cty. 1979).

[165]*See* Mental Health Reports, vol. 3, #23 (Nov. 28, 1979), at 1.

Chapter 18

PRIVACY, PRIVILEGED COMMUNICATIONS, AND CONFIDENTIALITY

Irwin N. Perr, M.D., J.D.

INTRODUCTION

Confidentiality, as a word of common usage, includes two elements referable to professional practice. It refers to communications told in secret, and it refers to communications told in trust. Secrecy and reliance on the .integrity, ability, and character of another is a characteristic of many professional relationships.

Privacy is an element of confidentiality; it broadly expresses the quality of seclusion, exclusion, or isolation — a state of being free from the intrusion of others, something intimate, and certainly something not available for public use or control. Thus, the element of privacy is the bedrock of confidentiality, which in turn is a principle that protects privacy.

Privilege refers to the protection offered under certain circumstances by the law to selected communications — that is, such communications are safeguarded from legal incursions. Creation by the law of a privileged communication is necessary to make the offer of confidentiality a meaningful one.

Many professions in their relations with those for whom they provide services (patients, clients, customers) expressly or implicitly offer secrecy or privacy as an element of the interactions. Newspapermen protect sources; police reassure their stoolies; clergymen offer the solace and sanctuary of their special role. Churches have provided not only physical sanctuary but also mental sanctuary. Confessionals are not only characteristic of many religions but are widely recognized as useful and essential by the public at large.

On the other hand, the law has long been guided by the principle that the courts have a right to every man's evidence and that law without truth is law without justice. When the law allows for exclusions to the availability of all possible information, it does so because the injury of violating confidential relationships is felt to be a greater social harm than the benefit to justice of access to information. Where to draw the line, what to protect or not to protect, has become a battleground for social and legal philosophers. Each group and each person may have a very specific interest or need, which may be contrary to that of another group or individual. The inherent clash of interests and conflicting social policies have formed a continuing battleground with the control of privacy at stake.

The goals of a police investigator, a prosecutor, a defense attorney, and a physician all involved with the same data are quite disparate. Professional or occupational function does not exist in a vacuum. Society changes; the means of recording and storing information and the loss of the one-to-one professional relationship subsequent to group and interdisciplinary team efforts have made the maintenance of privacy more difficult. Big government and intrusive government may be more efficient, but they also are more frightening in their power and their capacity to affect freedom of movement and thought. The courts and the legislatures periodically attack our freedoms intentionally or otherwise in the name of some other social good. The example of the harassment of the press is increasingly a poignant one. Americans have been sensitized to the demands of power and resist cooperating even with such a mundane matter as census taking, such is their fear of unbridled authority, a fear that history shows is well justified.

Anglo-American jurisprudence has long recognized the need for attorneys themselves to be able to consult confidentially with their clients without the fear that someone will have access to those very communications. Even here, a balancing is offered with the right of discovery to certain informational matters that will be used at the ultimate public decision-making process—the trial. Even trials themselves may be restricted for certain purposes if it is felt that certain types of public exposure will be unnecessarily deleterious to the parties. Such restrictions interfere with the public's right to know and provide a base for possible abuse by the very fact of suppression.

Nonetheless, the well-accepted right of attorney-client privilege is an essential ingredient of our legal system — most often spelled out in state statutes that prevent an attorney from testifying about communications made to him by his client or his advice to his client. Attorneys may testify with express consent of the client, and if the client testifies on the same subject voluntarily, an attorney may be forced to testify. After the death of the client, the right to privacy usually remains in the hands of the nearest of kin or surviving spouse or the executor or the administrator of the estate of the deceased client.

Clergymen have had a traditional protection from such incursions — more marked in practice than by law. The British did not spell out such a protection, but the American states have generally provided a statutory right to privacy to religious counseling. These laws provide for a priest-penitent or clergyman-parishioner privilege similar to that of the attorney-client. Courts have been loath to use clergymen as sources of information. A confession by a person about his committing a crime to his clergyman will be excluded from the legal process. However, such communications, to be protected, must be ones that are based on such a trust relationship. Thus, in New York, where a politician-priest was involved in allegations of criminal activities, the politician-priest was not allowed to hide behind the priest-penitent relationship.

The narrow use of privilege for court purposes is insignificant compared to its overall effect. The existence of a privilege statute allows those privileged to refuse to accede to any administrative or purportedly legal demands for information. If a party possessing information refuses to deliver the data, the ordinary procedure would be to use a subpoena or some similar court order to obtain the information. Once legal procedure is invoked, the privilege comes into play. Therefore, the ramifications of the existence of a privilege statute extend far beyond the narrowness of court procedures. Investigations by authorities are precluded by those protected by privilege; the opportunity for fishing expeditions for information to be manipulated or abused is minimized.

EVOLUTION OF THE DOCTOR-PATIENT PRIVILEGE

Physicians traditionally were not included in the ranks of those whose professional endeavors were protected by privilege. In 1776, a surgeon attempted to refuse to testify about an alleged past patient on the grounds of confidentiality. In this particular case, the court was seeking evidence of a prior marriage by the duchess of Kingston. The physician was forced to testify, the court stating: "If a surgeon was voluntarily to reveal these secrets, to be sure he would be guilty of a breach of honor, and of great indiscretion; but, to give that information in a court of justice, which by the law of the land he is bound to do, will never be imputed to him as any indiscretion whatever."[1]

Nonetheless, the clamor by physicians for patient protection was recognized by the first American statute espousing a doctor-patient privilege, that of New York, in 1828, proclaiming the following: "No person duly authorized to practice physic or surgery shall be allowed to disclose any information which he may have acquired in attending any patient, in a professional character, and which information was necessary to enable him to prescribe for such patient as a physician, or to do any act for him as a surgeon."[2]

This has been followed by many statutes throughout the country. Various states and courts have endorsed the principle, despite opposition from a group of attorneys who have opposed privilege. Wigmore, in his highly influential work, has spelled out what he feels should be limitations on the privilege.[3] Thus, he feels that a privilege may be justified under certain conditions:

1. The communication must originate in a confidence that it will not be disclosed.
2. Confidentiality must be essential to the satisfactory maintenance of the relationship.
3. The relation must be one that the community believes should be fostered.

---

[1]20 How. St. Trials 355 (1776).

[2]N.Y. Rev. Stat. 1828 II 406; Past III, C. VII, Art. 8, S. 73.

[3]Wigmore, EVIDENCE (3rd ed., Vol. 8, S 2380-91, 1940).

4. The injury to the relationship from disclosure of the communication must be greater than the benefit gained for the correct disposition of the litigation.

Psychiatrists in particular have indicated their need for protection of their work with patients. On a number of occasions, courts have recognized the justification for a right to privacy and have used this principle to allow suppression of information obtained by psychiatrists for a variety of purposes.

Thus, in 1952, Roy Grinker, an eminent psychiatrist, was upheld by a lower court judge in his decision to allow Dr. Grinker not to testify, the judge stating, "There is a vital difference in respect of communications between a psychiatrist and his patient and communications between the ordinary physician and his patient."[4] Similar decisions at lower court levels have been reached in Ontario, England, and elsewhere.

An English psychoanalyst who was involved in such a case wrote the following:

> When I was subpoenaed to give evidence in the High Court about someone who was alleged to be a former patient of mine, I was placed between two conflicting moral obligations. I had to decide whether to obey the Law or to abide by the rules of professional conduct. I complied with the subpoena by attending Court, but I decided I could not answer any questions about the "patient," and I made all arrangements, including having a barrister to plead in mitigation of sentence, for the possibility that I should be sent to prison for contempt of court. In the event, although my silence probably did constitute a contempt, the judge declared he would not sentence me, saying it was obviously a matter of conscience. In this he was acting within the discretion the law allows him. Though I had no legal privilege, I was in effect given the same freedom to remain silent usually allowed to priests for the secrets of the confessional . . .
>
> Some of the United States have a law prohibiting psychiatrists from giving evidence about a patient without the patient's written permission, but this honourable attempt to protect the patient misses the essential point that he may not be aware of the unconscious motives impelling him to give permission. It may take months or years to understand things said or done during analysis, and until this is achieved it would belie all our knowledge of the workings of the unconscious mind if we treated any attitude arising in the analytic situation as if it were part of ordinary social

---

[4]Civil Docket 52 C. 2535 (Cir. Ct., Cook County, Ill., June 24, 1952).

interchange. If we allow and help people to say things with the ultimate aim of helping them to understand the real meanings underlying what may well be a temporary attitude engendered by the transference, it would be the crassest dishonour and dishonesty to permit unwarranted advantage to be taken of their willingness to avail themselves of the therapeutic situation.[5]

He also discussed the problem of psychiatric notekeeping, which may not necessarily be the same as the recording of objective data, particularly when one is reporting feelings, goals, and reactions. These matters are not only subject to change but may be determined by unconscious factors, concluding that, "Justice, as well as our ethic, is likely to be best served by silence."

This uniqueness of psychiatric information was noted by Guttmacher and Weihofen:

The patient's statements may reveal to his therapist much more than the patient intends or realizes. The psychiatric patient confides more utterly than anyone else in the world. He exposes to the therapist not only what his words directly express, he lays bare his entire self, his dreams, his fantasies, his sins, and his shame. Most patients who undergo psychotherapy know that this is what will be expected of them, and that they cannot get help except on that condition. It is extremely hard for them to bring themselves to the point where they are willing to expose the dark recesses of their mind to the psychiatrist; often patients have undergone therapy for a year or more before they reveal anything significant. It would be too much to expect them to do so if they knew that all they say — and all that the psychiatrist learns from what they say — may be revealed to the whole world from a witness stand.[6]

The sensitivity of psychiatric or mental health information has been recognized in about ten states with special privilege provisions as well as in numerous mental health commitment statutes, which provide for confidentiality of records dealing with hospitalization or treatment authorized under the act.

ETHICS AND PENALTIES FOR VIOLATION OF PRIVACY

In addition to the privilege protections of privacy, both the profession and the guardians of the profession have recognized the

---

[5] Psychoanalyst subpoenaed. 2 Lancet 777–778 (Oct. 16, 1965).

[6] Guttmacher, M. and Weihofen, H., PSYCHIATRY AND THE LAW. W. W. Norton & Co., New York, 1952.

professional imperative involved in maintaining privacy.

Hippocrates, in the famous oath attributed to him, did not quibble in his assertion of professional responsibility.

> Whatever, in connection with my profession, or not in connection with it, I may see or hear in the lives of men which ought not to be spoken abroad I will not divulge as reckoning that all should be kept secret.

This was modified by the Principles of Medical Ethics of the American Medical Association (Section 9), which states, "A physician may not reveal the confidences entrusted to him in the course of medical attendance, or the deficiencies he may observe in the character of patients, unless he is required to do so by law or unless it becomes necessary in order to protect the welfare of the community."

The American Psychiatric Association has adopted the same principle with this annotated elaboration:

> Psychiatric records, including even the identification of a person as a patient, must be protected with extreme care. Confidentiality is essential to psychiatric treatment. This is based in part on the special nature of psychiatric therapy as well as on the traditional ethical relationship between physician and patient. Growing concern regarding the civil rights of patients and the possible adverse effects of computerization, duplication equipment, and data banks makes the dissemination of confidential information an increasing hazard. Because of the sensitive and private nature of the information with which the psychiatrist deals, he must be circumspect in the information that he chooses to disclose to others about a patient. The welfare of the patient must be a continuing consideration.

> A psychiatrist may release confidential information only with the authorization of the patient or under proper legal compulsion. The continuing duty of the psychiatrist to protect the patient includes fully apprising him of the connotations of waiving the privilege of privacy. This may become an issue when the patient is being investigated by a government agency, is applying for a position, or is involved in legal action. The same principles apply to the release of information concerning treatment to medical departments of government agencies, business organizations, labor unions, and insurance companies. Information gained in confidence about patients seen in student health services should not be released without the student's explicit permission.

> Clinical and other materials used in teaching and writing must be adequately disguised in order to preserve the anonymity of the individuals involved.

The ethical responsibility of maintaining confidentiality holds equally for the consultations in which the patient may not have been present and in which the consultee was not a physician. In such instances, the physician consultant should alert the consultee to his duty of confidentiality.

Ethically the psychiatrist may disclose only that information which is immediately relevant to a given situation. He should avoid offering speculation as fact. Sensitive information such as an individual's sexual orientation or fantasy material is usually unnecessary.

Psychiatrists are often asked to examine individuals for security purposes, to determine suitability for various jobs, and to determine legal competence. The psychiatrist must fully describe the nature and purpose and lack of confidentiality of the examination to the examinee at the beginning of the examination.

Psychiatrists at times may find it necessary, in order to protect the patient or the community from imminent danger, to reveal confidential information disclosed by the patient.

Careful judgment must be exercised by the psychiatrist in order to include, when appropriate, the parents or guardian in the treatment of a minor. At the same time, the psychiatrist must assure the minor proper confidentiality.

When the psychiatrist is ordered by the court to reveal the confidences entrusted to him by patients he may comply or he may ethically hold the right to dissent within the framework of the law. When the psychiatrist is in doubt, the right of the patient to confidentiality and, by extension, to unimpaired treatment, should be given priority. The psychiatrist should reserve the right to raise the question of adequate need for disclosure. In the event that the necessity for legal disclosure is demonstrated by the court, the psychiatrist may request the right to disclosure of only that information which is relevant to the legal question at hand.[7]

If a physician or a psychiatrist were to violate the ethical mandate protecting privacy, such a breach might then be the basis for action by the professional association. Thus, such a breach might result in a reprimand, suspension, or expulsion from the relevant professional group. The importance of this principle is shown in that the preceding statement of the American Psychiatric Association is the longest and most detailed in the position paper.

In addition to professional associations, another most important guardian of the medical profession is the state medical licensing

---

[7]The Principles of Medical Ethics with Annotations Especially Applicable to Psychiatry. American Psychiatric Association, Washington, D.C., 1973.

board. State medical boards have the authority broadly to discipline physicians who violate ethics or engage in unprofessional conduct. In addition, twenty-one states specifically provide that willful betrayal of a professional secret is grounds for revocation of a medical license. One state, Utah, provides for the same penalty as long as the communication lacks the patient's consent, thus not requiring willfulness (although the exact interpretation is not clear, as the Utah courts apparently have not interpreted the statute).[8]

In a related vein, actions for damages may ensue. At least one state, Michigan, has made disclosure punishable by a fine, imprisonment, or both.

Civil suits for violation of privacy have occurred in a number of states. Some of the cases are ambiguous, involving such matters as release of information to insurance companies or to third parties, one example being a Utah case where a physician released information on the character of a patient to other parties who were interested (the physician of a couple whose daughter had become involved with an expatient).[9]

A unique case involving the misuse of the physician as information seeker for law enforcement purposes was the notorious *Leyra v. Denno* case in New York, where a psychiatrist, masquerading as a jail physician, obtained damaging admissions.[10]

The problem of access to hospital records was the concern of a California court, which pointed out that in that state legislative action was a response to "a public awareness and concern that proliferation of governmental snooping and data collecting is threatening to destroy our traditional freedoms. Government agencies seem to be competing to compile the most extensive sets of dossiers of American citizens. Computerization of records makes it possible to create cradle-to-grave profiles of every American."[11]

---

[8] Morris, R. C. and Moritz, A. R. DOCTOR AND PATIENT AND THE LAW, C. V. Mosby, St. Louis, 1971, pp. 287–288.

[9] Berry v. Moench, 8 Utah 2d 191, 331 P. 2d 814 (1958).

[10] Leyra v. Denno, 347 U.S. 556 (1954), People v. Leyra, 302 N.Y. 353, 98 N.E. 2d 553 (1951).

[11] Appeal Court Rules for Hospital in Patient's Privacy Rights Case. FEDERATION OF AMERICAN HOSPITALS REVIEW 12(3):9 (June, 1979).

The court stated further that "The individual's right to privacy encompasses not only the state of his mind, but also his viscera, detailed complaints of physical ills and their emotional overtones. The state of a person's gastrointestinal tract is as much entitled to privacy from unauthorized or bureaucratic snooping as is that person's bank account, the contents of his library or his membership in the NAACP."

The right to privacy was also recognized in another context when a book by a psychiatrist about a patient was suppressed by the court in *Doe v. Roe.*[12] The court stated the following:

> A physician who enters into an agreement with a patient to provide medical attention impliedly covenants to keep in confidence all disclosures made to the physician in the course of examination or treatment. This is particularly true of the psychiatric relationship, for in the dynamics of psychotherapy the patient is called upon to discuss in a candid and frank manner personal material of the utmost intimate and disturbing nature ... He is expected to bring up all manner of socially unacceptable instincts and urges, immature wishes, perverse sexual thoughts—in short, the unspeakable, the unthinkable, the repressed. To speak of such things to another human being requires an atmosphere of unusual trust, confidence, and tolerance.

An Alabama case,[13] in a state without a privilege statute, asserted a qualified duty by a physician not to reveal information to an employer, noting an implied contract to maintain confidentiality.

COURT DECISIONS
CLARIFYING PRIVILEGE PRINCIPLES

Several California cases have dealt with aspects of doctor-patient privilege not ordinarily considered in earlier cases. Traditionally the doctor-patient privilege has operated on an all-or-none basis. If the patient testified on the subject matter or authorized release of information, then generally the medical file and information known by the physician involved were provided in their totality. One problem is that patients do not know what is in their files. Information provided by others in establishing diagnosis is includ-

---

[12] Doe v. Roe, 400 N.Y.S. 2d 668 (1977).

[13] Horne v. Patton, 237 So. 2d 824 1973.

ed. Extraneous diagnoses or nonrelated but emotionally potent information may be made public. The notes of the physician reflecting his own thinking or speculations may also be included.

As discussed in a previous article,[14] the *Lifschutz* case clarified the extent to which courts may make public information obtained by waiver of privilege. A former patient of a psychiatrist sued a third party for assault and battery, claiming physical injuries and emotional suffering. He had been seen for six months, ten years earlier. When subpoenaed, the psychiatrist not only refused to disclose any information or records but declined to state whether the man had ever consulted him. There was no claim of, or waiver of, privilege, but because the patient had put his mental health in issue, the trial court ordered production of the psychiatrist's records and ordered him to answer questions on deposition. Numerous writs and appeals resulted, as many psychiatrists throughout the United States contributed to the psychiatrist's defense fund. In his appeal to the California Supreme Court, he argued that he had a right to refuse to disclose confidential communication regardless of the wishes of the patient. The court rejected this plea, reaffirming the right to privilege as that of the patient. Lifschutz also claimed that compulsion would seriously affect psychiatrist-patient relationships, but the court pointed out that it was the patient who had introduced the issue of mental status and had not objected to the psychiatrist's testimony. Of particular interest was the refusal to extend to the psychotherapist the same privilege permitted to clergymen in California, wherein a clergyman has an absolute right not to disclose information and where the law would not compel a clergyman to violate the principles of his church (unfortunately without a corresponding concern that a psychiatrist might be compelled to violate the principles of his profession). While asserting that the psychiatrist-patient privilege was limited by the need for truth in litigation where there was a claim for mental suffering, the court indicated that judges must use discretion in determining relevant information and avoiding unnecessary embarrassment. The burden is on the patient to show that a

---

[14] *In re* Lifschutz, 85 CAL. RPTR. 829, 467 P.2d 557 (Cal. Sup. Ct., 1970), discussed in 22 THE CITATION 49 (Dec. 1, 1970); LEGAL MEDICINE ANNUAL 1971, edited by Wecht, C., Appleton-Century-Crofts, N.Y. (1971), p. 339.

given confidential communication is not related to the issue raised "since only the patient knows the nature of his emotional problem and the content of the psychotherapeutic communications" (quoted from *The Citation*); psychiatrically this conclusion is most dubious. The court did affirm limitations on disclosure of information to relevant matters and indicated that psychiatrists and their patients can apply to the trial court to limit the scope of inquiry.

In the *Roberts* case,[15] the court held that the mental or emotional condition of a patient was not put in issue in a personal injury case where the patient did not claim damages for emotional distress or mental suffering. She had been under psychiatric treatment, but the court refused to allow discovery of past psychiatric treatment merely to ascertain whether the psychiatric condition had decreased tolerance to pain or to look for complaints similar to those being litigated. That case also noted that a consent form authorizing the furnishing to an insurance company of reports "regarding the medical history, physical condition and treatment rendered" to the patient did not waive the psychotherapist-patient privilege.

The *Robertson* case dealt with an effort to avoid the necessity for a treating psychiatrist to testify, with Robertson claiming that an independent examiner could provide the necessary information.[16] The plaintiff-patient allegedly had suffered emotional trauma and injuries from an automobile accident in which her mother and brother were killed. Undertaking treatment after the accident, Robertson realized that he might be expected to testify. Both the patient and Robertson wished to avoid such court disclosure. The patient thus saw another psychiatrist for a separate examination for purposes of a possible trial. Robertson was subsequently subpoenaed to testify, however. He refused to do so on the basis of the patient's desire and the availability of other psychiatric testimony. On the basis of the *Lifschutz* case, the trial court excused him from testifying. It indicated that a court should use discretion in weighing the interest of both parties, take precautions to protect the confidentiality of the psychotherapist-patient communication at

---

[15] Roberts v. Superior Court of Butte County, 107 CAL.RPTR. 309 (1973).

[16] Reported in PSYCHIATRIC NEWS, Feb. 2, 1972, p. 3.

the discovery stage of the litigation, realize the medical necessities of the patient, and consider that psychiatric information may be obtained by means other than the examination of the total course of psychotherapy.

The court of appeals overruled the trial court, fearing dissimulation to an independent psychiatric examiner that examination of the psychotherapeutic record would aid in preventing. The court did indicate that "shocking" or "bizarre" revelations might be excluded.

Robertson and the Northern California Psychiatric Society (NCPS) then appealed to the California Supreme Court. The NCPS argued that constitutional rights were ignored by the appellate court, that the privacy of the patient was being violated, and that psychiatric information could be obtained from independent examining sources. Robertson claimed an unconstitutional invasion of the patient's right to privacy and his own right to due process in the practice of his profession.

Robertson[17] in response to a personal inquiry, reflected his distress in an earlier case in which a patient dropped a lawsuit for vertebral fracture sustained in an automobile accident, fearing that certain past but nonrelevant behavior would be revealed at trial. He indicated, in his own case, that the appellate court had authorized total disclosure at the discovery phase of the trial (depositions), while seemingly limiting alleged protection to the trial itself (which the former procedure would negate). After the state supreme court accepted the case, the defendant insurance carrier agreed to settle for the full amount asked by the patient.

The Northern California Psychiatric Society has prepared a guide for psychiatrists on how to handle a subpoena.[18] This guide quotes that portion of the *Lifschutz* case reflecting support of the United States Constitution in upholding confidentiality:

> We believe that a patient's interest in keeping such confidential revelations from public purview, in retaining this substantial privacy, has deeper roots than the California statute and draws sustenance from our constitutional heritage. In Griswold v. Connecticut, the United States Supreme

---

[17] Personal communication from J. B. Robertson to the author, Apr. 6, 1972.

[18] NCPS Task Force on Confidentiality Statement, approved Mar. 1, 1972.

Court declared, "Various guaranties [of the Bill of Rights] create zones of privacy" and we believe that the confidentiality of the psychotherapeutic session falls within one such zone.

The *Caesar* case also involved an attempt to limit testimony on the grounds that the plaintiff, although giving a waiver, had provided only a technical consent and that revealing the patient's confidences would be harmful psychologically and detrimental to her future well-being.[19] The lower court pointed out that the doctor had treated the plaintiff for a condition attributable to the accident in question.

An unusual Washington case involved a court decision that a witness, admitting symptoms of psychiatric disability, had thereby waived the physician-patient privilege for all communications with an evaluating psychiatrist, a treating psychiatrist, and a police department appointed psychiatrist.[20]

STATE LAWS
ON DOCTOR-PATIENT PRIVILEGE

About three dozen states have some type of doctor-patient privilege. Another three dozen have a psychologist-client statute, usually modeled on the attorney-client statute of those states. Apparently these have been interpreted in terms of previous interpretations of prior doctor-patient statutes. Some states have special provisions for social workers or marriage counselors.

An interesting California case was that of *Simrin v. Simrin*,[21] in which a rabbi, functioning as a marriage counselor, was granted the right to claim a privilege where, prior to counseling, he had both parties agree not to call him to testify in any subsequent divorce proceeding. The public policy in favor of preserving marriages through counseling was considered to be greater than the policy against a contract to suppress evidence.

---

[19] Reported in PSYCHIATRIC NEWS, Mar. 7, 1973.

[20] Liebert, J. A., Lustgarten, M. V., Kimbrough, C. A. and Bever, L., Court Ordered Waiver of Privileged Communications. BULLETIN OF THE AMERICAN ACADEMY OF PSYCHIATRY AND THE LAW, submitted for publication.

[21] Simrin v. Simrin, 233 Cal. App. 2d 90, 46 CAL. RPTR. 376 (Dist. Ct. App., 1965).

Ten states now provide for psychiatrist or psychotherapist patient privileges.

While various laws will be presented briefly to reflect some of the characteristics of such laws in different jurisdictions, the reader must be alert to the requirements in his own state and the possibility that changes may have occurred since the time that the references on this subject were collected.

The current New York law states that a person authorized to practice medicine, registered professional nursing, licensed practical nursing, or dentistry shall not be allowed to disclose information that was acquired professionally and that was necessary for the provision of such professional service.[22] An exception is the release of information about a deceased patient where there is no objection or where the privilege was waived by next of kin, by a judge where the interests of the personal representative are deemed adverse to the estate of the deceased, and in a will contest. An interesting exception to such release is "information which would tend to disgrace the memory of the decedent." By case law, New York has clarified the statute by indicating that a patient waives his privacy privilege by testifying concerning his condition or brings or defends an action in which his condition is affirmatively put in issue.[23]

Pennsylvania has a very archaic statute protecting information that doctors obtain "in attending the patient in a professional capacity and . . . which shall tend to blacken the character of the patient." Also to be determined is "whether material emerging in the context of treatment, when presented in the courtroom situation, would blacken the patient's character."

At least three states (North Carolina, Virginia, and Maine) would allow disclosure for the proper administration of justice or, to put it differently, at the discretion of the judge if the material is needed for proper disposition of the case. This, of course, provides very little clear-cut protection.

The North Carolina statute states, "Provided that the court either at the trial or prior thereto, may compel such disclosure if

---

[22]N. Y. Civ. Prac. Law, S. 4504.

[23]Lynch v. County of Lewis, 68 Misc. 2d 243 (Sup. Ct. Lewis Co., 1971).

in his opinion, the same is necessary for proper administration of justice."

Some jurisdictions differ in their protection of information in criminal, as opposed to civil, cases or in their differentiation of type of criminal case. For example, the District of Columbia does not allow the privilege in a criminal case where the accused is charged with causing the death of, or inflicting injuries upon, a human being and the disclosure is required in the interests of justice. Wisconsin does not allow privilege for homicide cases, but it will allow such protections in other criminal cases. California provides no protection in a criminal proceeding under the doctor-patient statute but does so under its psychotherapist-patient statute.

Although Alabama has a protection for utilization review committees, it does not have a statutory privilege. It does recognize a qualified privilege in view of the *Horne v. Patton* case already mentioned (*see* note 13). Alaska, Idaho, Montana, Texas, Virginia, and Washington apply the privilege only to civil actions. Illinois excludes privilege for any criminal action involving murder by abortion and other abortion issues, as well as for child abuse charges.

New Jersey's doctor-patient statute, a relatively new one effective in 1968, allows for exceptions for commitment of a patient because of mental incompetence, will contests, where the condition is an element of a claim or defense, where information is required to be reported by law, or where there has been prior testimony on the same subject.

A number of states spell out exceptions for malpractice suits, where the mental or physical status is an element of a claim or defense, in will and estate issues, where the subject matter has been waived, where a condition is reportable, for mental hospital commitment, and where the examination has been ordered by a court.

A number of states now have specified psychiatrist-patient or psychotherapist-patient statutes, including Georgia, Tennessee, Connecticut, Illinois, Massachusetts, California, Maine, Texas, Florida, Maryland, and New Mexico. In addition, a number of others spell out confidentiality or a psychiatrist-patient privilege in their mental health codes. (For example, Michigan includes the latter in its mental health rules.) Some states with such privileges have no doctor-patient privilege (examples are Florida, Connecticut, Georgia).

While California's doctor-patient privilege does not cover criminal situations, the psychotherapist-patient privilege does. Although one state may define a psychotherapist as a physician who devotes a substantial portion of his practice to psychiatry (Massachusetts), another may define a psychotherapist as a psychiatrist or psychologist (California). Maine limits the privilege to a communication to a board-certified psychiatrist, the only state to do so.

Illinois has a very complicated statute governing mental health records, one similar to that espoused by the American Psychiatric Association.[24] Similarly, the American Bar Association Commission on the Mentally Disabled[25] has prepared a bill with restrictive protections, particularly for minors—albeit that bill raises the problem of the age of consent for release of information by minors—another issue that has come to the fore but has not been often dealt with statutorily. This issue is discussed by Weinapple and Perr in the article, "The Right of a Minor to Confidentiality: An Aftermath of Bartley v. Kremens."[26]

The APA bill uses age twelve as a simple dividing line for capacity to authorize release of information (and thus for waiver in a legal situation). The Illinois statute requires written consent by both the recipient (from age twelve to age eighteen) and the parent or guardian. If the recipient refuses to consent under these conditions, the therapist may allow such release if he or she feels that consent is in the best interest of the recipient and the parent or guardian agrees. In any event, this is another cumbersome issue related to the release by a patient of what would otherwise be privileged information. One noteworthy feature of the Illinois law on mental health records is the exclusion of a therapist's personal notes, including information from other parties and speculations,

---

[24] APA Model Bill on Confidentiality of Health and Social Service Records. AM. J. PSYCHIAT. 136(1):138–144 (Jan., 1979).

[25] MENTAL DISABILITY LAW REPORTER. 2(4):480–481 (Jan.–Feb., 1978).

[26] Weinapple, M. and Perr, I. N., The Rights of a Minor to Confidentiality: An Aftermath of Bartley v. Kremens. BULLETIN OF THE AMERICAN ACADEMY OF PSYCHIATRY AND THE LAW, in publication.

from any legal process.

While Illinois under its psychiatrist-patient privilege includes communications with all members of a patient's family, Massachusetts refuses the privilege in a child custody case in which either party raises the mental condition of the other party as part of a claim or defense and the psychotherapist believes that disclosure is necessary because the mental condition of the patient would seriously impair his ability to care for the child (and it is more important to the interests of justice that the communication be disclosed than that the relationship between the patient and the psychotherapist be protected).

A recent article stated that Illinois, Rhode Island, and the District of Columbia specifically protect communications in group therapy;[27] on the other hand, a Virginia case excluded protection for marital or group therapy under the Virginia statute because more parties were involved than a doctor and a single patient.

RECENT FEDERAL PROPOSALS

In recent years, several bills have been introduced at the Congressional level to effect a national standard for the protection of privacy. Although all these bills espouse a right to privacy, their content belies their intent. Not only do numerous exceptions vitiate the right of confidentiality, but they in essence are fraudulent in that they would mislead those who would rely upon them, particularly in reference to a vast array of law and order procedures. The bills go much beyond a narrow concern for privacy; they also provide access to medical records for patients and an opportunity for patients to correct allegedly erroneous data in their records, as well as creating a set of standards to protect privacy through rigid rules requiring authorized release of information—followed by a list of exceptions to the requirement of patient authorization. None of the bills deals with the broad dimensions of privilege in matters such as joint treatment, civil litigation, wills, and so forth. The greatest defect is the ambiguity in criminal matters and the opportunity for abuse by the govern-

---

[27] Note, Virginia Court Ruling Stirs Concern About Confidentiality Protections in Group Therapy. HOSPITAL AND COMMUNITY PSYCHIATRY 30(6):428 (June, 1976).

ment itself. The most important element of these bills is not the misleading statement of principles, it is the long list of stipulations allowing medical information to be scrutinized without permission—the aptly named exceptions.

Proposed H.R. 3444 is a lengthy bill dealing with health care providers. It would allow release of information to agents of a facility to carry out their duties; to health care providers in connection with health care services; to next of kin; for the health and safety of another person; for research and statistics activities to meet medical emergencies or prevent a crime or in compliance with a judicial order in inquiry of a violation of a law by the research unit; for government investigation of a facility; and for investigations of fraud, abuse, waste, audits, evaluation, and payment. Similarly, exceptions exist (1) for third party payers, (2) compulsory to legal process, and (3) when the individual and the government are parties to a suit.

The picture becomes more complicated with numerous exceptions for law enforcement authorities. The presence, location, and general medical condition may be released if a person does not object or if the inquiry is pursuant to a legitimate law enforcement inquiry. The door is open to administrative summonses, subpoenas, search warrants, and judicial subpoenas; to prevent serious property damage or flight; to the FBI, Secret Service, Armed Forces (for people in the Armed Forces), penal authorities (for those so incarcerated), Veterans Administration (for those in VA facilities), and grand juries.

S-865 is a similar bill but would allow release of information [Sec. 310(6)] to "any local unit of government of any state, or any officer, employee, or agent thereof, but does not include a state legislature." Thus, theoretically, a city mayor could arrange to obtain records of a citizen by making him the subject of an investigation.

S-503 would allow access to information where the data could indicate that the patient "may have been involved in, or a victim of, a violation of law." Thus, the records not only of alleged criminals would be open to fishing expeditions but also those of alleged victims—certainly a most unusual breach of privacy. Specific reference is also made to the needs involved in conducting foreign counterintelligence.

These laws would supersede state laws and therefore would render all existing state laws and protections inoperative. Thus, if adopted, the result would be a marked diminution of legal protection of confidentiality in many states.

H.R. 2979 is a bill that would not exclude additional protections by federal, state, or local law and would specifically protect medical records relating to psychiatric, psychologic, or mental health treatment. Exceptions under this law include employee use, medical consultation, the fact of admission, where needed in health research situations, and audits and evaluations. Once again, there would be no privilege for a variety of law enforcement functions— investigation of fraud, abuse, or waste; in assisting in the location of a suspect or fugitive in a legitimate law enforcement inquiry; for judicial-administrative purposes (civil or criminal procedures where the individual is a party); and for the usual summonses, subpoenas, and search warrants.

A later, extensive bill introduced in the House, H.R. 5935, clarifies some of the matters raised in the earlier bills and allows for much more flexibility. It is the only bill that defines a patient as a living individual, thereby opening up records of the deceased. It does allow for restriction by federal, state, or local laws on the "disclosure of medical information relating to psychiatric, psychological, or mental health examination, care, or treatment." It further allows a state to prohibit disclosure of medical information under that part of the bill dealing with exceptions. (It is not clear about that part of the bill dealing with procedures, resulting in possible ambiguity.)

This bill is permissive. It states that hospitals "may" release information when requested under the various exceptions including the usual long list of law enforcement agencies. This places the responsibility and power in the health facility but at the same time makes the health facility peculiarly vulnerable to pressure by governmental authorities. Records of one patient could be obtained to seek information about crimes possibly committed by other patients. One of the most striking sections in the bill is Section 132, dealing with subpoenas, summonses, and search warrants. Part *a* states that a medical care facility *may* disclose information, while part *c* states, "Nothing in this section shall be construed as authority for a medical care facility to refuse to comply with a valid, administrative summons, subpoena, or warrant, or a valid judicial summons, subpoena, or search warrant." Thus, the bill is inherently contradictory.

Another interesting clause allows for information to be obtained at federal medical care facilities by the uniformed services to determine eligibility of a member of the uniformed service for service, promotion, assignments, or training (this without the person's knowledge or permission).

Numerous other exceptions for law enforcement purposes are specified. H.R. 5935 lacks clarity in that it is permissive both for states and health facilities. In the absence of state action, health facilities would be placed in a very awkward position in attempting to fend off law investigators without any standards or criteria. No consistency would be present. Because of its optional nature, release of information might open the door to litigation by parties whose records were revealed under circumstances that are injurious to the individual. The individual might claim that the health facility used inappropriate professional judgement. Other matters dealing with procedure, notification, and time factors will not be delineated here.

The major point to be made here is that the proposed federal bills either diminish protections existing in many parts of the country or create an ambiguous situation where certainty is desirable. Second, they adopt the premise that law enforcement investigations supersede the right to privacy; therefore, they propose changes that are inapposite to their stated intent. Third, they do not deal with many legitimate areas of privacy—areas where protections should reasonably be allowed.

Special circumstances deal with security and foreign intelligence. One particular area with broad social implications is the need to know the location and approximate status of those who have threatened selected federal officials. American history does leave one with a sense of disquiet in this regard. Yet, American history does not seemingly provide past cases where such information would have made any difference.

The use of a federal standard is a possibly treacherous one for those interested in civil rights and patient privacy. Unless carefully considered, it can result in a loss of civil rights, as the discussion of the proposed bills would indicate. Fear of government would be magnified. One might speculate, for example, on the effect of such legislation on federal employees and their sense of security in seeking therapy for themselves. Abuses in this area have already occurred; these bills would make vulnerable state and local employees, certainly a matter that might discourage an individual from seeking treatment in timely fashion. Law and order pressures themselves are threatening, and once passed, an inappropriate bill might be difficult to alter. Professional persons can lobby in their own states for improvement by pointing to achievements in other states. This would not be possible if there were a national rule. One might even attack the constitutional basis for such acts that loosely declare that medical care is a matter of interstate commerce and therefore subject to federal regulation. This is, of course, a fiction necessarily used for the exercise of federal power. Those who fear centralized power and who shudder at the track record of government in so many recent years should feel compelled to oppose militantly the imposition of such regulations.

Testimony on behalf of the American Psychiatric Association, American Psychological Association, and the National Association of Private Psychiatric Hospitals before a congressional committee affirmed the attitudes of interested professional groups towards proposed federal standards.[28] The statement noted one study of college students in which it was concluded that "limited confidentiality significantly inhibited self-disclosure." These groups, of course, focused on psychiatric or mental health communications, accepting the belief that a higher standard of protection is needed for such professional endeavors. One might argue that such protections should be maintained for all medical patients. The mental health professionals have duly noted the specific protections now offered for alcohol and drug abuse programs. Despite such rules, one New York psychiatrist went to jail to prevent access to the

---

[28] Statement by Marcia K. Goin before the House Ways and Means Subcommittee on Health, April 17, 1980.

records of a drug clinic. In another New York case, a crisis intervention center's funds were suddenly withdrawn when the state auditor was refused access to identifiable records without patient consent. Patient records were seized at a San Francisco general hospital based on a telephone call from an anonymous informant about a conversation about a planned crime. A warrant was used to obtain records on all patients seen during a specified period and to obtain photos and fingerprints of all those who visited the clinic. The possibility of police surveillance is considered to be potentially devastating to drug treatment programs. More recently, records of patients seen by private psychiatrists have been seized amidst great protest. The mental health professions continue to be threatened by continuing assaults on the doctor-patient relationship.

RECORDS AND DANGEROUSNESS

Related to the law and order provisions so zealously sought by some lawmakers is the fantasy that criminality in a violent society can be lessened if only disturbed psychiatric patients can be identified. The Tarasoff case in California has promulgated the principle that therapists must warn potential victims of violence,[29] allegedly in accordance with professional standards that are nonexistent. Failure to do so may result in a claim of responsibility against a therapist. This bizarre excursion of the law has resulted in a beginning crescendo of lawsuits as therapists are being intimidated into public revelation of patient communications.

RECOMMENDATIONS FOR A MODEL PRIVACY ACT

A model privacy act should state that communications involving health care matters may not be released without consent and should be private and immune to *all* legal action except the following:

---

[29] Tarasoff v. Regents of the University of California, 118 CAL. RPTR. 129, 529 P. 2d 553 (1974); often known as Tarasoff I: Tarasoff v. Regents of the University of California 131 CAL. RPTR. 14, 551 P. 2d 334 (1976) — Tarasoff II.

1. To accomplish psychiatric hospitalization, involuntary or otherwise, or evaluation to weigh the necessity for such
2. To inform relatives, next of kin, or appropriate parties about the general condition of the patient, in conformance with medical, psychiatric, or mental health practice
3. To communicate with other physicians and care providers involved in the management of the patient, in conformance with professional practice
4. To intervene in emergency situations where there is apparent significant threat to life, health, or property, the discretion being that of the care provider
5. To aid in the settlement of will disputes where testamentary capacity is at issue
6. To clarify, as necessary, eligibility for insurance benefits after the death of the patient and to provide information necessary for disposition of claims on behalf of or on the estate of the deceased patient
7. To report those diseases stipulated by law for public health purposes or to make available medical records of minors in accord with abuse or neglected child acts
8. In civil litigation where the patient is a party and the illness is a basis of a claim or defense. This exception shall not apply to any action for damages for pain and suffering alone that does not include a claim based on consequences or treatment of a mental condition as an element of such pain and suffering. This exception shall also not apply to domestic relations cases involving divorce, separation, or custody.
9. In a criminal case where mental or physical disease is an element of the defense or where clarification of such status is required for procedural reasons. This shall include fitness to stand trial and related issues.
10. As reasonably necessary for medical and statistical research
11. As reasonably necessary to establish the basis for payment by third parties, public or private
12. As reasonably necessary to establish conformity with the policies of government-supported programs
13. As reasonably necessary to effectuate peer review or similar review of hospital or physician procedures

In addition, clarification for protection needs to be provided for group therapy, conjoint therapy, marital therapy, family therapy, and child guidance therapy. Multiple therapies raise the issue of protection of a group of parties. Similarly, clarification of minor status and authority to release information needs to be included in any privacy statute so that protection is not lost in the hazy ambiguity of an unspelled authority to release.

Another element not to be omitted is the explicit restriction of information to matters pertinent to the release of information and careful exclusion of prejudicial or inflammatory data, whether or not relevant to the needs of the situation.

CONCLUSION

The subjects of privacy, confidentiality, and privilege continue to occupy members of the legal and healing professions. Therapists are continually confronted with the need to advance and maintain patient care, one element of which is the unique relationship of therapist and patient. Cross currents of legal trends and social issues sometimes advance and sometimes nullify this goal.

Legal protections for privacy have slowly and torturously evolved over periodic opposition. This positive development has been marked by the great disparity that exists from state to state. The imposition of a national standard would clarify the confusion that exists between jurisdictions. However, as review of proposed legislation has shown, the content of such a national bill might well be less protective than many existing state statutes. In addition, a federal law once enacted would in all probability be less amenable to alteration or modification than a state statute.

Those who look upon confidentiality as a necessary cornerstone for the appropriate provision of medical services will continue to press for clear-cut guidelines, which will inform patient and physician alike of their rights. The principles of an adequate privilege bill should reflect carefully the very specific and limited exceptions allowed by law. Otherwise, the concept of privacy and freedom becomes just a sham.

BIBLIOGRAPHY

Dewitt, C.: *Privileged Communications between Physician and Patient.* Charles C Thomas, Springfield, 1958.

Perr, I. N.: Current Trends in Confidentiality and Privileged Communications. *Journal of Legal Medicine, 1(5):*44–47, Feb., 1974.

Perr, I. N.: Confidentiality and Consent in Psychiatric Treatment of Minors. *Journal of Legal Medicine, 4(6):*9–13, June, 1976.

Perr, I. N.: Congressional Proposals and the New Assault on Privacy. *Bull. Am. Acad. Psychiatry Law, 7(2):*iv–vii 1979.

Perr, I. N.: Doctor-Patient Confidentiality—Suggested Legal Protections. *Bull. Am. Acad. Psychiatry Law, 7(3):*iv–viii, 1979.

Slovenko, R.: *Psychotherapy, Confidentiality, and Privileged Communication.* Charles C Thomas, Springfield, 1966.

Slovenko, R.: Privileged communication. In *Psychiatry and Law* Little, Brown and Co., Boston, 1973.

Chapter 19

CONSENT

JONAS R. RAPPEPORT, M.D.

Is it better for a patient to suffer the consequences of schizophrenia with its hallucinations, delusions, ideas of reference, and suicidal ideas, or is it better to take haloperidol and risk suffering with dystonia, akathisia, hyperreflexia, opisthotonos, oculogyric crises, or persistent tardive dyskinesia?[1] This is the dilemma that the patient may be faced with when an attempt is made to obtain his informed consent after one has clearly shown him, in writing or explained in detail, all the possible side reactions and complications from this dangerous medication.[2] Consent is defined as, "An act of reason, accompanied with deliberation, the mind weighing as in a balance the good or evil on each side.... It means voluntary agreement by a person in the possession and exercise of sufficient mentality to make an intelligent choice to do something proposed by another.... It supposes a physical power to act, a moral power of acting, and a serious, determined and free use of these powers."[3]

There are many different types of consent. The names they are given depend on who is doing the cataloguing. Rada has listed four types: implied, presumed, vicarious, and informed.[4]

Implied consent might occur when a patient comes for a physical. It is assumed or implied that by his presence there he has given his permission for routine laboratory work, as blood tests, chest x-ray, etc. There are also implied consent laws usually related to state functions such as licensing. For instance, in Maryland con-

---

[1]*Physician's Desk Reference*, 32nd ed., 1978, p. 1083.

[2]Rogers v. Okin 478 F. Supp 1342 (D.Mass. 1979) (appeal pending).

[3]*Black's Law Dictionary* (Rev. 4th ed., West Publishing Co., St. Paul. 1968).

[4]Rada, Richard T.: Informed Consent in the Care of Psychiatric Patients, *Journal of National Assoc. Private Psychiatric Hospitals,* 8:2, 1976.

sent for a Breatholyzer® test, if suspected of drunk driving, is implied when a person accepts his driver's license, or he forfeits his license for ninety days.

Presumed consent is that which occurs in situations where the patient is unconscious. It is presumed that he would give consent to emergency treatment if he were conscious.

Vicarious or substitute consent is that given by a parent of a minor or an officially appointed guardian of an incompetent patient.

Last, there is *informed consent,* where the individual is fully informed and makes a decision based on all of the necessary information. Regardless of how we might define consent, the basic concept involved is that an individual has, in some manner or other, given permission to allow another person to perform an act upon him. The essence of this concept is based upon the inviolate right of an individual to control what is done to him.

Consent does not seem to have been much of an issue in the medical-legal arena except for experimental surgery until the beginning of this century. The American Hospital Association monograph on informed consent states, "Four cases are often cited as progenitors of the informed consent doctrine."[5] The four cases cited, covering the period from 1905 to 1914, represent surgery performed without prior disclosure of the nature or scope of the operations. *Mohr v. Williams* involved an operation upon the plaintiff's left ear despite consent for a right ear operation only.[6] "The court held that unless a jury found that the patient had consented, either expressly or impliedly, to the challenged operation, 'the act of defendant amounted at least to a technical assault and battery.'"[7] The fourth case, *Schloendorf v. Society of New York Hospital,* contains Judge Cardoza's oft quoted statement on consent, "Every human being of adult years and sound mind has a right to determine what shall be done with his own body; and a surgeon who performs an operation without his patient's consent commits an assault, for which he is liable in damages. . . . This is true, except in cases of emergency where the patient is unconscious, and where it is neces-

---

[5] Ludlam, James E.: Informed Consent, Amer. Hospital Assoc., Chicago, 1978, p. 20.

[6] Mohr v. Williams, 95 MN 261 (104 NW 12 1905).

[7] *Id,* at 271 (104 NW 12 p. 16.).

sary to operate before consent can be obtained."[8]

Thus, the die was cast for a long series of cases that did not detail what constituted consent until the 1960 case of *Natanson v. Klein*.[9] As you can see, the law moved at a very slow and deliberate pace. In *Natanson* the court held that the physician "was obligated to make a reasonable disclosure to the appellant of the nature and probable consequences of the suggested or recommended cobalt irradiation treatment, and he was also obligated to make a reasonable disclosure of the dangers within his knowledge which were incident to, or possible in, the treatment he proposed to administer."[10] However, the court further noted that his duty of disclosure is limited to those disclosures which a reasonable medical practitioner would make under the same or similar circumstances. The concept of risks and benefits was thus clarified. Also, the standard of disclosure was a medical standard.

This remained until 1972 with the cases of *Canterbury v. Spence*[11] and *Cobbs v. Grant*.[12]

In *Cobbs v. Grant*, the court said that the duty is one of reasonable disclosure of the available choices with respect to the proposed therapy and of the dangers inherently and potentially involved in each of these procedures. The standard is set by law rather than by physicians, who may or may not impose it upon themselves. This was the beginning of the concept that the standard is no longer that which the physician or his colleagues might use but a standard that may be set by law. The courts have come up with a catch 22 situation indicating that the scope of the disclosure required defies simple definition. They then stated that there were at least four primary areas in which the patient should be informed:

1. Risk of death
2. Risk of serious bodily harm
3. Problems that might occur during recuperation
4. The alternatives to surgery

---

[8] Schloendorf v. Society of New York Hospital, 211 NY 125 (105 NE 92 1914).

[9] Natanson v. Klein, 186 Kansas 393 (350 P.2d 1093, 1960).

[10] *Id*, at 410 (350 P.2d 1093 p. 1106).

[11] *Canterbury v. Spence, 464 F.2d 772 (D.C. Cir. 1972)*.

[12] Cobbs v. Grant, 8 Cal 3rd 229 (502 P.2d 1 1972).

The court said that the patient's right of self-decision is the measure of the physician's duty to reveal. The final legal test must be whether there is a causal relationship between the failure to give material information and the injury, that is, would the patient have refused if he had been so informed?

In the *Canterbury v. Spence* case a young man who had severe back difficulties agreed to surgery without being informed of some of the risks, particularly that of partial paralysis. On his second postoperative day, he fell when voiding, unattended. A few hours later he was paralyzed from the waist down. He was once again operated on but was left with weakness of his extremeties as well as incontinence. In testimony Dr. Spence indicated that the disabilities suffered by the patient actually stemmed from his preoperative condition symptomatized by the swollen and nonpulsating spinal cord found at the original operation. The doctor further stated that even without the trauma, falling from the bed, paralysis can be anticipated "somewhere in nature of 1%," a risk he termed "a very slight possibility." He felt that "communication of that risk to the patient is not good medical practice because it might deter patients from undergoing needed surgery and might produce adverse psychological reaction which could preclude the success of the operation." The court felt that the testimony indicated that neither the patient nor his mother had been told about the risk of paralysis; therefore, this was "a prima facia case of violation of the physician's duty to disclose which Dr. Spence's explanation did not negate as a matter of law."[13] The court, after speaking of Judge Cardoza's comments, went on to say, "True consent to what happens to one's self is the informed exercise of the choice, and that entails an opportunity to evaluate knowledgeably the options available and the risks attendant upon each."[14]

Furthermore, "the average patient has little or no understanding of the medical arts, and ordinarily has only his physician to whom he can look for enlightenment with which to reach an intelligent decision. From these almost axiomatic considerations springs the need, and in turn the requirement, of a reasonable

[13] *Supra* note 11, at 779.

[14] *Supra* note 11, at 780.

divulgence by physician to patient to make such a decision possible."[15] The court held the following: "In our view, the patient's right of self decision shapes the boundaries of the duty to reveal. That right can be effectively exercised only if the patient possesses enough information to enable an intelligent choice. The scope of the physician's communications to the patients, then, must be measured by the patient's need, and that need is the information material to the decision. Thus, the test for determining whether a particular peril may be divulged is its materiality to the patient's decision: all risks potentially affecting the decision must be unmasked. And to safeguard the patient's interest in achieving his own determination on treatment, the law must, itself, set the standard for adequate disclosure."[16] "There is no bright line separating the significant from the insignificant: the answer in any case must abide a rule of reasons. Some dangers—infection, for example—are inherent in any operation; there is no obligation to communicate those of which persons of average sophistication are aware."[17] "The privilege does not accept the paternalistic notion that the physician may remain silent simply because divulgence might prompt the patient to forego therapy the physician feels the patient really needs."[18] For the motivated physician this is indeed a burden. It is difficult to accept a patient's refusal of treatment that you are convinced will help him, knowing that his refusal is based upon information that you were forced (by law?) to give him.

What, in fact, does the patient understand and recall? George Robinson and Avraham Merav of Montefiore Hospital conducted a study in which they made a conscientious effort to obtain fully informed consent from all of their patients undergoing cardiac procedures.[19] They made a tape recording of the informed consent conversations, made, of course, with the knowledge and permis-

---

[15] *Supra* note 11, at 780.

[16] *Supra* note 11, at 786.

[17] *Supra* note 11, at 788.

[18] *Supra* note 11, at 789.

[19] Robinson, George, and Merav, Avraham: Informed Consent: Recall by Patients Tested Postoperatively. *The Annals of Thoracic Surgery, 22(3),* Sept. 1976, p. 209–212.

sion of the patients, two days prior to the operation. They included the diagnosis and nature of the patient's illness, the proposed operation, surgical techniques to be employed, prosthetic devices to be used, risk of death resulting from the procedure, potential complications of the operation and devices, if applicable, benefits of the proposed operative procedure, alternative methods of management, and their chances for failure or success. They obtained acknowledgment by the patient of his understanding of all explanations and answered any questions he had. Then, between four and six months following the operation, twenty patients were selected for re-interview to determine their capacity to recall each of the details. The patients had convalesced uneventfully after satisfactory operations and a postoperative course. The ages ranged from thirty-five to sixty-six. These were patients who had valve replacements and so forth. Six categories of questions that had been discussed prior to surgery were asked the patients in a nonsuggestive manner. These covered diagnosis and nature of illness, proposed operation, risk of the procedure, potential complications, benefits of the proposed operation, and alternative methods of management. The poorest scores were achieved in the single category of potential complications, where there was only a 10 percent primary recall. Patients were then given suggestions as to the appropriate answers and then tested for secondary recall. Correct answers then increased to 23 percent out of a possible 100 percent. The average recall in all six categories was 29 percent for primary and 42 percent for secondary. They say, "Thus even with the influence of suggestion and a point by point review of every item covered in the original interview, patients could remember only 42 percent of the items that had been covered in the informed consent interview." Later they say, "Errors made by patients in the repeat interview had qualitative differences. They may be described as failure to recall; positive denial of the truth; fabrication, or the assertion of an untruth or falsehood; and errors of attribution." Therefore, in this study we see that despite meticulous efforts by the surgeon, the patients fail to recall accurately what had transpired in their preoperative interview. In this manner the cross of malpractice hangs on the beleagured physician involved in a consent case.

In a study, "Informed Consent in Voluntary Mental Hospital Admissions," Olin and Olin say, "The authors studied the amount of understanding that 100 mental hospital patients had of a voluntary admission application they signed upon entering the hospital. Only eight patients were rated as being completely informed of the terms of the contract at the time of admission; 15 of 33 patients re-interviewed about ten days after admission showed increased understanding. Minimal differences were found between 81 state hospital patients and 19 private hospital patients. The finding that few voluntary patients are fully informed to give consent to hospitalization poses a dilemma because of the trend to give personal responsibility to the patient."[20] Once again, the amount of understanding of these individuals is quite limited. It is interesting to note that after a period of time in the hospital the patients seem to have a greater understanding, but still over 50 percent of them did not really understand the situation.

Recently an editorial appeared in *Science,* which was entitled, "Informed Consent May Be Hazardous to Health."[21] It stated, "If protection of the subject is the reason for obtaining informed consent, the possibility of iatrogenic harm to the subject as a direct result of the consent ritual must be considered. The current legalistic devices, which are designed in part to limit subject recourse; intensify rather than solve the dilemma."

For us in psychiatry the issue of consent has been a particular problem, specifically when it has, in recent times, been associated with the concept of the right to refuse treatment. The problem is compounded because many of our patients may not be able to give a truly informed consent due to their lack of competency.

Roth, who has done so much work on the issue of consent, has clarified the problem with the issue of competency. He published two articles in the March 1977 issue of the *American Journal of Psychiatry,* "Tests of Competency to Consent to Treatment" and

---

[20]Olin, Grace B. and Olin, Harry S.: Informed Consent in Voluntary Mental Hospital Admissions. *Am J. Psychiatry, 132(9),* Sept. 1975 p. 938–941.

[21]Loftus, Elizabeth F. and Fries, James F.: Editorial, Informed Consent May be Hazardous to Health, *Science, 204,* April 6, 1979.

"Towards a Model of the Legal Doctrine of Informed Consent."[22, 23] In his first article, "Tests of Competency to Consent to Treatment," he points out that "the concept of competency, like the concept of dangerousness, is social and legal and not merely psychiatric or medical." He then states that a perusal of the literature and judicial commentary would indicate that there are five basic categories that are important in considering competency to give consent, competency being one of the variables in the consent decision: (1) evidencing a choice, (2) reasonable outcome of choice, (3) choice based on rational reasons, (4) ability to understand, and (5) actual understanding.

Some of these, of course, overlap, and all of them are extremely difficult to evaluate. One, of course, can get into such conundrums about what to do if the patient understands the risks but does not understand the benefits, an example being a forty-nine-year-old woman whose understanding of treatment was otherwise intact when informed there was a 1 in 3,000 chance of dying from ECT replied, "I hope I am the one." In his discussion Roth states that, "It has been our experience that competency is presumed as long as the patient modulates his or her behavior, talks in a comprehensible way, and remembers what he or she is told, dresses and acts so as to appear to be in meaningful communication with the environment, and has not been declared legally incompetent. In other words, if the patients have their wits about them in a layman's sense, it is assumed that they will understand what they are told about treatment, including its risk, benefits and alternatives." In conclusion he says, "The search for a single test for competency is a search for a holy grail."

In his next paper, Roth speaks of a model of a legal doctrine of informed consent. He points out the difficulties in determining the patient's competency, i.e. his degree of understanding in making the final decision. "I believe that the final decision has to be on the patient's decision and then the doctor's assurance to himself that

[22] Roth, Loren: Tests of Competency to Consent to Treatment. *Am. J. Psychiatry, 134(3),* March 1977, p. 279–284.

[23] Roth, Loren: Towards a Model of the Legal Doctrine of Informed Consent. *Am J. Psychiatry, 134(3),* March 1977, p. 285–289.

he does, in fact, have a valid consent." As I pointed out, the catch 22 is that judicial opinions do not squarely confront or discuss the meaning of their requirement for competency. Roth describes an objective model for consent, which would not focus on the patient's understanding but on his capacity to function as an average person. The disorganized psychotic would probably not be able to give consent. An alternate subjective model focuses entirely on the patient's actual understanding of the information supplied. Being psychotic, for example, would be irrelevant.

Obviously, in psychiatry we have a greater problem than in surgery. It is quite clear that the cases are becoming increasingly difficult and great in number, particularly in view of recent "right to refuse treatment" cases. *Rennie v. Klein* requires "such consent forms shall state in plain language the right of voluntary patients to refuse treatment and the qualified right of involuntary patients to refuse and to have their refusals reviewed within the hospital, and by the independent psychiatrist as described in this order. Each form shall also state all known short-term and long-term side effects of the drug to be consented to, and may be supplemented by informal discussion by hospital staff with the patient concerning the risks and benefits of the drugs."[24]The side effects of all psychotropic drugs used in a hospital are to be posted or made available in each ward. There are, of course, provisions for the incompetent patient in terms of emergency care and appointment of a guardian and even a situation where the patient can be considered functionally incompetent.

> A treating physician may certify in an involuntary patient's record that the patient is 'functionally incompetent' because he is unable to provide knowledgeable consent to treatment, although he has not been declared incompetent by a court of law. These cases must also be referred to the Patient Advocate. . . . No voluntary patient may be medicated who does not sign a consent form or who orally refuses. . . .[25] The Patient Advocates must be supervised by an attorney and psychiatrist in the Office of the Commissioner. The Advocates may be trained attorneys, psychologists, social workers, registered nurses or paralegals, or have any equivalent experience. They must be given training in the effects of psychotropic

---

[24]Rennie v. Klein, 476 F.Supp 1294, 1313 (D. N.J. 1979).

[25]*Supra* note 24, at 1314

medication and the principles of legal advocacy. The Office of the Commissioner shall hire and pay psychiatrists to review the decisions to forcibly medicate involuntary patients. . . . The medical director, any treating physician or other member of the hospital staff may encourage a patient to consent to and take medication; however, force or the threat of force may not be used unless forced medication is allowed for a patient under the terms of this order.[26]

[If] involuntary patient refuses . . . after all in-hospital procedures are exhausted, or where an involuntary patient refuses intermittently and the hospital seeks to give medication on a continuous basis, the hospital may seek permission to involuntarily medicate by bringing the patient before the Independent Psychiatrist. . . . The patient must have at least five days between the first refusal to a staff nurse or physician and presentation to the Independent Psychiatrist. The Independent Psychiatrist may hold an informal proceeding. . . . No compulsory access to witnesses or cross-examination need be permitted, although the Independent Psychiatrist may request hospital employees to appear if he deems this necessary. . . . The Independent Psychiatrist shall issue a written determination in each case, basing any decision to override the patient's privacy right on the four factors outlined in the court's November opinion."[27]

The nice thing about *Rennie* is that the final decision is made by a psychiatrist, and patients ordinarily will not have to be declared incompetent. Even so, *Rennie* is being appealed because it is too restrictive and creates many problems.

The more recent decision, *Rogers v. Okin,* is much more troublesome in that this court, U.S. District Court, Massachusetts, establishes more stringent requirements and clearly sees psychotropic medication as mind altering. "Because the drugs' purpose is to reduce the level of psychotic thinking, it is virtually undisputed that they are mind altering."[28] It is curious that the court was unable to conceive of psychosis as being mind altering and medication as reconstituting the altered mind. Perhaps the psychiatrists and their lawyers failed in conveying this to the court.

In this opinion, Judge D. J. Tauro handed down, on October 29, 1979, a decision that, if it stands on appeal, could cause substantial changes in the functioning of psychiatric hospitals. The opinion

---

[26] *Supra* note 24, at 1313.

[27] *Supra* note 24, at 1314–1315.

[28] *Supra* note 2, at 1360.

deals generally with the right to refuse treatment, so parts of it touch upon my topic of consent. "The defendants, their agents and employees, are restrained from forcibly secluding or medicating the plaintiffs and all other inpatients of the Austin and May Units, and successor units, of the Boston State Hospital without the patient's consent or the consent of the patient's guardian, if any, except where there is a substantial likelihood of, or as a result of, extreme violence, personal injury or attempted suicide. . . . "[29]

The decision covers the forced use of medication and seclusion in nonemergency situations on voluntary and involuntary patients. "Although they have a right to receive treatment when confined at a state mental institution, they, nonetheless, have a constitutional right to refuse such treatment."[30]

The court seemed persuaded that tardive dyskinesia was a common side effect of these psychotropic drugs, even though none of the litigants suffered from it. Therefore, this, too, made these drugs dangerous. With reference to the ability to give consent, the court said, "The weight of evidence persuades this court that, although committed mental patients do suffer at least some impairment of their relationship to reality, most are able to appreciate the benefits, risks, and discomfort that may reasonably be expected from receiving psychotropic medication."[31] "Related D.M.H. regulations do recognize in absolute terms the competence of committed persons to manage their affairs and participate in a variety of challenging activities. That recognition tilts the scales in favor of presuming, as well, the competence of a committed mental patient to make treatment decisions, absent an adjudication to the contrary."[32]

In the ruling, the court stated the following:

> This court concludes, therefore, that committed mental patients are presumed competent to make decisions with respect to their treatment in non-emergencies. Given an adjudication of incompetence, a guardian may exercise for and on behalf of a committed mental patient any rights he

---

[29] *Supra* note 2, at 1342.

[30] *Supra* note 2, at 1352.

[31] *Supra* note 2, at 1361.

[32] *Supra* note 2, at 1362.

may have to make treatment decisions in a non-emergency.[33]

In making medication decisions, a guardian would not act as a third person, but would merely stand and act in the place of the patient. The patient's right is not to get a guardian. It is to be free from unwarranted government intrusion. The guardian is merely a means for protecting that freedom.... Given an emergency, plaintiffs concede that the Commonwealth would have a right to forcibly medicate any committed patient, competent or otherwise. Thus, plaintiffs contend that the Commonwealth's interest in preserving order and safety at the Hospital is adequately served as well.[34]

This court holds, therefore, that a committed mental patient may be forcibly medicated in an emergency situation in which a failure to do so would result in a substantial likelihood of physical harm to that patient, other patients, or to staff members of the institution.[35]

Whether or not the ideas are sick appears of no concern to the court.

As a practical matter, therefore, the power to produce ideas is fundamental to our cherished right to communicate and is entitled to comparable constitutional protection. Whatever powers the Constitution has granted our government, involuntary mind control is not one of them, absent extraordinary circumstances. The fact that mind control takes place in a mental institution in the form of medically sound treatment of mental disease is not, itself, an extraordinary circumstance warranting an unsanctioned intrusion on the integrity of a human being.[36]

The court seems to support vegetative custodial neglect.

Given a non-emergency, however, it is an unreasonable invasion of privacy, and an affront to basic concepts of human dignity, to permit forced injection of a mind-altering drug into the buttocks of a competent patient unwilling to give informed consent. That type of treatment is not necessary to protect the general public, since the patient has already been quarantined by commitment. Of course, there being no emergency, the hospital community is in no danger. The only purpose, therefore, of forced medication, in a non-emergency, is to help the patient. The desire to help the patient is a laudable if not noble goal. But, a basic premise of the right to privacy is the freedom to decide whether we want to be helped, or whether we want to be left alone. It takes a grave set of circumstances to

---

[33] *Supra* note 2, at 1364.

[34] *Supra* note 2, at 1362.

[35] *Supra* note 2, at 1365.

[36] *Supra* note 2, at 1367.

abrogate that right. That a non-emergency injection in the buttocks may be therapeutic does not constitute such a circumstance.[37]

Although testimony indicated that only 12 of 1000 patients refused medication and then only briefly, Applebaum and Gutheil have reported severe chronicity and loss of valuable treatment time in refusing patients.[38] This was a bad decision. Let us hope the appeal court is reasonable.

The important point for my purposes in citing the preceding material is that the issue of consent has reached its acme in psychiatry in the right to refuse treatment situations. Can we now anticipate an increasing number of civil suits for assault and battery based on the patient's claim that he did not give his consent to that injection in a nonemergency situation? Based on all I have said, the problem could be overwhelming. Hopefully, such a time will not arrive, because most of our patients are grateful for their treatment once they have recovered. It seems that law and psychiatry may be suffering from bilateral scotoma, that is, each of us seems to have our blind spots. Some of the conditions on the May and Austin Wards of the Boston State Hospital (*Rogers v. Okin*) were deplorable—flooded bathrooms, understaffed, unheated, etc. Could we not expect the court to be upset and question our therapeutic ideals? In the *Rennie* case, nursing personnel were proven to have beaten Mr. Rennie. After they were reprimanded, Mr. Rennie was still kept on the same ward. The state of New Jersey had originally agreed to establish a review system for refusing patients. The court discovered that the state had actually done nothing to implement the program. Where is our good faith? Behind our blind spot?

I have tried to discuss consent from its recent historical roots to its current posture and its requirements for full informed consent. I have touched on the right to refuse treatment issue and its implications for consent. As we enter the 1980s in our litigious country, I suspect we will hear more about consent suits and

---

[37] *Supra* note 2, at 1369.

[38] Applebaum, Paul S. and Gutheil, Thomas G.: Drug Refusal: A Study of Psychiatric Inpatients. *Am. J. Psychiatry, 135(3),* March 1980, pp. 340–346.

problems in obtaining informed consent. Patient package inserts and similar approaches may reduce the psychiatrists' liability and burden. Perhaps patients will not be scared off. Perhaps patients will accept more responsibility for their care. Perhaps we can help the law resolve this problem so medical care will not suffer.

In closing, in the words of Shakespeare, "We must not make a scarecrow of the law, setting it up to fear the birds of prey, and let it keep one shape, till custom make it their perch, and not their terror."[39]

---

[39]*Measure for Measure,* act III, scene 1, Line 1.

Chapter 20

ECT AND INVASIVE THERAPIES

JONAS ROBITSCHER, J. D., M.D.

Lawyers and militant patients who attempt to curb the power of psychiatrists divide therapies into two categories—those which are invasive or intrusive and therefore require supervision and control and those which are not invasive and intrusive and therefore can be imposed on unwilling patients in their own interest. The distinction between the intrusive/invasive and the nonintrusive/noninvasive therapies is not as clear cut as many would make it; in fact, I would argue that all therapies are invasive.

Psychiatrists invade their patients' lives and minds in the act of relating to them as psychiatrists. The lobotomist of the 1950s inserting his leucotome into the frontal lobes of his patient was unquestionably invasive. But, the transference reactions of a patient in psychoanalysis may lead to changes that are equally profound; the behavior and the life of the patient may be equally changed. The verbal and even the nonverbal productions of the therapist— thoughts, feelings, directions, suggestions, interpretations—all invade. The overcoming of resistance in analytically oriented psychotherapy is an invasion; so is the forced change of methods of feeling and reacting produced by behavior modification.

Yet, although any therapy that is effective will invade the patient in some way, the militant patients' groups and the lawyers who are attempting to curb psychiatrists are referring to somatic therapies when they call for a curb on invasive therapies—in particular, the outmoded lobotomy and three currently practiced more sophisticated modalities: psychosurgery, electroconvulsive therapy, and

Presented at the Annual Meeting of the New York State Chapter of the American Academy of Psychiatry and the Law, entitled Psychiatric Treatment and the Law, New York University Medical Center, New York, January 19, 1980.

Dr. Robitscher died in 1981.

drug therapy when the drug is injected into or forced upon the patient.

These therapies are patently invasive. They can be and often are inflicted on patients who have no power to argue, resist, or defend against them. Psychosurgeons apply radioactive materials or cutting instruments to excise portions of the brain. Psychiatrists pass electric currents through the brain to interrupt thoughts and memories. Behavior modifiers — psychiatrists and psychologists — apply milder electric currents or other painful stimuli to the calf or some other part of the body or give emetics as aversive conditioners. Psychiatrists dose patients or inject drugs that work their way into the cells and bathe the synapses of the brain. Psychiatrists literally get under their patients' skins.

One ranking of psychotherapies from the least to the most intrusive and coercive — qualities that are roughly equivalent to invasiveness — is as follows: milieu therapy, individual and group verbal psychotherapy, drug treatment, behavior modification, electroconvulsive therapy, electrostimulation of the brain, and psychosurgery. The one qualification I would make in this ranking is that one particular form of drug therapy, the use of a long-acting injectable, Prolixin®, is much more invasive or intrusive than other forms of drug therapy and should be considered on a par with ECT.

Early psychiatrists had all sorts of unpleasant ways of invading their patients. Mercurials and purges were used to expel the disease; tartar emetic was used as a nauseant and emetic to help the patient rid himself of evil humors. At the time of the American Revolution, the chief methods psychiatrists used were dosing, purging, and, in the modality of bloodletting, cutting. Benjamin Rush, the father of American psychiatry, advocated a "caustic applied to the back of the neck or between the shoulders, and kept open for months or years. The remedy," he said, "acts by the permanent discharge it induces from the neighborhood of the brain."[1]

We all know of some of the drastic remedies that psychiatrists have forced on patients. Until the time of the Civil War, bloodlet-

---

[1] Gregory Zilboorg, *A History of Medical Psychology* (New York: W. W. Norton, 1941), p. 548.

ting continued to be a favorite treatment. In the 1890s sterilization and castration began to be utilized to cure sexual pathology, and the early years of this century saw the perpetration of a focus of infection theory that led to the removal of teeth, tonsils, the appendix, and portions of the colon.[2]

Some of the treatments that psychiatrists have forced on their patients in the past 200 years include flagellation, twirling in revolving chairs, sudden immersion in cold water, exposure to high pressure streams of alternating very hot and very cold water, laxatives, irritant plasters, and poultices. Treatment methods discussed by Wilhelm Griesinger, a leading German neurologist and psychiatrist of the mid-nineteenth century, were cupping, leeching, douching, cold plunge baths, poultices and plasters, belladonna, quinine, purgatives, emetics, bitters and tonics, ether and chloroform, and the application of galvanic electrical current.[3] The nineteenth century saw two models of psychiatric treatment pitted against each other—the model of the doctor forcing treatment on patients in the context of the traditional medical authoritarianism and a new model, advocated by only a few psychiatrists, of moral treatment, enlisting the cooperation of the patient and appealing to his or her sensibilities. Our use of drugs, electroconvulsive treatment, and psychosurgery stems from the authoritarian and more typically medical tradition.

The beginning of modern somatic treatment and of psychopharmacology came with the introduction of bromide salts in the 1850s; chloral hydrate was added next to the treatment schedule followed by the barbiturates, which for half a century were the chief drugs used for psychiatric patients. In the period before the introduction of modern psychopharmacological agents in the 1950s, these and electroconvulsive therapy were the main somatic treat-

---

[2] In the 1920s in the United States, Henry Cotton popularized the focal infection theory, and thousands of patients had their teeth and tonsils removed as psychiatric therapy. Eventually Cotton came to believe that mental symptoms were caused by an overly long colon that allowed food to remain undigested and become a source of poisons in the system, and a multitude of state hospital patients—the exact numbers are not known—had portions of their colons removed. Jonas Robitscher, *The Powers of Psychiatry* (Boston: Houghton Mifflin, 1980), pp. 85–86.

[3] Wilhelm Griesinger, *Mental Pathology and Therapeutics* (London: New Sydenham Society, 1867, facsimile ed. New York: Hafner Publishing Co., 1965), pp. 470–483.

ment methods; since then, the introduction of the major tran-
quilizers and of antidepressants has led to an even greater reliance
on drug therapy. The new psychopharmacology also led to a
displacement—only temporarily—of electroshock therapy and the
elimination of the lobotomy. A recent article in *Time* is headlined:
"Comeback for Shock Therapy?" The subhead reads: "Its unsa-
vory reputation may be changing."[4] Without good statistics, many
psychiatrists have a feeling that use of ECT is very much on the
upswing after its recent period of relative unpopularity.

The crusade against invasive therapies centered initially on
psychosurgery as represented by the lobotomy, a technique pio-
neered in the 1930s by Egas Moniz in Portugal and simplified and
popularized by Freeman and Watts in the United States. Peter
Breggin, a Washington psychiatrist opposed to psychosurgery in
all its forms, has given us a "probably reliable" estimate of 50,000
lobotomies done in this country over a period of a decade.[5] The
introduction of Thorazine® led to the phasing out of the lobotomy,
but since then, what Breggin has called the second wave of
psychosurgery has arrived—the use of new and sophisticated surgical techniques, developed originally to deal with intractable
pain and symptoms of Parkinson's disease, to alter emotions, behavior, and personality. Perhaps 500 experimental psychosurgical
procedures are now done each year, all on voluntary and presumably
competent and informed patients.

Patients were not protected from psychosurgery in the 1960s and
early 1970s; the procedures were done for episodic dyscontrol,
sexual crimes of violence, and other psychiatric indications on
prisoners and on patients in hospitals for the criminally insane
and Veterans Administration hospitals.

A stop to this kind of invasive treatment was effected through
the decision in the *Louis Smith* case, known in law books as *Kaimowitz
v. Michigan Department of Public Health*. Several aspects of the
ruling bear attention. First, although it was a decision of a court of

---

[4] *Comeback for Shock Therapy?* Time, Nov. 19, 1979, p. 76.

[5] Peter Breggin, The Return of Lobotomy and Psychosurgery, *Congressional Record*, Feb. 24,
1972, E1602–12. Reprinted in *Quality of Health Care—Human Experimentation*, Hearings
before Senator Edward Kennedy's Subcommittee on Health, U.S. Senate. (Washington, D.C.:
United States Government Printing Office, 1973).

first impression and never was appealed, the case has had great precedential effect because it is (as far as I know) the only case dealing with the propriety of psychosurgery; it has been much quoted and cited.[6] Second, although the jurisdiction of the court only extended as far as the boundaries of Wayne County, Michigan, the case led to the general awareness that physicians were performing psychosurgery experimentally on captive populations, and this in turn led to the end of this practice. Third, the case stands for two propositions that are highly debatable—that a potentially coercible individual, such as a prisoner or inmate of a hospital for the criminally insane, can never give consent or have consent supplied for him for a procedure that is extremely invasive, irreversible, experimental, and potentially risky, and that the power to formulate one's own uncontaminated thoughts is protected by the first amendment.

More recently the *Kaimowitz* case has in effect been overruled by the National Commission for the Protection of Human Subjects. Its final report, issued in 1976, was unexpectedly favorable to psychosurgery. It recommended that experimental psychosurgery be continued under carefully supervised conditions, and it advocated that the Secretary of Health, Education and Welfare support such research financially.[7] J. Kenneth Ryan of Harvard Medical School, chairman of the Commission, said, "We saw that some very sick people had been helped by it, and that it did not destroy their intelligence or rob them of feelings. Their marriages were intact. They were able to work. The operation shouldn't be banned."[8] The Commission saw the *Kaimowitz* holding, that no

---

[6] Kaimowitz v. Michigan Department of Public Health, Civil No. 73–19, 434–AW (Cir. Ct. Wayne County, Mich., July 10, 1973), summarized at 42 U.S.L.W. 2063. In addition to the Kaimowitz case, there have been at least two cases based on alleged bad effects of psychosurgical procedures; in 1975 an unsuccessful malpractice action was brought against Dr. Robert Groff, the former chairman of the department of neurosurgery at the University of Pennsylvania, and in 1979 an unsuccessful action was brought against Dr. Vernon Mark and Dr. Frank H. Ervin for alleged malpractice in a 1966 to 1967 bilateral amygdalotomy performed at Massachusetts General Hospital.

[7] *Protection of Human Subjects: Use of Psychosurgery in Practice and Research: Report and Recommendation for Public Comment,* Fed. Reg., May 23, 1977, pp. 26318–32.

[8] Barbara Culliton, Psychosurgery: National Commission Issues Surprisingly Favorable Report, *Science,* Oct. 15, 1976, pp. 299–301.

prisoners and involuntarily held patients could give a valid informed consent to experimental psychosurgery, as overly restrictive, saying, "With respect to the question of safety and efficacy, it is clear that the information presented to the court in 1973 differs significantly from that which has been presented to the Commission." It recommended an absolute right for prisoners and mental patients to refuse psychosurgery, but also a right to give informed consent to the procedure. Psychosurgery, according to the Commission, is "an opportunity to seek benefit from a new therapy."

In spite of this go-ahead for psychosurgery, the procedure is apparently not now being sponsored by the government. At one time research was funded both by HEW and the Law Enforcement Assistance Administration of the Department of Justice, which raised the anxieties of the civil rights minded, and is only being done on voluntary patients who are not in institutions and who are considered fully competent and informed.

Proponents of psychosurgery have said we are denying freedom to sexual psychopaths, violent prisoners, and others included in the category of criminally insane by not allowing them to consent to psychosurgery. They have reversed the traditionally liberal point of view, which sees psychosurgery as restrictive of freedom and the law as protective of freedom and claim that by giving patients the freedom to think in socially unacceptable ways we are only ensuring that we will be forced to continue to deprive them of physical freedom. But, in spite of the protests of psychosurgeons, neurologists, and some psychiatrists, most psychiatrists feel that psychosurgery is extremely invasive and drastic and do not object to the right of patients to refuse this treatment or even its outright interdiction.

The question then arises, How different is ECT from psychosurgery? Very different, most psychiatrists say. Most psychiatrists see electroconvulsive therapy as an effective treatment method, given so frequently that it can hardly be called unusual, so harmless in its application that it cannot be called drastic. They are therefore both surprised and affronted when this treatment method is attacked, regulated, and restricted. In particular, they react with strong feeling when legislatures and courts find ECT so adverse to the interests of and so unacceptable to some patients that they have begun to extend to them the new legal concept, "the right to refuse" ECT treatment.

The campaign against the unrestricted use of ECT goes on on four fronts. First, legislatures are beginning to set up special procedures allowing patients to challenge any attempt to have ECT forced upon them; California is an example.[9] Second, the civil commitment statutes of some jurisdictions are including protection against the imposition of ECT. In Wisconsin, for example, before ECT can be used, patients must be consulted, and they must have a chance to consult with their attorneys or guardians. (Incidentally, the Wisconsin statute, although ambiguous, could be read to deny the possibility of a substituted consent, no matter how irrational the patient might be.)[10] Third, some so-called right to treatment cases — *Wyatt v. Stickney* is an example[11] — have imposed limitations on the use of ECT. Finally, two recent cases, *Rennie v. Klein*[12] in New Jersey and *Rogers v. Okin*[13] in Massachusetts, have used language to give patients in one case a limited right and in the other case an absolute right to refuse drug therapy that by implication would be equally or even more applicable to ECT.[14]

Why the great difference in the perception of ECT by psychiatrists on the one hand and legislators and courts on the other? Should psychiatrists be given a free hand in administering this treatment, or should patients and their representatives have veto power? We are involved in a growing debate on the subject, and the intensity of the conflict and the effort to curb the use of ECT are both escalating.

The historical background of ECT is well known. It was developed by Cerletti and Bini, who in 1938 discovered that an alternating current sent from temple to temple for one-tenth to one-half of a second produced a strong shaking convulsion, like the convulsion of grand mal epilepsy, and that the patient lost consciousness and on regaining consciousness showed confusion and loss of memory,

---

[9] Cal. Ann. Welf. & Inst. Code, §§ 5326.7, 5326.75, 5326.8, 5326.85 (West, Supp. 1980).

[10] Wis. Stat. § 51.61 (1)(k) (1977).

[11] Wyatt v. Stickney, 344 F. Supp. 373 (M.D. Ala. 1972).

[12] Rennie v. Klein, CA–772624, D.C. N.J., Sept. 14, 1979.

[13] Rogers v. Okin, CA 75–1610–T, D.C. Mass., Oct. 29, 1979.

[14] Both of these cases are now on appeal to the respective circuit courts of appeal.

which was cumulative with the administration of further shocks. A lesser known fact of psychiatric history is that Benjamin Franklin, the inventor of other amenities of modern living, had suggested the use of shock as early as 1785 and had himself been the recipient of perhaps the first ECT treatment. Franklin was one of a number of scientists of his day who experimented with electricity as a cure for a variety of diseases, including neurological disorders and epilepsy. He administered mild, galvanic shocks to other parts of the body, not the head; there was no thought of producing convulsions. A friend in America wrote to Franklin and asked if shocks could be useful for mad persons. Franklin in reply recalled an incident when a paralyzed man had been brought to his chamber at Passy to be shocked. Because so many of the patient's friends had come with him, Franklin was crowded into a position under an iron hook, which hung from the ceiling to within two inches of his head. When he discharged two large jars to give the patient the shock, he, not the patient, received the charge. He described the event as follows: "I neither saw the flash, heard the report, nor felt the stroke. When my senses returned, I found myself on the floor. I got up, not knowing how that had happened. I then again attempted to discharge the jars; but one of the company told me they were already discharged, which I could not at first believe, but on trial found it true. . . . A small swelling rose on the top of my head which continued sore for some days; but I do not remember any other effect, good or bad."[15]

Franklin reacted to his friend's letter by getting in touch with an electrical operator, who under French government sponsorship was using electricity to treat epileptics and other neurological conditions and suggesting to him that he try electric shock for madness, but we do not know of any further development in response to the suggestion. We do know of widespread belief for a century and a half in the efficacy of electricity not used as shock therapy but as an invigorator with reported good results. In America S. Weir Mitchell used electrotherapy as part of his rest cure, and Freud, when he started his private practice, like the other neurol-

---

[15] Franklin letter of April 29, 1785, quoted in letter by Walter Ford, Franklin and ECT. *Psychiatric News*, July 21, 1978, p. 12, from *Connecticut J. of Public Safety*, June, 1956.

ogists of his time and place, utilized the electrotherapeutic approach as described in the textbook of Wilhelm Erb. As this kind of use of electricity was passing into disrepute, new, nonelectrical shock therapies—insulin shock, Metrazol®, and Indoklon®—were being used to produce convulsions, and the marriage of electrical and convulsion-producing therapy finally occurred, as we have seen, in the work of Cerletti and Bini.

Fink has described the growth of the use of ECT, advanced by Cerletti and Bini as a cure for schizophrenia in 1938 and extended to depressive psychoses, involutional depression, and mania, then to endogenous depression, then to patients with suicidal thoughts and intentions. "Soon," Fink says, "trials were reported in patients of all ages, from childhood to the senium; and in all mental conditions including the neuroses, psychopathies, drug dependence, and organic psychoses."[16] Indeed, in my opinion, ECT became our most overutilized psychiatric treatment method, given for more cases where it is not indicated than for those where it is indicated.

In 1948 Gordon listed fifty theories for the efficacy of ECT; since that time many more sophisticated explanations—some of them focused on such neurohumoral factors as acetylcholine, the catecholamines, and serotonin—have been advanced.[17] The popularity of ECT increased as the practice of modifying seizures with muscle relaxants became popular by 1950, but the introduction of reserpine and chlorpromazine in the early 1950s and subsequent reliance on drug therapy led to the temporary eclipse of ECT, especially in its use by state hospitals (although many private hospitals and individual practitioners continued to use it heavily), and during this period of decreased use many variations were tried to reduce the complications—the combination of shock with electronarcosis, the use of subconvulsive currents, the unilateral placement of electrodes to reduce the effect on memory function.

Before the use of modified shock there was a great fear of such complications as death, fractures, muscle sprains and strains, chipped

---

[16]Fink, M.: A History of Convulsive Therapy. *Psychiatric J of the Univ. of Ottawa, 4:* 105–110, 1979.

[17]*Ibid.*

teeth, as well as fears of the treatment itself and of memory loss and regression. Since that time, the treatment has been seen as much safer and less fear inspiring. Death is an infrequent event and usually results from cardiac complications, which were stated in a 1955 study to be common, affecting 8 percent to 75 percent of patients depending on premedication and other factors, but rarely severe.[18] We have very inexact figures on the death rate from ECT. According to some frequently cited but probably not very authoritative statistics, it is only one in 60,000 persons, compared with one in 18,000 from a tonsillectomy.[19]

A study of 259,000 treatments in England showed one death per 29,000 treatments.[20] A study in Denmark gives a similar fatality rate, one in 25,000 treatments. Since these figures are for treatments, not patients,[21] and since the average patient according to an American study receives ten treatments,[22] the fatality rate would appear to be possibly as high as one in 2,500 patients, and higher when we take into consideration that many patients have more than one course of treatment. Peter Breggin, one of ECT's most vocal critics, has said that "in some studies the treatment has a mortality rate of 1:1,000, among all patients given the treatment, and a much higher rate in high-risk populations, such as older individuals and individuals with cardiovascular, respiratory, or central nervous system disease." He believes this information should be part of the informed consent protocol.[23]

The mortality rate is less than the anticipated suicide rate in untreated patients but still does not justify giving the treatment to patients for whom the risk is unacceptable or would be unacceptable

---

[18] Leioxs, W. H., Jr., et al.: Cardiovascular Disturbances and their Management in Modified Electrotherapy for Psychiatric Illness. *N. Engl. J. Med,* 252:1016–20, 1953, cited in a recent editorial in the *Journal of the American Medical Association,* APA Task Force Report, *supra.*

[19] Chemotherapy and ECT. *Hospital & Community Psychiatry,* 30:827–828, 1979; Scarf, Maggie: Shocking the Depressed Back to Life. *New York Times Magazine,* June 17, 1979, p. 34.

[20] Barker, J. C., and Baker, A. A.: Deaths Associated with Electroplexy. *J. Mental Science, 105:* 339–348, 1957.

[21] Grosser, G. N. et al.: The Regulations of Electro-Convulsive Treatment in Massachusetts: A Follow-up. Departmental Report, Department of Mental Health, Mass., 1974.

[22] Heshe, J., and Roeder, E.: Electroconvulsive Therapy in Denmark. *Br. J. Psychiatry,* 128:24–245, 1976, cited in Electroconvulsive Therapy. *JAMA, 242:*545–46, 1979.

[23] Breggin, Peter: *Electroshock: Its Brain-Disabling Effects* (New York: Springer, 1979), p. 208.

if they were capable of rationally evaluating it. Some of the studies do not sufficiently distinguish between the fatality rates of unmodified and modified shock. Most medical authorities—but not patients—now, in contrast to Breggin's view, consider the risk of death as "negligible."[24]

There has been general agreement that ECT is an effective treatment for psychotic depression, catatonia, and mania. There is much disagreement about its efficacy for obsessive thinking, suicidal preoccupation, neurotic depression, personality disorders, and schizophrenia, a condition for which it is widely used. In 1947 the Group for the Advancement of Psychiatry stated that "abuses in the use of electro-shock therapy are sufficiently widespread and dangerous to justify consideration of a campaign of professional education in the limitations of this technique, and perhaps even to justify instituting certain measures of control."[25] Recently the American Psychiatric Association has issued a favorable Task Force Report, which according to Breggin "was written with the clear intent of improving the image of ECT. . . . It laments public criticism of the treatment and legislative intent to enforce informed consent, and it questions the motives of those who criticize the therapy. It urges discarding the time-honored name 'shock treatment' because it arouses fear, and further argues that even 'convulsive therapy' is inappropriate because the muscles are relaxed during the treatment." He also criticized the APA Task Force on the ground that its composition was dominated by some of the best-known advocates of ECT.[26]

The attack on ECT continues on a number of fronts—the general public is afraid of it, and this is reflected in legislation and legal advocacy, groups of former patients campaign against it and recount their own bad experiences, some psychiatrists oppose it.

---

[24]Clare, Anthony: Therapeutic and Ethical Aspects of Electro-Convulsive Therapy: A British Perspective. *Int. J. Law Psychiatry*, 1:237–253, 1978, at 243. A minority of psychiatrists continue to rate the risk of death from ECT as far from negligible. *See* Breggin, Peter: *Electroshock*, Chapter 4.

[25]GAP (Group for the Advancement of Psychiatry): "Shock Therapy," Letter, Sept. 15, 1947, quoted in Fink, *supra*.

[26]Breggin, *Electroshock*, pp. 14–15, commenting on American Psychiatric Association, *Task Force Report 14: Electroconvulsive Therapy*, Washington, D.C., APA, Sept. 1978.

Breggin, following up his attack on psychosurgery, has written a book marshaling all the antishock arguments.[27] Most psychiatrists show their lack of enthusiasm for this treatment by failing to use it; an APA Survey showed that only 16 percent of the respondents had personally administered ECT in the previous six months and that only 22 percent had administered it or recommended its use to psychiatric residents in the previous six months, a less than strong endorsement of this treatment method.[28]

One of the main arguments against ECT is that it is given to patients with conditions not amenable to convulsive therapy. We should note that many commentators believe ECT only deals with symptoms, not with causes; its beneficial effects often seem to be only temporary and require reinforcement at intervals. Its use almost always precludes the discovery of dynamic psychic causes and conflicts, and it usually closes out the option for interpersonal therapy in which a transference develops and is explored and attempted to be resolved. A major argument against ECT is that it sometimes results in long-term and even permanent memory deficit, and although most psychiatrists who have studied this deny any permanent effects, patients and some literature references state this is a real phenomenon.[29] It should be noted that although the APA Task Force found there was no division of informed opinion about the efficacy of ECT in properly selected cases of severe depression[30] (although it did find that there is inadequate information[31] or that not all opinion is in agreement about its use for other, nondepressive, conditions[32]) and also found that the risks and side effects when it is property administered can be minimized,[33] it also stated that patients subjectively report persistent memory loss[34] and that 41 percent of psychiatrists responding to its questionnaire agreed (and only

---

[27] Breggin, *supra* note 26.

[28] APA *Task Force Report, supra.*

[29] *See* Breggin, *Electroshock, supra* note 26.

[30] *Task Force Report,* pp. 15–16.

[31] *Supra* note 30, at 18.

[32] *Supra* note 30, at 23–26, 31–45.

[33] *Supra* note 30, at 145.

[34] *Supra* note 30, at 66–68.

26 percent disagreed) that it is likely that ECT produces slight or subtle brain damage.[35]

When the large number of conditions for which ECT has been or is being given is compared with the few conditions for which there is general agreement that it is effective, it becomes apparent that ECT is often given for inappropriate reasons. When I was on the staff of a suburban Philadelphia hospital that had a nursing school, the treatment of choice, dictated by the chief of psychiatry, for nursing students who had acute psychotic breaks was an immediate course of ECT to make them docile enough so they could be sent home to their parents as cured or in remission; no one followed up these girls to see how long the cure lasted, and no member of the staff was able to do more than inaudibly mutter his expression of opposition to this kind of treatment. A psychiatric journal report, how typical we cannot say, describes a fifty-seven-year-old housewife who complained of abdominal pains, epigastric discomfort, a fitful sleep pattern, and deteriorating initiative. She was hospitalized, given ECT three times weekly for three months and twice weekly for another month and given outpatient ECT each Saturday morning for more than two years. When she was examined then by outside consultants, she was suffering from severe dementia, loss of spontaneity, and profound memory deficit, but her psychiatrist did not readily accept the recommendation that ECT be discontinued. Instead, he warned against further loss of affect and said that the confusion was part of the treatment. ECT was stopped, and eleven months later the patient had an improving sensorium, memory, and spontaneity, and somatic symptoms that became worse after the discontinuance were alleviated by antidepressant drug therapy.[36]

Following is one more example of the abuse of ECT. Phillip Frazier was a twenty-year-old Oklahoma former high school basketball star who murdered a fellow worker and was convicted and given a ten-year sentence and sent to the administrative section of the Oklahoma State Penitentiary, with prisoners who are disciplinary problems. He was diagnosed as schizophrenic. Periodically

---

[35] *Supra* note 30, at 4.

[36] Regenstein, Quentin, et al.: A Case of Prolonged, Reversible Dementia Associated with Abuse of Electroconvulsive Therapy. *J. Nerv. Ment. Dis., 161:*200–203, 1975.

he was transferred to Eastern State Hospital in Vinita, Oklahoma, where his condition was stabilized by drugs. The time spent in the hospital did not count toward his parole, so he was given shock treatments to stabilize his condition so that he could be returned to prison and serve enough of his sentence to appear before the parole board. Not surprisingly, the shock left him as bad off as, or worse than, he was before, hallucinating Jesus and asking for sixty teabags for lunch.[37]

It is very easy to make a case for ECT; it is the treatment of choice for psychotic depression after other methods have proved ineffective; it is sometimes lifesaving. Nevertheless, this is an intrusive and drastic method of treatment, which has many disadvantages. We impose it on incompetent patients on the fiction that if they were competent they would want this for themselves, but if they knew all the indications and contraindications, many of them would not want ECT. They would want a long trial of other therapies, if necessary, in a safe place where suicide could be guarded against. ECT, like drug and other somatic therapies, is aimed at stamping out florid symptoms and returning patients to their prepsychotic level of functioning. Such psychiatrists as R. D. Laing and John Weir Perry have hypothesized that psychosis is an attempt by the individual to break away from an intolerable and ineffective state of functioning and that the psychosis has reparative value. Perry has said that the prepsychotic state of tension experienced by the individual represents a more pathological state than the psychotic disorganization we call the sickness.[38] Psychiatrists who see psychosis as reparative believe that only an interpersonally based patient-therapist relationship (made much more difficult by ECT, sometimes facilitated by drug therapy but often not even attempted when drugs are relied on), which utilizes verbal therapy and understanding of the meaning of symptoms, rather than the suppression of symptoms, will help the patient reach a more satisfactory adjustment. Boyer and Giovacchini, for example, have said that the regression of the patient and the development of a psychotic transference are necessary elements in the cure of schiz-

---

[37] Ward, Steve: Litigant Bewildered in $2 Million Lawsuit. *Tulsa Tribune*, Dec. 1, 1979, p. 1.

[38] Perry, John Weir: *The Far Side of Madness* (Englewood Cliffs, N.J.: Prentice-Hall, 1974).

ophrenic patients.[39]

I would want for myself a combination of drug and verbal therapies if I were psychotically depressed, and I would not be comfortable in ordering anything less than this for my patients, even if I were in a position to completely dictate their treatment. Only in an acute life-threatening situation or after the failure of a comprehensive trial of other therapies would I recommend ECT.

Peter Breggin's book on ECT, *Electroshock: Its Brain-Disabling Effects*, states that the basic question in the ECT controversy is whether there is complete recovery from the acute organic brain syndrome phase. He cites cases from his personal practice, animal experimentation data, human autopsy studies, human brain-wave and neurological studies, and clinical and research reports, which he says confirm that in addition to the retrograde amnesia that proponents of ECT concede is caused by ECT, there is other permanent mental dysfunction.[40]

Breggin believes that studies showing ECT effective for psychotic depression and for the prevention of suicide lack scientific credibility and that whatever good effects are obtained can be explained on grounds other than the efficacy of the treatment. Although proponents of ECT will find Breggin's position extreme, he raises many points that deserve serious consideration. He recommends rigid controls over the use of ECT, but he would allow it for voluntary informed patients who choose the treatment (in spite of his belief that patients who pick this treatment risk sacrificing their highest mental functions).[41]

Whether or not we agree with Breggin, we can safely say that with a treatment method of literally so much power, the patient deserves protection from its misuse and overuse and also deserves the right to enter into his, or more usually her, own treatment decisions. Psychiatry has asserted that commitment should not be merged with the incompetency decision, that psychosis does not mean that there is lack of testamentary capacity or criminal responsibility. It cannot now assert that patients who are commit-

---

[39] Boyer, J. Bryce, and Giovacchini, Peter: *Psychoanalytic Treatment of Schizophrenic, Borderline and Characterological Disorders* (New York: Jason Aronson, 1980).

[40] Breggin, *Electroshock*, p. 74 ff.

[41] *Ibid*, p. 211.

ted have lost all right to participate in their own treatment decisions. Certainly voluntary patients should have full right to assent to or decline any treatment recommendation. How should we deal with involuntary patients?

It comes difficult to doctors who are by temperament and training authoritarian to adjust to the new age of consumerism to say that even irrational patients have something to contribute to their treatment plans. And it is ridiculous to say that a wildly delusional or hallucinatory patient should make decisions about whether he should or should not receive Thorazine® or haloperidol. When patients meet the criteria for application of ECT, that is, when they are psychotically depressed, when a combination of drug and verbal treatment has not been helpful, and when a life-threatening emergency is present, which cannot be treated in any other way, psychiatrists should have the authority to use their best treatment modality—in this case, shock—to deal with the situation. In all other situations we must yield to our legalistic critics and seek patient consent and go through a review process if our recommendation and the patient's wishes remain unreconciled. In particular, when shock is used on young patients, new patients, schizophrenic patients, on personality disorders, on neurotic depressive patients, we must have some safeguards to ensure that the treatment is in the interest of the patient, not merely being applied because this is the therapist's preferred treatment method, because longer term relationship therapy is too expensive, or because Blue Cross and Blue Shield will pay for three weeks of hospitalization, enough for shock but not for other treatment methods.

Following is an outline of some of the safeguards we need to see that shock is not misapplied:

1. We need a central registry of shock treatment, with names coded to protect confidentiality so that we have reliable statistics on how often this method is used, the range of stated indications, the range of length of courses of treatment. We need to establish, in addition, the frequency with which any one psychiatrist uses shock—for many or most of his patients, for none, or for some quantity of patients in between. Patients are entitled to this information. They are entitled to know if their psychiatrist gives shock more or less frequently than other psychiatrists do. Perhaps a psychiatrist's rarely or never giving shock—I place myself in this

category—is as indefensible as a psychiatrist's using shock on a majority of or many of his patients. In either case, the patient needs this information if he is to determine whether the treatment is in his best interest.

2. We need follow-ups on shock patients. We need to know how effective the treatment is, how long the good result is maintained, how often patients need repeat courses of treatment. We must get a better concept of whether shock merely deals with symptoms—scatters and dissipates them—and whether the natural course of the depressive condition is for the symptoms to reform and regroup, or whether the patient can hope for a definitive cure. If all we are doing is to dissipate feeling and thought so that patients forget that they are living a life of intolerable pain and do not feel it necessary to do anything to deal with the causes of the pain, we are truly, as critics say, working to maintain an untenable status quo, not working in the interest of growth and change.

3. We need a clarification of the uses of ECT. Is psychotic depression truly, as I think, the only major indication for the treatment? Should it be used for manic excitement, catatonia? How long should other therapies be applied before the decision to go to shock is made? We are now operating a laissez faire system in which each psychiatrist makes his own rules for the indications of treatment, and that to me seems an intolerable situation.

4. We need a system of patient appeal and peer review so that patients or their representatives can object to ECT.

5. We need insurance and third party payment plans that will pay as much for out-of-hospital treatment by longer term methods as for the shorter term inpatient treatments, because we know that the ability to complete a course of treatment within the three weeks of hospitalization provided for in many insurance plans is one of the chief determinants that this kind of therapy will be used.

In addition to psychosurgery and ECT, drug therapy has often been described as invasive. Some patient advocates have used the terms drastic and intrusive to describe drug therapy. Psychiatrists see drug therapy as standard and benign treatment. Should patients be given as much protection, as extensive a right to refuse treatment for drug therapy, as for psychosurgery and ECT? Most psychiatrists feel that many patients who refuse drugs will, after a trial of therapy, recognize that their refusal was irrational and be willing to take drugs. However, it must be conceded that drugs are greatly overutilized, that overmedication turns patients into apathetic ghosts of their potential selves, that the side effects of drugs can be more disabling than those of ECT, and that depot injection tranquilization—the use of fluphenazine—can be easily seen as much more intrusive and more drastic than other drug therapies.

We have noted the two recent cases that have focused on forced medication and the ruling in one case that involuntary patients who refuse medication can only be given medication by force in emergency situations and that the guardians of incompetent patients can substitute their refusal to treatment for the refusal of the patient[42] and the ruling in the other that involuntary patients have the right to refuse medication, subject to the opinion of an independent reviewing psychiatrist.[43]

Both of these are federal district court cases now on appeal. They represent a threat in the mind of most psychiatrists, but mental health lawyers see them as great advances in the definition of patients' rights. The Massachusetts decision, the more sweeping of the two, would be difficult for most psychiatrists to live with. The New Jersey decision also seems unsatisfactory because it allows an outside independent psychiatrist to review all protested drug decisions, an expensive and cumbersome process.

Nevertheless, after we have finished working out our rules to allow patients to resist ECT, we will have to pay attention to the right to refuse treatment more generally and to face our most difficult issue—to what extent should drug treatment be included in the concept of the patient's right to refuse. By their overreadiness to utilize ECT and drugs and to rush to treatments emphasizing rapid suppression of symptoms rather than patient change and growth, psychiatrists have forced and are forcing patients and their advocates to place curbs on the scope of their power, and in order to live with this new consumerism and patient advocacy, they will have to recognize the legitimacy of some of the complaints and move rapidly to establish their own regulation before it is imposed upon them.

---

[42] Rogers v. Okin, CA 75–1610–T, D.C. Mass., Oct. 29, 1979.

[43] Rennie v. Klein, CA–772624, D.C. N.J., Sept. 14, 1979.

Chapter 21

A FORMULA FOR SANE PROCEDURES FOLLOWING ACQUITTAL BY REASON OF INSANITY

STEPHEN RACHLIN, M.D., ABRAHAM L. HALPERN, M.D.,
and STANLEY L. PORTNOW, M.D.

In earlier papers, Halpern commented extensively about misuse of psychiatry in situations of hospitalization following acquittal by reason of insanity.[1-3] With illustrative examples, he demonstrated how courts, in "adjudicating" medical findings, make decisions concerning discharge, which are, at best, antitherapeutic. That the judicial system retains control serves to keep in hospital persons for whom the clinical staff can find no evidence of mental illness.

In this communication, it is our purpose (1) to review in somewhat greater detail one such case, wherein the differences between psychiatric findings and their judicial interpretations were brought into bold relief and (2) to propose major changes in current practices relating to individuals acquitted of crime by reason of mental disease or defect. Such revisions, we believe, constitute a rational approach to the handling of insanity acquittees and will help restore public confidence in both the criminal justice system and the psychiatric profession.

---

[1]Halpern, A. L.: The insanity defense: A juridical anachronism. *Psychiatr Ann, 7(8)*:41–63, 1977.

[2]Halpern, A. L.: The fiction of legal insanity and the misuse of psychiatry. *J Legal Med, 2(1)*:18–74, 1980.

[3]Halpern, A. L.: Uncloseting the conscience of the jury: A justly acquitted doctrine. *Psychiatr Q, 52*:144–157, 1980.

THE TORSNEY CASE

Phase One

On Thanksgiving night 1976, New York City Police Officer Robert Torsney, an eight-year veteran of the force, was one of several men responding to a man-with-a-gun call in a housing project in Brooklyn. Upon arrival upstairs in the apartment building, no such individual was located, so the officers involved returned to the streets to continue their search. As a precautionary measure, Torsney, who is white, kept his hand on his gun. He then fatally shot a fifteen-year-old black youth, who was approaching him and who, he maintained, pulled a chrome-plated gun from his belt. After this act, Torsney, apparently oblivious of the magnitude of what had happened, followed no accepted police procedures and simply returned to his patrol car. This was reportedly the first time he ever had to fire his weapon in the line of duty. It is critical to note that no man with a gun was ever found, nor was the pistol that Torsney said was in the possession of the youngster. Torsney was charged with murder in the second degree.

After being out on bail for a year and showing no problems in community adjustment, Torsney was found not guilty by reason of mental disease or defect. At the trial, one psychiatrist stated that he showed a tendency to hysterical dissociation, while another opined that he was suffering from psychomotor epilepsy. The jury chose to accept the latter explanation.

In accordance with law,[4] Torsney was immediately remanded to the custody of the commissioner of mental hygiene and sent to the Mid-Hudson Psychiatric Center, a secure facility for the evaluation and treatment of patients who are involved with criminal law questions such as dangerousness, competency, or responsibility. Upon admission there, he was found to be symptom free and suffering from no mental disease. After a brief period of observation, he was transferred to the Creedmoor Psychiatric Center in New York City, as it was felt that he did not require that degree of security provided by Mid-Hudson and could be more appropriately managed at the local, community-based state hospital.

When admitted to Creedmoor in March, 1978, once again no

---

[4]Criminal Procedure Law of the State of New York, Sec. 330.20 (McKinney Supp. 1977).

evidence of mental illness was found. The diagnosis of hysterical neurosis, dissociative type, in remission, was offered. A more complete mental status examination failed to reveal any disorder of thought or affect or, indeed, any other abnormalities. It was concluded that there were no current signs or symptoms of mental disease, and the diagnosis of adjustment reaction of adult life, in remission, was made. After two months, the Creedmoor staff, in accordance with applicable regulations, convened an internal special review committee to study the case of Mr. Torsney. They concluded that he had never shown any evidence of mental illness and was not dangerous to self or others. This group supported the diagnosis of adjustment reaction in remission. The personal examination of the director of Creedmoor also revealed no evidence of mental illness or dangerousness.

At this juncture, Departmental procedures call for the appointment of an independent review panel to advise the commissioner on whether or not he should petition the court for the patient's discharge or release on condition. This panel is to consist of two board-certified psychiatrists, at least one of whom shall have had five years postcertification experience in forensic psychiatry, and a certified social worker. Its task is to review all available information, discuss the patient with various members of the treatment team, and evaluate the patient. In making its report, the panel is charged to address specifically the issue of the patient's dangerousness, since the absence thereof is the only criterion under present New York State law by which the insanity acquittee may be released.

One of us (S.R.) wrote the report of this independent review panel. In it, we noted that Torsney did not see himself as ill or in need of treatment and that he was aware that posthospital life would be fraught with uncertainties. The mental status examination showed no clinically significant abnormalities, and we concluded that there was no present evidence of mental disease or defect. Our recommendations were that he not carry a gun again and that continuing treatment be provided in order to assist him to deal with the anticipated stresses he would face in the community. Commenting that his history contained no dangerous behavior other than the offense in question, that he had shown no difficulty controlling impulses nor any inappropriate hostility, and that none of his recorded behavior was in any way harmful or threatening, we concluded that he could be released without danger and had fully recovered from the entity that led to his acquittal.

Upon receipt of this report, the commissioner, in July, 1978, applied for Torsney's release on conditions specified previously. The court, in accordance with the provisions of Section 330.20 of the Criminal Procedure Law,[5] and at the request of the District Attorney, exercised its option to appoint two independent psychiatrists to evaluate the patient and report directly to the court. One such expert was another of the authors (S.L.P.).

In his report, he commented that Torsney was more prone to action than to feeling and had some impairment of judgmental capacity. The event in question was seen to be related to fear, anger, and impulsivity. He found nothing in Torsney's condition at the time of his interview that would warrant continued hospitalization and commented that the patient was neither psychotic nor dangerous. The recommendation was for a program of gradual release via a series of passes from the hospital, followed by reevaluation.

Phase Two

The Supreme Court of Kings County (Brooklyn) conducted nine days of hearings in this matter and listened to eighteen witnesses. In his memorandum opinion of December 20, 1978, Justice Yoswein noted that the applicable burden of proof was a preponderance of credible evidence and fell on the petitioner, the Department of Mental Hygiene, as represented by the Attorney General.[6] It was stated that all witnesses concluded that the patient was neither psychotic nor dangerous to himself or others. Indeed, the evidence showed that Torsney was not suffering from any mental illness during the entire period of his hospitalization.

In ordering Torsney released on condition that he not be permitted to carry a gun, that he should no longer be a peace officer, and that he continue in outpatient treatment for five years, Justice Yoswein wrote, "We cannot simply throw away the key on patients who have at one time been found not guilty by reason of mental

---

[5] Criminal Procedure Law of the State of New York, Sec. 330.20 (McKinney Supp. 1977).

[6] *In re* Torsney, Supreme Court, Kings County, Memorandum by Yoswein, J., Dec. 20, 1978.

illness or defect and commit them to an institution as a result thereof. Such action would be a total rejection of modern medicine and psychiatry for the purpose of effecting a punishment where someone had disagreed with the underlying verdict."

The district attorney, who had been perhaps the most active participant in the proceedings and had, in fact, called most of the witnesses, immediately appealed the decision, filing a lengthy brief to show cause why the order should not be enforced pending appeal.

Using, in part, material more than two years old, the district attorney's brief made much of psychodynamic inferences relative to personality characteristics and structure, rather than diagnoses.[7] Commenting that the patient's condition had not been treated, the district attorney concluded that Torsney's dangerousness remained unchanged. The district attorney relied more heavily on psychological examination results than on psychiatric evaluations and chided the physicians involved for disregarding the test findings. The psychiatric testimony, therefore, was believed to be irrelevant to the issue of dangerousness. Further demonstrating his confusion, the district attorney stated, "This personality disorder was consistently diagnostically referred to as either a hysterical neurosis, dissociative type, or a transient situational disturbance, both stress-related conditions," from which Torsney had not yet recovered, despite being in remission.

Questioning the independence of the panels involved and alleging that their conclusions were of little value, the district attorney contended that "petitioner suffers from the personality disorder of hysterical neurosis, dissociative type. This condition, while not amounting to legal insanity, has made and continues to make the petitioner dangerous to the community." He went on to rely heavily on the reports of the court-appointed independent psychiatrists, especially that portion counseling against immediate release. Since most of the professional witnesses recommended that Torsney not carry a gun, this was, in hyperbolic fashion, taken to mean that there was recognition that his condition had not changed.

---

[7] *In re* Torsney, Supreme Court of the State of New York, Appellate Division: Second Department, Brief in Support of Order to Show Cause.

Clearly, the district attorney considered the "relevant illness" to be a personality disorder, despite Torsney's not being so diagnosed throughout his clinical course. This, it was felt, rendered him dangerous and unfit for release. The "disorder," variously referred to as "disability," was in reality, as previously stated, personality traits, which we, as psychiatrists, were criticized for failing to consider as mental illness!

In opposition, Torsney's attorney simply reiterated that no witness considered him to be dangerous, and none had recommended against his release.[8] Pending decision by a higher court, Torsney remained confined to Creedmoor Psychiatric Center.

Phase Three

On February 5, 1979, the five-judge Appellate Division announced its unanimous decision, concluding that the determination of Special Term (of the Supreme Court) was not supported by the weight of the credible evidence.[9] Relying on a section of the Mental Hygiene Law that defines dangerousness as the standard for (brief) emergency involuntary hospitalization being "mental illness for which immediate inpatient care and treatment in a hospital is appropriate and which is likely to result in serious harm to himself or others . . .",[10] they decided that, under these criteria, Torsney required further hospitalization. Asking that the petitioner must prove that he will not in the future commit a dangerous act, the appellate division cautioned the lower courts "not to be circumscribed by the mere conclusions of expert witnesses on the issue of the detainee's danger to himself or others."

Some errors of fact are also contained in this decision. It was stated that the court-appointed psychiatrists were the only experts not in the employ of the department of mental hygiene; the independent review panel consisted of three additional such persons. The diagnosis of impulsive and explosive personality disorder relative to stress was attributed to the independent psychia-

---

[8] *In re* Torsney, Supreme Court of the State of New York, Appellate Division: Second Department, Brief in Opposition to Application for Stay Pending Appeal.

[9] *In re* Torsney, 66 A.D.2d 281, 412 N.Y.S.2d 914 (1979).

[10] Mental Hygiene Law of the State of New York, Sec. 9.37 (McKinney 1978).

trists, notwithstanding that their reports contained no such assertion. Furthermore and again in apparent disregard of the independent review panel, the court believed that only one of the psychiatric expert witnesses (S.L.P.) gave consideration to the stress Torsney would likely face upon release, although it is elsewhere in the decision stated that the independent review panel had commented on this issue. An additional misunderstanding is reflected by the assertion that, despite a one and one-half hour interview with Torsney, the panel "conducted no independent psychiatric examination . . ."

Overturning the trial court's decision, the appellate court recommitted Torsney to the custody of the commissioner after it concluded that he continued to suffer from a dangerous personality disorder. In so doing, it ordered the department of mental hygiene to prepare a treatment plan designed to surmount this condition and, in a footnote, indicated that if this goal were abandoned, further judicial review could be had. Another footnote seems also to show the court contradicting itself; while again referring to mental hygiene law criteria for hospitalization, it is stated that an insanity acquittee in confinement need not meet these standards and shall be involuntarily hospitalized, if considered dangerous, even if not mentally ill or in need of treatment. With reference to Torsney, of course, it is at least curious that in three years with the United States Marine Corps and eight with the New York City Police Department he had a clean record with no marks against him.

At this juncture, fortunately, the appeal to the state's highest court was taken over by the commissioner of mental hygiene rather than the attorney general. The work on behalf of Torsney was under the control of the then deputy commissioner and counsel, William Carnahan, one of the nation's acknowledged legal experts in the field of mental health law. He and his staff extended their work beyond the one patient to include approximately 230 other insanity acquittees confined within the state hospital system.

In an outstanding brief,[11] they pointed out (again) that the evidence that Torsney was neither clinically mentally ill nor dan-

---

[11] *In re* Torsney, Court of Appeals of the State of New York, Brief for Petitioner-Appellant.

gerous remained uncontradicted and that the ruling of the appellate division "represents a total disregard of the essential testimony of every single witness, and was arrived at by selectively excerpting from the record in a manner that distorts not only the entire record, but also the testimony of virtually every witness." Reiterating what we have already stated previously, the department's brief also noted the absence of any medical diagnosis of personality disorder, and how S.L.P.'s recommendation for a prerelease program mysteriously became translated into a need for further hospitalization.

Rejecting the appellate division's conclusions that the state had failed to investigate and treat Torsney's illness, the brief recounted how every expert who examined the patient failed to find evidence of the disorder that the court had presumed to exist. Even if it was present at one time, there was no disagreement that, at the time of the evaluations, he had recovered. Impulsivity was correctly stated not to be a condition (certainly not a disease or defect within the meaning of the law) and not to be equated with dangerousness.

The second major point made in the department's brief was the impropriety of continuing hospitalization for someone who may be deemed dangerous, but not mentally ill. Reference was made to the court of appeal's own decision in a previous case,[12] that mental illness was still a necessary condition for continued confinement of individuals acquitted by reason of insanity. Hospitals, we can agree, are (and should be) for the ill, not for the alleged dangerous but not ill. A personality flaw, it was concluded, does not distinguish Torsney from the rest of society.

Phase Four

Carnahan personally argued the case before the court of appeals in April 1979. Originally there was a 3 to 3 split among the judges, and when the court was brought to its full strength by the addition of its seventh member, reargument became necessary. On July 9, 1979 the court announced its decision with the anticipated 4 to 3 vote.[13]

---

[12] People v. Lally, 19 N.Y.2d 27, 277 N.Y.S.2d 654, 224 N.E.2d 87 (1966).

[13] *In re* Torsney, 47 N.Y.2d 667, 420 N.Y.S.2d 192 (1979).

The plurality concluded that the patient was to be released because he was not found to be dangerous as a result of mental illness and did not suffer from the postulated personality disorder. They held that the purpose of commitment of those found not guilty by reason of mental disease or defect was a narrow one; that is, to determine the mental condition of the person committed on the date of the acquittal, for such time as may be necessary to permit examination and report, and for the conduct of a hearing on that issue. The court of appeals majority disagreed with the appellate division's conclusion that a dangerous but not mentally ill person could continue to be confined in a state hospital.

Noting that in New York insanity is a defense rather than an affirmative defense and, therefore, all that acquittal by reason of mental disease or defect really means is that the prosecution failed to prove beyond a reasonable doubt that the defendant was sane, not that the jury found mental disease, the court held that continued hospitalization beyond that necessary for prompt examination and report required the same standards of illness as does civil commitment. Citing both *Jackson*[14] and *Baxstrom,*[15] their decision was that Torsney was entitled to release, absent any finding of present dangerousness by reason of mental illness, and that the sole act for which he was acquitted could not be used to justify his continued confinement.

For the first time in any court opinion in the matter of Torsney, due credence was given to the medical conclusion that, despite the presence of emotional conflicts, the patient was symptom free. On the issue of the weight of credible evidence, the court of appeals found "abundantly clear" that every opinion offered at the hearing substantiated the absence of mental illness and/or dangerousness. They ordered that Torsney be released pursuant to the conditions originally imposed by Justice Yoswein.

In a concurring opinion, Judge Meyer, the newest member of the court and the deciding vote, expressed the additional thought that continuing commitment of insanity acquittees under the criminal procedure law can take place only in accordance with the

---

[14] Jackson v. Indiana, 406 U.S. 715, 92 S.Ct. 1845, 32 L.Ed.2d 435 (1972).

[15] Baxstrom v. Herold, 383 U.S. 107, 86 S.Ct. 760, 15 L.Ed.2d 620 (1966).

provisions of the mental hygiene law, that is, a finding of present mental illness of sufficient severity to warrant involuntary hospitalization.

The three dissenting Judges, in a rather lengthy opinion, stated their belief that Torsney may still suffer from the same symptoms as were present in 1976 and should, therefore, have further rehabilitation within a psychiatric institution. This, it was felt, should continue apace until he proves that he no longer has the symptomatology that made him dangerous: "We would, therefore, be unwise to bind our legal determinations to psychiatric theories . . . which are designed to deal with medical rather than legal problems." They went so far as to equate symptoms with "mental defect," and to state that, therefore, nothing had changed over time as far as Torsney's dangerousness was concerned. Apparently, these judges believed that, despite there being no such incident ever happening prior to the present episode, one could very readily occur again. Difficult to disprove, but equally impossible to support.

DISCUSSION

The majority of four of the seven judges on the court of appeals was all that was necessary for Torsney to be released from Creedmoor Psychiatric Center under the conditions set forth by the trial court after it conducted extensive hearings. However, we should not forget that the three dissenters on the highest court, combined with the five from the appellate division, constitute a majority of eight out of the twelve appellate level judges involved in this case, and thus fully two-thirds of these jurists managed to conclude, despite unanimous medical evidence to the contrary, that Torsney was mentally ill, dangerous, and in need of continued involuntary inpatient psychiatric treatment. How frightening!

As psychiatrists, we cannot help but find it unacceptable to be ordered to treat a condition that has been medically determined not to exist. No hospital should have a patient imposed on it unless a need for that level of care has been demonstrated. Under present law, at least in New York, that possibility was a temporary reality based on judicial misuse and misinterpretation of clinical data.

For the moment, let us put aside the issue of abolition or replacement of the insanity defense and the surrounding debate, since presently its retention is a fact. What, then, can we recommend to ease the potential that this has for abuse of the mental health system?

RECOMMENDATIONS FOR CHANGE
The Trial Phase

First, we suggest that insanity be made an affirmative defense. That this is legally acceptable is attested to by the fact that in quite a number of jurisdictions it is the law and has been declared constitutional by the United States Supreme Court in 1952[16] and again in 1977.[17] Indeed, it is likely that the original M'Naghten criteria were in the nature of an affirmative defense. Consider the wording: "Presumed to be sane ... until the contrary be proved to their satisfaction ... " and "It must be clearly proved that, at the time of the committing of the act, the party accused, etc. ... "[18] By virtue of having to demonstrate the presence of insanity, it may be more likely that those who successfully assert such a defense will have a mental illness. We are, of course, aware of the observation that jury decisions in this regard are not always made based on relevant psychiatric issues.[19, 20] In any event, entry into the mental health system will be a bit more difficult, and the patient, once having proven his illness, cannot then easily challenge the physicians to demonstrate his continuing sickness.

We would further recommend a change in the statute in order to mandate, especially if requested by the defendant, the informing

[16] Leland v. Oregon, 343 U.S. 790 (1952).

[17] Patterson v. New York, 432 U.S. 197 (1977).

[18] Daniel M'Naghten's Case, 8 Eng. Rep. 718 (1843). Cited by Carnahan, W. A.: Legal perspectives on the insanity defense, in The Insanity Defense in New York: A Report to Governor Hugh L. Carey. State of New York, Department of Mental Hygiene, Albany, Feb. 17, 1978.

[19] Singer, S. J.: A treatment and proposal concerning the insanity defense in New York (mimeographed), Sept. 1979.

[20] Pasewark, R. A., Pantle, M. L., and Steadman, H. J.: Characteristics and disposition of persons found not guilty by reason of insanity in New York State, 1971–1976. *Am J Psychiatry*, *136*:655–660, 1979.

of the jury as to the potential disposition should they render a finding of not guilty by reason of mental disease or defect. There is no reason why they should have to guess or conceivably be misinformed and misled by self-appointed experts in the jury room.

Postacquittal Confinement

The broadest issue we wish to address, although one that "has not exactly set the legal or psychiatric world on fire,"[21] is that of disposition, i.e. what happens to the individual following acquittal.

Only recently has wide recognition been given to the problems that develop when "patients" who do not belong in hospitals are sent there by courts. An ad hoc study group in New York,[22] of which one of us (S.R.) was a member, chose to address this as the principal issue needing resolution, with support for this position coming from a psychiatrist who worked with such patients on a day-to-day basis and who commented that indefinite hospital confinement may be more restrictive than a set prison sentence.[23] Wright, former Assistant Commissioner for Forensic Services in the New York State Office of Mental Health, has written that "placing these individuals in mental hospitals is detrimental not only to the hospitals but also to other patients, the individuals themselves, and, not to be forgotten, to the aims and needs of society at large."[24] There exists the clear danger that hospitals housing insanity-acquittees will become more and more like prisons, to the detriment of treatment services for all patients.

Currently, the person found not guilty by reason of insanity (NGRI) has only one placement option available in New York, and that is state hospitalization. On the other hand, a variety of possibilities confront one who stands convicted, such as condi-

---

[21] Perlin, M. L.: Après the acquittal, le deluge: Release procedures and allocation of the burden of proof in subsequent review hearings following a finding of "not guilty by reason of insanity" in State of New Jersey v. Hetra Fields. *Bull Am Acad Psychiatry Law*, 7:29–38, 1979.

[22] Kaiser, D. B.: Report of the ad hoc Committee for Legislative Input of the Working Committee on Forensic Problems, New York Downstate Area (mimeographed), Oct. 10, 1979.

[23] Crain, P. M.: Position statements on the insanity defense (mimeographed), Apr. 7, 1979.

[24] Wright, J. B.: Problems in administering the insanity defense, in The Insanity Defense in New York, *supra* note 18.

tional release or probation. For anyone else in the criminal justice system, even if sentenced to a term in a correctional facility, the court and the prosecutor no longer play a major decision-making role insofar as disposition is concerned. It is only the insanity acquittee who has to go back to court to gain his freedom. Indeed, if determined not guilty by any other successful defense, the individual is immediately freed from custody, no matter how mentally ill or dangerous he might be.

We believe that disposition should be in accordance with treatment needs, with due regard to public safety. A finding of NGRI is certainly not sufficient cause to presume that the individual involved has a mental illness or, if he does, that inpatient care is required. One does not create a treatment plan based solely on past history; present findings are most germane. If hospitalization is warranted, then, in the oft-quoted words of the Supreme Court in *Jackson*, "At the least, due process requires that the nature and duration of commitment bear some reasonable relation to the purpose for which the individual is committed."[25]

Should the NGRI patients be an exceptional class? Should some special procedures be required? Certainly one must be mindful of the public need to be protected from unnecessary harm. Pasewark et al. have shown that only a slight majority of those found NGRI are murderers and that, most often, the victims of their violence were family or friends.[26] In their series, 69 percent of the patients were diagnosed as psychotic. As long as the issue of exculpatory insanity continues entrenched in our legal system, it is our view that illness, not crime, should determine what happens to those adjudicated NGRI.

A number of recommendations for modification of the New York statute[27] relative to the disposition of the NGRI has just been issued by a committee of The Association of the Bar of the City of New York.[28] This group, which was composed mainly of legal

---

[25] Jackson v. Indiana, 406 U.S. 715, 92 S.Ct. 1845, 32 L.Ed.2d 435 (1972).

[26] *Supra* note 20.

[27] Criminal Procedure Law of the State of New York, Sec. 330.20 (McKinney Supp. 1977).

[28] Mental Illness, Due Process and the Acquitted Defendant. Report and Recommendations by the Special Committee to Study Commitment Procedures and the Law Relating to Incompetents of The Association of the Bar of the City of New York, Apr. 1979.

professionals, based its report on an update of a prior German and Singer study[29] with specific reference to New York law.[30] Their work was completed prior to the court of appeals' decision in Torsney[31] but published after it and at the time that we were preparing this paper. Although extensive revision of the procedures governing the release and retention of insanity acquittees was recommended, the committee's report, we feel, falls short of what is required for a rational and psychiatrically acceptable system. For example, according to the committee, the acquittee is to be treated as any other civil patient, yet he is nevertheless precluded from receiving treatment in a facility other than one under the control of the department of mental hygiene. Furthermore, their proposed statute gives unnecessary power to the local prosecutor to subvert, oftentimes for political purposes, the psychiatrically indicated disposition.

The Torsney case was the third from New York's highest court to affirm that, following acquittal by reason of mental disease or defect, automatic commitment to the state hospital for a brief period for the purpose of examination and report is acceptable.[32, 33, 34] Indeed, a federal court upheld the New York statute only in light of such interpretations.[35] It is our observation that these decisions have had little practical effect.

We therefore propose that immediately after a finding of NGRI, a hearing be held to determine the presence or absence of mental illness. If it is demonstrated that the presumption of continuing insanity can be rebutted and that the individual no longer suffers from mental disease or defect, he should immediately be freed from custody. If the finding is that he is mentally ill but not

---

[29] German, J. R., and Singer, A. C.: Punishing the not guilty: Hospitalization of persons acquitted by reason of insanity. *Rutgers L Rev, 29:*1011–1083, 1976.

[30] Singer, A. C., and German, J. R.: Report to the Special Committee on the proposed revision of Section 330.20 of the Criminal Procedure Law, in Mental Illness, Due Process and the Acquitted Defendant, *supra* note 28.

[31] *In re* Torsney, 47 N.Y.2d 667, 420 N.Y.S.2d 192 (1979).

[32] People v. Lally, 19 N.Y.2d 27, 277 N.Y.S.2d 654, 224 N.E.2d 87 (1966).

[33] *In re* Torsney, 47 N.Y.2d 667, 420 N.Y.S.2d 192 (1979).

[34] People *ex rel.* Henig v. Commissioner of Mental Hygiene, 43 N.Y.2d 334, 401 N.Y.S.2d 462, 372 N.E.2d 304 (1977).

[35] Lee v. Kolb, 449 F.Supp. 1368 (W.D.N.Y. 1978).

dangerous, within the definition found in the civil statute,[36] then as with any other patient a medical decision is rendered whether his treatment needs would best be met by an available hospital, day program, private practitioner, clinic, or other modality, and this disposition would be implemented. It must be noted that in many cases the individual has been out on bail pending trial and involved in therapy; compulsory commitment has the potential of undoing those gains which have already been achieved.

In the situation where the insanity acquittee is found to be both mentally ill and dangerous, the type of offense with which he was charged should come into consideration. If that act was nonviolent, the patient should be hospitalized either on a voluntary or involuntary basis in an appropriate facility. State hospitalization should not be the only course of action possible; there is no reason why these individuals could not be treated in private institutions, general hospitals, or other suitable inpatient setting. When, on the other hand, the persons were involved in crimes of violence and continue to be mentally ill and dangerous, this special group, *pro bono publico*, requires unique treatment overriding the individual's right to liberty. *This is the exceptional class.* These are the people who must, in our opinion, be involuntarily hospitalized under special court order with release possible only under the stringent provisions outlined later in this article.

We are aware that it is precisely within the sphere of the determination of dangerousness that courts have shown significant mistrust of the opinions rendered by psychiatrists. Indeed, one can readily find cases in which courts have rejected clinical opinions of nondangerousness.[37-40] The New York Court of Appeals, in the Torsney case,[41] has stated that the act for which the patient was acquitted could not be determinative of present dangerousness, while New Jersey's highest court held that said event was "power-

---

[36] Mental Hygiene Law of the State of New York, Sec. 9.37 (McKinney 1978).

[37] *In re* Torsney, 66 A.D.2d 281, 412 N.Y.S.2d 914 (1979).

[38] People v. Corrente, 63 Misc.2d 214, 311 N.Y.S.2d 711 (1970).

[39] *In re* Miller (Sherman), 73 Misc.2d 690, 342 N.Y.S. 2d 315 (1972).

[40] *In re* Miller (Sherman), 46 A.D.2d 177, 362 N.Y.S.2d 628 (1974).

[41] *In re* Torsney, 47 N.Y. 2d 667, 420 N.Y.S.2d 192 (1979).

ful evidence of potential dangerousness."[42]

At the postacquittal hearing, if the psychiatrists agree on the continuing dangerousness by virtue of mental disease of one accused of a violent act, as noted previously, involuntary hospitalization should be obligatory, with the patient entitled to all of the procedural due process granted to any other patient. In the case of disagreement by the psychiatrists, the judge would have the option of ordering inpatient evaluation at any facility willing to receive the individual to resolve the dispute. Surely a thirty-day period would be adequate for this purpose, given the (unfortunate) reality that, with most other applicants for hospital admission, the decision is made in thirty minutes. At least one court had made this limit part of its order,[43] and one of us (S. R.) can personally attest that it worked without any major problems. Other jurisdictions have similarly established time frames.[44]

Is personality disorder exculpatory mental illness for which inpatient care is indicated? This is what was suggested by the appellate division in the Torsney case.[45] We think that such a diagnosis in and of itself should not automatically lead to the assumption that an insanity defense or hospitalization is justified. If someone with a personality disorder has a transient psychotic episode, he may be eligible for an insanity plea. If that acute episode has fully resolved by the time of trial, he should, upon a verdict of NGRI, be set free.

Release Procedures

Turning our attention to procedures for the release from a hospital of one adjudicated NGRI, we contend that for all other than the exceptional category that we have defined previously, discharge should be in accordance with usual clinical practice, without reference to a court.

For the NGRI patient, discharge continues to be primarily

---

[42] State v. Fields, 77 N.J. 282, 390 A.2d 574 (1978).

[43] People v. McNelly, 83 Misc.2d 262, 371 N.Y.S.2d 538 (1975).

[44] Singer, A. C. and German, J. R.: Report to the Special Committee on the proposed revision of Section 330.20 of the Criminal Procedure Law, in Mental Illness, Due Process and the Acquitted Defendant, *supra* note 28.

[45] *In re* Torsney, 66 A.D.2d 281, 412 N.Y.S.2d 914 (1979).

based on judicial rather than psychiatric considerations, and the adversarial approach is utilized. This is the case in most,[46] but not all[47] jurisdictions. Recently, the New Jersey Supreme Court reaffirmed that decisions in this regard are "for the court, not the psychiatrists."[48] With reference to release from the hospital of an NGRI patient, Brooks has commented that, "It is likely that no other aspect of American law puts so formidable a set of obstacles in the way of a petition for freedom."[49]

It is interesting that in expressing their dissatisfaction with the disposition of insanity acquittees, a group of legal professionals indicated that the standards for release were too lax.[50] We disagree. Psychiatrists are not about to discharge whimsically from the hospital patients who had been involved with the criminal justice system. In the words of Justice Pashman of the Supreme Court of New Jersey, "Surely a psychiatrist would not allow a patient to come and go as he pleased when the doctor was convinced that his patient was bent on and capable of perpetrating a violent crime."[51] If an error should be made, ordinary standards of professional practice can be brought to bear on any decision as to potential liability for untoward events. It should go almost without saying that due process is mandatory in any redress against a physician who acted in good faith. Absent negligence, as would be the case under any other set of circumstances, the hospital staff should not be held liable for any erroneous decision to release. Doctors cannot be guarantors.

It is only the situation of the person charged with a violent crime, found NGRI, and determined to be both mentally ill and dangerous that calls for distinctive release procedures. Even in

---

[46] Brooks, A. D.: *Law, Psychiatry and the Mental Health System.* Boston, Little, Brown & Co., 1974.

[47] Perlin, M. L.: Après the acquittal, le deluge: Release procedures and allocation of the burden of proof in subsequent review hearings following a finding of "not guilty by reason of insanity" in State of New Jersey v. Hetra Fields. *Bull Am Acad Psychiatry Law,* 7:29–38, 1979.

[48] State v. Fields, 77 N.J. 282, 390 A.2d 574 (1978).

[49] Brooks, A. D.: *Law, Psychiatry and the Mental Health System.* Boston, Little, Brown & Co., 1974.

[50] Burton, N. M., and Steadman, H. J.: Perceptions of the insanity defense, in The Insanity Defense in New York, *supra* note 18.

[51] State v. Carter, 64 N.J. 382, 316 A.2d 449, 457 (1974).

this case, we are firmly of the view that the district attorney should have no role whatever. A prosecutor simply has nothing to contribute to the decision-making process relative to release from medical care of one found not guilty.

When, in the exceptional class, the treatment team and attending psychiatrist feel that discharge is indicated, there should be mandatory medical review. Three independent psychiatrists, certified by the American Board of Psychiatry and Neurology and selected on a rotating basis from a panel of volunteers maintained by the local district branch of the American Psychiatric Association, should be appointed to evaluate the patient. For this task, they ought to be paid their usual and customary fee in order to allow people of the highest caliber to participate. If this board agrees unanimously with the plan, the hospital should have the authority to release the patient conditionally with provisions made for adequate continuing treatment as an outpatient.

Where there is a dispute among the psychiatrists or where there is expressed the unanimous opinion that the patient should remain hospitalized, that patient would, at his option, have recourse to court in order to seek his discharge. This should be a civil proceeding and be conducted by a judge other than the one who presided at the original trial and postacquittal hearing. Courts have split with regard to the question of who should bear the burden of proof in such situations. In New York, this burden has been held to be the petitioner's[52] while in the neighboring state of New Jersey, it is the state that must prove the need for retention in a hospital.[53] Our feeling is that the person who seeks to continue the inpatient status must demonstrate that this is necessary. Inappropriate retention can only be viewed as punitive and, therefore, unacceptable. Preponderance of the evidence would appear to be a sufficient standard to protect society, as represented by the attorney general's, not the district attorney's, office.

The court could send the patient back to the hospital if such were supported by credible medical evidence, but this would not be permissible where at least one psychiatrist did not so recom-

---

[52] *In re* Lublin, 43 N.Y.2d 341, 401 N.Y.S.2d 466, 372 N.E.2d 307 (1977).

[53] State v. Fields, 77 N.J. 282, 390 A.2d 574 (1978).

mend. Of course, after a hearing, the court could decide to discharge the patient notwithstanding psychiatric expert testimony to the contrary. If the outcome is conditional release, the patient might be required to be followed by a private physician, community mental health center, state Office of Mental Health clinic, or any other suitable outpatient setting. The treating person would, as a matter of obligation and to assure accountability, submit progress reports to the court at appropriate periodic intervals, with proper regard for confidentiality.

Where the hospital staff believes that the NGRI patient needs to remain and he himself disputes this, he should have available the full panoply of procedures already outlined. This process should be accessible to him at such times as a civil patient's involuntary status would be scrutinized.

CONCLUSIONS

All of the foregoing is, of course, academic if there is to be a more basic change in the laws relating to the insanity defense, such as replacement by diminished capacity.[54-58] Such a route would take the person who is now our NGRI patient out of the mental health system initially. Whether or not this is what the public wants is something that will have to be decided by the usual political process involved in effecting statutory change. The only issues then left would be the identification of those individuals who can be released on probation for treatment in the civil mental health system and the determination of how the treatment needs of those remaining within the correctional setting can best be met.

In summary, it is our view that the time has come for a drastic

---

[54]Halpern, A. L.: The fiction of legal insanity and the misuse of psychiatry. *J Legal Med, 2(1):*18–74, 1980.

[55]Singer, S. J.: A treatment and proposal concerning the insanity defense in New York (mimeographed), Sept. 1979.

[56]Crain, P. M.: Position statements on the insanity defense (mimeographed), April 7, 1979.

[57]Kolb, L. C.: Reflections on the insanity defense, in The Insanity Defense in New York, *supra* note 18.

[58]Carnahan, W. A.: Changing the insanity defense, in The Insanity Defense in New York, *supra* note 18.

revision of the procedures governing the handling of individuals acquitted by reason of insanity. If condemnation and punishment are not to be the hidden denominators, no semblance of rationality is possible unless we (1) clearly distinguish the insanity acquittee who has committed a violent act from the one who has not and (2) establish specific dispositional policies depending on the degree of mental illness. Nor can the principles of medical ethics guide the psychiatrist in his work with this patient population if a court has the power to impose mental hospital confinement on a person who has been found *not* to be mentally ill by the treatment staff. The recommendations we offer in this article constitute a most sweeping departure from prevailing procedures. They are, nevertheless, nothing more than is required if fundamental fairness and compassion are to be the measure of how we deal with those who are acquitted of crime by reason of insanity.

Chapter 22

COULD OLIVER WENDELL HOLMES, JR., AND SIGMUND FREUD WORK TOGETHER IF SOCRATES WERE WATCHING?

Samuel Gorovitz, Ph.D.

When I was asked to speak to this group, my initial reaction was to realize that I know very little about law, very little about psychiatry, and nothing about forensic psychiatry. But, I thought it would be an interesting area to think about. Then I was told, "You've got to come up with a title right away, because we've got to get a program out. Please make the title as specific as you can." My main objective in picking the title was to minimize constraint on myself—to pick a title that would enable me to subsume under it any remarks that I happened to develop in connection with psychiatry and the law. But, as it turned out, it seems to me, the title fits rather well what I want to consider.

I want to begin with Dr. Michels' closing point to the effect that forensic psychiatry may well be dangerous, a force for evil, conceptually incoherent, and illegitimate. Take Oliver Wendell Holmes, Jr., as symbolic of judicial wisdom, of the quest for truth in the service of justice. That well-known champion of civil liberties is, as far as I can tell, the jurist it is most fashionable to quote in forensic psychiatry circles. Freud is the exemplar of the psychodynamic hypothesis, of the willingness to go beyond the descrip-

This chapter is one of four presentations made on the theme "Ethical Issues in the Practice of Forensic Psychiatry" on January 17, 1981, at the Fifth Annual Conference of the Tri-State Chapter of the American Academy of Psychiatry and the Law. Other speakers were Robert Michels, M.D., Barklie McKee Henry Professor and Chairman, Department of Psychiatry, Cornell University Medical Center, New York; Alan Meisel, J.D., Associate Professor of Law and Psychiatry, University of Pittsburgh, Pittsburgh; and Jonas R. Rappeport, M.D., Clinical Professor of Psychiatry, School of Medicine, University of Maryland, Baltimore. Only Dr. Gorovitz's chapter was available at the time of this publication.

tions of observable behavior to conjectures about the conditions of mind that are causally related to that observable behavior. Where does Socrates come into the picture? He represents the question whether psychiatry can legitimately be in the employ of the courts. (I am talking now about the historical Socrates, not Socrates as a vehicle for the development of the views of Plato in the middle and later dialogues, but the Socrates of the very early dialogues about his trial and death.)

Students find it challenging to be asked to read of the trial and death of Socrates and then be asked what is significant about him. Wherein lies the Socratic heritage, when the man disclaims any positive doctrine about any substantive issue? The answer is that Socrates did provide change in the agenda of questions. He redirected philosophical inquiry. He fashioned new standards of adequacy for the answers. He exhibited a relentless unwillingness to compromise in the quest for truth. He displayed humility about his own knowledge and about knowledge in general. He had a particular interest in judicial proceedings—which is unsurprising considering his circumstances. He had, perhaps above all, a commitment to self-examination. Socrates made his mark debunking the pretentions of the ostensibly wise. It was not a particularly effective strategy for gaining the friendship of influential people, however.

Why would one ask the question that constitutes the title of my remarks? Socrates would view forensic psychiatry with his relentless, probing, skeptical eye. He would ask, as Dr. Michels implicitly asks in his closing remarks, Is the activity of forensic psychiatry even legitimate? Can the assumptions on which this activity rests bear scrutiny? Is there perhaps a conceptual conflict that is unresolvable?

Let me mention some of the issues that support this skeptical view of the joining of psychiatry and the law. It is well known that psychiatry has many powers. I gather the book of the year in the area is Robitscher's widely discussed book on the powers of psychiatry.[1] There is also widespread skepticism about the legitimacy of the claims made by psychiatrists—both about individual

---

[1] Robitscher, J. *The Powers of Psychiatry,* Boston: Houghton Mifflin, 1980.

cases and about psychiatry as a discipline. It may well be that you have to be outside psychiatry to realize how widespread that skepticism is. And, of course, there is skepticism about forensic psychiatry in particular. The question of whether it can bear scrutiny seems to arise with increasing frequency as the profession increasingly coheres into a visible discipline.

Now, I come to it from outside, quite naive. I thought it might be useful not to apologize for that but to claim it has certain advantages. Let me illustrate. Consider, for a moment, a different professional activity—that of surgery. Psychiatrists, being physicians, have a comfortable familiarity with the practice of surgery. What would it be like to view it without that comfortable familiarity, to view it as one genuinely naive, looking at it anew with literally no understanding and no preconceptions about it? I think we can perform the following exercise:

> Imagine a distant planet on which life is like that on earth, with one major exception: there is no illness or injury. People live to a standard age of, say, 90, and then quite predictably they instantaneously die. There are lawyers to write wills and morticians to handle funerals, but the role of the physician is unknown. Now imagine a visitor from such a place asking one of our physicians what he or she does. "I'm a doctor" is the natural reply. "Of what?" asks our visitor, thinking perhaps of philosophy, history, the natural sciences, and the rest of the disciplines in which one can be a doctor. Our physician replies, "Why, of *medicine*." The answer does not help, for our visitor does not understand. "I treat sick people, cure illness, save lives," explains the physician to no avail. At this point, the baffled visitor might well propose an empiricial solution. "Don't try to explain any more; just let me follow you around for a while and observe what you do. That way I'll be able to see for myself what the practice of medicine is."
>
> The visitor might well see the following events. The physician approaches a virtual stranger in a small, austere room. The stranger, who has been waiting a long time, looks up anxiously, yet with some relief, as the physician enters. Calling the stranger by a first name, the physician introduces himself as Doctor Whatever, and directs the stranger to remove his clothes. The events that then ensue, perhaps over many days, strike our observer as barely credible; the physician examines the exterior of the stranger, and then begins to examine the interior, placing instruments of various kinds in all the existing orifices, and from time to time creating new orifices for the purpose. The physician directs the stranger to eat certain poisonous chemicals. The stranger complies, but his cooperation seems to do him little good. The physician perseveres, causing tubes to be

connected to the victim, through which additional chemicals are inserted. At one point, the victim is stabbed with a sharp weapon, through which poison is inserted into the body, rendering him unconscious. The physician's henchmen then seize the fallen victim and cart him off to a room filled with various instruments — the visitor is reminded here of the Tower of London — and the punishment then escalates. The physician cuts the victim open and looks over the interior parts. He steals one or more of them, discarding them or sending them away, and sews what is left of the victim back together. Only many days later is the victim — perhaps one should say prisoner — let out on parole.

We could not blame the observer for concluding that the practice of medicine is a part of the penal system — indeed, the part that metes out the most severe punishments and humiliations to the worst among Earthly criminal elements. He might then observe that on his planet, there are also criminals from time to time, but that the kind of invasive physical and psychological abuse he has just witnessed has long since been rejected by the judicial system as not befitting a humane and civilized social order.

"No, no," our physician protests. "It isn't punishment. This has nothing to do with the penal system. These are not prisoners or criminals."

And the visitor replies, "Then what you people call the practice of medicine I would describe as felonious assault."

Of course, this little story rests entirely on the assumption that the visitor does not understand what he is seeing; he does not know that the actions performed by the physician are designed to benefit the patient. Indeed, he does not understand the notion of being a patient. He simply observes behavior, and makes of it what he can. But *we* know what is going on, so the story strikes us as ludicrous (except where it strikes a familiar chord). Yet it makes a point, for physicians do things that *would* be felonious assault except under very special circumstances of justification. And, of course, the story also rests on the particular episodes the visitor chanced to see. He might well have witnessed scenes of obvious kindness instead. Still, we can understand the observer's reaction; we can sense how cruel and primitive medical practice could look to one who came to it with no prior understanding of its purpose or justification.[2]

In providing an understanding of that meaning and providing an explanation of that justification, we confront fundamental issues too easily overlooked when we maintain the comfortable familiarity that we usually have as we consider medical practice. To pursue this line further would involve looking at the underlying

---

[2] Gorovitz, S. *Doctors' Dilemmas: Moral Conflict and Medical Care*, New York: Macmillan, forthcoming, Spring 1982.

assumptions of medical practice. I do not want to do that here; that is a different agenda. Among the issues we would confront if we did pursue it are the value of life, why it is good to protect and preserve it, whether that is always the case, the relative importance of health in competition with other things that people value, and other such fundamental issues with respect to which physicians commonly operate on the basis of conventional and unexamined assumptions.

What happens if we step back now from inquiry into the practice of medicine, and look naively, from the outside, at forensic psychiatry? What do we see? We see, in the first place, that it is not a new dispute. Ninety years ago, discussing a man named Claggart in the story *Billy Budd*, Herman Melville wondered whether Claggart's behavior could have arisen from "a depravity according to nature," and he went on to say that our juries have at times—

> Not only to endure the prolonged contentions of lawyers with their fees, but also the yet more perplexing strife of the medical experts with theirs. . . . But why leave it to them? Why not subpoena as well the clerical proficients? Their vocation bringing them into peculiar contact with so many human beings, and sometimes in their least guarded hour, in interviews very much more confidential than those of physician and patient; this would seem to qualify them to know something about those intricacies involved in the question of moral responsibility; whether in a given case, say, the crime proceeded from mania in the brain or rabies of the heart. As to any differences among themselves these clerical proficients might develop on the stand, these could hardly be greater than the direct contradictions exchanged between the remunerated medical experts.[3]

And Melville went on—

> Who in the rainbow can show the line where the violet tint ends and the orange tint begins? Distinctly we see the difference of the colors, but when exactly does the one first blendingly enter into the other? So, with sanity and insanity. In pronounced cases, there is no question about them. But in some . . . cases, in various degrees . . . less pronounced, to draw the exact line of demarcation few will undertake—though for a fee some professional experts will. There is nothing namable but that some men will undertake to do it for pay.[4]

---

[3]Melville, H. *Billy Budd,* New York: Signet, 1961, p. 39.
[4]Ibid., p. 61.

Forensic psychiatrists have been accused of being hired guns, people willing to trade on their professional credentials to give testimony to support the objectives of whoever hires them. As Nancy K. Rhoden put it, "Psychiatrists are in general well healed beneficiaries of the status quo."[5] The hired gun charge is supported by the observation that it is a rare court proceeding indeed when one side offers psychiatric testimony and the other side says, "Well, we couldn't find any psychiatrists willing to speak in support of our side." Somehow, there is always one willing to speak in support of that side, too. Indeed, I am told that proficient attorneys know which psychiatrists to call, depending upon which kind of case they have and which side of the case they are on. Some psychiatrists can apparently be relied upon to give testimony supportive of particular positions.

The picture I am painting so far may not at this point appear flattering. But, the charge that forensic psychiatrists are hired guns, engaged in an immoral practice by selling to the highest bidder the illusion, based on their credentials, that they have knowledge relevant to the legal proceeding is not the most serious charge. A more serious charge is that they are worse than hired guns, because hired guns can at least do what they contract to do. Hired guns can deliver what they represent themselves as offering. The charge against forensic psychiatry is that they *would* be hired guns if they really knew anything. But, because there is always directly conflicting testimony in forensic psychiatry, it is all a sham. So, in their attempt to convey their services as hired guns, they are fraudulent pretenders to an illusory competence, who defraud not only the courts but even their employers. Conjoin that with the powers that forensic psychiatrists have, and the argument for dangerousness builds.

What are those powers? Forensic psychiatrists render opinions with respect to such matters as competence to stand trial, competence to refuse medical treatment, testamentary competence, abortion, the military draft, custody suits, civil commitment, insanity defenses, annulments of marriages, and workmen's compensation

[5]Rhoden, N. "Psychiatry, Heal Thy Self," *The Hastings Center Report*, vol. 10, no. 6, December 1980, p. 44.

claims. That is quite a substantial list of matters that have to do not just with how people feel, but with their fates in a very fundamental sense.

Finally, psychiatrists are notoriously resistant to self-criticism. I find even practitioners of clinical medicine more inclined to admit to mishandling of cases than it seems to me psychiatrists are. One reason may be that a psychodynamic account of why the patient was resistant to treatment is much easier for psychiatrists to fashion than it is, say, for a surgeon to fashion a fictional physiological account of why the operation went wrong. And yet, psychiatrists are promoters of self-examination in others! There seems to be a kind of discordance, unless I misperceive.

So, the claim is that forensic psychiatrists are to some extent fraudulent, to some extent self-deceivers, resistant to self-criticism, that they are betrayers of the physician's commitment, that they trade deceptively on their status as physicians, not only in the opinions they render but in the way in which they gather evidence. I noticed with some interest that even Dr. Michels, who is as sensitive and insightful as anyone, referred to *patients* and to psychiatrists interviewing *patients*. He said, quite appropriately, that he does not like to see psychiatrists interviewing and interrogating their *patients*. That very criticism is symptomatic of the problem. Why should anyone think it is appropriate to view the subject of that kind of psychiatric interrogation as a patient? If I hire a moonlighting psychiatrist to paint my house, he may paint it for an agreed upon fee, and we may have interactions; that does not make me his patient. Now, if a psychiatrist, because he is an employee of a lawyer, is trying to get some facts from the lawyer's client, what justifies invoking the concept—and all it entails—of a patient in connection with that transaction? Indeed, that very way of perceiving it emphasizes the inherent deception that can result from the social expectation that the physician is a doer of good, someone who acts in the interest of and is protective of the patient. The forensic psychiatrist is not functioning as a provider of care any more than the house painter is, though they both have medical degrees. The difference is that the forensic psychiatrist deceptively trades on his being a physician in a way in which the moonlighting psychiatrist painting a house does not.

That may be as much of this sort of thing as you will sit still for. So, let me stop at this point and say that, coming from the outside, bringing to bear the uninformed, naive view, that is how forensic psychiatry looks. I invite you to think about it. Now I will explain why I told the story of how surgery might look to the visitor from another planet. I suspect that you found the story easy to follow; it was easy to get the point. Perhaps if I had just moved directly to this outside view of forensic psychiatry, you might not have viewed such an outside perspective as at all credible.

It is true that a more sympathetic and informed view of forensic psychiatry is possible. I do not think human behavior, despite its complexity, its marvelous richness, is wholly resistant to understanding. I think there is such a thing as psychiatric insight. But, it is important to realize that forensic psychiatry, like medicine in general, is in its adolescence. Let me say what I mean by that. It is characteristic of adolescence—and this is one reason why it is so difficult to be an adolescent or to have one—that there are recently acquired powers of great magnitude, conjoined with the lack of the wisdom and maturity required for employing those powers appropriately. Part of what the adolescent has to learn is how to use the abilities that have suddenly developed. Medicine is in similar circumstances. The powers of forensic psychiatry are also now great. I suggest that forensic psychiatry has not yet collectively developed the wisdom and maturity to put those powers into perspective.

I would love to spend the next hour or two talking about the very rich, provocative, and insightful remarks that Dr. Michels made about medical education. I will resist that temptation until another occasion, however, and limit my attention to two stages of moral sophistication that have to be separated. They are quite distinct, and both should be involved in medical education. One is the development of sensitivity to the reality of ethical problems, seeing that they exist, and recognizing what they are. Second, and this is a subsequent and separate stage, is the development of some competence in dealing with them, some wisdom about how to respond to them. Medical education and the medical profession have done much better on the easier task of developing sensitivity and recognizing the existence of these problems. The forensic psychiatry community, as far as I can tell, has similarly identified most of the moral and ethical problems that beset the practice of forensic psychiatry. As a profession it seems to me to be at that first stage, and ought to be commended for that.

Socrates' most widely known remark is probably the claim that the unexamined life is not worth living. Let me suggest that if Socrates were observing forensic psychiatry today, he might make the analogous remark that the unexamined profession is not worth serving, thereby to invite the continuing examination of forensic psychiatry. There are many hard questions that the individual practitioner must face. In giving testimony, shall I reveal facts that I believe true and relevant to the case, or shall I obscure them because I know that revealing them will damage the objectives of the client and lawyer who employ me? Such questions can be very difficult for an individual on the stand. But, I suggest that there is a need to shift the focus, to consider questions of collective responsibility, questions that are not addressed to what individual forensic psychiatrists do in the course of day-to-day practice but that should be reflected on by forensic psychiatry as an emerging discipline. I will move very quickly through some of these questions. They are the sort that I hope will infuse our discussion, so I will not dwell on them here. I want then to conclude by making a number of assertions that perhaps will provoke further discussions as well.

Perhaps no question is more fundamental than this: To whom is the forensic psychiatrist's obligation? Whom does he serve? It is the double agent issue. Even to speak of a double agent is to understate the complexity of the case. Dr. Michels spoke of four different goals and the four different roles that might be involved. There is a dramatic difference between taking your obligation to be that of serving the goals of the lawyer who hires you, on the one hand, and taking it to be the transmission of truth to the court on the other. If your obligation is to provide psychiatric wisdom to the best of your ability to the court, you may do very different things than what you will do if you take your goal to be to help the lawyer win his case. That question, it seems to me, ought to be discussed at length and reflectively and openly by the profession.

Second, do the obligations undertaken by physicians conflict with the complicity of forensic psychiatrists in the adversarial system itself? One way to put a sharp focus on this is simply to say the forensic psychiatrist is playing a role in the service of a larger institution, the adversarial system. It, too, is open to scrutiny and to objection. If you know that your lawyer's client has committed a murder, and you have learned these facts from psychiatric interviews and perhaps other supporting evidence, do you keep still when another man is on his way to his death, having been convicted and sentenced to capital punishment for that crime you know he did not commit? Now that is a problem for lawyers, not just for psychiatrists. One dispute in the legal community concerns precisely whether there are moral limits to the pursuit and advocacy of the client's interest. Is a lawyer acting rightly and defensibly when he pursues his client's interest at the cost of another man's life, or reputation, or wealth? That is no easy question; it strikes at the very heart of the adversarial system. As you buy into that system as forensic psychiatrists, are you perhaps betraying commitments that you have undertaken as physicians? That is a very difficult issue to sort out, and I do not mean to suggest by raising it that the answer is easy. I do mean that it should be addressed tenaciously by the profession of forensic psychiatrists.

There are other issues regarding which some position should emerge. Should commitment nullify the right to refuse treatment? How should the conflict be resolved between a patient's interest and that patient's civil liberties, or between civil liberties and societal interests? If commitment in involuntary treatment is ever justified, and I believe it is, why not mandatory outpatient treatment? Why such professional silence on this issue? What about the chronic, young mental patient? With a high suicide rate and a very high rate of readmission, such patients seem to provide a paradigmatic case for benefit from involuntary treatment. If commitment can be justified, why not the milder measure of partial commitment—that is, commitment to mandatory outpatient treatment? What is remarkable is not that the community of forensic psychiatry opposes it, but that, as far as I can tell, the issue is not being pursued with any vigor. What are the collective responsibilities of the community of forensic psychiatry with respect to such issues?

There is a Board of Forensic Psychiatry now, a new instrument. What will you do with it? Will it have an impact on training? Will it have an impact in defining the role of the forensic psychiatrist? Will it mandate, for example, as a condition of conformity to professional ethics, that the forensic psychiatrist unambiguously inform the subject of his investigation that he is not in the role of physician, and that the subject is not a patient? These are among the questions that the profession must address.

A number of points remain that I would like to assert for your contemplation.

1. There is an important difference between what forensic psychiatry knows collectively and what individual practitioners know. That is true, of course, in all professions. For example, forensic psychiatry collectively knows that the ethical issues I have mentioned are important. Individual practitioners may not. That is a gap worth contemplating, especially considering that each forensic psychiatrist acts in behalf of the profession as a whole whenever he acts as a forensic psychiatrist.

2. Dr. Michels spoke quite persuasively this morning about the difference between ethics as the acting out of personal choice and personal values, and ethics as derived from the conventions adopted by the profession of which one is a part. But does the role one plays exempt one from personal moral responsibility? He did not claim that it does, but I want to make sure that no one makes that fallacious inference. "This is how it's done in the profession" is not an airtight justification or moral defense of any particular form of behavior.

3. I call your attention next to what I view as the bad practice defense, another sham in the discussion of medical ethics. Many times when I ask practitioners of clinical medicine about a particular piece of behavior, they say, "Oh, but that's bad medical practice. Good doctors don't do that." The implicit suggestion is that therefore it is not a problem. Nevertheless, you cannot simply eliminate from the agenda of issues that you must consider those sorts of behavior which you view as bad practice, dismissing them on the grounds that they do not conform with the canons of good practice that you and your colleagues follow in your professional lives. The presence of bad practice is a reality in every dimension

of medicine, and it is a collective responsibility of medicine to be concerned about it. Forensic psychiatry is no different.

4. What are the limits of your craft? I suggested, in backing off the harsh, naive view of forensic psychiatry I described earlier, that there are things that forensic psychiatry can legitimately do, but it does not follow that forensic psychiatry can accomplish everything it represents itself as being able to do. The profession of forensic psychiatry should take a hard and honest look at what the limits of the craft are, and then, having come to some view of what those limits are, it should look at another question. What should follow from a recognition of those limits, in terms of what behavior individuals are willing to perform for a fee and in terms of what the collective position of the profession should be about what is and what is not legitimate?

This kind of inquiry requires a bit of sophistication. For example, one should not take comfort in the simplistic refuge of slogans about personal liberty. There is a distinction, well known in philosophy, between freedom *to* act in various ways and freedom *from* constraints of various sorts. Freedoms from are as important as freedoms to. One recent article in psychiatry spoke of commitment to freedom, that is, of limiting patients' freedom to act in order to enhance their freedom from various kinds of constraints. This kind of inquiry also requires honesty in the analysis of your objectives, including the psychiatrist's self-interested motivation. Self-interested motivation is not illegitimate, but it is too easily overlooked.

5. I want to move, finally, to the question of guidelines, because there is a fundamental point on which everything I have said previously builds: You can never circumvent the distress and anxiety associated with ethical dilemmas by fashioning professional guidelines—conventions of practice adopted by the profession as setting the limits within which individual practitioners can legitimately move. No set of guidelines can be adequate to handle the problems that arise where the guidelines are incomplete or in conflict, as they inevitably will be. I am not arguing against the usefulness of the movement to fashion guidelines for the profession. What I am saying is that you cannot separate the intent to fashion those guidelines from fundamental issues in moral phi-

losophy and in political philosophy — such issues as how important individual liberty is in comparison with individual well-being of other sorts, how legitimate the adversarial system is, or how pure the physicians' pursuit of medical activities must be. Psychiatrists do all sorts of things, such as consultation for political campaigns, advertisers, the CIA, or the State Department. What are the appropriate limits of that? So far, they do not give testimonials on television for breakfast cereals. Why not? If Ben Spock had been willing to endorse Cheerios® cereal, he would have gotten a handsome fee, you can be sure. Think very hard about why we object to that, and then ask whether those reasons place constraints on the behavior of psychiatrists in the court.

In fashioning guidelines for the profession, you must reflect values that you have already addressed and identified; otherwise, you will not know what kinds of guidelines to adopt. Should they be guidelines that reflect just the achievement of good consequences? Should they be guidelines aimed solely at doing good, or not? Should they be guidelines aimed at protecting individual integrity and individual rights no matter what the cost is in terms of doing good? Those are difficult and fundamental issues. Certainly philosophy does not have the answer to them and should not pretend to. Yet, it is hard for me to imagine how a profession such as forensic psychiatry could find the answers without some collaboration that goes beyond the confines of law and of psychiatry. I hope that these remarks will help promote some continued discussion.

NAME INDEX

355

SUBJECT INDEX

A

Actualities
    as standard for assessing dangerousness, 49–50
    definition of, 49
Addington v. Texas, 230, 241, 242, 243, 260
Adolescent (*see* Psychiatrist, child and adolescent)
Adoption
    qualifications for, 210
Advocacy
    civil rights and
        discussion of, 24
Advocacy, child (*see* Child advocacy)
Affairs, domestic (*see* Domestic affairs)
Alcoholics Anonymous, 48
Alexander & Murdock v. United States
    discussion of, 101–105
Alliance for the Liberation of Mental Patients v. Fong, 250
Amendment, constitutional (*see* individual amendments)
American Academy of Psychiatry and the Law, ix, x, xi, 12, 23, 42, 44, 80, 82, 216, 239, 340
American Association of Psychiatric Services for Children, 185
American Bar Association, 14, 279
    Committee on the Improvement of the Law of Evidence, 139
American Bar Association Journal, 12
American Board of Psychiatry and Neurology, 338
American Civil Liberties Union, 24, 175
American Hospital Association, 290
American Law Institute, 114, 234, 236
    Model Penal Code rule, 8
American Medical Association, 269
American Psychiatric Association (A.P.A.), 185, 186, 245, 260, 269, 270, 279, 284, 313, 314, 338

American Psychological Association, 284
American Society for Adolescent Psychiatry, 185
Amicus curiae
    child and adolescent psychiatrist as, 162
    definition of, 162
Anderson v. State, 145
Apomorphine
    use of
        court case concerning, 31
Association of the Bar of the City of New York, 333
Authority
    public attitude toward, 25

B

Ballay, 55
Balson v. Davis, 241, 249, 250
Bannister v. Painter, 220
Bartley v. Kremens
    discussion of, 59, 63, 64, 66, 184
Baxstrom v. Herold, 329
Beckwith v. Sydebotham, 87
Before the Best Interests of the Child (Goldstein, Freud, Solnit), 167
Behavior modification (*see* Conditioning, aversive)
Behavior, violent
    interventions designed to prevent
        classification of, 50
Bellevue Psychiatric Hospital
    pilot study conducted at, 39–40
Bender gestalt, 93
    use of, 100, 106, 203
Berry v. Chaplin, 116
Berry v. Moench, 271
Beyond the Best Interests of the Child (Goldstein, Freud, Solnit), 167, 178
Billy Budd (Melville), 345
Blue Shield
    coverage provided by, 21, 318

361